MURDER MACHINE

A TRUE STORY OF MURDER, MADNESS, AND THE MAFIA

Gene Mustain
and
Jerry Capeci

AN ONYX BOOK

for Doreen, forever

for my wife, Barbara, and our children, Matthew, Jenna, and Craig

and for those *New York Daily News* strikers who stood tall and chased the bullies out of town

ONYX
Published by New American Library, a division of Penguin Group (USA) Inc., 375 Hudson Street, New York, New York 10014, USA
Penguin Group (Canada), 90 Eglinton Avenue East, Suite 700, Toronto, Ontario M4P 2Y3, Canada (a division of Pearson Penguin Canada Inc.)
Penguin Books Ltd., 80 Strand, London WC2R 0RL, England
Penguin Ireland, 25 St. Stephen's Green, Dublin 2, Ireland (a division of Penguin Books Ltd.)
Penguin Group (Australia), 250 Camberwell Road, Camberwell, Victoria 3124, Australia (a division of Pearson Australia Group Pty. Ltd.)
Penguin Books India Pvt. Ltd., 11 Community Centre, Panchsheel Park, New Delhi - 110 017, India
Penguin Group (NZ), 67 Apollo Drive, Rosedale, North Shore 0632, New Zealand (a division of Pearson New Zealand Ltd.)
Penguin Books (South Africa) (Pty.) Ltd., 24 Sturdee Avenue, Rosebank, Johannesburg 2196, South Africa

Penguin Books Ltd., Registered Offices: 80 Strand, London WC2R 0RL, England

Published by Onyx, an imprint of New American Library, a division of Penguin Group (USA) Inc. Previously published in a Dutton edition.

First Onyx Printing, July 1993
30 29 28 27 26 25 24

Copyright © Gene Mustain and Jerry Capeci, 1992, 1993
All rights reserved

 REGISTERED TRADEMARK—MARCA REGISTRADA

Printed in the United States of America

Prologue

It was about six p.m., already pitch black out, and one of those wet stingy snows was coming down hard. Mr. Todaro parked his car in the street in front of the crew's clubhouse. He was an older gentleman, sixty, I think. What was about to happen to him was, well, to me it was something out of Auschwitz. Roy had ordered Freddy, who was like Roy's servant, to lure Mr. Todaro to the clubhouse by making him think Roy had a used car to sell. But actually Roy was going to kill him so that the man's nephew, a friend of Roy's, could take over Mr. Todaro's film-production business. Roy was always available for this kind of work. After the first few, I think he started enjoying it.

Anyway, it's dark and it's snowing and as expected Mr. Todaro sees Roy's guy Freddy waiting outside and says hello. They start walking toward the clubhouse. Now, there is a picture window with venetian blinds next to the doorway, and as Freddy's walking he sees someone inside the clubhouse pinch the blinds and look out. All he sees is the person's eyeballs; it's eerie and he begins to quiver. He knows Mr. Todaro is going to die, but he's never seen Roy DeMeo murder before.

Mr. Todaro goes in first. There is a living room off the hallway that leads to the kitchen. As soon as Mr. Todaro is past the opening to the living room, Freddy is startled to see someone he knows, Chris, leaping out into the hallway with a butcher knife in his hand; it was an almost balletic move. Chris, by the way, was the first kid to join Roy's crew; at the moment, he doesn't have any clothes on, except for his Jockey shorts. He always worked in his underwear because he didn't want to bloody his clothes. Freddy starts to wet his pants—he believes Chris is going to stab him—but no, Chris just grabs him by the arm and wings him out of the way. "You, over here!" he says.

Freddy then sees Roy DeMeo coming out of the dark from the other end of the hall, just gliding along, and he's got a gun in one hand and a white towel in the other. He just glides up and shoots dumbfounded Mr. Todaro in the head, and before the man even hits the floor Roy is wrapping the towel around his head to prevent the blood from spurting all over. Then Chris comes over and stabs Mr. Todaro in the heart. Many times. "That stops it from pumping blood," Roy tells Freddy, who's still shaking. The murder only takes a few seconds, but of course they're not done yet. They're going to make Mr. Todaro disappear.

Some other kids in Roy's crew appear from somewhere, and they all drag Mr. Todaro's body across the kitchen and into the bathroom, where they put it in a bathtub. Now, before they begin cutting Mr. Todaro up, they have to wait forty-five minutes or so, until his blood congeals. Dismemberment isn't so messy that way, Roy tells Freddy, like Freddy was a medical student. So they wait. Maybe they even ordered a pizza, I don't know, but we do know they did that once while waiting. One of the men waiting actually lived in the clubhouse. The others called him Dracula, and not just because he had silver hair and a deep voice.

As I indicated, Mr. Todaro was one of those free-lance jobs that Roy and the crew did. There were a lot of those. But normally they were out making money for a gangster named Nino. You knew Nino was a gangster soon as he walked into a room; he was a murderer too, but did not do as much killing, and so far as we know, was not present for any of the dismemberments at the clubhouse. Neither was Dominick, who was the guy Nino used to collect his cash and keep an eye on the DeMeo crew. When Dominick was a little boy, Nino practically stole him from his father. Dominick went on to be a Green Beret war hero in 'Nam, and was a tough guy, but he did not have a killer's eyes. Roy and his crew, they all did.

Eventually, Mr. Todaro's body was taken out of the bathtub and placed on either a tarpaulin or one of those swimming-pool liners they sometimes used. Then Roy and his crew sawed the man apart, put him in garbage bags and took him to the biggest dump in Brooklyn. It was like a disassembly line. None of Mr. Todaro was ever seen again. This butchery went on all the time. It was systematic. The system was, you know, almost ceremonious. And they used to talk about the kick they got from it, the high, the power. They used to say killing made them feel like God.

Of all the horrifying stories about Roy DeMeo and his crew, the murder of Mr. Todaro is the one that stays in the mind of FBI Special Agent Arthur Ruffels. While telling it in the main conference room of FBI headquarters in New York City, Ruffels—a former high school teacher—rose to his feet to mimic the killers' movements. His audience—other agents, their boss, and the authors of this book—was spellbound. The room felt colder than before. Ruffels had transported us to a charnel house.

"They were the scariest people we've ever seen," he continued, sitting down. "Just in Roy's crew there were five people you'd have to call serial killers."

This was in the fall of 1989. It was our first major interview for a story we came upon while researching a previous book on John Gotti, the ex-hijacker who bludgeoned his way to the top of the underworld and became a household name because of his winning streak in courtrooms. Poking into Gotti's past, we found a transcript of a conversation secretly recorded by FBI agents in which Gotti's brother Gene said he and violent John were afraid to take on Roy DeMeo because Roy had "an army" of killers. At the time the comment was made, only a few cops and residents of certain neighborhoods even knew the crew existed. But who were these people so notorious in their malignant realm that even the Gotti brothers were afraid? And what had they done?

Out of the search for those answers comes this story about the most foul and prolific gang of murderers in the modern history of the United States. The Roy DeMeo crew was the coming together of an uncommon union of killing spirits; Roy and his followers killed for profit, for revenge, and finally, for fun. Many of their victims were themselves criminals, but many others were innocents who simply strayed into their merciless path, or who committed particular acts—such as insulting someone in a bar—that agitated the hairiest triggers anyone would want to encounter.

Jules Bonavolonta, supervisor of the FBI's organized crime squads in New York, opened that first interview this way: "We speculate this group killed in excess of two hundred people. A great many were just innocent people who got in the way, who just wandered in, who just happened to witness something. In other words, wanton killing. With no remorse."

Officials of the FBI, the New York City Police Department, and other agencies that eventually joined forces and tried to put the DeMeo crew out of business faced monumental obstacles because witnesses to some of the murders never came forward and because so many victims, such as Mr. Todaro, were never found.

The gang was unique not just for its violence, but also for its pedigree. Some of the most important members were still teenagers when they joined. One was a champion racecar driver. One had taken and passed the cops' entrance exam; another's brother was a cop. One more was the product of an upright Jewish family; his brother was a doctor. The gang's leader was smart enough to be a doctor—and his favorite uncle was a prominent New York lawyer.

This story will tell who the gang members were, how they got together, how they killed, and how they were brought to justice, one way or the other. It also is the story of many of their victims, including a teenage beauty queen, a college student, and a father and a son short of money and long on naiveté.

The saga unfolds across a raw and treacherous landscape that stretches from Kuwait to Beverly Hills and from New York to Miami—and against the background of a ponderous criminal justice system that frequently misfired, and not just because of the usual bureaucratic nonsense. Some heroic cops and prosecutors battled the DeMeo crew, but some cops not so heroic aided and abetted it.

Two men that Special Agent Arthur Ruffels mentioned while describing the demise of Mr. Todaro—Nino and Dominick—are central to the story. Nino's full name was Anthony Frank Gaggi; he was what Roy DeMeo wanted to be—a top Mafia gangster. His roots extend to Lucky Luciano and the dawn of organized crime in America. Strictly speaking, Dominick was Nino's nephew, but son was closer to the truth, for better and for worse.

It is because of Dominick that we are able to tell many parts of the story. We met him in an elevator at a federal courthouse. In our earlier book on John Gotti, he was mentioned in one paragraph in which we described him as a thief, loanshark, and drug addict. The characterization came from a legal document.

"So you're the guys who called me a thief, a loanshark, and a junkie?" he said.

We were happy there were cops in the elevator with us, and that he began to smile. "There's more to the story," he added.

It was the first few seconds of eventually hundreds of hours of conversations with Dominick Montiglio. They were conducted in separate cities around the country and at pre-arranged times on the telephone. He never refused to answer a question. As with the other sources for this book, he was not paid any money.

"All I want is for someone to lay it out the way it was," he said at the outset. "Then maybe my kids can understand what happened to me."

All the characters in this book are, or were, living people. Almost all their conversations come from hundreds of interviews with one or more of the participants, or from some half million pages of official documents, public and secret. A few are based on what people recall being told. As memory is never really completely infallible, no nonfiction book can be, but we have endeavored to make this one as true as experience and judgment enable.

The land is full of bloody crimes,
and the city is full of violence.

—The prophet Ezekiel

Only the dead know Brooklyn.

—Thomas Wolfe

I

LOVE
AND WAR

CHAPTER 1

Uncle Nino

Dominick grew up in a house dominated by his Uncle Nino. It was a roomy house but not fancy, just a rectangle of bricks the color of dried blood sandwiched between others like it on an ordinary street in Brooklyn, New York, the Borough of Churches and Homes. The Gaggi clan, mostly one generation removed from Sicily, occupied three floors but shared a common kitchen and a common wariness for the world beyond what they called "the bunker." From 1947 when he was born, and on through the Eisenhower years, Dominick lived there with his mother, another uncle, his grandparents, assorted aunts and cousins—but Uncle Nino, who had an opinion about everything, was always boss of the bunker. Early on, Dominick's father had lived there too, but he was a drunk and a bum and had run away when his son was about age three, or so Uncle Nino always said.

To outsiders and little boys, Nino Gaggi was a successful car salesman. With no children of his own until his nephew was nine, he was affectionate and attentive, if always aggressively and profanely blunt-spoken. "Your dad was a drinker, he treated your mother, my sister, like shit," he would tell the boy.

Growing up, Dominick sought particulars, but Uncle Nino always blocked inquiry with further condemnation. His mother Marie was gentle, but not much more forthcoming; she would say her husband was a good man, but they had a hard time living together and the marriage just never worked out—next question please. Once in a great while, though, she gave up a biographical detail. So her son came to know his father, Anthony Santamaria, a popular boy from the neighborhood, who served in the Army Air Corps and then fell in love with his mother after coming home a hero from the war.

When Dominick began showing some athletic ability, his mother also gave him a tiny silver boxing glove his father had given her. It was inscribed, "Army Air Corps Boxing Champ—1943."

The boxing glove became a cherished memento because, in time, Dominick recalled his father only as someone recalls a few scenes from an obscure play seen years before and therefore has trouble deciding what the story line was. His earliest memory was of the boxer coming home one night, tweaking him on a cheek, then stumbling into the bathroom and puking like a baby. Bombed out of his mind, Dominick concluded as he and the memory got older.

The second memory was more a sequence of scenes, probably from his fourth year, 1951, sometime after his father left the bunker, when they were allowed to see one another on Sundays. His father was living a few blocks away, back home with his parents, but after Dominick was dropped off the reunions usually led to the Magic Lantern, a rowdy local tavern, where the Army Air Corps champ defeated all comers, bare-fisted, for money and drinks.

Dominick never forgot his father telling him during one of these jousts that he would prefer living with him, but it was impossible so long as it meant living with Uncle Nino too. "He wants me to do things I'm against," he said.

"Like what?"

"Some things you can't understand yet."

Anthony's brother-in-law and estranged wife threw fits when they heard about the Magic Lantern; consequently, Dominick never spoke to his real father again. The boxer stayed in the neighborhood a while and occasionally his son saw him walking along—but as his Uncle Nino and mother Marie had instructed, he crossed the street and avoided him like the man had chickenpox.

The boy felt terrible, but his mother said life is terrible sometimes. "The man is a fucking bum," Uncle Nino added, bouncing the little bambino on his knee. "I'll take care of you now."

Obviously, Dominick was too powerless to protest and too ignorant of family history to wonder if this was the right course for his life.

* * *

Antonino Gaggi came to life on a hot-tempered summer's evening in 1925. He was the third and last child of Angelo and Mary Gaggi, who lived in a cold-water walkup on the Lower East Side of Manhattan, a brawling area of immigrant angst. In time, his first name became Anthony, but its original form yielded his nickname—Nino.

Some avenues on the Lower East Side were known by letters, so it also had a nickname, "Alphabet City." The Gaggis lived on Twelfth Street, near Avenue A and the neighborhood's noisy hub, Tompkins Square Park. Angelo Gaggi, a placid man from Palermo, ran a barber shop. His iron-willed wife was a sweatshop seamstress who quit work to stay at home with Nino and her other children—two-year-old Marie and one-year-old Rosario, later known as Roy.

It was a hard life in a hard neighborhood. The couple wanted out as soon as possible, but the Depression hit and things got worse. Men stopped getting haircuts as often and Angelo laid off barbers he employed. As soon as little Nino was able, he was put to work sweeping up and polishing the shoes of men lucky enough to have jobs.

With the suspicious clans huddled together, with their common anxiety but different languages and strange rituals, the dense streets were always filled with disagreement. Children on virtually each block formed gangs known as "mobs." Kids without the stomach for fighting were lucky to arrive at school with their milk money.

In 1932, seven-year-old Nino posed for his first Holy Communion photograph at the Roman Catholic church across the street; the photograph showed no trace of cowardice in his face, nor evidence of a lost fight. The camera did capture a remarkably handsome, utterly rigid child appearing to possess great discipline. It was proof he had inherited his mother's willful personality.

On the other hand, Nino's brother Roy resembled, both in appearance and demeanor, their father, a slender man with a prominent Adam's apple and a weak chin. Nino's sister Marie was somewhere between—solid and plain like her mother, but like her father, reserved and inclined to resign herself to situations.

Mary Gaggi was so struck by Nino's photo—he was such a manly boy—she spent a few scarce dollars and made it a postcard she mailed to relatives. Because his mother doted on him, and Nino took advantage, Nino's sister thought he was a mama's boy. The accusation always caused a prominent vein left of his jugular to swell—its thickness was how people measured little Nino's anger.

As his sister and brother had, Nino attended public school the first three grades, then transferred to the parish school behind the church across from his home. Besides after-school chores at his father's shop, he delivered flowers. By age ten, he roamed the Lower East Side confidently and was hanging out at Tompkins Square, the neighborhood *piazza* at Avenue A and Tenth Street.

This was the domain of Alphabet City's toughest gang, the Tenth Street Mob; its boss was a wild thirteen-year-old, Rocco Barbella, a ferocious fighter who took on much older boys before large crowds in the park. Later on, as Rocky Graziano, he became middleweight boxing champion of the world.

Many fighters came out of the neighborhood, but only Tenth Street spawned two middleweight champions. The second was Jake LaMotta, with whom Nino became friendly before Jake, like Rocco, was sent to reform school. The professional handle Jake adopted, "Raging Bull," captured all the fury of Alphabet City.

The mobs aligned along turf and ethnic lines, which was why a boy from Twelfth Street and Avenue A ran with the boys from Tenth Street. With fists and sticks, the Tenth Street Mob fought the Avenue B Mob, the Eleventh Street Mob, and anyone who had a smart remark. They swiped fruit from pushcarts and clipped candy from newsstands, and when the mostly Irish cops of the day grabbed them, penalties were administered on the street.

Nino never complained that he was given an official beating, but he developed a seething grudge against cops. Given the anti-cop grousing that went on in his father's shop, a beating was not required. All the official plundering of Sicily through the ages made contempt for authority a Sicilian tradition. Passing cops on the street, Nino sneered and swore under his breath.

It was obvious that the cops operated according to a

double standard. The men who ran the neighborhood's gambling, loansharking, and fencing rackets operated in plain sight. It was obvious the "rackies" were prosperous. Lucky Luciano, the biggest gangster in New York City, was out of an Avenue A walkup. So it was natural that Nino emulated that life and stood on streetcorners flipping coins, mimicking George Raft as menacing Guido Rinaldo in a big film of the day, *Scarface* (the story of Al Capone, a New York-born rackie).

Nino's mother Mary knew the phenomenon. She grew up in the similarly disgruntled Hell's Kitchen neighborhood on Manhattan's West Side. One of her playmates was George Raft, and she always joked to Nino that her old friend became a movie star just by being himself and every other Guido Rinaldo on the corner.

Nino's father Angelo was even more acquainted. A cousin of his, Frank Scalise, was a powerful gangster and an associate of the nation's most infamous men—Luciano, Capone, Meyer Lansky, Dutch Schultz. Scalise sat at the table when those men met and divvied up the rackets among "families" of criminals that collectively became known as the Mafia. Milquetoast Angelo did not move in such circles, but he and Scalise played together in Palermo as kids, emigrated about the same time, and still socialized at each other's homes out of a yearning for old-country camaraderie.

When Scalise came to Twelfth Street, neighbors buzzed over his car, clothes, and jewelry. How he made his living was not a polite topic, but an Alphabet City child did not need to be told when someone was "connected." The sight of Scalise entering the Gaggi walkup boosted Nino's standing with the corner boys.

With audacious solemnity, he told them: "I only want two things when I grow up. I want to be just like Frank Scalise and when I die, I want to die on the street with a gun in my hand."

The boys were well aware that death on the street was an occasional fact of that life. Now and then, people came running up to the church across the street from Nino's house to inform the pastor that some rackie had been shot and was lying mortally wounded and in need of extreme unction, the church's last rites.

When Nino was almost fourteen, he graduated eighth

grade. Though contemptuous of the work, he began barbering hair in his father's shop; between that and his florist's delivery job, he had spending money for the first time. Leaving childhood behind, he became acutely interested in the image he projected; he began dressing as sharp as funds allowed, and when his eyesight deteriorated, he chose spectacles so dark they appeared to be sunglasses.

He also learned to play dice but decided gambling was not for him; he could not bear losing and hated handing over money to anyone. He was intrigued, however, by the loansharks who circled the dice games, charging the foolish gamblers up to five percent interest, or "vig" (for *vigorish*), a week. He saw that taking advantage of a sucker's weakness was what the rackets were about.

Unlike his siblings, he did not even try high school; low regard for education was another immigrant Sicilian tradition—especially if work was waiting at home, and Nino's parents provided that when they announced to his dismay that the family was moving to rural New Jersey, where they had bought a small farm.

Nino stewed on the farm. In 1942, after war broke out in Europe and Asia and after his seventeenth birthday, he tried to escape by enlisting in the Army. He was five-feet-eight, one hundred sixty pounds, and muscular from hard labor, but he was rejected during the physical exam because he was too nearsighted. This hardened the chip on his shoulder about men in uniform.

In New Jersey, the adults did not adjust well to a farming life either. As Angelo Gaggi later said, they were city people who barely knew a hoe from a rake. After two years they gave it up but decided against returning to the Lower East Side. Some of their relatives had since moved across the East River to Brooklyn, the promised land of immigrant families.

In 1943, Angelo and Mary found a house they liked in Bath Beach, an Italian neighborhood on the southwest coast of Brooklyn. It was a roomy but bunker-like brick house, and affordable—one hundred dollars down secured a mortgage for eight thousand five hundred and fifty. The deed was placed in the name of the eldest child, Marie, the one who understood English best.

Compared to Alphabet City, Bath Beach was a paradise. One hundred years earlier, it was a fashionable resort area for the wealthy and even by 1943 there were still only a few windswept marshes between the Gaggi bunker on Cropsey Avenue and the Atlantic Ocean. Coney Island and all its amusement parks lay only a couple of miles away.

Bath Beach adjoined Bensonhurst, a larger, similar community of immigrants beginning to make it. In both, merchants and residents replicated the culture of their old Sicilian and southern Italian villages. Tiny cafes and fruit-and-vegetable stands lined commercial streets; in residential areas, fig tress grew in backyards and grape vines formed canopies over makeshift carports.

Eighteen now, Nino scouted opportunity. Not to his parents' surprise or particular alarm, he turned to his father's connected cousin, Frank Scalise, whose influence had continued to grow; he was a leader of the city's largest Mafia gang and had made a fortune as a loanshark. His customers included many top politicians and union officials, so Nino got a job on a truck dock; in hardly any time he was a supervisor. He hated it as much as the farm but worked hard and added ten more pounds of muscle. He bossed older workers with confidence and never tolerated sloth or tardiness.

Angelo Gaggi opened up another barber shop, and his wife and daughter got work in a dress factory. His other son, Roy, who had enlisted in the Army but was sent home after a training-camp injury, sold peanut dispensers to local bars; Roy had grown up in the shadow of his younger brother and would stay there.

Over the next two years Nino cultivated his connection to Scalise. At age twenty, he quit his job on the truck dock—but not on paper. He was made a ghost employee as a favor to Scalise. The phony job covered him with the tax man and he began a full-time life on the sly. To his parents he was still just devoted son Anthony—a respectful young man, as handsome as George Raft, strong and self-assured, and destined to find what best suited him. Mary Gaggi especially felt that way.

Like her brother, Marie Gaggi had matured into an attractive person, brunette and shapely. When the neighborhood men came home from war in 1945, she fell in love with Anthony Santamaria, a local legend whose boxing skills were regularly on display in barroom exhibitions.

Nino was scornfully unimpressed. His childhood friends Jake LaMotta and Rocky Graziano were now marquee professional fighters, not barroom hacks. He derided Anthony Santamaria as having no future; the boxer was just a deliveryman for a butcher shop. The man also drank too much, in Nino's exaggerated estimation. Nino did not drink liquor at all; he did not like losing control. He did not smoke, either. He prided himself on having no personal vices.

Marie resented her brother's heavyhanded opinions; Anthony Santamaria was always a gentleman around her. Late in 1945, they married and he moved into the Gaggi bunker. Nineteen months later, their only child was born. Marie incorporated her gentle father's name into the infant's, Dominick Angelo Santamaria.

Anthony Gaggi was the only adult in the bunker who did not rise early in the morning to go to work, so he became Dominick's primary babysitter. Nino made his money at night, loansharking in the bars and poolhalls of Brooklyn and doing whatever else came along. At home, his business was not discussed. He had a new car, cash, clothes, and no job; that said everything. His parents accepted life as it came. This way everything was normal. Everyone in the bunker was the same way—including Anthony Santamaria, who just tried to keep his distance.

In 1950, however, the relationship between brothers-in-law, strained from the start, grew frayed. It happened after Nino developed what would be a lifelong interest in the money to be made in the automobile business—one way or another—and asked Anthony to help stage a phony car accident so that Nino could defraud an insurance company. Anthony refused, and Nino began complaining that Anthony was a freeloader who abused Marie.

With most men, Anthony would have answered these accusations with fists, but he feared Nino might strike back with bullets. At the bunker, he kept going his own way, but since everyone ate in the common kitchen, it was hard. A cold war Anthony had no chance of winning set in; in time, with no money to take his wife and child away, he became sullen and defeated. He got deep into the bottle, began staying out late, arguing with his wife, and by 1951, his marriage was on the rocks and he was history.

For all intents and purposes, twenty-six-year-old Nino became the father of the four-year-old Santamaria boy, Dominick.

No one ever sat Dominick down and explained why and how Nino was different from other men. He was left to learn by osmosis, to read between the lines and keep his mouth shut.

What indirect lessons there were came in the form of pointed remarks—such as when Dominick, shortly after entering the first grade, said to Nino that he wanted to be a policeman someday. On his way to Public School 200 each morning, he had enjoyed friendly encounters with cops changing shifts at the precinct stationhouse across from the school.

"I hate cops," Nino huffed. "No one in our family has ever been a cop."

When Dominick, after hearing about the Korean War at school, next said he wanted to be a soldier, Nino said people were fools to die for anyone but their families. Because Uncle Nino was so sure about everything, his nephew was in awe of him.

Dominick was age seven the first time the police came to his house. In his room one night, he woke to a frightful racket. He knew but a few words of Sicilian, but they included "Police!" which his grandfather was screaming repeatedly. He then heard a door slam, someone thrown against a wall, and Nino swearing loudly. His mother came and sat with him until he stopped bawling; some men had just come to see Uncle Nino, she said.

In truth, Anthony Gaggi had been arrested and taken away in handcuffs, not by police, but by the FBI; he was accused of running an international stolen-car ring out of the used-car lot he had opened in a nearby neighborhood—no doubt with the backing of Frank Scalise, who had become the number-two man or underboss of the city's largest Mafia family.

Scalise lived in the Bronx, north of Manhattan, but supervised the family's various branches, the largest of which was in Brooklyn. Nino was not a "made" member of the family yet, and by tradition would not be until he demonstrated he was a capable money-earner and a killer.

The car operation showed the former. Over two years, Nino and two others created phony registrations for dozens of nonexistent Cadillacs, then dispatched thieves to steal ones that matched. The hot Caddys' vehicle identification numbers were replaced, new license plates obtained with the bogus registrations were installed, and within hours they were on their way to some cash customer in Florida, Georgia, Texas, or Mexico.

Nino was released on bail in a few hours. The next morning, no one in the bunker mentioned the FBI raid of the night before; everything was normal, though Dominick went off to school with a first inkling of what Anthony Santamaria might have meant when he said Nino wanted him to do things he was against. Meeting expectations, he kept the revelation to himself.

The stolen-car case dragged on nearly three years, with all the classic earmarks of Mafia tampering. Witnesses suffered sudden memory loss; codefendants who pleaded guilty either refused to testify against Nino or changed their stories from grand jury to trial. By early 1956, the federal prosecutor was left with a shell of a case and a jury found Nino not guilty. Nino did not take the stand, adhering to the first vow a potential made man must make, absolute noncooperation with official authority.

While the case pended, Nino also took another vow—to love and honor Rose Mary Pezzella, a stunning blond telephone operator whom he married shortly before his twenty-ninth birthday. She was eight years younger, a ringer for Betty Grable, and had lived with her parents atop a furniture shop a few doors from his used-car lot. She and Nino had to petition the judge in Nino's case to permit Nino to leave the state for a honeymoon, after which they took over the first floor of the bunker, forcing Dominick and his mother to smaller accommodations on the second floor. The couple's first child, a boy, was born a year later.

Though a neighbor lady had become Dominick's chief babysitter, Nino still looked after him if the neighbor was unavailable and the other adults were still at their jobs. If he had business to conduct or people to see, he took his nephew along. At family events, the boy had bounced on Scalise's knee many times, listening to folk tales of

Sicily and the suffering of its people, but now he began to meet others with whom Nino would rise to power, men he was encouraged to regard as uncles.

The first was Paul Castellano. Ironically, his father owned the butcher shop that once employed an upstairs tenant, Anthony Santamaria, as a deliveryman. After his wife divorced him, however, Anthony had quit and was gone from the neighborhood by the time Dominick returned to the shop to visit Uncle Paulie. By appearances, Paul was following his father into the meat business, but he also was top aide to Carlo Gambino, who ran Scalise family business in Brooklyn. Carlo, a sly Sicilian who arrived in America in 1922 as a cargo ship stowaway, and Paul were cousins, and Paul had married one of Carlo's sisters. Carlo was fifteen years older than Paul, who was a decade older than Nino.

To Dominick, Nino always described Paul and Carlo simply as "important men" it was an honor to know. Several times Dominick joined them and others for afternoon espresso, and by the way the men seemed to defer to Uncle Carlo, a quietly spoken man with a notably large beak, he sensed that Carlo was almost as important as Frank Scalise.

Once, as one of these sitdowns ended and Dominick said goodbye to Carlo, Nino described him as a smart boy with the speed of a deer. The boy never forgot Carlo's reply: "Smart like a fox, that's good. The fox recognizes traps. But a deer? It's better to be a lion than a deer. The lion scares away the wolves. If you are a lion and a fox, nothing defeats you."

As any boy would, Dominick accepted Carlo's observations as original thoughts, and for several years quoted them to friends. Not until much later did he learn that Carlo was cribbing from the philosophy of Niccolò Machiavelli, the Italian Renaissance statesman. Carlo had found a veneer for his life in Machiavelli's famous treatise, *The Prince:* Whatever a ruler has to do to gain or hold power, he must do.

Through the mid-1950s, Nino's body began showing the effects of a basically sedentary life. About the only exercise he got was taking his pet boxer "Prince" for a walk; he was still handsome, but now round-faced and jowly; he still had the smooth skin and inky black hair of his youth, but his muscles sagged and he had ballooned to about two hundred pounds, which did not lie well on a man five feet eight inches tall; he still drank only wine, but with a multicourse dinner.

With his broad shoulders, dark wavy hair, brown eyes, and high strong cheekbones, young Dominick was emerging as a chip off the Anthony Santamaria block—right down to the small gap between two upper front teeth. Even though active and athletic, he also was a bit chunky around the middle.

In school, the boy made friends easily and caught on quickly. One day in 1957, his tenth year, he came home all excited and wearing a blue button with the word "President" stenciled across it. He rushed to tell Nino how he had been honored by his classmates.

"Guess what happened!" he asked, so impatient he supplied his own answer, "I got elected class president!"

"What does the class president do?"

"I take care of the class when the teacher leaves the room. If anyone's bad, I write their name down."

Nino frowned. "That just means you're a rat."

"A rat?"

"A rat! A stoolpigeon! You can't be a stoolpigeon. No one in our family can be a stoolpigeon. You go back and tell your teacher you can't be no class president."

"But I was elected," Dominick said meekly.

"It isn't for our family. Tell the teacher you can't do it."

The next day, Dominick did as ordered. His teacher asked why many times, but he never gave a straight answer. His evasiveness was proof that the lessons he received at home were having their effect. Telling the truth would have made him a stoolpigeon against Uncle Nino.

In Bath Beach, as when they lived on the Lower East Side, the Gaggi clan were members of the local Catholic parish, Saint Finbar's, but as before, only the women and the children went to mass regularly. As Nino's mother had with him when he was a boy, Dominick's mother exposed him to the church's doctrine and ceremonial rituals, but as with Nino, not to much effect. For instance, he never made the connection between his surname, Santamaria, and the Feast of Assumption, when Mary was said to have been assumed from earth straight to heaven.

When at his confirmation ceremony on May 5, 1957, Dominick became a "Soldier of Christ," the day was more a revelation of familial relationships than a reflection of any religious significance. The ceremony began with him and other children lined up outside the church with the adults they had selected as their godfathers and godmothers, their protectors in life should anything happen to their parents. Home movies show that the man Dominick had chosen was wearing a nifty charcoal suit, a red silk tie, and a red carnation—and that he was fidgeting with his dark glasses, as if nervous. Nino Gaggi had not been in Saint Finbar's for some time, but when a drum and bugle corps signaled the ceremony's start, he put a godfatherly arm around Dominick Angelo Santamaria and marched inside.

Even though Dominick had begun to notice, after the family got its first television set, that Uncle Nino always cheered the villains, his mental picture of his godfather was still blurred. A few weeks after the confirmation ceremony, however, it was brought violently into focus by a sequence of events. One afternoon in June 1957, a distinguished-looking man, dapperly dressed in pale yellow slacks and matching shirt, was buying peaches at his neighborhood deli in the Bronx when an assassin came from behind and shot him four times. The victim, Frank Scalise, was sixty-two years old.

The next day, in his home, police found one hundred photos of him vacationing in Italy with Lucky Luciano, the former hero of Avenue A, who ten years before had been deported as an undesirable alien for helping bring the Mafia from Sicily to New York. They also recovered his loanshark "book," a ledger of illegal loans that included the names of some twenty prominent officials.

In Bath Beach, Marie Gaggi told her son that Scalise had "passed away," but at the wake in the Bronx, Dominick learned the harsher reality and overheard Scalise's fiery brother Joseph vowing revenge. Not much later, the Gaggi family traveled to the Bronx again, this time to comfort the family of Joseph Scalise, who had disappeared.

"He left last Friday and just never came home," Dominick heard one of the sobbing relatives say, as his highly agitated godfather huddled in a corner with many grave-looking men.

Some weeks later, with still no trace of Joseph Scalise, a gangster named Albert Anastasia was assassinated in a Manhattan hotel. The press reacted as though Mayor Robert F. Wagner himself had been killed. No one tried to shield Dominick from the radio or television coverage, and he concluded that the adults intentionally decided to let him learn the hard truths about Nino and the important men from strangers.

The news reports identified Anastasia as the leader of New York's biggest criminal gang; his former righthand man was Frank Scalise, whose brother Joseph was also presumed murdered; all the murders were part of a war between two gangs; the new boss of the Anastasia gang might be Carlo Gambino, who was "sly like a fox."

This last report struck Dominick like a thunderbolt, and he added a silent kicker: And strong like a lion!

After Anastasia was in the ground, Nino announced it would be best if the Gaggi family stayed inside the bunker a few days. Filled with new information, Dominick knew that a siege was on, and took it as a test of his bravery and loyalty. Holed up, the family passed the time as normally as possible by playing cards and games. The only discordant note was sounded by Dominick's mother, whom he heard complaining to her parents about the stupidity of "that life" of her brother's.

Although it was like sitting around waiting for a bomb to go off, Dominick managed to act as normal as anyone. The boy, who had lately taken an interest in music, even tried lightening the mood by singing for them his favorite song, "Little Darlin'."

Naturally, no one ever openly discussed what was happening outside the bunker. One day, the siege was over and that was it. Dominick felt he passed his tests and had survived real peril. He began feeling wiser and somehow more special than his classmates at Public School 200; he was a keeper of secrets so big he could never even admit to having them.

The next two years were comparatively uneventful. If there was still a power struggle in the underworld, Dominick could not tell by the demeanor of Nino—nor Uncles Carlo Gambino and Paul Castellano, when he saw them at lunches and family occasions. It was a happy time of music, sports, and friends.

He added "At the Hop" to his repertoire and formed a neighborhood group, The Tuneups. His fireplug body was put to good use as a catcher in the Bath Beach–Bensonhurst Little League, and he stole a first kiss from a girl at Coney Island. He began to develop keen pride in his Brooklyn heritage; he had come along at the peak of the borough's fame—people from Brooklyn were making it big in every walk of life. He had heard Nino say many times, "If they're not from Brooklyn, they're farmers," and he adopted the cocky saying as his own. Only cool kids came from Brooklyn.

When Dominick turned twelve, however, his mother announced stunning news. She intended to marry Anthony Montiglio, a man she had been dating, and move out of Brooklyn. Dominick liked his future stepdad. Like Anthony Santamaria, Anthony Montiglio was an Army Air Corps veteran; he had taken the boy sightseeing to West Point and given him a football. Still, the news was breathtaking. After the marriage, the couple was buying a house in Levittown, thirty miles east on Long Island, and she might even have a baby.

As the shock wore off, Dominick began looking on the move as an adventure. Without hearing her say so, he knew his mother was happy to put some distance between herself and "that life" of Nino's, where people were killed or just disappeared. Though silently attracted to one aspect of Nino's life—the daring uniqueness of it—he decided some distance was probably good for him too.

After his mother's marriage, she asked him to use the name Dominick Montiglio when it was time to enroll in another school. Because he did like his stepdad and wanted to please his mother, and although he was not legally adopted, he agreed.

The new family left for Levittown in the summer of 1960, unaware that Nino was about to revenge a personal loss, close the books on an underworld power struggle, and become a made member of what was now the Gambino Mafia family—all in one vicious stroke.

In October, a lawyer for a gangster named Vincent Squillante told newspaper reporters that his client was missing. Squillante was president of the trade group rep-

resenting the city's private commercial waste cartel, and
had been identified as a major drug dealer in testimony
before the United States Senate rackets subcommittee in
Washington. In Bath Beach, however, he had also been
identified as the man who shot Frank Scalise and then
lured a revenge-minded Joseph Scalise to the same fate.

Officially, the disappearance remained a mystery, but
many times over the years Anthony Gaggi gave this account to people he trusted: "We surprised him in the
Bronx. We shot him in the head, stuffed him in the trunk,
then dumped him for good."

Nino and his accomplices took the body to the basement of a building on Tenth Street in Alphabet City,
Nino's old neighborhood. There, in the building's furnace, the former member of the Tenth Street Mob cre-
mated the man who killed his childhood hero.

In Levittown, one of the nation's first postwar-style suburbs, Dominick Montiglio became an all-American teenager.
He delivered newspapers, flipped hamburgers at a Mc-
Donald's, hung out at the mall, played varsity football, and
lost his virginity in a grassy field behind school.

The only blemish was a period during his freshman
year when he rebelled against his stepfather's authority
and began ditching school. After much pleading from his
mother, he began to behave, but had missed so many
classes that he spent the next three years making up cred-
its. During that time, his mother gave birth to two children, Stephen and Michele, who grew up not knowing
their busy older brother had a different father.

The activity Dominick enjoyed most was his music.
His voice was now low and mellow, and at fourteen he
joined some other boys who had performed at dances and
weddings. They called themselves The Four Directions;
they liked the songs of black singers, and that became
their hook—white boys who sounded black.

One night, they tried out a new song in a shopping-
center alcove that simulated an echo chamber. Two doors
away, the owner of a liquor store chain was impressed;
he offered to back them with money for stage clothes and
expenses. In weeks, the boys were looking aces and singing in popular Long Island nightclubs, warming up
crowds for concerts by The Shirelles and Little Anthony &

The Imperials, premier black groups of the era. The Four Directions began getting stars in their eyes.

Anthony Gaggi, however, tried to keep Dominick's feet on the ground. "The music business is a rotten dirty business," he would say during family reunions in Brooklyn.

"I don't care about the business, just the music," Dominick would reply to no avail.

The Montiglios and the Gaggis got together nearly every Sunday, particularly after Nino's father Angelo died of a heart attack in 1962. The Montiglios always went to Brooklyn because Nino hated driving on the busy Long Island Expressway. Marie Montiglio put up with it because otherwise she would never see her mother, now living alone in the apartment above Nino and Rose. Her husband Anthony put up with it too, for Marie's sake.

Dominick thought his uncle's attitude about the music business was hypocritical; the musicians he was meeting were saying that "Mafia people" were making moves on the music industry. He believed it because some Italian-American singers he regarded lightly seemed to be on the radio all the time. They were proof it was possible to manufacture a hit out of a bad song. All it took was enough cash to grease a disk jockey's palm.

The Four Directions were certain of stardom when, after an audition, a record company agreed to record a song a friend had written, "Tonight We Love." The words were original, but the music was a knockoff of a Tchaikovsky piano concerto.

Sales were modest, but the record got the group into another studio, where they sang backup vocals on an album by Mitch Ryder & The Detroit Wheels, a popular group. The album included a big hit, "Sock-It-To-Me," but the song Dominick liked most was, "A Face in the Crowd," for which he did the vocal arrangement.

Friends said it was a fitting song because Dominick had impressed them as so unusual in one regard. Moving from singer to athlete to student to McDonald's grill man, he seemed to take on a different persona at each stop. It was not just the clothes or the uniform that changed, it was the body language, speech, and manners. His friends called him a chameleon.

One night, the Four Directions got giddy on Thunderbird wine and decided to crash Carnegie Hall in Manhattan. The forty-five-minute drive sobered them up some, however, and they decided to just hang outside the Carnegie entrance. Doing so, they noticed an overhang that reminded them of the echo chamber created by the alcove at the shopping center where they sounded so good and the liquor distributor discovered them. It was an omen.

"Tonight, we love," the boys began, straining their voices, banging Tchaikovsky's notes against the concrete and steel. As they continued, a few people stopped and applauded. But as a concert crowd poured out of the theater and swelled around, they suffered stage fright. They stopped singing and ran off.

A few blocks away, a limousine pulled alongside them; a chauffeur got out and said his boss was in show business and wanted to meet them. The Four Directions returned to Carnegie Hall and met June Havoc, hostess of a television variety show.

"I'd love you to be on my show," she told them.

Just like that, the Four Directions made their television debut; it led to other shows—including an American Bandstand–type show in Cleveland, where the guests also included a young couple, Sonny & Cher. Dominick chatted with both, but the Indian-looking Cher, with her peculiar beauty and black hair to her buttocks so unnerved him he never remembered anything she said.

Promoting "Tonight We Love," The Four Directions also played Arthur, a club in Manhattan owned by actor Richard Burton's former wife, Sybil, and the Uptown Theater in Philadelphia, a famous black club whose audience clapped them to two encores.

Still, The Four Directions' act was limited.

To make it big, they had to have a runaway hit record and to establish their own image. They could not make it big singing only other groups' songs. A friend in another group wrote them a song they thought would do the trick, but the label that had recorded them before was not interested. The limited success of "Tonight We Love" was not enough to overcome the perception that all they were was a warmup act. Dominick believed the real reason was that four other Italian-American singers for the label, the very hot Four Seasons, did not want it promoting potential rivals.

Believing the group just needed one more break, Dominick asked Nino for help. He thought that with one telephone call to Uncle Carlo, Nino could make it happen. He believed Carlo already controlled a record company in New Jersey; in the clubs, he had heard such stories and in newspapers, read more. He felt guilty invoking his blood connection to "that life"—but not too guilty. He did have talent.

"All we need is this one little push, someone to make the record," he told Nino.

"I don't think that business is for you."

"I told you it's not the business, it's the music."

"All they do in that business is drugs and women. It's not for you—forget about it."

The patronizing attitude was infuriating. Dominick raised his voice against Nino for the first time. "Who are you telling me what's good for me?"

"You came here with your hat in your hand."

"So it would be cooler if I was a murderer and ran around the streets being a loanshark, is that it?"

Nino moved closer to Dominick. "I think you should watch what you say."

"Loanshark is okay. Professional artist, forget about it."

"You better leave now or I'm gonna pop you in the nose."

Dominick left the bunker angry and humiliated. He detested everything his uncle was, and himself for trying to use him.

The Four Directions stayed together another year, but never went any farther than they had already gone. In their disappointment, they began to resent each other. They bickered over who had the best voice and the number of leads each sang. When Dominick was seventeen, they disbanded.

That same year, 1965, Dominick graduated from Mac-Arthur High School in Levittown. Frustrated by the dead end of his musical career, he wanted something new and dramatic but had no idea what. Angry at Nino and sour on New York, he wanted to run off but had no idea where. He had the ability for college but not the desire or discipline. Bitterly, he declined Nino's offer to help him get a job. Adrift, he found work on his own, an assembly-line job at the Grumman Aircraft Corporation.

Meanwhile, a friend joined the Army Reserves and began telling Dominick about an elite unit, the Green Berets, the Army had recently formed. The Berets were superstar warriors; at the time, in Vietnam, they were helping put down a Communist revolution.

It sounded exciting to Dominick, daring and unique. He also had a heroic self-image and was genuinely if naively patriotic; moreover, he was spontaneous. On Valentine's Day, 1966, he left Grumman in a defiant mood after arguing with the foreman. On his way home he saw a recruiting center. He stopped and went inside. He walked past the Coast Guard and the Marines before locating the Army. The Four Directions breakup had not completely shattered his confidence. "I want to be a Green Beret," he said.

The recruiter thought he was joking and started to laugh.

"Just because you want it doesn't mean you get it. It ain't that easy."

"Didn't ask if it was easy."

"Okay. I can't guarantee you Green Beret. All I can guarantee you is basic training. After that, if you want to be a Green Beret, you must volunteer and be accepted for advanced infantry, then Airborne Ranger school, then Special Forces school—that's Green Beret—but only if they want you."

"Great! Where do I sign?"

That night the new recruit told his stunned mother, "If you're going to go to war, you might as well go all the way."

His mother did not like the bravado; it reminded her he had some Anthony Gaggi qualities. But as the shock wore off, Anthony Gaggi was the reason she became supportive. She feared her restless son might eventually turn toward Nino's world. The Army put him on a different path. "Just remember to stay alive," she said.

Puffed up, Dominick went to Brooklyn to tell Nino, and got a reaction only partially expected. "People are getting killed over there, you idiot! And for what? To prop up a bunch of rice farmers? It's insane!"

"I know it sounds corny to you, but I am going to fight for my country." Dominick paused. "Like my dad did, and my stepdad."

"They were stupid too. Don't fight for generals, fight for us. If you want to die, die for your family."

Dominick was startled by Nino's last words. For the first time, it sounded as though he was referring to the Gambino family, not the Gaggi or Montiglio. He felt anger, surprise, fear, and pride all at the same time and was momentarily speechless.

"I ain't going to die," he finally said, then marched away.

CHAPTER 2

Bully Boy

Not long after Dominick left for the Army, Nino became acquainted with a young man with neither the looks nor the talent for the music business. Roy Albert DeMeo had a lot of other qualities that impressed Nino, however—intelligence, energy, resourcefulness, and by age twenty-five, a lot of experience with the things that interested Nino—cars, loans, and money.

Roy did not wear this completely on his sleeve—not yet, anyway—but down deep he also had a mean and bitter streak, a bully's heart capable of beating even more ruthlessly than Nino's.

They met when Roy came to Bath Beach one day to visit his mother, a widow who had recently moved into the home of a widowed friend who lived a few blocks from the bunker. Nino already knew of Roy, because Roy was already a minor criminal legend in certain parts of adjoining working-class neighborhoods east of Bath Beach—Flatlands and Canarsie. Nino heard about him from friends in the much smaller Lucchese Mafia family, which controlled tow truck companies, junkyards, and car theft operations in that part of Brooklyn and which was historically close to the Gambino family because children of the two bosses had gotten married.

Always on the alert for new business partners, as was Roy, Nino sent a message through mutual acquaintances for Roy to stop by the next time he was in Bath Beach. Roy did not need a second invitation. Anthony Gaggi was a made man in the Gambino family, the city's most important, and Roy was nothing if not ambitious and opportunistic. He did not intend to spend his life hanging out at junkyards, the horizon he saw with the Lucchese family.

Roy also was a man who liked to keep up with the

Joneses, and he made enough illegal money to afford it. In 1966, he left Brooklyn and settled in the suburban haven of Massapequa Park on Long Island, moving into a substantial home he custom-built on three adjacent lots on Park Place. He did a lot of the work himself, because among all his other still-developing qualities Roy was adroit with tools. He lived there with his wife Gladys, who was already regretting having married Roy six years before but was also accommodating to it, and their children, who were about to number three.

It was quite a feat for Roy to raise the necessary couple of hundred thousand to buy into exclusive Massapequa Park; even if the house was not in the absolute best part of town, Massapequa Park was still where Carlo Gambino himself owned a country manor, to go along with his Brooklyn apartment. Roy drove by the old legend's house many times through the years, but as ambitious as he was, he never dared to drop in without an invitation—which never came because Roy was not even on the bottom of the totem pole yet.

With his egg-shaped face, slicked-back hair, and lumpy build, Roy looked more like an indifferent civil servant than a prosperous young gangster. But as many people already knew, it was hard to be indifferent about Roy; they either liked him, or kept their distance, usually out of fear. Though overweight, Roy was incredibly strong and a wicked sucker-puncher in a bar fight.

He was also a criminal anomaly in that he was raised in an ordinary middle class family—an extraordinary one once you went beyond his parents; his mother never worked, but his father, who died when Roy was nineteen, was a sternly law-abiding laundry company deliveryeryman whom Roy stopped getting along with once he hit his teenage years and set much higher financial goals for himself.

Other relatives of Roy, however, were distinguished professional men. One uncle, a former top prosecutor for the Brooklyn District Attorney, was a professor at Brooklyn Law School. Another uncle ran a Buick dealership. His father's cousin was the medical examiner for New York City, a big job. Roy's mother, who he did get along with, always wanted him to be a doctor too, he always said.

"Ya know somethin'?" Roy would say later in life, "I am just my family's black sheep." *Ya know somethin'?* was a phrase he put at the front of many sentences, as if he wanted people to concentrate on the unique statement he was about to make.

From Massapequa Park, Roy still drove his new Cadillac in to Brooklyn each day, back to his base of operations and his roots. His office was a blue-collar bar, Phil's Lounge, that was just a few blocks from his childhood home in Flatlands. He rarely had a drink at the bar, though Roy did like a drink at home after the day's scheming was done. He also was a familiar sight at neighborhood hangouts like Benny's Candy Store, Jimmy's Restaurant, and a bowling alley for nostalgic Brooklyn Dodgers' fans, Gil Hodges Lanes. Roy may have gone to live next door to the Joneses, but since high school and for the rest of his life he worked among the Profacis, the DiNomes, the Foronjys, the Dohertys—all friends and acquaintances from his below-twenty years.

Flatlands was a historic neighborhood. Roy's childhood home was five blocks from where the first Dutch settlers in Brooklyn built their village square. Saluting a town in Holland, the explorers christened the settlement New Amersfoort, but that name eventually gave way to one descriptive of what attracted them—flat land. The treeless plains of that far western section of mid-seventeenth-century Long Island suited the Dutch, who were inexperienced at clearing forests.

The land was occupied by Delaware Valley Indians known as the Canarsee, meaning "fort" in their language. The main encampment of the Canarsee was across a narrow inlet of the Atlantic Ocean to the east, and so the area across the inlet from Flatlands became known, with a variant spelling, as Canarsie.

At the start of the twentieth century, nonfarm families began moving into Flatlands. The first subdivisions were built in the 1920s; by 1941, when Roy's family arrived, most of the community was paved over. From Bath Beach, Flatlands was seven miles northeast along the Brooklyn coastline and connected by roads built on original Canarsee trails.

Roy's family moved into a very bunker-like red-brick

house on Avenue P when he was just a month old and the fourth baby of Anthony and Eleanor DeMeo. Their other children were a girl two years older than Roy and two boys, one ten years older, the other seven. As in Nino Gaggi's case, and as was common then, a few of Roy's relatives, an uncle, aunt, and two cousins, also lived in the house, on the top floor. Everyone had been residing in Williamsburg, an older Brooklyn neighborhood directly across the East River from Manhattan that had been settled by their Neapolitan ancestors.

Because of Roy's father's steady delivery job, the family was no better or worse off than most of their similarly employed and hard-working neighbors—mostly second-generation immigrants of Italian and Irish background. Still, like everyone else, the family watched its pennies, especially after Eleanor gave birth to her fifth and final child, another boy, in 1950. As Roy would, all the DeMeo kids took after-school jobs as soon as they were old enough.

As Roy approached his tenth year, his second-oldest brother, who was named after his father Anthony, took a job as a soda jerk at a popular local fountain. Anthony was nicknamed Chubby; he was short but very broad and muscular in the upper body from working out with weights. Everyone on the block loved Chubby and thought he was the most promising DeMeo kid. Roy's mother actually dreamed of Chubby becoming a doctor before Roy. Roy's father was putting away all his overtime so his namesake could attend college, a first in their branch of the family. They could only help one, and it was going to be Chubby.

Sixteen-year-old Chubby slipped Roy a free chocolate shake now and then, but not too often because Roy was already grossly overweight. Other kids taunted him about it. ''Hey little fat boy, why don't you roll on over here,'' some of the older brats in the Foronjy house one door away or the Duddy house across the street would yell out at Roy as he left for parish school a few blocks away.

Because of his weight, Roy was so slow afoot that sooner or later most of the neighborhood's jerks got around to terrorizing him; a favorite game, especially if some girl was within sight, involved three or more morons sneaking up on Roy from behind; while two held his arms, a third pulled his britches down.

None of this ever happened, however, when Chubby DeMeo was on the block. And even if he was off mixing shakes, some jerks were made to pay the price later. The more bulky Chubby got from lifting weights, the less Roy was bothered. Naturally, Roy began to idolize his powerful, popular brother.

Roy's Roman Catholic parish school, Saint Thomas Aquinas, was only four blocks from home. All the DeMeo kids went there until they were old enough for public high school. Roy was an inquisitive student, if a bit too talkative in class, and he got good marks. The school also tried to hammer home the values of religious devotion and patriotism; ''For God and Country'' was carved into the school's cornerstone.

Like Chubby, Roy was more patriotic than devout. In 1951, after war broke out in Korea, seventeen-year-old Chubby caused his parents worry by volunteering for the Marine Corps. Still, they were proud, and he was a dashing sight in his dress blues. Roy told friends of his plans to enlist too, but this changed when only a few months after Chubby set sail for Korea, two Marines in dress blues knocked on the door of the house on Avenue P and said Chubby DeMeo had been killed in action.

The neighbors always talked about how there never was another happy day in the DeMeo home after that. Roy's mother stopped talking and sat weeping in her bedroom for three months. No one ever saw a smile on Roy's father's face again either. Roy was devastated too but began to express his hurt in ways that surprised neighbors.

At Saint Thomas Aquinas, Roy began picking on the younger, smaller kids for no reason but the anger inside. He continued to get good grades, but he became a fat little bully boy. At home, neighbors began to hear violent shouting between Roy and his father Anthony.

Roy's new ways were not the only problem. His father had instructed Roy to avoid all contact with three boys about his age who lived two doors away, the Profaci brothers. Their uncle was Joseph Profaci, a well-known Mafia boss; on Friday nights a lot of well-known gangsters came in Cadillacs to the Profaci home on Avenue P to play poker. Anthony DeMeo knew well of the Profaci crowd because one of his brothers, Albert, was a top prosecutor for the Brooklyn District Attorney and had tried to send many of them to jail. Roy owed his middle name to Uncle Albert.

Roy, however, liked the Profaci boys and liked to sit on the stoop with them as all the gangsters arrived in their big shiny cars. They looked as dashing to Roy as Marines in dress blues once did.

"That was my brother Chubby's mistake," Roy would say later on, "believing all that Marine bull-shit."

Roy's father slapped him a few times for violating his order not to hang out with the Profaci brothers, but the slaps were no match for the thrill Roy got watching the gangsters come and go. Besides, Roy's mother did not feel the same about the situation as her husband; she was good friends with the mother of the Profaci boys. The boys were not gangsters, she tried pointing out to him; in fact, all were smart students headed for college.

In 1955, Roy graduated eighth grade and enrolled in James Madison High School, one of the city's best. Its graduates, determined to fulfill the dreams of their immigrant grandparents and parents, included two Nobel Prize winners, environmentalist Barry Commoner, writer Irwin Shaw, writer-producer Garson Kanin, and many other notables in their fields—including popular New York deejay Bruce Morrow and several more writers and reporters, lawyers, politicians, and actors. The singer Carole King was one class ahead of Roy.

Roy was slimmer now, but hardly svelte. His anger was more under control, but when unleashed in a street fight, it was something few classmates wanted to see. Roy scratched, gouged, kicked, did anything possible to get the advantage. All of that occurred outside school, however. In school, Roy earned good conduct, punctuality, and perfect attendance awards many times. Except for his father, he seemed to respect people with power; on his report cards, his teachers wrote that Roy was "dependable," "well-behaved," and "coopera-tive."

Some teachers even thought Roy was a bit of a brown-noser. Throughout high school, he was a room assistant and lunchroom guard—"stoolpigeon" jobs similar to the one that, in 1957 in Bath Beach, had gotten newly elected class president Dominick Santamaria/Montiglio in such trouble with his Uncle Nino.

Disappointing his mother, who wanted him to try and become the doctor Chubby was supposed to be, Roy elected to concentrate on manual arts in high school. His impatience to get out of his father's house and begin making money was too strong for him to think about committing himself to eight or more years of study. It certainly was not because he could not cut it academically. Competing against some of the city's ablest college-bound students in mandatory academic classes, he scored well above average.

With students in shop classes, Roy talked about the Profaci crowd; with students in biology class, he talked about his Uncle Albert, the prominent prosecutor and a man who had power. Uncle Albert's name was frequently in the newspapers, most notably for putting away some brainy boys from Williamsburg who murdered a vagrant, apparently on a lark. In what was known as the "Thrill-Kill Case," Albert DeMeo defeated the bigtime Manhattan defense lawyers hired by the boys' wealthy parents.

One irony of Albert's work, of course, was that he prosecuted friends and relatives of Roy's friends, the Profaci boys, including Joseph Profaci, their uncle. Albert, however, lost more of these cases than he won. A characteristic of Mafia cases, he complained often enough for Roy to hear, was that witnesses "get up on the stand and don't say what they said to the grand jury."

Roy never forgot that indirect lesson or its implication: The witnesses had been intimidated, and the technique worked.

At James Madison, Roy was an honor student in manual arts. The curriculum plan permitted him to leave school early in the afternoon to work, so at age fifteen he found a part-time job stocking shelves and delivering groceries on a three-wheeled bicycle for Banner Dairy, a local grocery store.

The store manager, Charles Healey, a young Marine just home from Korea, did not understand why Roy sneered about this until he learned about Chubby from other teenagers. Roy also impressed Healey as one of the hardest workers he ever met. When Roy made deliveries, he loaded the bike with twice as many orders as anyone else. Soon, he was making up to one hundred dollars a week—great money for a teenager in 1956.

Working in the store, Roy slimmed down further; like Chubby, when he was that age, he also put on muscle. In the basement of Banner Dairy, he began weightlifting one-hundred-pound cartons of Ivory Snow detergent boxes, the heaviest in the store. He called it "working out with Ivory large," and it became a ritual. The store manager and others gathered to watch him work out.

"Okay, Roy," Healey would say, "that's eleven, one more and you break your record."

Roy broke his record many times, but eventually lost interest in weightlifting. Gradually, he put on weight again, but retained his Ivory-large upper body strength.

Healey, who became a cop and then a United States marshal in Brooklyn after his days at Banner Dairy, once teased Roy about a much larger kid he also employed there: "You better not fool around with Dave, he'll knock you on your ass."

One day, Roy and Dave started teasing each other; it got out of hand and Roy attacked his opponent so ferociously—scratching, gouging, kicking—that Healey became frightened. He and some of his other stockboys managed to pull Roy away but not before Dave was a pulpy mess.

"Roy is scary," Healey said after he sent Roy home and Dave was carted away.

While still in high school, and with delivery money to burn, Roy started loaning money to friends and eventually to anyone who asked. His reputation as a dirty fighter—newly reinforced by accounts of his attack on Dave—assured prompt payment of principal and vig. Loansharking was just the sort of contaminant Roy's father had in mind when he ordered Roy to avoid the Profaci boys, and one day not long after it began, neighbors saw Roy and his father slugging it out in the middle of Avenue P.

By his senior year, Roy was carrying cash around in brown paper bags and driving a not-too-used Cadillac. He was the star of the manual arts crowd at James Madison and would pick up the tab for beer bashes, which he enjoyed. He loved showing off his money; it made him feel powerful. More and more teens short of cash on date night borrowed money, and by the time he graduated in 1959, Roy was, for someone eighteen, fairly prosperous. He told the yearbook editors that his career goal was business.

Because he was overweight and not the most handsome guy in Flatlands, Roy was not successful with neighborhood girls. Soon after graduating, he married one of the first who ever said yes to a date. Her name was Gladys Brittain; she was petite, quiet, two years older, and cute. She also was a good person and out of a respectable family, so Roy's parents were happy for him and her. As his oldest brother and older sister had, Roy left the house on Avenue P, leaving only a younger brother at home.

Between his job and the loansharking, Roy was able to rent a nice apartment not far away; at Banner Dairy, he became assistant manager and occasional apprentice to the man who ran the butcher shop. The man taught Roy how to slice apart whole steers quickly and efficiently.

Roy was just marking time at Banner Dairy, however. By now, he fully intended to make his living as a loanshark. There were just too many suckers out there, and he kept putting more money "on the street," as he described it.

On the night of December 12, 1960, Anthony DeMeo, Roy's fifty-five-year-old father, was found dead in a subway car, felled by a heart attack as he went to work. Roy did not wish his old man ill, but he got over the death more quickly than he did Chubby's. And when his mother took her youngest son and went to Italy for a few years, to grieve and live with relatives near Naples, Roy suddenly had no immediate family members around.

Roy and Gladys, however, had already started building their own family, and in five weeks time, Gladys gave birth to a baby girl, the first of three children she had during the next eight years. Roy was wild about his kids—less so, over time, his wife. They got married before they really knew one another well, a particular problem for her because, while she knew about Roy's loan business, she never meant to marry a fullfledged criminal, which is what Roy became during this time. She shut her eyes to it, however, and stayed married for the kids' sake and her own. Roy did provide, copiously.

Roy began launching his career in crime from Phil's Lounge, the neighborhood bar a few blocks from his old home in Flatlands. With an eclectic assortment of friends, acquaintances, loanshark customers, and even some of the jerks who taunted him when he was just a slow little fat boy, Roy had been hanging out at the bar since graduating from high school. At one time or another, the crowd included the three Profaci brothers, the five Foronjy brothers, the three Doherty brothers, and the three DiNome brothers—all except the DiNomes were from Avenue P.

Some in the crowd, such as the Profaci boys, were actually college students and not around as often. Others, such as one of the Doherty boys, had joined the police force, but John Doherty still came around. His brother Charles tended bar once in a while. The group also included a future burglar, an electrical contractor, a tailor, a sportswear retailer, and in the case of one of the older Foronjy brothers, Richard, a Hollywood actor in such films as *Prince of the City* and *Serpico,* but only after he got out of prison for an armed robbery conviction.

Roy's best friend at the time was Frank Foronjy, the future electrical contractor. Frank was interested in guns, and had begun to collect them. He taught Roy about various weapons, and Roy would eventually become a collector too, in a more elaborate way and for different purposes of course. Once he became interested in guns, Roy practiced firing them and became good and fast, especially after John Doherty, who was police-trained, showed him the finer points of the combat-firing position.

One of Roy's friendships showed that he was capable of sympathy for people who had been tormented as he was when he was young. He had gone out of his way to befriend one of the DiNome brothers, Frederick, who came from the wrong side of the tracks in Canarsie, an area known as Pigtown because even in the early 1960s swine farms were still prevalent there. Freddy was a mechanic at a Canarsie gasoline station where Roy and others from Phil's Lounge bought their gas cheap.

Freddy never made it past fourth grade because school doctors failed to diagnose a dyslexic condition that made it difficult for him to understand letters and numbers. Instead, they classified him as a slow learner and threw him in with students who were actually retarded. Some people, but not Roy, made fun of the lean and gawky mechanic because he never did learn to read or write and because he sometimes acted like his synapses were not firing, the way some mentally disabled kids do. He was, however, a genius with cars; unable to make sense of manuals, he still made engines purr and built new ones out of others' junk.

Freddy was twelve days younger than Roy; his mother had died about the same time as Chubby DeMeo. Roy invited him and his brother Richard, who was not much of a genius about anything, to stop by Phil's Lounge anytime. Roy's benevolence made Freddy a fiercely loyal friend. "Roy is the smartest guy I know," he would tell everyone. "I would do anything for Roy."

The friendship had its rewards. Freddy had already done two years in jail for stealing a truckload of batteries. And he was not just a mechanic when Roy met him; he was a car thief working for the Lucchese Mafia men who ran the Canarsie junkyards. Freddy specialized in Volkswagens—parts were scarce, therefore valuable. Freddy also stole motorcycles whenever he or any of a group of motorcycle hounds he rode with needed a spare part. The motorcyclists were known as the Aliens of Pigtown.

Through Freddy, Roy began meeting a vast new array of possible loanshark customers—thieves, robbers, hijackers, all manner of lowlifes. Through Freddy, Roy even met some of the Lucchese Mafia gangsters who ran the junkyards. He was not that impressed.

Eventually, all these people made their way to Phil's Lounge, joining the cops, firemen, and other city workers from the neighborhood who came to socialize and make a bet with the bar's bookmakers. For Roy, working this crowd was like shooting ducks in a pond. Soon he had so much money on the street and so much coming back on a regular basis that he quit Banner Dairy.

From age twenty-two on he never worked another legitimate day. He began stealing cars with Freddy not because he needed the money but to learn the business; same thing with the break-ins he committed with a friend from the Avenue P crowd. Working the bar crowd, he also fenced stolen cars and other property. In time he became a kind of concierge of crime in Flatlands and Canarsie, the person to see for this or that.

Making his deals, Roy emphasized the making of relationships just as much. Relationships produced benefits beyond the immediate deal, he always said. "My business is just buying and selling," Roy began to say to Gladys and everyone else—including his mother, after she returned from Italy and moved into the home of her good friend Mrs. Profaci, who was a widow now too and living in Bath Beach.

In 1965, Roy began demonstrating what was to be a lifelong paranoia about the Internal Revenue Service—the only arm of the law that really scared him. He could not just fail to file, as many criminals do, because he had already demonstrated a filing history while working at Banner Dairy. So Roy, through his relationships, worked out deals with a couple of friends who owned small businesses to carry him on their books as an employee. The trick was deciding how much salary to claim; the more salary, the more taxes, and naturally he wanted to pay the smallest possible tax. This became a trickier equation as Roy made plans to build a house in Massapequa Park—how to avoid IRS suspicion that his lifestyle exceeded his income while still chiseling every dime he could.

At Gil Hodges Lanes one day, before the move to Massapequa Park, Roy sought out a former Saint Thomas Aquinas classmate who was now an IRS agent. He asked how the IRS conducted "net-worth" cases—how it proved someone spent more than they reported as income. "How would you make such a case against a guy who said he made his money gambling?"

The agent put Roy off—one of the rare times Roy was unable to develop a relationship—and it angered him. When he later ran into the agent at a wake for a mutual acquaintance, he loudly and sarcastically proclaimed to a group of mourners that "stoolpigeons" were in the room and he was leaving.

After building his house in Massapequa Park, and despite his worries about his fictional returns, Roy was the most successful twenty-five-year-old that he knew—with the possible exception of Freddy DiNome. With money made from stolen Volkswagens, Freddy had built a race car and become a star on the professional drag-racing circuit. Late-night television commercials promoted the appearances of "Broadway Freddy" at local and national race tracks; he was making one hundred thousand dollars a year.

In 1966, after his first get-acquainted meeting with Anthony Gaggi, Roy set his sights on becoming a member of the Gambino Mafia family; from his Uncle Albert's old stories and his contacts in the Luchese family, he already knew a lot about its history.

After winning the power struggle that followed the assassination of Albert Anastasia, Carlo Gambino had inherited an army of some two hundred fifty made men and at least that many collaborators. They controlled a network of gambling, fencing, and prostitution operations and held key positions with labor unions and trade groups in the garment, construction, food, and private sanitation industries. Men dealing drugs were ordered to stop—or be killed. Carlo believed that the severe penalties attached to drug crimes pressured defendants to become informers.

Since Carlo's takeover, the family's influence had spread like a virus. Carlo orchestrated schemes affecting everyday life in many ways: from monopolistic practices that added a few dollars to the cost of clothes and food to the bid-rigging, bribes, and threats that added many thousands to the cost of unloading ships and building skyscrapers. The racketeering produced cash for loansharking; the family became an underground Citibank for people unable to get legitimate loans. Carlo's men borrowed from him at low interest, then loaned the money out at high interest; their books yielded regular income—and business opportunities that fed the virus.

Nino Gaggi was a good example. By 1966, he received hundreds of dollars a week in interest from loans to jewelry shops, truck companies, and many clients in the car world—repair shops, used-car lots, gas stations, and automobile dealerships. The customers knew that if they failed to meet their obligations they had to invite their unforgiving banker into their businesses, and thus Nino had become a secret owner of a restaurant in Manhattan, a film-processing lab in Brooklyn, and another Manhattan operation that made and distributed counterfeit copies of X-rated films.

Although doing well, Nino wanted more. That's what the game was about. And that's why he wanted to meet the dynamo from Flatlands who was making so much he had already built a fancy home, whereas Nino was just beginning to scout out property in Florida on which he intended to build a deluxe getaway for himself, Rose, and their children.

It increased Nino's status in the family if he also earned more for Carlo and Paul. By Mafia tradition, a soldier was obligated to give his capo a negotiable percentage of his earnings, just as the capo was expected to do the same with his boss. Predictably, nearly everyone cheated, but the more money one earned, the less it hurt to give some up.

To test a possible relationship, Nino proposed that he and Roy co-make a loan to one of Nino's customers, a used-car dealer who wanted to expand. Roy jumped at the chance and promised to pick up the man's payments and faithfully bring Nino's share to him. That way, dependable Roy would get to see Nino more.

That same year, 1966, Roy began building another relationship that eventually led him to the business Carlo Gambino had banned—drug dealing. Like the one he had with the pitiable mechanic who became a successful dragracer, Freddy DiNome, this relationship was with a person he felt sympathy for—a sixteen-year-old kid with a huge chip on his shoulder because he was short and Jewish, when he wanted to be tall and Italian like all his friends.

Just as with Freddy, Roy met Chris Rosenberg at a gas station in Canarsie, and he could see that underneath the chip the kid was ambitious and smart—for one thing, he knew who Roy was. Chris was making a few bucks dealing marijuana, and Roy loaned him some money so he could deal in larger amounts.

Through the late 1960s, Roy continued to nurture his relationship with Nino. They made more loans together and Roy found new markets for Nino's counterfeit X-rated film operation. Roy and Nino each had what the other wanted. Roy was a moneymaker; Nino had influence. Working for Nino, Roy would have Gambino family cachet, which would enhance his moneymaking, especially if he too ever became a made man. So, by 1970, Roy was working for Nino—and giving him hundreds a week just for being his boss.

During that time Roy also brought Chris Rosenberg along, loaning him money for more drug deals and selling off the cars that Chris and his friends stole to his connections in the Canarsie junkyards. Chris introduced his friends to Roy, and by 1972, Roy was the Fagin of Flatlands, with his own loyal crew of young drug dealers and car thieves.

It was not all business, however. Roy and his young friends got together socially. They went to watch "Broadway Freddy" race and to Frank Foronjy's farm, where they learned to shoot the guns Roy had begun collecting. His collection, which was more like an arsenal, included machineguns, automatic rifles, shotguns, and silencers for the handguns. Roy also invited them to Massapequa Park for barbecues—generally, the only time Roy let people see him get drunk. None had ever seen a house like Roy's, at least not from the inside, where all the floors were marble. Roy now even employed a gardener and a maid, and the food and drink he offered were always top shelf.

Like diminutive Chris, the young men closest to Roy were all good-looking characters, if in a dangerous sort of way. The contrast between them and Roy was actually remarkable. Where he was dowdy and lumpy, they were chiseled and sleek. Some years later, someone videotaped one of the elaborate barbecues, which were by then a DeMeo crew tradition. No one ever said Roy ever made amorous moves on his crew, but in the videotape—as he ate, drank, and swapped stories with his crew—he looked like a man who might pay handsome young men to hang around—not for actual sex necessarily but for the hint and scent of it.

Roy had begun cheating on Gladys with some of the

barmaids who worked at his office in Flatlands. It began happening after Phil's Lounge came up short of cash and Roy stepped in with six thousand dollars and became the secret owner as the bar was reborn the Gemini Lounge. On paper, the bar was owned by one of the Doherty brothers from Avenue P, Charles, the one Roy was closest to. It was incorporated as Charley D's, but before it opened, Doherty, a horoscope fan, decided his astrological sign provided a better name. Another Doherty brother, Daniel, helped out with the bartending, and so did another one of the Foronjy brothers, also named Charles.

Roy's new friends knew he was unfaithful because he bragged about it. Success with women was something Roy never experienced as a teenager, but now that he had money and status (at least in the Gemini Lounge context) Roy discovered that some plain Janes would jump into bed with him. Because his marriage was more one of convenience anyway, he never lost a guilty moment over these one-hour stands in an apartment next to the Gemini. Even if his marriage was a good one, he probably would not have felt guilt, given the gross remarks he would make about his tawdry conquests. "I made her do things you wouldn't believe and then I fucked her in the ass," Roy would tell his young friends. With Roy, sex was money; it was a way to show how strong he was.

Roy's neighbors did not fail to notice that a lot of young men were always pulling into Roy's driveway in fancy sportscars. But they were too discreet to comment on it in front of Roy and accommodating Gladys, who were actually a popular couple on Park Place. If Roy noticed his neighbors raking leaves, he offered extra trash bags. When he cleaned his garage, he invited them to take what they wanted before tossing anything away.

The front porch of the DeMeos' two-story, bay-windowed house offered a lovely view of a sloping tree-lined yard, around which strong-armed Roy personally erected a corral-type fence. During holidays, the house was decorated inside and out, and an outdoor speaker system played seasonal music. Gladys, who loved being a mother if not Roy's wife, marked every holiday with special batches of cookies for all the Park Place kids.

The neighbors were also too polite to comment on the house's sophisticated alarm system, or the iron bars across the windows, or the irony of Roy saying he was going to his office when everyone else was coming home from theirs. His neighbors only saw the jovial, helpful side of dependable, cooperative, and well-behaved Roy.

When the Hanes boy was struck by a car in the middle of the block, Roy was the first adult on the scene. He comforted the injured boy and took him to a hospital in nearby Amityville. Gladys told neighbors that Roy was still shaking when he came home because the Hanes boy was a playmate of their son Albert, who had inherited Roy's middle name (Roy's prominent lawyer-uncle's first name).

"Roy kept saying he did what he did because that could have been Albert out there bleeding on the street," Gladys said.

When some older boys began parking their cars around the corner from Park Place at all hours of the night and using the woods in a state park behind Roy's house for pot parties, Roy swung into action. With his German shepherd watchdog Champ at his side one night, he went into the woods and confronted the teenagers.

"I don't want any drugs in my neighborhood! Get the hell out and don't come back! Never!"

The neighbors figured the rumors about Roy, that he was a "big racketeer" in Brooklyn, must have reached the teenagers because they never did come back.

Occasionally, Roy and Gladys hosted parties for everyone on the block. The biggest party every year was on the Fourth of July and always featured an illegal fireworks display—which always drew a wink from the local cops. The next day Roy would be out in the street, sweeping up Roman Candle fragments. One year, a neighbor complained that some large rockets landed on his roof, and Roy promised to eliminate them the following year, which he did.

Roy had to swindle a lot of money to support this life, but that was no problem. In partnership with Nino, or his crew, or sometimes on his own, he was constantly panning the landscape for opportunity. For instance, in 1972, he joined the Boro of Brooklyn Credit Union and within months had talked his way onto the board of directors; he soon showed some of his colleagues how they could earn something on the side by using the credit union as a laundering service for drug dealers Roy had met; with the others' connivance, Roy also dipped into credit union reserves to finance loans in his mushrooming book. Roy's book was still anchored in the car business, but it was soon to include a dentist, an abortion clinic, a flea market, and two restaurants.

Unknown to Roy, someone in the credit union complained about what was going on there, and for the first time Roy's name entered an official police file. That same year, an informant caused an FBI agent to place a sparse note in bureau files: Two men known only as Nino and Roy had muscled their way into a company that processed X-rated films. It was the first time the name "Nino" appeared in any official file too.

Viewed from another angle, the note was even more significant. This newest scheme of Nino's and Roy's would lead Roy over the bridge separating those who merely steal from those who kill. Nino had already crossed it; once Roy did, removing the last barrier to unrestrained criminality, the bully in him would surface again, in new monstrous ways.

Paul Rothenberg's X-rated business was a natural extension of the counterfeit film business Nino already had, for which Roy had been finding new markets. It was also a perfect extortion target; it was lucrative, yet small, uncomplicated, and only semilegitimate.

With a partner, Rothenberg owned two film processing labs. The labs served commercial clients, but also producers of X-rated and in some cases clearly pornographic movies, by the standards of New York's obscenity laws.

Rothenberg, age forty-three, had been arrested four times, pleading guilty in one case to possessing what a judge described as "the worst type of hardcore pornography." He was believed to be the largest processor of blue movies in New York and charged as much as thirty dollars per film. He lived with his wife and three children in a swank community on Long Island.

One of Roy's loanshark customers told him about Rothenberg's business. On a spring day in 1972, Nino and Roy visited Rothenberg at his companies' Manhattan headquarters. In the meeting, Nino would be the good cop, Roy the bad.

Nino suggested to Rothenberg that with his and Roy's connections they could help improve his business, if only he would make them silent partners. Rothenberg said no thanks and laughed. Roy then slapped him across the face like Rothenberg was just a kid at Saint Thomas Aquinas who had been disrespectful. In his hand, Roy also had a pistol, from his collection.

Rothenberg could hardly complain to the police, so he and his partner began paying Nino and Roy several hundred dollars a week, the amount depending on the number of films they processed each week.

Rothenberg hated being squeezed. A woman friend later told police she heard him arguing on the telephone once with someone he described as a partner who was taking too much money from him.

"I just finished paying this guy off and he wants more," Rothenberg said to her.

The arrangement lasted a year, until the labs were raided and Rothenberg and his partner, Anthony Argila, were arrested. The police took films they valued at two hundred fifty thousand dollars, films with titles like *Deep Throat—Number Five*.

"We don't think we're doing anything wrong," Argila told police. "We're just making a living."

Wrong or not, both faced several felony charges—and heavy prison time. Nino and Roy instantly realized that they too were in serious trouble, if either Rothenberg or Argila decided to reveal how they were extorted.

The day after the raid, Roy met Rothenberg at a diner and gave him twenty-five hundred dollars toward his legal defense. It hardly seemed appropriate under the circumstances, but Roy also gave him a gold ladies' wristwatch festooned with diamonds and asked him to try and fence it. The watch had been stolen in a one million dollar hijacking at Kennedy Airport a few months before.

In a few days, after sifting records confiscated in the

raid, the police came back to Rothenberg and Argila and asked about checks made out to Roy DeMeo and cashed at the Boro of Brooklyn Credit Union.

"Business expenses," Argila said.

"Extortion payments," Rothenberg said.

Rothenberg then refused to say any more. Over the next few days, a Manhattan assistant district attorney called Rothenberg's lawyer to urge him to urge his client to cooperate. Rothenberg might help his own case if he gave information about a Mafia extortion scheme. Several meetings to discuss the proposal were scheduled, then canceled—the last on Friday, July 27, 1973.

That night, Roy called Rothenberg and scheduled a meeting on Sunday morning at a diner near both their houses. Roy told him he wanted his hot ladies' watch back, but in reality Nino had decided Rothenberg had to be killed and had ordered Roy to do the job. Roy had already demonstrated he was an earner; it was time to see if he possessed the other necessary made-man trait, the murdering one.

Roy was more than ready to oblige. The murder would seal his alliance with Nino and put him on the Gambino fast track. So, in Roy's mind, murder, like sex and money, became just a way to show power.

At the diner, Roy sat in his car and waited until Rothenberg arrived in his. Getting straight to the task, he ordered Rothenberg out of his car at silencer-equipped gunpoint, marched him into an alleyway and fired two bullets into his head with the calm of an executioner. No muss, no fuss. No mistakes, no guilt.

Rothenberg's partner, Anthony Argila, was boating when the murder occurred. In interviews with detectives, he made statements that were proven to be lies. He denied even knowing Roy, but detectives tailing Roy after the murder saw them meet twice. Argila knew his partner was thinking of cooperating, but Argila had decided it was safer to keep quiet, which he continued to do.

When police questioned Roy, he told them only his name and address. With Argila afraid for his life, Roy was confident the case would go no further, and it never did. Roy's partner, the man known only as "Nino," was not even identified.

For thirty-two-year-old Roy, the murder was an epiph-anous moment. He tried explaining it to his young fol-lowers. "Ya know somethin'? After you kill someone, anything is possible."

CHAPTER 3

Hill 875

The first time Dominick Montiglio was ever in an airplane, he jumped out—and what a glorious feeling it was when his parachute popped and he was just a kid's balloon floating in the pillowy sky above Fort Benning, Georgia. He yelled like he was back on Coney Island: "Airborne! Airrrborrrne!"

Beside him other recruits floated down too. He had passed basic and advanced infantry training and was in Airborne Ranger school, the third leg of his quest for a Green Beret. The spontaneity of his enlistment aside, he was on a mission to prove himself right and Nino wrong.

He was immune to the era's budding antiwar movement. His new buddies were the same. Soldiers in other units had begun greeting each other with the word "Peace." Not Rangers. They said, "War!" When they sang Ranger songs on long humps across Georgia's clay plains, it was with fervor generals dream about. "I wanna be an Airborne Ranger! I wanna live the life of danger!"

The reward at the end of those humps was having to recite the Ranger Creed while bellying through a trench a hundred yards long and full of excrement, mud, and garbage. "I accept the fact that as a Ranger my country expects me to move farther, faster, and fight harder than any other soldier. Readily will I display the intestinal fortitude required to fight on to the Ranger objective and complete the mission, though I be the lone survivor."

Though I be the lone survivor was the phrase Dominick began quoting to people back home.

After seventy-seven days of physical torture and mental abuse, the formerly chunky boy from Brooklyn by way of Levittown graduated Ranger School with a lean, hard body, a supremely confident attitude, and a two-pack-a-day Camel habit; his buddies nicknamed him

"Stubby" because he was only five-feet-eight but strong as a tree trunk.

Next came the John F. Kennedy Special Warfare Center at Fort Bragg, in North Carolina. He learned how to throw a hatchet and to use two hundred sixty-seven other instruments of death, from garrotes to .50 caliber machineguns. He was cross-trained in two specialties—light weapons and silent warfare. When he finally got his Green Beret, he was a land-based stealth fighter.

Unaccompanied by any members of the Gaggi family, the Montiglio family saw him off at an airport in New Jersey the day he left for South Vietnam. The goodbye had a double-edged poignancy because his mother Marie had recently been diagnosed as having Hodgkin's disease, a cancer for which treatment was then limited. Her doctors had told her she might live several more years, or only a few—it was impossible to tell.

"You can't die before I do," she told her son.

"Though I be the lone survivor, Mom," he said. "Promise."

At the time, counterinsurgency was the primary Green Beret mission. They parachuted into enemy territory to blow up convoys, capture prisoners and spread disinformation. On one such mission two months after he arrived, Dominick saved a life and, so far as he knew, took one for the first time. As he ran to a helicopter extraction, a Beret behind him was wounded by a sniper; he turned and saw the sniper racing toward the man to finish him off. He ran back, shot the enemy dead, and carried his comrade away. The man survived, and Dominick won his first medal, a Silver Star.

Later, he won a Bronze Star for saving a patrol from an ambush and helping to destroy a machinegun nest while under heavy fire. A writer heard about it and called him a "rawhide rough" hero in a magazine story picked up by a newspaper back home. The more combat he saw, however, the less the medals meant. The only medal he wore without unease was his Combat Infantryman's Badge because it was awarded for being under fire thirty straight days; to him, it was a greater measure of bravery than a single feat.

He survived his tour, then volunteered for special patrol duty with the 173d Airborne Brigade, his home unit.

Patrol members were known as LURPs, a twist on the acronym for their specialty, Long-Range Reconnaissance Patrol. As a Green Beret, he had done the same kind of hide-and-seek soldiering as the LURPs.

He became close to his LURP team's five other members, and after surviving a second tour, volunteered for a third to be with them. Home on leave, he broke the news to his mother, but she did not complain because he also said he intended to make a career of the Army and stay in at least twenty years. In the shadow of her terminal illness, she found more peace of mind in him going back to war than worrying about him drifting toward Nino's world once Hodgkin's disease finally claimed her.

Nino, of course, was appalled. "You really are an idiot," he told his nephew, "but a lucky one."

Nino's barbs did not sting like before because Dominick was certain he had won his respect. Nino might not have answered any of the six letters he wrote to him from Vietnam, but Dominick detected admiration in his uncle's voice when Nino probed for details about the medals and how he survived combat.

Dominick would cite training, prudence, teamwork, preparation, and luck—never the secret survival mantra he had adopted. In times of stress, when he was buried in some foxhole, hiding from the enemy or hoping the next mortar shell would land elsewhere, he would pull his poncho around like a boy hiding under the covers and, adapting an old story from Uncle Carlo, would repeat to himself, over and over, "I am the lion and fox. I am the lion and the fox."

In the summer of 1967, the twenty-year-old sergeant left for Vietnam again. His unit was now in the Central Highlands of South Vietnam. In the jungle hills west of Dak To, some twelve thousand North Vietnamese Army regulars had massed in order to seduce the U. S. forces into a fight, and late that summer the NVA got its wish.

It was the worst fighting of the war so far. The NVA had rigged the hills with tunnels and bunkers enabling them to withstand superior American firepower and mount a series of wicked artillery assaults and ground attacks. A one-hundred-sixty-four-man company of the 173d Airborne was reduced to forty-four. Many dead were dismembered during the artillery barrages; after one,

Dominick and others who knew their friends' tattoos were ordered into mobile morgues and asked to identify body parts.

The experience haunted him for days. He could not erase the images, nor his guilt for feeling relieved his arms and legs were not on display. After more skirmishes, he was awarded the Army's second-highest medal, the Distinguished Service Cross, which was pinned on him during a battlefield ceremony that included a symbolic tribute to the dead—one hundred twenty-six empty pairs of Ranger boots in neat eerie rows.

By fall, the U. S. command was certain the NVA had retreated to sanctuaries in Laos and Cambodia. In November, Dominick's six-man LURP team was ordered to scout a hill where commanders felt an NVA remnant was protecting the retreat. The hill was on the western edge of Cambodia and since it rose eight hundred seventy-five meters above sea level, was known by the Army as Hill 875.

LURP teams often stayed in the jungle up to two weeks before being helicoptered out. Their job was to get information and, if feasible, ambush enemy patrols. LURP warfare was constant tension spiced by moments of total terror, forgetting the one hundred degree temperatures, the ants, leeches, and mosquitoes, and the jungle's one hundred thirty-one varieties of poisonous snake, harmless until they sensed movement.

Dominick was his team's point man, the one who surveyed the landscape ahead for signs of life and death. He carried a shotgun because of its wide shot pattern at close range; he looked for bushes leaning the wrong way, rocks recently overturned, trees with suspicious branches. To his teammates, he had described his skill on point as "reading between the lines," a gift from his Uncle Nino, about whom little else was ever said.

On November 18, 1967, the patrol's tenth day on Hill 875, Dominick came around a bend in a trail and saw a series of manmade steps—short stalks of bamboo tied together with vines—running up and away from the trail, then vanishing in the bush; they appeared freshly made, and were the enemy's way of moving men and firepower up and down the hill in a hurry.

Following the steps, the team soon found an empty bunker. It appeared connected to a tunnel, which probably led to caves where the enemy had hid during American bomb attacks. Dominick decided the enemy was hiding now, letting the LURPs up the hill. He said to Uncle Ben, the LURPs' team leader, "They're not gonna hit us. They don't fucking want to."

"Not yet," Uncle Ben agreed.

"Bad vibes here," said Bones, the team's radio man.

Moving up, the LURPs found more empty bunkers, tunnels, and finally, an enemy base camp, recently abandoned, judging by campfire ashes. Evaluating the findings, commanders at Dak To decided the enemy had indeed kept a force on—or under—the hill to cover a retreat across the border. They ordered the 2d Battalion of the 503d Infantry, a thousand men, to the foot of the hill. They were to move up in the morning and look for a fight. The LURPs were told to spend the night where they were, halfway up.

At dawn, the jungle began to vibrate as preparatory shelling of bunkers pinpointed by the LURPs signaled the start of the assault. At 9:43 A.M., about five hundred men—Companies C and D of the 2d Battalion—began moving up. The LURPs were to monitor the action from above. It was their eleventh consecutive day in the bush; Dominick noticed he was running low on food and water.

Bones's radio soon crackled with urgent voices. A point man for one of the assault companies had been shredded at point blank range. When his friends went to get him, enemy gunners popped up and shot them down. Others tried advancing in greater numbers, but were pinned down and suffered heavy casualties. Company A of the 2d Battalion, protecting the rear, was then decimated by an NVA unit that circled in behind.

On Bones's radio, the LURPs heard the doomed Company A commander frantically shout that he was under fire from all sides and in danger of being overrun. They heard the stutter of automatic fire, swearing, screaming, then only static.

"Holy fuck," Dominick said. "They're wasted."

Down the hill, the rest of the 2d Battalion was surrounded. Each time troops tried moving in any direction they were mowed down. In much larger numbers than

Dak To commanders anticipated, the enemy was everywhere, racing up and down steps, dashing through tunnels, and popping out of bunkers to prevent escape. They had avoided contact with the LURPs until they had something to risk dying for: hundreds of Americans in an ambush.

The 2d Battalion was squeezed into a shrinking perimeter and exposed to a mortar rain. Bodies piled up in craters. The living tried hiding under the dead. Forty-man platoons became ten-man squads; eleven of thirteen medics died; all sixteen officers went down, eight permanently. Ten helicopters trying to deliver ammo and evacuate the wounded were shot out of the smoky sky.

The LURPs could do nothing but monitor the carnage on their radio. With the bombing and shelling between them and the battalion, they could not help. With the hill under NVA control, they could not run. They felt like prisoners as friends were tortured in the next cell, but their lives were now on the line too. Even if able to reach Dak To without the NVA eavesdropping on captured radios, Dak To did not have a way to extract them. Choppers still flying would be trying to help the men under fire. The LURPs were stranded and, in all likelihood, also surrounded.

As night fell they moved into a thicket and laid a "kill-zone" of defensive booby traps. The slaughter below continued several hours. When the explosions stopped, the wind carried the moaning of mangled men up to the LURP hideout. For a while, single gunshots rang out as wounded paratroopers not yet dragged to cover were executed by the NVA. After the shots died down, the wind brought the odor of burning opium, the enemy's tranquilizer. The LURPs now knew they would have a few hours of peace.

A damp chill settled over Hill 875. When it came Dominick's turn to try and sleep a couple of hours he curled up and pulled his poncho tightly around. "I am the lion and the fox. I am the lion and the fox. I am the lion and the fox."

The LURPs stayed in their hideout for two days and used the rest of their food and water. On the morning of the third day, as a ghostly blue haze draped the jungle, they heard muffled voices and clanging noises—the enemy was moving fresh troops out of the caves and down the hill, where the battle still raged.

The 4th Battalion, sent in to rescue the 2d, was also pinned down. Several more helicopters had been shot down, and wounded men were dying for lack of medical help. As enemy bugles signaled the start of more combat, Uncle Ben, the LURP leader, called a meeting to evaluate their predicament. Without food and water, it was useless staying hidden. They had to try to escape while they had the strength to fight.

Transmissions on the team's radio indicated that a force of many thousand NVA controlled the hill. The NVA could easily spare as much as a company, two hundred men, just to shadow the LURPs and "make sure we don't get away," Uncle Ben said.

"They know where we are. They know we have to move. When they hit us, we have to spread out and keep movin'. Move and fire. We ain't gonna lay down for the motherfuckers."

The LURPs moved out. Ten minutes down the hillside opposite the battle, they heard movement and dove for cover just as automatic fire erupted in front. Dominick heard bullets whizzing past his ears make a clicking sound as they broke the sound barrier and then a slapping sound as they slammed into bamboo.

The LURPs scattered. One of them began firing the team's omnipotent M-60 machinegun, which spewed deadly splinters of stalks and branches in all directions. Dominick looked up to another eerie sight: enemy dead dangling upside-down from trees like slaughterhouse steers. They had tied themselves to the branches so mere wounds would not fling them from their perches.

"Spread out!" Uncle Ben shouted. "Move and fire!"

The LURPs raced through the thickets, ducking and spraying fire. Changing directions to confuse the enemy, they ran right into them—pumping his shotgun, Dominick pulverized several at close range. The men took turns saving each other's lives, picking off NVA who popped up behind. They ran, ducked, and fired for forty minutes—it seemed like hours—until return fire ceased.

Soaked and aching, the LURPs gathered together. The jungle was absolutely still. All the birds and animals had long since left it to the humans. From the radio they learned another battalion was moving up their side of the hill, meaning they would soon be exposed to preparatory bombing and shelling. Uncle Ben then mapped an escape route that snaked through the worst fighting of the last few days. Low on ammo, they moved out again.

Progress was slow. They slithered through an evil-smelling area defoliated by napalm, whose powdery residue penetrated their fatigues. With nightfall, they hid again. Dominick shook from oncoming dehydration; his lips were cracked and bloody; his legs felt napalmed. But his ears hurt the most, because of the nonstop explosions all around the hill. He covered them with his hands as he tried digging a hole in the jungle floor with his elbows. Agonizing hours later, the noise stopped; he rolled on his back and stared at the stars, a body waiting for the coffin to be closed.

At first light, shell-shocked and dying of thirst, the LURPs moved out. Dominick was down to three shotgun shells and a single clip in his .45 caliber handgun. They came under fire immediately; rocket-propelled grenades exploded in the trees. Dominick saw Bones the radio man go down. He saw Uncle Ben run toward Bones, then fall. An NVA soldier popped up out of a bush and aimed at Dominick, but Uncle Ben popped back up and shot him dead. Dominick dove beside a tree, fired at bushes that moved, then stopped, saving his last ammo for when the enemy was upon him. When the ammo was gone, he would unfasten the machete he carried and die hand-to-hand like a Samurai.

When a seeming lull came, he realized his legs were exposed and got up to move just as a grenade exploded five meters behind, knocking him out instantly. Shrapnel tore into his back and legs and a gush of air kicked his legs forward and lifted him several feet into the sky before he crashed to earth like an Airborne Ranger whose parachute never opened. It was November 22, 1967, the day before Thanksgiving.

There was a military quality to Nino's life now that would have surprised his point-man nephew. From the beginning, Mafia bosses had organized their families along a rigid chain of command. It started at the bottom with "soldiers" like Nino. They formed squad-like "crews" that reported to "capos" or "captains," who reported to an "underboss," who reported to the boss.

To Nino's benefit, the system was altered when Carlo became general. To appease Albert Anastasia loyalists, Carlo appointed an Anastasia protégé as underboss, but limited his authority to certain crews that in time became known as the "Manhattan faction." Paul Castellano, Nino's capo, answered directly to Carlo, and over the years Carlo's brother-in-law, cousin, and longtime confidant became the de facto underboss of the family's "Brooklyn faction."

Nino, of course, was well positioned anyway because he had worked for Carlo and Paul since the early 1950s. He and Paul were close friends now too; Paul, age fifty-two in 1967, was godfather to Nino's son Frank; his daughter Connie was godmother to Nino's daughter Regina. Nino had recently purchased a lot on a private island in Florida, near Paul's getaway condominium in Pompano Beach and was making plans to build a Roy-type home there.

Seemingly, Nino's special relationship with Paul also boded well for the future. Although the Manhattan faction might disagree, Paul was the logical heir apparent to sixty-seven-year-old Carlo. Because of his proximity to power, Paul had the best overall perspective on the family's disparate operations. He had also proven himself an able businessman, having spun his father's pork store into a chain of butcher shops plus a wholesale meat company that supplied most of the chickens on Brooklyn dinner tables. He was a major loanshark too; his book, worth several hundred thousand dollars, rivaled even Carlo's.

All the while Dominick was in Vietnam the Montiglios continued to visit the Gaggis in Brooklyn on Sundays, particularly after Nino's sister learned she had Hodgkin's disease. In between, there were birthdays, holidays, and special events like Nino's wife Rose giving birth to her fourth and last child, a boy.

Despite the frequency of visits, Anthony Montiglio, an inspector for a Department of Motor Vehicles facility near Levittown, had an arm's-length relationship with Nino. It was defined soon after Anthony and Marie were married. Nino asked if he could hide some money in a bank account in Anthony's name, and Anthony refused. Because he had no way to make his brother-in-law's life miserable, the way he had Anthony Santamaria's, Nino just grumbled for a while, then forgot about it.

The motor vehicle inspector had developed a better relationship with his warrior stepson, but because he felt destined to lose any competition with Nino in which the reward was Dominick's undivided loyalty and respect, he never tried to mount one. He also did not think Dominick had the will to refuse Nino a tainted favor the way he had.

"Nino will try to win Dominick over someday," he was always warning Marie.

Overweight once, Nino was svelte and taut now. He exercised in a gym he had installed in the bunker's basement. He squeezed his own orange juice, did not eat vegetables out of a can, and still drank only wine. His world was notorious for men who like Roy cheated on their wives, but he was a loyal husband. He doted on his children, three boys and a girl, but demanded good behavior. His Cadillac and his clothes were always immaculate.

His personal dress did fit the gangster stereotype: rakish suits, ties that matched pocket squares, shoes that clicked, and a dazzling collection of watches, rings, and bracelets. With his dark eyeglasses, which changed with each suit, he sparkled. The style was so deliberately slinky that when he strolled with Rose into a status-conscious place like the 21 Club in Manhattan, where Chuck Anderson, the maître d', was a friend and a loan-shark customer, it seemed he wanted people to know he was a gangster.

Though no one in his family knew just how ferocious he was, because they did not know how he had incinerated the killer of Frank Scalise, Nino's temperament was still a family wonderment. One day, he was in his car on Eighty-sixth Street in Bensonhurst, waiting for his brother Roy's wife to exit a delicatessen. As she did, some neighborhood teenagers whistled and hooted; she was a dark-haired version of the pretty and blonde Rose Gaggi. One of the raucous teens was Vincent Governara, a former classmate of Dominick's at Public School 200.

Judging the catcalls a personal insult, Nino waded into the teens with a hammer kept under his front seat; he swung wildly several times before Governara, who was a boxer, flattened him with a nose-breaking right hook. After coming home from the hospital, the prominent vein on the left side of Nino's neck appeared ready to explode as he vowed to his brother: "I'll get that punk some day. I'll kill the little motherfucker."

Marie shook her head when she heard the story—the offense was so slight, the response so exaggerated. "I don't want Dominick working for you when I'm gone," she told Nino during a rare departure from the normal decorum of dinners in Brooklyn. Besides the obvious reasons, she had other grounds. "Dominick is Americanized now. You can't control him. He won't go by your rules."

"All I want is for Dom to survive that silly damn war."

"He will," she said.

In another example of family wonderment, Dominick did. Late on the day he was knocked out and severely wounded on Hill 875, four dazed LURPs carrying him and Bones the radio man staggered into a Ranger camp at the base of the hill. Just when the LURPs were on the ropes, the NVA had retreated and let them slip away. Dominick woke up two weeks later in a military hospital and after several more weeks of treatment was awarded another medal. Bones recovered too. They and the others were believed to have killed at least fifty enemy fleeing down the hill.

Early in 1968, still in the Army, he left Vietnam. He was to report to Fort Bragg in North Carolina next, but went home first. His mother hosted a homecoming party in Levittown; Nino, maintaining his policy of never going to Levittown, did not attend.

The next day, Dominick went to Brooklyn to pay his respects. His anger at Nino's refusal to help his music career had faded in the wake of Army triumphs; he even attributed some of his success to growing up with Nino and living through dramas like the siege in the bunker during the gangland war of 1957. Apart from Nino's tirades, Dominick had always enjoyed his company. Making people come to him was just the price Nino charged; since Dominick had proven himself right about the Army and Nino wrong, it was easy to pay.

Nino invited him to accompany him, Paul Castellano,

and their wives to a stage show at the Waldorf-Astoria Hotel in Manhattan. "Wear your uniform, your beret, and all your medals," he said.

The hypocrisy was amusing, but Dominick did as ordered, and marveled at the squad of Waldorf waiters who doted on his party's perfectly positioned table. He got the idea, which was true, that the Gambino family practically ran the hotel workers' union.

In a few weeks, after a physical examination by an Army doctor in North Carolina, Dominick was told he would not be allowed to parachute again because of knee injuries suffered on the hill. Angrily, he made an abrupt decision later questioned but not retracted: "That's the end of the Army for me," he told the doctor.

To his mother's dismay, he wound up right back in Brooklyn. With only a few months left on his enlistment, the Army assigned him to a military police unit at Fort Hamilton, a small base whose main gate was a mile from Nino's house in Bath Beach.

He enjoyed his new assignment—tracking down AWOLs, rounding up drunk soldiers in Times Square—and with the bunker so nearby, began taking some of his meals there. Naturally, Nino moaned that having an MP at the dinner table was the same as having a cop—and got even more belligerent when Dominick said he intended to take the New York State Police entrance exam after the Army.

"I'll be upstate someplace, writing speeding tickets."

"Bullshit! A cop is a cop!"

Marie Montiglio urged her son to go to college, preferably one far away. "Mom, I know what you're trying to say, but don't worry," he told her. "That life of Nino's is not for me."

Recently, Marie's disease had produced some discolored bumps on her arms, making everyone anxious about how much time she had left. Wanting to please her, Dominick searched for a college that would admit someone with lackluster high school grades and found a junior college in Miami, Florida. He announced plans to enroll there after his discharge.

By appearances, Nino demonstrated only an avuncular interest in Dominick's life. He never mentioned Gambino family matters in his presence or introduced him to

Roy DeMeo or any of the men who worked for him. "Uncles" Carlo and Paul were always presented in a social context, such as when, at another dinner, Nino tried to get Dominick interested in Paul's handsome daughter Connie.

Dominick liked Connie, but felt no spark. His spark came on another occasion, when he went to Nino's for a birthday party for a cousin. Nino set the stage by inviting the family babysitter, a neighborhood girl whose father owned a bar in Manhattan. Dominick froze when he saw her sitting crosslegged on a chair in his grandmother's apartment. She was drop-dead pretty, with Cher-like black hair to her buttocks and skin the color of café au lait; her brown paisley minidress evoked shapely dreams. He felt she belonged in a slick Italian magazine ad, draped over a red Ferrari, and he fled to the floor below, speechless.

Recouping, he asked Nino, "Who is that lady!"

"Our babysitter, Denise Dellisanti. Denise of the saints. A beautiful name, a beautiful girl, why don't you go talk to her?"

In a while, the former LURP gathered his courage and walked back up the steps where Denise was. He remembered little of their conversation, only that she was seventeen years old, youngest of five daughters and a freshman at St. John's University in Queens. Apart from beautiful, she was smart, sweet and gentle, and her last name was so apt: *Dellisanti*. Denise of the saints.

In six weeks, he asked her out. They saw a movie, then went to Nino's house for coffee. He took her home at half past ten in the evening; she lived with her parents and had an eleven o'clock curfew. They quickly moved from dating to relationship, but did not make love. She was against it outside marriage. Dominick, head over heels, did not try to persuade her otherwise.

The FBI might not know about Nino, but Denise's parents did. They knew some of his loanshark customers and were therefore neither fond of him nor his nephew. They allowed Denise to babysit only because the Gaggis lived nearby and paid her well. Dominick resented the prejudgment, but did not mention their hostility to his volatile uncle.

Dominick was still in the Army when Nino first asked

for a tainted favor, which was cast as a matter of honor. A dentist who lived and worked in the neighborhood had made a suggestive remark to one of his patients, Rose Gaggi; Nino interpreted it virtually as attempted rape and informed Dominick he was going to plant a stick of dynamite beneath the dentist's front porch.

"He insulted my wife and your aunt. This'll tell the guy he should get the fuck out of the neighborhood before he really gets hurt. We'll sneak over there tonight. You watch my back."

Knowing Nino and having heard the Vincent Governara story, Dominick was less surprised by Nino's overreaction than his assumption he would help. But because a porch, not a person, was the target, he watched Nino's back. Some days after the message went off, the dentist did pack his bags and move away.

Dominick never mentioned the incident to Denise and never talked about his uncle's shadowy life, except obliquely, in a language a neighborhood girl like Denise well understood. "It's funny about people in that life," he would say. "You can tell who's in it just by the way they are, but if that person is friendly and treats you well, they're just good people."

Everyone liked Denise. At St. John's, a fraternity elected her "Miss Mu Gamma Delta." She invited Dominick to be her date at the installation and the party following. With his close-cropped Army hair, he felt out of place; people his age were adopting hippie looks and attitudes as 1968 wound down.

At the party, he experienced his first Vietnam flashback. He was standing against a wall, drinking a beer, watching everyone dance, when the room exploded and body parts flew everywhere. He sank to the floor and covered his face. Denise kneeled beside him.

"Are you okay? The war?"

"Yeah, no, worse than that."

She hugged him. "I think I'm just overwhelmed by change," he finally said. "It was so bad over there, but here I am with you and I'm so happy. It's like I was in hell, and now I'm in heaven."

"I love you."

"I love you too." His eyes were moist. "You make

me so happy I cried. I can't believe it. You wanna dance?''

''Whatever you want.''

On December 16, 1968, Dominick was honorably discharged, but emotionally he would never leave the Army. It dominated the self-portrait in his mind's eye and made him confident of his own wit, luck, and strength. His sudden meltdown at Denise's party was just an aberrant consequence of combat that would fade. Still, he began submerging some of his military identity because he also was attracted to the countercultural drumbeat of the time. He would never attend an antiwar rally, but did begin wearing long-sleeve shirts to conceal the paratrooper tattoo on his right forearm.

He was filled with optimism, but except for his relationship with Denise, he would not succeed at much. He enrolled at Dade County College in Miami, but rarely attended class. He and a few similarly minded veterans spent most of their days high on LSD and listening to music in the squalor of a ghetto dive they rented. One spring day, unexpectedly, Nino and Rose showed up. They were in Florida overseeing construction of their sumptuous winter home.

Dominick was embarrassed, and he was surprised that Nino spared him a harangue on his unkempt appearance and surroundings. ''Why don't you come home?'' his uncle said instead, adding that he was about to buy a small Italian ices business in Brooklyn. ''You can run it, as long as you cut your hair and straighten out.''

When Dominick telephoned his mother and mentioned the offer, she warned him away. She recalled reading somewhere that someone in that business had recently been shot dead at his desk.

''Only in Brooklyn can making ices get you killed,'' he replied, too lightly for her.

''That's your uncle's life,'' she snapped. ''Don't forget it.''

Tired of his mother's worries, Dominick came up with a new idea. In a letter to Denise, he suggested they run away together and make a new life for themselves in San Francisco. He had visited there on one of his leaves home; it was where he first saw an exciting new breeze sweeping the country, where he first felt out of step. Musically, San Francisco was also a center of innovation, and he wanted to give that part of his nature one more chance. He described it as a fairytale land where dreams came true.

When Denise said maybe, he left Florida and rented a small apartment near her parents' house in Brooklyn. Nino had filled the Italian ices job, but Dominick saw no harm in accepting another job his uncle offered: doorman and assistant "greeter" at the 21 Club in Manhattan, where Nino was influential because of his relationship with Chuck Anderson, the maître d', who owed Nino money. Dominick had met Anderson, the "Mr. New York" of the city's gossip columns, at parties at Nino's house. Nino had described him as a war hero whose relatives grew up with Al Capone.

The 21 Club was a glittery restaurant patronized by celebrities, politicos, and old men with young women on their arms. Dominick hated it; he felt like a servant and quit after two months. "Too many assholes," he told Nino.

Nino and Paul got him membership in the waiters' union; he hired out as a bartender at banquets and weddings but felt like a servant again and quit after a few weekends even though he was trying to save money for a new start in San Francisco.

Nino got him another job with a small landscaping company owned by the brother of a Castellano soldier, but the work was irregular and mundane. In high school, Dominick had hustled at a McDonald's to make a few bucks, but common labor was now below his Green Beret self-esteem. Being unemployed, rather than underemployed, was easier on his ego.

His ego kept the California fund from building too quickly and aggravated Denise's parents' opinion of him. When he indicated to them through Denise that he wished to discuss marrying her, they sent back a message: Don't even bother.

"They say Michele has to get married first," Denise reported, referring to an older sister, "before they even think about letting me get married."

It was Denise who proposed a solution. One night soon, as they were parked in a lover's lane along the

Brooklyn shoreline, she said: "We don't need anyone's permission. Let's elope!"

Dominick happily agreed and suggested they leave immediately and get married somewhere along the way to California.

"No, we have to do it before we leave. If we leave together, we'll sleep together, and I want to be married first."

"Let's do it then! I'm dying to get out of Brooklyn."

Eighteen-year-old Denise had been charmed by his depiction of San Francisco. She had more flower-child in her than he. She was ready to take a break from college. Her grades were superior; she could go back anytime. "California, here we come," she cried.

The couple got a marriage license and confided their plans to Marie Montiglio, who was elated. She urged them to make her a grandmother right away and volunteered to speak on their behalf to Denise's parents.

"Don't bother, it won't do any good," Denise said.

Without Denise's parents' okay, the pastor at Saint Finbar's in Bath Beach refused to officiate. So did the pastor of the Montiglio parish in Levittown. The couple randomly visited a Protestant church near Levittown. The minister married them the next day, January 19, 1971.

After the newlyweds broke the news to everyone else, Dominick's mother hosted a reception in Levittown. All the Montiglios were in a gay mood. Denise's parents appeared funereal. Nino refused to come because Dominick had not informed him beforehand.

Once in San Francisco, Dominick and Denise discovered they could not afford the city's rents and had to settle for nearby Berkeley. Still, they quickly exhausted their meager funds, but just when they were thinking of coming home, the owner of their apartment building offered Dominick a job as the building's superintendent. It came with free rent, and Dominick could do the work just about when he pleased. He and Denise made love, did drugs, went to concerts, explored northern California. For a year, they had their fairytale life.

Denise was an incredible partner—strong, loyal, and supportive to the point of selflessness. Deciding they could use more money than he made as a building super, she took a job as a supermarket checkout clerk, and continued to keep her own education on hold when he began attending Merritt College in Oakland as a full-time music student. His interest had turned to jazz, and she bought him a twelve-hundred-dollar saxophone.

He quickly became skilled on the sax, and he and four other students formed a group, the Brooklyn Back Street Blues Band. All became interested in a new sound, "fusion," a marriage of jazz and rock. Frank Zappa came to one of their sessions at a school seminar and encouraged them to record a demo tape. The result was astounding. Their compositions roared and sailed in many directions, yet held onto unifying themes. It was intricately plotted music, but raucous and chaotic—like combat.

The Back Street Brooklyn Blues Band sent their tape to all the record companies, and waited, and waited. "These assholes say it's too avant-garde," Dominick bitterly complained to Denise. "We ain't marketable. We ain't Frankie Valli."

Marie and Anthony Montiglio, and their children Steven and Michele, arrived for a visit in the summer of 1972. Marie used almost all her home movie camera film on landscapes along the way. Arriving in Berkeley, Anthony took over the camera. The movie, the last in the Montiglio family collection, ended with Marie, two fingers of her right hand crossed in a gesture of hope, knocking on the door of her son's apartment.

Marie's health had declined significantly, but nothing was said for fear of scaring the children. Dominick's boss gave the visitors keys to a furnished apartment and they wound up staying six weeks. Between Marie's illness and Dominick's disappointment with another stalled music career, it was a bittersweet time.

After the Montiglios left, Dominick and Denise went to see the new hit film *The Godfather*. Inevitably, he identified with the character Michael Corleone, the Mafia don's youngest son, a war hero who first appears in the movie wearing a military uniform. The character's family and relationship dilemmas were instantly familiar. The heroic way he becomes like his father and takes command of what is portrayed as a dark but peculiarly noble world was an irresistibly appealing fantasy.

"It wasn't about gangsters," Dominick solemnly told Denise on the way home. "It was about family."

Within days, the couple made two major decisions—to try and make a baby and to return to New York, where they found an apartment near his dying mother's house. Dominick's Brooklyn Back Street Blues Band tape and his saxophone went into storage with his Four Directions memorabilia and Vietnam medals. Later, he went to Saint Finbar's in Bath Beach for the first time in a long while and became godfather to Nino's youngest child—a boy named Michael.

In December 1972, Marie Montiglio entered a hospital. She hung on several weeks. "I will not die until my first grandchild is born," she told Dominick before, at age 52, she slipped away.

That same day, too late to tell her mother-in-law, Denise learned from her doctor that she was pregnant. Having prepared for the bad news, Dominick tried concentrating on the good, but it was impossible; he had never felt life's cycle of pain and beauty more profoundly.

Marie was laid out at the Cusimano & Russo Funeral Home in Bensonhurst. The first night of the wake, after everyone left, a gaunt man with drinker's eyes came in by himself. Mortician Joseph Cusimano tried to shoo him away.

"Please," the man said. "I used to be married to her."

"What's your name?"

"Santamaria. Anthony Santamaria."

"Sorry, we're closed, come back tomorrow night."

Early the next night, Cusimano told Dominick a "bum" claiming to be Marie's first husband had come by—"Says his name is Santamaria."

"If he comes back, let him in," said Dominick. Since coming home, he had extracted a few more details of his parents' breakup from his mother. These made him want to hear his father's side of the story, but he had put off looking him up. On the last night of his mother's wake, he waited until everyone left, and then some more, but no more mourners came by, not until after he left too.

Former Army Air Corps boxing champ Anthony Santamaria came in a few minutes later, and Cusimano led him to the casket, where he stood silently for several minutes. "Thank you," he said, then shuffled away, back to a sister's house in North Brooklyn.

Hearing about it the next day, Dominick wondered if his father hid in the shadows until he left because he wanted to mourn in private, or because his son used to cross the street to avoid him. He was denied any answer because his father was soon found frozen to death next to a pile of cardboard in an empty lot. His sister buried him without telling his son. "He just decided to lay down and die of a broken heart," she told her friends.

Marie Montiglio's death created a wrinkle for the Gaggi family. The deed to the bunker had been placed in her name in 1943. No other owners were ever added. That meant her husband had the strongest legal claim on the property, but he never raised the issue. Officially, Marie died without any assets. Even so, the deed was a problem if the Gaggis ever wanted to sell the house.

As his sister lay dying, Nino had promised to look after her children Steven and Michele. Dominick, he said, was a big boy who would take care of himself. "Let him," she said.

A few days after the funeral, however, Nino asked Dominick his plans. Dominick said he and Denise were returning to California to have their baby and another go at a music career. He said it without much conviction.

Nino said a father-to-be could not afford any more drift. "I'm buying a car service; you could run it for me," he said.

Private car services were a booming business in New York, thanks to the declining state of subways and the practical unavailability of taxis in any borough but Manhattan. "It's time to settle down," Nino said. "You belong here in Brooklyn."

Twenty-five-year-old Dominick asked for time to think; replaying the conversation in his mind, it was hard not to compare himself to Michael Corleone and Nino to Vito, Michael's father. Fantasy aside, the car service was a legal business venture. It was a job with some dignity. On the other hand, California was a cloudy picture. His rent-free deal was gone; his band had broken up.

Once Dominick made all his rationalizations, only his dead mother's wishes stood in the way, but he told Denise it was possible to work for Nino without getting too deep into "that life." Denise had accepted the inevitability of this moment since his romantic assessment of *The Godfather*. Her parents had opposed marriage because he might turn out like his uncle, but she had married him and loved him deeply. In her twenty-one-year-old mind, Dominick could be a rogue, but not a criminal. A week later, he accepted Nino's job. Miss Mu Gamma Delta accepted a full-time role as wife and mother and never returned to school.

Pleased, Nino asked, "Where you gonna live? You can't stay in Levittown. Why don't you move in here?"

The top floor of the Gaggi house was open. Denise liked the idea. It was a large apartment. She had spent many nights in it babysitting and had met her husband a few steps below. Early in 1973, they moved in. He had begun life on the bottom floor, moved to the middle when his father left and now, after his mother's death, was on the top—back home in the bunker.

Nino gave him two hundred dollars a week to manage the car service, but deducted one hundred sixty-five a month as rent. Dominick was miffed—his mother had helped pay off the mortgage on the bunker—but accepted it as another example of Nino's confounding ways: He gave with one hand and took with another. Nino also purchased the couple furniture worth two thousand dollars, but docked Dominick's salary seventy-five a week to pay for it.

Denise delivered a baby girl on August 1, 1973. She and her husband wanted to honor his late mother, but thought it might be bad luck to name the infant Marie. They decided on Camarie, the "Ca" having no special meaning, but making for a pretty name.

Not then and not ever did Nino sit Dominick down and explain the outline of his world. He never gave a speech about Carlo Gambino controlling an empire through crews of soldiers led by captains and capos reporting to an underboss. He merely pulled back a curtain, a little at a time. Once in a while, however, he would quote lines from his favorite movie, *The Godfather*. His favorite was the ailing don's speech as he passed the torch to son

Michael, "I don't regret my life. I refused to be a fool dancing on a string held by all those bigshots . . . I don't apologize."

"That's me," Nino would say. "I don't apologize."

CHAPTER 4

Swing of Things

Lingering in the amber light near the entrance to the Villa Borghese, the restaurant on the corner, Anthony Gaggi appeared to be waiting for dinner companions. Some passersby, neighborhood people in the know, might have speculated he was a gambler debating whether to return and chase his losses at the craps game underway in a house one door away. No one was aware how dangerous it was just being near him.

It was minutes before midnight, March 2, 1975, two years after Marie Montiglio's death. Nino occupied the northwest corner of Twentieth and Bath Avenues in Bath Beach. A block west on Bath, the shift was changing at the New York Police Department's 62d Precinct stationhouse, the "Six-Two." Nino was two blocks from home, and close to settling an old score.

On Twentieth, at the corner, he saw a maroon Plymouth. Inside, a small dot of light snaked across the windshield; a man was barely visible on the front seat. Nino was pleased—the job was underway. Then he noticed the car was illegally parked by a hydrant, making it an easy mark for quota-filling shift-ending cops from the Six-Two. His pulse quickening with this overlooked wrinkle, he peered beyond the car, expecting to see his normally reliable partner, Roy DeMeo. But Roy was nowhere in sight.

Nino grew more agitated. Roy was the job's rear sentry; if strangers came along that way, he was to tap on the Plymouth's trunk and warn the man inside to douse his penlight and duck down—the same as Nino's role at the front. The man inside was placing an explosive device under the front seat and rigging it to the driver's-side door.

The car belonged to a smalltime craps player, Vincent

Governara, the teenage boxer who broke Nino's nose after Nino tried to assault him and his friends with a hammer because they rudely admired a pretty woman, Nino's sister-in-law—twelve years ago.

Tonight, Nino was tying up a loose end in his ordered life, making good on a vow: "I'll get that fucking punk someday." His embarrassment and defeat at the hands of a neighborhood teen were blemishes in his morning mirror; he never doubted he would remove them when the time came, and finally it had.

After the fight, Governara's family had moved away. A few months ago, however, one of Nino's men—aware of his leader's grudge—saw Governara driving in the neighborhood; he tried following to find where he lived, but lost him in traffic. En route to Nino's this night, the man had spotted the Plymouth again, parked two blocks away. Governara had come to Nino.

But where was Roy? Nino's telltale neck vein bulged. Shaking down pornography distributor Paul Rothenberg, and then murdering him to protect Nino and himself from exposure, Roy had been effective and ruthless, a good partner to have. But lately, as the worst of his fears came true and the IRS began investigating his fairytale tax returns, Roy had grown jittery and started taking Valium. Nino, who shunned even aspirin, had scoffed that an IRS investigation was just a board game played by lawyers, but Roy refilled his prescription.

Nino now concluded that Roy was panicking again; worried the man in the car might make a mistake and blow them all up, he had wandered into the Villa Borghese on the pretense Governara might be inside, eating a late dinner. Roy was watching out for himself and exposing his partners to detection.

The shadowy figure of a man, too slim for Roy, suddenly appeared on the sidewalk. He was just a passerby, approaching the car from behind. Nino began to move forward, to tap on the hood and warn the man inside to duck down, but saw he was going to be too late. The man in the car, his work over, was sliding across the front seat toward the passenger door; he opened it and stepped out just as the passerby strolled by.

For an instant, the men were face to face, but the passerby quickly averted his eyes and moved on, a wise way to be in Brooklyn, according to legend. If called as a witness, he would not have been able to identify the man he saw leaving the car—Dominick Montiglio.

Dominick had told his wife it was possible to work for Nino without getting too deep into "that life," but here he was, at age twenty-seven, hitting bottom. This time he was helping blow up a person, not a porch. In the minds of Nino and Roy, however, he was merely opening the door to the clubhouse, making his debut. Murder was just his final rite of passage.

Heart racing, he joined Nino on the corner and angrily whispered, "Where the fuck was Roy? The fucking guy dogged it!"

On the heel of these words, Roy emerged from the restaurant.

"Where the fuck you been?" Nino demanded.

"Makin' sure the kid wasn't in there."

"Fuck you, the guy eats at White Castle. He ain't anywhere but the crap game. Some guy got up in Dom's face 'cause of you."

Roy offered to make amends, show power. "All right, so let's go get that guy."

"Fuck you, let's get outta here."

Roy resented the implication that he had been cowardly. He thought he had acted smartly. It was dumb to stand behind a car while someone inside it played around with a grenade. Here he was trying to help Nino get his revenge and all he got was grief. "Nobody was gonna bother that car. This is Brooklyn."

The men walked to Nino's house and waited on the front stoop for an explosion.

Dominick had inserted toothpicks in the locks of the car's other doors so Governara would have only one to open, and on the inside pull-up lock of that he had tied string connected by fish hooks to the grenade's pin. He was certain of an explosion, but not a fatal one. It was a concussion grenade, meaning it did not spew shrapnel like a fragmentation grenade. The plastic housing of its black-powder charge melted on detonation. To accomplish its purpose, the shattering of brains, a concussion grenade was ideally used in a confined area, like a Hill 875 tunnel.

"When the guy opens the door, the energy has a way

out,'' he had told Nino and Roy. ''He might break his neck against the ceiling, but he might just get knocked out.''

The grenade came from Roy's arsenal of weapons, now hidden in the Gemini Lounge basement. Roy, saying he knew just as much about weapons as Dominick, insisted it would work; since meeting him eighteen months earlier, Roy also had frequently ridiculed Dominick's combat experience and all his ''Green Beret bullshit.'' Once, he broke into a mocking singsong, ''From the halls of Montezuma to the shores of Tripoli . . .''

''Roy,'' Dominick pointed out, ''that's the Marines, not the Army.'' Roy had never mentioned Chubby DeMeo to Dominick.

About the grenade, Roy had bitingly said, ''It'll work, this ain't no Vietnam, this ain't like over there in Vee-at-nam.''

About one o'clock in the morning, with all still quiet, Roy left for his Massapequa Park home, his Valium, and a stiff Cutty. If IRS investigators had interviewed his neighbors, they might have learned that at various times he told them he worked in the used-car business, the construction field, and food retailing. He never mentioned the Boro of Brooklyn Credit Union, where he was now president of the board of directors, or the S & C Sportswear Corporation, a Brooklyn company that listed him as an employee. Naturally, he never mentioned the Gambino Mafia family, where much to his chagrin he was still an associate, not a made man.

Alone with Dominick, Nino said, ''Don't ever forget what Roy did tonight.''

''How could I? He left me in a bad spot.''

''Like they say in the Army, he left his post, don't ever forget that.''

Dominick felt a chill, not from the words, but an uninvited thought: What if Governara did not leave the game until morning? Public School 200 was a block away. Kids would be passing by, like he and Governara were twenty years ago when they were classmates waving to Six-Two cops. In their haste to kill, the plotters had been insanely reckless.

The former LURP braced himself because he knew what thought would come next. More regularly now, violent images from Vietnam darted equally uninvited into his consciousness. One particular flashback kept recurring. In it, he saw himself picking up heads, arms, legs and intestines that slipped through his fingers as he sought to piece soldiers together, and now in the dark with Nino he flashed on little heads, arms and legs, and sank down on the stoop before he fainted.

"Everything okay?" Nino said.

"Just a little tired."

"Me too. I'm going in."

Alone now, Dominick decided to stay up and, if no explosion occurred by daybreak, remove the grenade. He had four seconds to re-pin it once he opened the door; more time could be bought by breaking a window and entering the car that way; somehow, it could be done.

He was growing accustomed to sleepless nights because he had also begun having nightmares. A recurring picture from these had been that of an artillery shell drilling a basketball-size hole through his chest. One night he awoke with such pain that he went to a hospital certain he was dying of a heart attack. The nightmares had gotten worse over the last year, and a few months ago he had finally sought help from the Veterans Administration.

A doctor prescribed the same drug Roy was taking, Valium, then wrote:

This veteran is suffering moderate to severe emotional reactions from his battle experiences in Vietnam. . . . Since his separation from the Army, he has functioned significantly below the level of a person of his intelligence and previous performance. . . . This pattern is quite the opposite of that which prevailed prior to combat, when he was active in sports, led his own musical group, and had an active social life. . . . His nightmares duplicate actual events he was involved in.

"Delayed stress syndrome" was the term used to describe the emotional turmoil many veterans experienced after coming home to a divided country whose politics reduced them to pawns, losers, or savages. Dominick did not see a connection between his stress and working for

Nino. Veterans who led Boy Scout troops suffered similarly. It was just another way his life had changed since he began managing Nino's car service.

The Plaza Car Service took part of its name from the shopping center where it was located. Kings Plaza, the first suburban-style mall in Brooklyn, was on the southern edge of Flatlands and was that community's, and Canarsie's, principal shopping district. At the car service office in 1973, Dominick met Roy DeMeo for the first time.

Roy arrived with Nino, who came by twice a day to count his dollars. Nino introduced Roy as a friend, but Dominick knew that if Roy was truly Nino's friend he would have met him earlier. Roy was clearly younger than Nino and also plainly deferential. Reading between the lines, he sized Roy up as a Gambino family partner of some kind. Where Uncle Nino was disciplined in speech and appearance, Roy was an immediate gabber, and his knit shirt also hung outside his trousers in a still-failing attempt to downplay an abdominal tire.

Relationship-conscious Roy chattered away. In a few minutes, Dominick knew where Roy grew up, where he lived, his kids' names, and that he had recently survived an automobile accident in which a woman was killed. And that on another occasion, driving home, he saw another accident and had stopped his car and assisted one of the injured drivers. "That guy turned out to be an FBI agent. Can you believe it? Me helping an FBI agent? If it had been an IRS guy, I would've let 'im bleed to death."

Roy also asked Dominick many questions about Vietnam—not so much the war but the weapons. "Do they really have 'scopes that see in the night now?" Roy asked.

"Sure," Dominick said. "I used 'em on point."

Roy invited Dominick to visit the Gemini Lounge, the renamed bar he secretly owned in Flatlands. "Good people there," he said, using code words Dominick well knew.

"Roy has a bunch of kids around him," Nino said later. "Real sleepers."

"Sleepers?"

"They look about twelve years old, but they're tough guys."

In a few weeks, when Nino took him to the Gemini Lounge for the first time, Dominick met the first of Roy's sleepers—but at five-feet-five, long-haired Chris Rosenberg did not appear that tough. Roy introduced him as "a friend in the car business" and while Roy and Nino huddled, the younger men talked.

Chris was cocky and ebullient. He said he had been "with Roy" since he was sixteen; he was now twenty-three; his "man" Roy was a major loanshark, although not as big as "your man" Nino. He borrowed money from Roy at three quarters of one percent interest and loaned it out to his own customers at three to five "points" a week. His customers were mechanics and body-and-fender men in Canarsie and Flatlands, where he owned an auto-repair shop.

"Need a car?" he asked Dominick. "I can get you a good deal on a Lincoln. 1973. Great shape."

At the time, Dominick owned a Jeep he bought in California. On the way home, he mentioned Chris's proposal to Nino.

"I don't want you to buy a car from Chris. It might be stolen. Chris and his friends deal in stolen cars."

Because Chris was with Roy and Roy was with Nino, Dominick concluded that Nino profited from stolen cars too, if only as a shareholder in Roy's operation. He took silent satisfaction in remembering that as a child he had suspected that Nino, when he owned a used-car lot, was somehow making money off stolen cars.

Nino, driving his third new Cadillac since Dominick came home from California, told Dominick a friend of his would give him a good price and favorable financing on a new car. The friend was a loan customer who owned a General Motors dealership in Brooklyn. Soon, Dominick was driving a new Oldsmobile Cutlass.

In a few weeks, Nino gave Dominick a fifty-dollar raise on the condition he start picking up the weekly payment of a loan customer in Manhattan. So, on Friday afternoons, Dominick began taking a few hours off from the car service and going to a familiar place, the 21 Club, to see Chuck Anderson, "Mr. New York." Anderson greeted him at a new level of respect, but never said why he owed Mr. Bath Beach twenty-five thousand dollars.

In 1974, Nino folded Plaza Car Service because the profit was not worth the bother. Staying on Nino's payroll, Dominick agreed to pick up his other loans, but not for any additional salary—"It's easy work," Nino said. Nino's customers were not repairmen or unreliable junkies, gamblers, and street criminals. Mostly, they were otherwise legitimate businessmen who had found themselves with too many accounts payable.

The developer of a dinner theater in suburban Westchester County, a few miles north of the Bronx, was a good example. He failed in a public offering of stock shares to raise the cash to complete construction of the Westchester Premier Theater in Tarrytown. For their agreements to perform, the developer then sold bargain shares with options to several entertainers, including Steve Lawrence, Eydie Gormé, and Alan King. Still, construction overruns at the thirty-five-hundred seat theater left him short.

A major investor, a connected Californian, contacted Carlo Gambino, who agreed to loan one hundred thousand dollars, which still was not enough. Another investor, the nephew of a Gambino captain who lived in Westchester County, then asked Nino to meet him at the theater to discuss another loan. Exposing Dominick to his first big Gambino family business deal, Nino asked Dominick to accompany him.

The second investor, Gregory DePalma, asked for a quarter-million-dollar loan. "A little steep," Nino said, "but I'll talk it over with Paul." A week later, he called Dominick downstairs to his basement office in the bunker and handed him a brown paper bag. "There is a hundred and twenty-five grand in there. Half of what they wanted. Take it to Greg DePalma. And you'll be goin' up there every week now to get the vig. Fifteen hundred. Make sure they don't try and cheat."

Collecting the weekly interest, Dominick learned that Nino and Paul were equal partners in the loan and were gambling that the entertainers scheduled to appear would keep the house packed, enabling the developer to meet his weekly payments and pay off his loans with them and Carlo. The theater opened in 1974 with Diana Ross as the attraction, but the week ended as a loss because the Dreamgirl had cost too much—two hundred fifty thousand dollars.

"We're right back in a hole," DePalma told Dominick.

The theater's California investor contacted a friend who was a childhood friend of Frank Sinatra, who agreed to a week of concerts for one hundred and twenty-five thousand dollars. Sinatra grew up across the Hudson River from New York in Hoboken, New Jersey, then a community much like the Lower East Side when Nino was growing up. He developed his act in New York clubs and like Rocky Graziano and Jake LaMotta was a cultural hero to Italian-Americans; a Sinatra performance in New York was a special event.

Carlo, Paul, Nino, Dominick, and their wives—and many other Mafia-connected men—attended Sinatra's opening night. Nino also brought his willful mother Mary, and all ate a pre-show dinner in the theater's VIP room. With their connections, they were assured the best stagefront seats; New York Governor Hugh Carey occupied their adjoining table and backstage everyone had their picture taken with Sinatra.

Ominously, however, even Sinatra's concerts were unprofitable. Even so, wanting to protect his, Paul's, and Nino's investments, Carlo approved another seventy-five-thousand-dollar loan. Nino gave the cash to Dominick, who took it to DePalma. "The vig's gonna be two grand a week now," Nino said.

In the meantime, when the new models came out, Dominick got another Cutlass because Nino got another Cadillac. He kept the car—and himself now—washed and waxed at all times; he was meeting substantial people and representing Nino. So he tried to look substantial; he had shorn his long hair and tossed all the ridiculous hippie outfits he owned. He was now a more manly rendition of his old Four Directions look—polished, swarthy, and with his high strong cheekbones and wide powerful jawline, handsome in a rugged way. Once again, he had demonstrated, as his high school friends once noted, an uncanny knack for completely changing his outward appearance; inside, he was feeling special again too. He was getting into the swing of things as a top assistant to one of the important men. Denise liked the new Dominick. She did not want to know any details, however, and he did not tell her many.

As the months went by, Nino kept opening the window on his world. Despite all he saw and heard growing up with Nino, despite the dynamite beneath the dentist's porch, Dominick only now began to appreciate what a dangerous man his uncle was. A telling moment came when Nino recalled his encounter with Dominick's former classmate, Vincent Governara, the teenage boxer who left Nino in the middle of Eighty-sixth Street with a broken nose.

Even telling the story, Nino seethed. "The day that happened, I promised myself, 'I will get that punk some day. I will kill that little motherfucker.' "

"Why not just give him a good beatin'?"

"Some things cost a little more."

When Nino and Rose left for a long stay at their now-complete luxurious Florida getaway, Dominick needed a place to stash all the cash he was collecting. Beneath a chest of drawers in his bunker apartment, he made a trap. In a few weeks, it contained sixty thousand dollars.

One night, Nino called and told him to fly to Florida with twenty thousand. Two robbers had accosted Nino and Rose in their retreat and taken all their cash. The robbers got away, but not without another demonstration of Nino's raging-bull nature.

The robbers believed the house was unoccupied, but rang the bell to be sure. When Rose opened the door, one wanted to leave, but the other pulled a gun and pushed his way inside. When Nino came to investigate, the robber without the gun yelled to the other, "Let's get the fuck out of here!"

"Who the fuck are you assholes!" Nino screamed.

"Shut the fuck up!" the gunman shouted back.

"Fuck you! Get the fuck out of my house!"

Unarmed, Nino rushed forward, but the gunman smacked him in the face with the pistol, then hammered the top of his head. Nino keeled over, incapacitated and bleeding; Rose tended to him while the robbers rifled the house.

Hearing Nino tell the story, and seeing his eyes as cold

and focused as they were when he spoke of Governara ("Judge a man by his eyes," Nino liked to say. "The eyes don't lie."), Dominick was certain the robbers were dead men if Nino ever learned who they were.

Back in Brooklyn, in 1974, the bond between Nino and Dominick grew stronger. The more Nino talked about the past, especially about Frank Scalise, the more Dominick began to feel like a descendant of a royal, if renegade, family. "Frank Scalise was the finest man I ever met," Nino said. "He was there with Luciano at the beginning of all this. Him and his brother Joe, they were two of the shooters on the St. Valentine's hits in Chicago. Capone used out-of-town talent on that, you know."

For the first time, Dominick thought of his lineage this way: Luciano, Scalise, Gaggi, Montiglio. "Didn't know our family was so famous," he said.

Nino's response betrayed his own romantic notions. "Growing up, all I ever wanted was to be like Frank Scalise and to die on the street with a gun in my hand."

"Like Frank did."

"Frank wasn't carrying. He didn't have a gun. But we took care of the guy who got Frank and Joe."

"Oh yeah?" Dominick probed a little further. Nino had come to the edge of a confession, a milestone in their relationship.

"The guy's name was Vincent Squillante. We surprised him in the Bronx. We shot him in the head, stuffed him in the trunk, drove to Tenth Street, and threw him in a furnace."

The statement was so casually matter-of-fact that Dominick saw that in Nino's mind the killing was not about murder—but evening the score, tying up a loose end. It became that way in his mind too. Squillante had killed two members of his family. Taking revenge was normal. Taking no revenge was abnormal.

"I'm glad you got the cocksucker," Dominick said.

While continuing to pick up Nino's loans, Dominick, at his uncle's suggestion, began working occasional days at a used-car lot on Long Island. The owner had a loan with Nino and Roy. "It's a good business for you to

learn,'' said Nino, the proprietor of a used-car lot when
he was twenty-seven, Dominick's age.

With the owner of the Long Island lot and one of the
employees, Dominick began attending automobile auctions in New Jersey. The cars came from new-car dealers
who wanted to move trade-ins off their lot. After one
auction, he accompanied the owner's employee to a car
repair shop in Canarsie; the shop, it turned out, was
owned by a friend of Roy's protégé, Chris Rosenberg.
The man from the used-car lot handed over blank forms
as Chris's friend gave him a wad of bills.

Dominick suspected Chris's friend was buying papers
he could use to make phony titles and registrations. Chris
confirmed this when he invited Dominick to take a look
at ''my car collection.'' The collection—five virtually
new Porsches and Mercedes—was stored on the second
floor of another friend's warehouse.

''They're tag jobs,'' Chris said.

''Tag what?''

''A tag job. We steal 'em, then change the vehicle
identification number and sell 'em as clean cars, with
clean titles.''

''How do you get the titles?''

''There's a hundred ways,'' Chris said.

Nino and Dominick began stopping by the Gemini
Lounge early on each Friday evening. Fridays, Nino
said, ''Roy and his crew get together and slice up the
money.''

The Gemini occupied the front half of the first floor of
a dreary two-story, rectangular brick building on a corner
lot in Flatlands; in a feeble attempt to mimic a chalet, a
contractor had placed a slanted wooden structure over the
second floor and dropped in an A-frame cutout on each
side. Whoever designed the outside of the bar tried to
carry out the chalet theme by painting the bricks white
and choosing Bavarian-style letters for the bar's logo.
The rest of the building stayed two shades of brown.

Inside, the Gemini was like a thousand other neighborhood bars in Brooklyn: It had a jukebox, a pinball
machine, ten worn stools by the bar, and maybe another ten tables with red-and-white vinyl checkerboard
coverings arrayed around a tiny platform where a small
band could perform. Hanging by the bar was the fa-

mous *New York Daily News* front page announcing the Brooklyn Dodgers' first and only World Series victory, in 1955.

Roy and his crew were seated around two adjoining tables like a board of directors. Dominick recognized Chris and a few other of Chris's body-shop friends, including the one who paid cash for blank car documents. Other faces were new and so young they appeared to belong to teenagers. Dominick was introduced to a Joey, an Anthony, a Patty, and some others he forgot.

Being with Nino, Dominick was greeted respectfully. As Nino and Roy stepped away to talk, he joined the others for a drink. It became clear that Chris, Joey, Anthony, Patty, and the rest had known each other most of their lives—they seemed to communicate with grunts, glances, and hand signals, as if they were part of some secret society.

"But they don't look so tough to me," Sergeant Montiglio told Nino on the way home.

"Well, they are and I don't want you hanging out with them. They're punks and drug-users. Any contact is on a business level only."

"What's their business?"

"Cars and drugs. Roy backs 'em."

Dominick already knew Nino was profiting from stolen cars, but drugs was new. Nino had railed against people who used drugs—he had recently walked out of a movie theater when a kid across the aisle lit a joint—but here he was in business with a man who bankrolled drug dealers.

Of course, Dominick had never told Nino that he had taken LSD, that he sometimes smoked marijuana and that while in California he had on a few occasions used a drug he really liked, if only he could afford it: cocaine.

Nino's admission was another example of the incremental way he raised the window on his world. He was preparing Dominick for a specific role. He wanted to spend more time in Florida, where he had his elegant home in Golden Isles, near Hallendale, plus a new issue of loans that had already caused a launderette to fall into his hands. While away, he needed someone to collect his

New York loans and, just as important, be his eyes and ears. It explained why he introduced Dominick to Roy and his crew, but did not want him to become too friendly.

One day, Nino asked Dominick if he knew Anthony Santamaria had died.

"I heard they found him in an empty lot somewhere."

"It's a good thing because I always meant to pop him someday. He treated your mom like a dog."

Though now aware that Nino aggravated some of his father's problems when they lived together long ago, Dominick did not make a reply. Any attempt to disturb Nino's facts invited tension, unwise now that he was living under the same roof and had spent the last two years accepting the trust Nino placed in him.

He was never able to fully decide whether this was a matter of inevitability, convenience, lack of character, or—even as ridiculous as it seemed—seeing himself as if he was in a fictional romantic movie. He did think himself a good case study for the question, What in his life does a man control and what is beyond him?—but his answers always got too complicated and lost to daily routine and finally ceased to matter. It was now a simple fact—Nino's life was his life, and it was a strangely good sign that Nino was so sure of his faith that in his presence Nino could discuss killing his father like the man was some sick animal.

"That's all in the past now," Nino added. "You'll be carrying the torch for me someday."

Near the end of 1974, Dominick spotted Vincent Governara's car, tried following it, but lost it in traffic. Lying to his stepdad Anthony Montiglio, still employed at the Department of Motor Vehicles, he asked him to run a license plate check on a car that sideswiped his and took off. The plate checked to an address from which Governara had moved, but Dominick, after checking it out, told Nino he was on the case.

"Good, I want to get the guy."

All the time Dominick was marching toward this bend in the trail, the delayed stress of Vietnam grew worse. Some nights he would bolt out of bed with images so vivid—intestines slipping through his fingers, shells burrowing into his chest—he was afraid to close his eyes again. It became impossible for Denise to sleep with him, and finally she urged him to see a Veterans Administration doctor, which he did on December 20, 1974.

In a report, Dr. James J. Canty wrote that his patient had delayed seeking help because Green Berets were not supposed to complain. Dr. Canty wrote: "I believe this veteran underwent extensive emotional trauma during his combat duty in Vietnam and that his life is still being very much disturbed by these experiences."

Believing the nightmares unrelated to "that life," even believing, as he told Denise, that the "action of 'that life' " might make the dreams go away, Dominick plunged on. On March 2, 1975, he saw Governara's car by the craps game next to the Villa Borghese Restaurant and went home to tell Nino, who called Roy, who came by with the concussion grenade, which, Dominick warned, might not do the job because its energy might escape when Governara opened the door to his car.

"If this is gonna bother you, let me know now," Nino said as the three men made their plan. "You don't have to help."

"No, I'll do it."

"Hey Dom, this ain't no Vietnam," Roy said.

"Gimme the fuckin' grenade."

Vincent Governara left the craps game about two o'clock in the morning, nearly two hours after Dominick booby-trapped his car. Roy was en route home, Nino had gone to bed, and Dominick was sitting on Nino's porch, wondering how to remove the grenade if it did not explode by morning, when Public School 200 kids would be all around.

Governara opened the driver's-side door of his car and sat directly over the grenade. The fish hooks had already pulled the pin. But while inserting the key into the ignition, the intended victim left the door open.

The explosion was tremendous and knocked Governara out immediately. Glass flew everywhere and the car collapsed on itself. A gush of air threw the victim up and out of the car, and across the street, where he landed, breaking a leg, but otherwise all right when he came to. Dominick had been right about the concussion grenade. And he was spared dismemberment dreams featuring children.

II

"That Life"

CHAPTER 5

Night of Knives

Roy DeMeo's young followers thought more highly of Dominick as Roy circulated the story of the attempt on Vincent Governara's life. Until then, Dominick was someone who rode his uncle's coattails. He might have been a Green Beret once upon a time, but he was an errand boy now; they on the other hand were active criminals, taking chances with the law. But booby-trapping a car on a busy street two blocks from a cop shop was a daring feat, even if the result was unimpressive. Roy's boys also admired the intensity of Nino's desire for revenge. They were the same way and, as they would soon show, capable of settling their scores with savage fury.

All of them grew up in Canarsie, a neighborhood with a chip on its shoulder. Prior to World War II, like Bath Beach, it was a resort area, but not for the wealthy. Its bawdy oceanfront amusement park, Golden City, was a playground for the most downtrodden immigrants, who carried on against the backdrop of a giant flaming dump where Brooklyn deposited most of its garbage. In marshlands near the water, squatters from Sicily and southern Italy lived in tin and tarpaper shacks and survived by fishing clams and raising chickens.

A trolley line from Manhattan, an hour away, made its final stop in Canarsie. It was the city's last frontier, its last open space, until the same postwar housing shortage that spawned instant-mix suburbs like Levittown ignited a building boom. Developers, however, coated Canarsie with the more urban look of adjacent Flatlands, creating a grid of mostly attached brick homes and boxlike apartment buildings. By 1970, about eighty thousand people lived there. Mostly, they were Sicilian, southern Italian, and eastern European Jewish immigrants, or their descendants—the clerks, mail carriers, bakers, tailors, and factory hands of New York.

Many had fled "changing" neighborhoods to the north and northeast—Brownsville and East New York. Immigrants from the southern United States and Puerto Rico had turned those communities darker in color and many violent clashes between old and new groups had occurred. It was especially true in Brownsville, where the Mafia had great sway. In time, however, even the most diehard Italians bailed out and relocated in Canarsie. In 1972, a good example was John Gotti, an up-and-coming member of the Gambino family's Manhattan faction, even though he lived in Brooklyn.

Like the Lower East Side in the early part of the century and Brownsville around midcentury, Canarsie in the 1970s incubated recruits for "that life." Some residents still resented any authority but the family, still distrusted governments, cops, even schools. They resisted the unreality of these notions in an urban, democratic society. And so, even by 1970, fewer than half of Canarsie's Italian male students had graduated from high school.

The lackluster achievement of its young did not stop Canarsians from caring about their schools when the Board of Education revealed plans in 1972 to bus thirty-two black grammar school students into all-white Canarsie. The Italian-American Civil Rights League, founded two years earlier by the boss of the Colombo Mafia family, helped lead a raucous but ultimately unsuccessful boycott. With the Arab-invader blood of Sicily in their veins, some of the protesters were only a shade whiter than some of the six- and seven-year-old black children.

The protesters screamed that busing was the beginning of the end of another neighborhood for them—and this time they had nowhere to flee. The Atlantic Ocean was at their back, and blacks and Puerto Ricans were bearing down from two directions; to the west was Flatlands, but it was built up and more expensive. Canarsians felt cut off; then, their hastily built neighborhood began falling apart. While most of their homes were built on concrete supports driven into bedrock below porous topsoil, sidewalks and streets were not—and these quickly became so buckled and lacking in repair that Canarsie, though new, appeared badly used.

The building boom unearthed evidence showing Canarsie to be unique in another way. Its dumps and marshlands were ideal sites for killers to dispose of their victims' bodies. Throughout the boom, so many remains were found at construction locations that it became an old story and the newspapers stopped writing it.

Canarsie also was a graveyard for junked cars, buses, and trucks. Whole blocks were given over to scrap metal dealers and salvage operators attracted by the comparatively favorable cost of commercial real estate. In Canarsie and to a lesser extent in Flatlands, main streets also featured, one after the other, businesses catering to every automobile need—transmission, brake, and muffler installers; engine rebuilders; custom paint and upholstery specialists; and body shops for foreign and domestic models.

In the early 1970s, a fever began to sweep through this culture of cars. Because of inflation, the price of even an ordinary new car shot up several thousand dollars, creating a black-market demand for stolen vehicles many sought to fill. A stolen car with counterfeit papers or an altered VIN (vehicle identification number) fetched a wondrous profit—given that it cost nothing to steal.

The era's economy, combined with the nature of the auto-repair industry, created another black market in replacement doors, hoods, fenders, trunks, and grilles. The prices that distributors charged for such parts were increasing at a faster rate than the price of new cars. By 1974, a ten-thousand-dollar automobile was actually worth twenty thousand in parts. This paradox, and two-hundred-forty-percent higher salaries for union auto-body men in just four years, made a routine fender-bender an expensive accident. Some insurance companies, trying to contain costs, urged auto-body shops to buy used parts—and, seeking to contain costs further, some of the shops began buying their parts from illegitimate suppliers, no questions asked.

So-called "chop shops" sprouted everywhere. In garages and shops throughout Canarsie and Flatlands, men with acetylene torches turned stolen cars into profitable piles of parts. The difference between new and chopped parts was substantial. A "nose clip"—grille, lights, and bumpers—might cost eight hundred dollars when ordered from a distributor, two hundred if purchased from a chop shop.

Auto theft became the fastest-growing crime in New York City and the nation. Besides the appeal of high profit, it was a low-risk crime requiring modest nerve and simple skills easily acquired in a body shop or gas station. New York's dense housing patterns also worked in the thief's favor; many drivers did not have garages, and cars left on the street or in open lots and driveways were easy pickings. The city's weak fiscal condition at the time was yet another advantage: With several thousand police officers laid off, the criminal justice system focused on violent crime; when a car thief was arrested, prosecutors and judges normally plea-bargained the case away to keep courthouse doors turning.

Seventy-seven thousand cars, a record number and eight percent of the national total, were reported stolen in the city in 1974. The young men gathered around Roy DeMeo, mostly high school dropouts from Canarsie, accounted for many dozen. The key member of the group, the one closest to Roy, was Chris Rosenberg.

Chris was five-feet-five and would try to gouge the eyes of anyone foolish enough to remark on it. He owned many pairs of platform shoes, not only because they were fashionable in the early 1970s, but because wearing them he walked with an obvious bounce, springing off his toes with each step, feeling as if he was elevating himself. Though short, he was wiry and strong and would attack bigger foes wildly and suddenly after lulling them with peaceful words—a Roy DeMeo–type trick.

In 1974, at twenty-three years, with his brown stringy shoulder-length hair, slightly droopy mustache, flowered shirts and bellbottom jeans, he looked like a heavy-metal guitarist. In appearance, he fit into the landscape when he cruised for female company in Manhattan's Greenwich Village, a mecca for the city's young. Two things, however, separated him from the crowd—his white Corvette and the .38 caliber revolver hidden inside.

Chris was not really his first name; it was Harvey. But he hated "Harvey," and for that matter, "Rosenberg." Calling him Harvey or Rosenberg was just as much an offense as commenting on his size. He hated being Jewish and was estranged from his parents because of it.

Growing up on a Canarsie block dominated by Italians, he came to believe that Jews were weak and timid like his father. While a boy, he asked friends and family to start calling him "Chris"—a clean-cut, heroic name not in use on his block—and because he was such a tortured and volatile little guy, they did.

It improved his self-image but not his temperament. He was in constant trouble in school and at home, where his mother tried in vain to coax him into showing respect for his heritage. His parents were not particularly observant Jews, but did enjoy taking family vacations at Jewish resorts in the Catskills, where Chris always acted up and picked on other Jewish kids. His parents eventually gave up on Chris, their eldest child, and let him go his way. They felt blameless; Chris's younger brother was well adjusted and a top student on his way to becoming a doctor.

Chris was as smart, if not as wise, and had an enterprising, entrepreneurial streak. At age thirteen, he was buying and selling marijuana among an older crowd that hung out at a gas station. He also had mechanical ability and learned how to repair cars inside and out. Then, at age sixteen, at the gas station in Canarsie, he met a friendly, tough-talking man who became a father figure to him, Roy DeMeo.

Roy was then only twenty-six, living well on Long Island but working hard on the underside of Canarsie and Flatlands, his old neighborhood. Chris knew Roy by reputation, especially as someone connected to the Lucchese Mafia men who owned Canarsie's junkyards and scrap-metal lots. Chris had dreams that someday he would be in the Mafia; he knew the notion was farfetched, because only full-blooded Italians, preferably Sicilians, were admitted. Still—"You never know," he would tell friends.

Idling at the station, Roy got to know Chris, who had moved from dealing in joints of marijuana to ounces. Roy liked Chris's ambition and how he bounced around with his chin out. He saw himself in Chris—a go-getter, confident of his effect on people, one way or the other. Eventually, Roy offered to loan Chris money so Chris could deal pounds of marijuana and grams of a more potent drug, hashish. Roy had tried both, but thought they were for stupid people; Roy stuck to his favorite drug, alcohol.

Over the next several years, Chris became a success, by the underside standards of Canarsie. Combining his car expertise with the money made from drug dealing backed by Roy, he opened his own business, a body shop. The name he chose was baffling to most of his friends, but showed that somewhere he absorbed something about psychological dysfunction: He called it Car Phobia Repairs.

Gradually, the body shop became a waystation for stolen and chopped cars. Roy provided Chris customers and connections to the junkyards—which were the illegal parts centers for the auto-body shops. Roy was paternal toward Chris, and although their ten-year age difference made big brother a more likely type of bond, he nurtured Chris like a son and took credit for his development. Chris was the first young man to be invited out to Roy's for a barbecue, the first to go to Roy's old friend Frank Foronjy's farm and practice shooting handguns and rifles.

"I made Chris what he is, but the kid's got a knack," Roy would boast to Nino.

"Why don't he get a haircut?" Nino would reply. "He looks like a fuckin' hippie."

By 1974, to strangers, Chris was sometimes introducing himself as "Chris DeMeo." He had moved into an upscale apartment in Flatlands, and was buying whatever gadgets and clothes he wanted and hiring kids to wash and wax his personal cars—the Corvette plus a Porsche. Many young thieves stole cars for him, including two full-blooded Italians who had become his closest friends, Joseph Testa and Anthony Senter. Chris met them when he was living in Canarsie and dealing joints. They were nineteen years old in 1974, four years younger than he. To strangers, he sometimes introduced them as "my brothers."

Joey, as he was known, and Anthony *were* like brothers—like twins—in some ways: Joey would start a sentence, Anthony would finish. They were fanatically loyal to each other; an insult to one provoked a payback from the other. They were always together and had grown up on the same Canarsie block, each in a turbulent home with a contemptuous view of the outside world's ways.

Anthony dropped out of high school before Joey did, but for the most part, Joey led and Anthony followed. Joey was two months older and quicker on his feet, one of nine kids born to a truck driver and his wife; he had five brothers—six counting Anthony. Joey also was more handsome. As he blossomed, he resembled the singer Frankie Avalon—except when he opened his eyes wide and broke into a wide mocking smile chilling to behold.

As with Chris, Joey's smile came when he wanted to smash someone's face, a frequent occurrence beginning when he turned thirteen and his mother died of a blood clot, leaving his father unable to cope with his brood.

Growing up, mutual friends liked Anthony more than Joey, but always ran to Joey when problems arose. When Joey was fifteen, a thirteen-year-old neighbor was mugged by a knife-wielding Puerto Rican kid from East New York. The victim complained to Joey, who rounded up Anthony, and a group led by Joey borrowed someone's car and spent the day searching for the assailant.

"No fucking spic can come on this block with a knife," Joey screamed as the car sped away. "I'll stick the knife up his ass!"

A year later, after Joey dropped out and began dealing dope and stealing cars, another kid on Joey's block complained that his teacher had too unfairly smacked him for smarting off in class. Joey went to the school, waited for the teacher to leave, and beat the daylights out of him.

Before completely casting his lot with Chris and Roy, Joey worked now and then as a carpenter's helper and, as Roy once had, as an apprentice butcher. He became skilled with knives, but almost died in 1973 in a knife fight in a bar with another Puerto Rican opponent. He was stabbed in the chest and suffered a collapsed lung that gave him respiratory problems for the rest of his life.

Anthony, more likable than Joey but equally vicious when provoked, hunted down the Puerto Rican and nearly beat him to death with his fists. Anthony was five-feet-eleven, two inches taller than Joey, and a lot more powerful physically. Before following Joey into Chris's and Roy's world, he worked for his father's small debris-removal business and his uncle's sanitation company. He had only one sibling, a sister. His parents were divorced when he was eight, then remarried one another when he was fourteen, but by then Anthony had been left to his own devices too, like Chris and Joey.

Anthony dazzled many neighborhood girls. Where Joey was conventionally good-looking in a Frankie Avalon way, Anthony was exotic and sensual. With his darker skin, thicker lips, and blacker hair swept back, he would have stood out less in Rome than in Canarsie. Though Joey was more dangerous, Anthony looked the part, and a few of the girls knew that he wore a tattoo of the devil on his right shoulder.

Because they were together so much, frequently at the Gemini Lounge, Joey and Anthony became known as the Gemini twins; it was a more apt nickname than people knew because, in Greek mythology, Zeus the Thunderer fathered two warrior sons, Castor and Pollux, and sent them on missions; their namesakes were the twin stars of Gemini, the third sign of the Zodiac. As time would tell, it was not much of a stretch to think of Roy as an ill-tempered Zeus and Joey and Anthony as his equally surly twin stars.

One of Joey's younger brothers, seventeen-year-old Patrick, known as Patty, sometimes tagged along with Joey and Anthony. He was a dropout too, but a wizard with cars, knowing more than his brother, or Anthony, or even Chris. At fourteen, with money made from a deli job, he had bought a junk car, repaired and rebuilt it, and sold it for a big profit.

The young Canarsie men did not fear the law, or respect it. Chris had picked up his first car-theft arrest in 1970. Joey got two the same year. Anthony already had three, the first when he was twelve years old. Chris's case started as a felony, but was knocked down to misdemeanor with only a fine. Another case, in 1971, for hashish possession, was flat-out dismissed, as was a case in 1972, when he was caught swiping a snowplow out of a garage. Joey and Anthony beat all their cases because they were juveniles at the time. So far, Patty had only been charged with assault, but that too had been dismissed.

By the time they all assembled under Roy's wing, they were by nature and experience primed for bigger and worse things. In 1974, backed by Roy, Chris began dealing two recent products in the street drug market—cocaine and methaqualone, known in tablet form as Quäalude. His connection was a young pharmacist who stole the drugs, including a potent form of pure cocaine then available for medical purposes, from his drug store. One night, the pharmacist arranged a fateful meeting; he introduced Chris to his car repairman, a young Rumanian immigrant named Andrei Katz.

Andrei Katz was twenty-two years old. In Flatlands, he ran the Veribest Foreign Car Service, a small shop near Chris's, for his father, a mechanic who did not speak English well. His father and mother, survivors of a World War II concentration camp, had come to Brooklyn in 1956.

Andrei was not a humble, straightlaced immigrants' son. He permitted customers to pay him with drugs and boasted that women instantly fell for him because his Gypsy features and accent were irresistible. He swaggered as much as any native son of Brooklyn, and when Chris said he could provide spare parts for Veribest, he knew the parts were stolen. He and Chris and the Gemini twins became friends and were soon snorting cocaine together. Once, they got so rowdy at Andrei's apartment that his neighbors called police and much pharmaceutical powder went down the toilet.

In the next two months, Andrei bought cocaine and a Porsche engine from Chris, Joey, and Anthony. In August, he bought a .38 caliber revolver from Chris and paid him seventy-one hundred dollars for a half-interest in eleven stolen Volkswagen vans—"tag jobs"—according to Chris. With Chris, Joey, and Anthony as his suppliers, Andrei also began dealing cocaine himself. They all became vulnerable to one another because of the knowledge each had of the others' crimes.

In September, a friend of Andrei's who had bought one of the tag jobs was stopped by police, who discovered the van was stolen. The friend led police to Andrei, who was arrested in October, but Auto Crime Unit detectives were less interested in a single case than a possible pattern. Andrei was told he might help himself if he provided information about an organized ring. After making bail, Andrei went home and fumed. Chris had done a lousy job retagging the van, the VIN plate was an obvious phony.

As soon as he learned Andrei was out on bail, Chris came by Veribest Foreign Car Service with Joey and Patty Testa. Andrei was with his younger brother Victor; Chris got straight to the heart of their dilemma.

"You better think about what you're going to say or do, or else you're going to get hurt."

"Fuck you! Get the fuck out of my shop!"

"I'm just telling you, watch yourself."

"Fuck you! I'll take care of you!"

The next day, Chris confronted Andrei at a Canarsie stable where Andrei boarded a horse. Andrei, his back against a wall of pride now, refused to bend. The problem was Chris's fault. Chris punched him in the mouth and took off. In a few more days, Andrei was pulled from his pride-and-joy dark green Mercedes by two men, then brutally pistol-whipped, blackjacked, and left in the street.

In a hospital, Andrei was incoherent for three days; part of his right ear was nearly severed. His face was so badly swollen, his brother and father would not let his mother see him. When finally able to speak, he told his brother that Joey and Anthony were his attackers.

"I will deal with it myself," he added. "And I am going to testify someday against Chris."

Out of the hospital, Andrei began carrying the gun he bought from Chris. He stopped dating and going anywhere alone. One night a woman he did not know called him and said a friend had told her about him and she wished to meet him. Andrei the self-anointed ladies' man was tempted but smelled a trap and backed out.

On November 13, 1974, shortly after Andrei's release, Chris was opening his garage door when a sniper opened up with an automatic rifle; Chris was hit three times, but luck was with him; a bullet bound for his chest became just a glancing wound when he spun around from the impact of one that struck his lower jaw and another that ripped into his right arm. He spent only a few days in a hospital, but his face was badly disfigured. Eventually, he underwent reconstructive surgery, but was not happy with the outcome. For the rest of his life he was bitter that he had to wear a beard.

The sniper fled without detection, but Chris was certain it was Andrei and he was right. Warily, the Canarsians began traveling in groups and always with weapons. Six days after the attack, a city jail guard walking by a car parked near the Gemini Lounge noticed a pistol in the waistband of one of three males seated inside—Joey, Anthony, and Patty. The Six-Three precinct sent police officer Alvin Root to investigate and he arrested Joey and Anthony, for possessing both loaded pistols and other weapons—Joey a knife, Anthony a blackjack.

At this point, another hardboiled product of Canarsie entered the drama: His name was Henry Borelli. The backyard of his home abutted the backyard of Joey's, and when Joey contacted him from jail, Henry ran right to court and got Joey and Anthony out on bail. At age twenty-six, Henry was practically an old man compared to them; he was also married and the father of two girls, but the boys liked him, and he was always a guest when Joey fired up the backyard barbecue. To a lesser extent, Henry was friendly with Chris, his more immediate contemporary; Henry had actually met Roy before Chris did and was quietly jealous of the way Chris had over the years become so close to Roy. Still, Henry had kept up relations with Chris and was one of his marijuana and hashish suppliers.

What impressed Joey and Anthony about Henry was that on occasion he traveled to Morocco to score the hashish. During his last trip to Casablanca, however, Henry had been arrested, fortunately while in possession of only a test amount. But the experience was so unsettling—he was released with a warning that if he came back and tried again, he would never leave—he was looking for another line of work. He was now indifferently employed at his father-in-law's car-service company; once, he had wanted to be a cop, and he had taken and passed the entrance exam, but when the city froze the hiring list during a budget crisis, he ruined any future chance with two arrests for petty burglary.

After Joey and Anthony got out of jail and Chris got out of the hospital, they all sat down with Roy and Henry to discuss the Andrei Katz situation and the weapons charges against Joey and Anthony.

Roy told the boys not to worry about the latter problem—his lawyer would (and did) get them off with just another slap on the wrist: probation. But Andrei was another matter. Having already told his boys that "anything is possible after you kill someone," Roy did not shock them when he said: "With what he knows about the cars, he can hurt you. Just kill the fucking guy. What're ya afraid of? Just whack 'im and get rid of the body. No body, no crime."

"I ain't afraid!" Chris said. "The asshole ruined my face!"

Joey and Anthony were not afraid either. Neither was Henry. Andrei had tried to kill Chris. It was all the motive they needed. Revenge was normal; taking no revenge was abnormal.

Chris said they needed a way to entice Andrei into the open. Andrei was still limiting himself to his home and to his father's body shop and traveling back and forth always with his brother. Henry, a ladies' man despite being married, said he knew an ideal lure, a pretty young woman who lived in Manhattan. They had been lovers and were still friends.

Henry called the woman and asked her to visit Andrei at the shop and flirt with him until the Rumanian asked her out. The woman halfheartedly agreed, then backed out, and the idea was dropped, for a while.

Meanwhile, in January 1975, at the Brooklyn district attorney's office, Andrei identified Chris as a major car thief. Chris learned of it within days from Roy, who was tipped off by someone who came to the Gemini Lounge one evening; without saying a word, the man stood in the shadows outside and waited for Roy—who was talking to Dominick Montiglio—to come over. Dominick was there on a collection for Nino. The men spoke about five minutes, then the stranger, who had curly hair and acne scars, left.

"That's my hook in the district attorney's office," Roy told Dominick. "He's a cop; he gets us information on anyone we need."

The hook was actually an auto crimes detective from Queens; his partner's brother was a bartender at the Gemini. He typified why Roy constantly sought relationships and why he always tried to exploit others' weaknesses. The cop liked to gamble on sports contests; Roy hooked him by telling a cousin, who now ran a bookmaking operation at the Gemini, to overlook the man's losses. It was not unusual for cops and firemen to come to the Gemini to place bets, sometimes while on duty; on the day of a big game, before betting closed, it was not unusual to see squad cars and fire trucks parked outside the Gemini.

After the cop in Roy's pocket left, the proposal that Henry Borelli made—to get a pretty woman he knew to lure Andrei into the open—was revived. Henry agreed to contact her again.

At age twelve, Babette Judith Questal had asked her friends to start calling her "Judy" because of a new television cartoon show starring a monkey named Babette. She was born upper middle class in Manhattan, but grew up in Long Island suburbs; she returned to Manhattan in 1970, to put a broken engagement behind her.

After first living on Twenty-seventh Street, she and a girlfriend moved to a ninth-floor apartment on Thirty-seventh Street, between Park and Madison Avenues, in well-to-do Murray Hill. Her building was on the same dense block as the Polish mission to the United Nations, around a corner from the West German consulate in New York and a few doors from the city home of writer William F. Buckley. Judy and her friend bought an old plaid couch and a Tiffany lamp, put candles and wicker all around, hung a poster from the musical *Hair!* and set about having a good time.

One rainy night in 1972, Judy happened to hail one of Henry's father-in-law's car-service cars. She struck up a friendship with the driver, who later introduced her to Henry, who was as casual about cheating on his wife as she was dating a married man. Judy by now had long forgotten her fiancé; at age twenty-five, she was a club-hopping party girl with a coquettish vibrancy and a Nancy Sinatra go-go boots look. After work, she and her roommate would sleep until ten o'clock, hit the discos until four in the morning, sleep a few hours, go to work, and then do it all over again. At the time, she was a secretary for the Katz Underwear Company.

Like Joey and Anthony, tall, dark, and handsome Henry presented an attractive image to the world. He was well built and fastidious about his grooming and clothes— a natural candidate for the door of the 21 Club—and Judy jumped out of her go-go boots at the sight of him. Years later, she did not recall if they made love on their first or second date, only that it was soon after they met.

Since breaking off her engagement, Judy had been daring in her choice of companions, who included some Hell's Angels, but Henry was something new and vaguely mysterious. He told her he had been imprisoned in Turkey for smuggling jewels and once asked if she would be interested in helping him smuggle stolen emeralds from Venezuela.

Henry, who had a fanciful side, was just making the most of his arrest in Casablanca, and Judy dismissed his comments as malarkey. She thought he was a harmless dreamer until one night he showed off a pistol he was carrying. Even so, she continued seeing him, but only a few months more. Between his marriage and her club life, the affair had no place to go. They agreed, however, to remain friends.

Their friendship was three years old when Henry dropped by her apartment in March 1975 to explain in further detail what he had proposed over the telephone months earlier. Judy noticed that Agatha, her Chinese pug who usually sat in visitors' laps, was frightened by Henry and had fled the room—but she listened to what he had to say anyway. A man named Andrei owed him money, Henry said, but whenever Henry tried talking to him, Andrei ran away or threatened to call the police.

"So I just want you to go and meet this guy and make a date with him. Then I can talk to the guy about making payment."

"Are you sure all you want to do is talk to him?"

"I wouldn't involve you in anything."

Judy drew what she regarded as a respectable line. "If you want to talk to him, I don't want to hear what you have to talk to him about—and I don't want it done in my house."

No problem, Henry said, offering to buy her a gift.

"No. If this is a favor, it's a favor, as long as you promise you're not going to hurt him."

Henry promised.

Two months and the attempted murder of Vincent Governara went by. Judy got telephone calls from Henry saying the matter was pending and to stay available.

Then, in May of 1975, Andrei upped the ante by testifying before a Brooklyn grand jury and spilling secrets about not only Chris, but Roy as well.

As with all grand jury testimony, it was supposed to stay a secret, but Roy got another visit from his hook, and Dominick arrived just as the crooked detective left.

When it came to the process of law, Roy liked to make it appear he knew as much as his famous lawyer uncle, and so Dominick heard Roy tell Chris that a grand jury investigation added up to nothing. However, if the case proceeded to trial and Andrei testified again, they had problems.

"We've got to take this guy out," Roy added. "He's got to go right away."

In the first week of June, Henry called Judy to say he needed his favor now.

"Do I really have to do this?" she asked.

"Yes, you really do."

Judy put down the phone and went shopping for a new outfit. She selected snug orange bellbottom pants and an orange and yellow plaid shirt—she thought she looked best in hot colors.

A plan emerged for Henry to pick her up at lunchtime on June 12 at her new secretarial job at the Bulgarian Tourist Office on East Forty-second Street in Manhattan—and drive her to Andrei's shop in Flatlands. On that morning, she donned her new clothes, added a brown wig with bangs and a white plastic umbrella with matching handbag. Although it was raining, she straddled sunglasses across the top of her head.

In Brooklyn, Henry and Judy picked up Joey. Henry and Joey then dropped her off near Andrei's shop; she was to walk in and ask about a nonexistent car.

"How will I know who Andrei is?"

"He has a mustache," Joey said.

"He'll have his name on his shirt," Henry said. "He's a good-looking guy."

"How do we know he'll ask me out?"

Henry and Joey smiled. "He will," they said, as a chorus.

A few blocks away, Judy left Henry's car and sashayed toward Veribest Foreign Car Service. Just inside, she saw Andrei on the phone and a young woman behind a desk.

The woman, Judy learned later, was Andrei's fiancée. Opposed to sex before marriage, the fiancée had reached an understanding with Andrei: He could date other women until he and she were married.

"I'm looking for a white Porsche that my girlfriend left here to be fixed," Judy announced.

"We don't have a car like that," the woman replied. Judy affected dismay, insisted they must. This caused Andrei to put down the phone—here was a walk-in requiring personal attention.

"Could I help you?"

"It's my friend's car, a white Porsche. I'm supposed to pick it up."

"Let me look in the back." Andrei smiled. Judy smiled back, pleased her effect was working so soon. "Come with me," he said.

The garage was small and had only a few cars, none to be mistaken for a white Porsche. "Here's my car," Andrei said, beaming beside his Mercedes, which she appraised as "very nice."

He said, "Maybe the car you're looking for is somewhere else."

"No, I was told it was here."

Well, it obviously isn't, he said, and Well, damn, some other friends dropped me off and I'll have to take a cab, she said.

Andrei took the bait. "Can I drive you home?"

"It isn't any problem. I'll find my way."

"Well, why don't we get together sometime?"

Pause. "All right, I guess."

"Do you like to dance?"

"You bet."

"Well, when?"

"How about tomorrow night?"

Andrei said great. Judy thought he looked like he had just won the lottery. She gave him a phone number a couple of digits off hers and said her name was Barbara. They made plans to meet outside her apartment building on Thirty-seventh Street.

In a strange whirl of shame and triumph, she left the garage and walked to where Henry and Joey waited. "He seems like a nice guy and he's good looking," she wanly said. "I hope you're just going to talk to him."

"That's all," Henry said.

Judy took the rest of the afternoon off and the men drove her to her apartment, where Henry took out a vial and laid lines of cocaine, which he and Joey snorted. It was the first time she saw Henry take cocaine.

The next day, a Friday the 13th, Henry telephoned Judy and said he would come by her apartment about seven o'clock that evening and wait outside for Andrei. She telephoned Andrei to confirm he would meet her in front of her building about half-past-eight.

Excited about his date, Andrei left Veribest early that day. He showered the day's grease off and put on brown platform shoes, a white shirt with beige geometric designs, and maroon bellbottom pants. He topped off the ensemble with a white and red neck scarf and a light pink sweater. Underneath, he was wearing what was described later by a doctor as silk, yellow ladies panties.

Traffic into Manhattan was slow and it was not until fifteen minutes after Andrei was due that Judy, surveying the street from her ninth-floor window, saw Andrei's dark green Mercedes moving slowly east along Thirty-seventh Street and then after a righthand turn disappearing onto Madison Avenue. In minutes, the car reappeared; probably believing Judy had gone inside because he was late, Andrei began to maneuver his car into the only available parking space, an illegal one by a fire hydrant.

Suddenly, a white Lincoln owned by Henry Borelli's father appeared and blocked Andrei's car at the curb. Three men jumped out, surrounded the Mercedes and flung open its doors. Judy recognized Joey Testa. She also recognized a smaller, wiry man she had seen with Henry once, but knew only as Chris. She did not recognize Anthony Senter, whom she had never seen before.

Andrei got out, but did not try to run.

From inside the Lincoln, Judy thought she heard a voice she recognized as Henry's say, "We just want to talk."

On the street, she saw Andrei hunch his shoulders and extend his arms as if in a shrug. She saw a rope come out and one of the men lift Andrei's arms above his shoulders. In another instant, Andrei was violently shoved into the Lincoln, which sped away.

A wave of guilt knocked Judy Questal onto her couch. She felt jolts of self-hate for her teasing manipulation of Andrei and her naiveté in trusting Henry. She remained by her window through the night to see if Andrei or anyone came for the Mercedes. She was afraid—and in too deep—to do much else.

In the morning, police officer Lewis Feirberg came upon a mysterious sight: an expensive car parked at an odd angle by a fire hydrant, sun roof up, doors open, leather jacket in plain view in the backseat. In the afternoon, as Judy watched, Andrei's beloved car was towed. Her thoughts ran wild, but the truth of his demise was beyond her ken.

The four kidnappers had driven Andrei to Queens. Andrei must have begun begging them to kill him as soon as they dragged him into the meat department of a Pantry Pride supermarket, where Roy was waiting. A friend of Roy's had given him access; Roy had told his crew they had to make sure Andrei was not seen again. As they all later described it, they had to make him "disappear." If his body was found, the police would naturally suspect them.

Nino's method had been incineration; the method that former butcher's apprentice Roy was going to use was dismemberment.

Dismemberment was not unheard of in the underworld, but even in the Mafia it was considered radical, and few had the stomach for it. For Roy, it was going to be just another way to show his power, and so it became that for Chris and Joey and Anthony too.

Only Henry had expressed any unease. "I'd shoot anybody for ya, Roy, but that, no thanks."

"It's just like takin' apart a deer," Roy said. "It's only a little weird if you do it while the guy's still alive."

The kidnappers had already decided to give Chris his revenge and let him prepare the victim for dismemberment. So as his would-be brothers Joey and Anthony held the quaking victim, and as Roy and Henry watched, Chris furiously drove a long butcher knife into Andrei's heart six times. The target area was deliberate—the quicker the heart stops pumping, the less bloody mess a victim makes.

As Andrei slumped to the floor, already dead, Chris

maniacally stabbed him fifteen times more in the back. Roy and Joey, the second former butcher's apprentice on hand, would now show the others how to dismember a corpse. Out came the boning knives and on went the white butcher coats and orange and yellow rubber gloves.

"We have to wait a little bit," Roy said, "until the blood gets hard."

Roy and Joey began stripping the body of its clothes; Chris and Anthony laid out some green plastic garbage bags and twine. Feeling nauseous, Henry went outside, ostensibly to guard a rear exit.

Violating his practice of never drinking while working, Roy took occasional shots from a quart bottle of whisky; so did the others as Roy sliced off the victim's head and he and Joey began sawing the torso apart limb by limb. Chris and Anthony wrapped the body parts in the garbage bags and secured them with the twine.

At one point, crazy with personal revenge for the gun-shot damage to his face, the bearded Chris took the victim's head and ran it through a machine for compacting cardboard.

After the sawing and packaging was over, Henry came back in and everyone methodically cleaned the Pantry Pride meat department. They swept and mopped the floor, scrubbed the sinks and knives, wiped extruded brain matter off the cardboard compactor. They then took the body parts, Andrei's clothes, and the empty whisky bottle and buried them under some rotten vegetables in a garbage bin behind the store.

The night of knives marked the real beginning of the DeMeo crew, a union of five killing spirits stepping across a wicked threshold. Roy had and would show the way, closely followed by devoted Chris and his loyal brothers, Joey and Anthony. Henry's queasiness hardly exempted him from having become a full partner, and as he would show, he was not at all queasy with guns.

It was the coming-together of a gang that other gangs would come to fear, and it might have passed officially unrecorded if the killers had not overlooked a detail: the garbage at the supermarket was not picked up on week-ends.

On Sunday, two days later, a bum foraging the garbage bin for food walked off with one of the packages, believ-

ing it was a discarded side of beef. Not far away, un-
wrapping it, he realized his mistake, dropped it and ran
off; in moments, when his dog began barking wildly, a
passerby found it and telephoned police.

Salvatore Napolitano, the first officer to arrive, went
to the garbage bin, unwrapped another package, then
quickly summoned a medical examiner, who unwrapped
eight more. At the scene, she laid the body parts on a
tarpaulin and pieced them together like a puzzle. The
body's genitals were missing and never found.

"A butcher or someone with knowledge of the anat-
omy of the human being did this," Detective Michael
Walsh told other cops after conferring with the medical
examiner. A top police official, Gerald Kerins, told the
media there had been a "frenzied, wild, vicious type of
attack."

At the city morgue, chief medical examiner Dr. Dominick DiMaio spoke into a microphone as he began conducting an autopsy, "Head is decapitated and flattened
into a pancake appearance. . . ." Years ago, a branch of
the DiMaio family began spelling the name differently.
Dr. DiMaio had no reason to know that this horror show
it was his duty to review had been directed by his cousin
Anthony's son, Roy DeMeo.

CHAPTER 6

Map of Murder

Coaxed by Henry, Judy Questal had wandered onto a landscape she knew nothing about, territory that was about to become a lot more violent. Had she known how Andrei Katz died, she would have never dialed the number of the Veribest Foreign Car Service on the day before his remains were discovered and, innocently as possible, asked the woman who answered if Andrei was there.

"Isn't he with you?" replied Andrei's accommodating and now irritated fiancée, believing she was talking to the flashy "Barbara" of two days before.

"He never showed up for our date, I never saw him."

"That's strange."

Judy did not know what else to say and hung up. On Monday, she called again; a man who said his name was George got on the phone and spoke sharply to her. "You better tell everything you know because the police are going to make it very very hard for you."

George asked for her last name and real phone number. Judy told a series of lies, the last being that she had only arranged to meet Andrei on Thirty-seventh Street; she really lived farther uptown, on Fifty-eighth Street. Then she hung up.

On Tuesday, she received a call from a man who always began telephone conversations the same way, with his name: "Henry." He apologized for not calling earlier. "I know you must have been nervous."

Judy was distant, and now concerned about sounding angry—maybe she was in jeopardy. "What happened? His car was there until the next day. What did you do to him?"

"He just got a beating and he's in a hospital someplace."

"I hope he's not dead because I can't handle that."

"Don't worry, he's not."

On Wednesday, from her desk at the Bulgarian Tourist Office, Judy called Veribest again, but got no answer. She called a business next to the shop. "There has been a death in the family over there," a man said. "Andrei died. He was in an accident."

The words took Judy's breath away. If her telephone had not immediately started to ring, she might have fainted.

"Henry."

Judy cringed and tried reclaiming her composure. She recalled that someone in her office had said the FBI tapped all the telephones of foreign businesses, especially tourist offices. She took Henry's number and hurried out to East Forty-second Street and onto a pay telephone. "He's dead," she began, "isn't he?"

"Yes."

Tumultuous Forty-second Street, one of the busiest in the world, forces people to notice what is happening around them. Beginning to grieve for her own neck now, Judy said, "The police are gonna be looking for me."

"Don't worry, whenever they find you, you just say that you don't know anything."

"Henry, I saw everything from my window. I saw somebody put something around Andrei's neck. I saw Joey. I saw the other guy—that Jewish guy, whatever his name is, Chris?—who else knows everything I know?"

"Only you."

"Are you going to try to do away with me, too?"

"Nothing's going to happen to you."

"What about your friends?"

"I'm the boss," Henry lied.

"How did you kill him?"

"I don't want to say anything about that."

The next day, after Andrei's remains were identified through dental records and the story made the newspapers, the doorman for Judy's building told her that detectives had come with questions for "a hooker named Barbara." Henry also called to say someone he knew in the police department had assured him that the cops would ask their questions a while, then forget about it. Even if they picked her up for questioning, all she had to do was say she did not know anything; no one in Andrei's shop could identify her.

In a few days, feeling she might skate free because the police had not come back, Judy left on a previously planned vacation to San Francisco. Beforehand, Anthony Senter visited her office and dropped off two hundred dollars and a have-fun message, courtesy of Henry. In San Francisco, she threw her Andrei-baiting outfit in the garbage.

Relief was short-lived. A girlfriend who had been visited by detectives called Judy at her hotel and said they wanted her for questioning. Finally realizing Henry was more than she bargained for—and that, as she had said, if Andrei was dead, "I can't handle that"—Judy came home. After confessing her role, she led police to the homes of Henry and Joey Testa, who were arrested. They identified themselves as unemployed carpenters and were jailed without bail.

Judy's story did not contain enough evidence to arrest either Chris or Anthony. Afraid he would be killed, Victor Katz kept quiet about Chris's threats against his brother. Checking out Henry and Joey, police learned about Roy, but found nothing linking him to the murder. Roy arranged for his lawyer, Frederick Abrams, to advise Henry and Joey. Abrams had ample political connections; his father was a judge and both were active in the local Democratic club that produced incumbent mayor Abe Beame.

Worried about police surveillance, Anthony Gaggi stopped going to the Gemini Lounge. Dominick, however, continued to go, to pick up cash for Nino from Roy. One night outside the bar, Chris discussed the murder with him as they admired Chris's Corvette. Chris was comfortable implicating himself because he knew Dominick had tried to kill Vincent Governara.

"Two of my guys are in jail because we killed some guy who shot me." Chris smiled. "Then we took him apart. Bit by bit."

Chris's boast was startling, but Dominick remained poised. Having adopted Nino's logic as his own, he believed that just as Nino's revenge was normal, it was normal for criminals to kill other criminals. This was how they maintained their own law and order. But was dismemberment normal? He did not think so, but he did not argue the point with Chris. ''Who got whacked?'' he said.

''Some old drug partner of mine. He was gonna squeal on us. So we had to get rid of him.''

''Because he broke the rules of engagement, right?''

''You got it. And after I got shot, we made a pact we weren't gonna get in any more fights, and we weren't just gonna kill the guy. We were gonna make 'im disappear.''

''I'm glad you guys are on our side,'' Dominick said, then got in Chris's Corvette and went for a ride.

As the plot to murder Andrei Katz unfolded during the first half of 1975, Paul Castellano—like Nino, he learned of the murder after the fact—walked into some legal trouble of his own.

Although Paul's true power in the Gambino family was still unknown to federal authorities, they had learned he was a major loanshark. In March, they persuaded a stock swindler facing fraud charges, who was married to one of Paul's nieces, to wear a secret recording device and tape Paul talking about his loans. In June, Paul was indicted, accused of charging a usurious one hundred fifty percent interest on one hundred fifty thousand dollars in loans over six years.

The swindler's name was Arthur Berardelli, and for a while Paul contemplated having him killed. He told Nino the job would be his but to try intimidation first. Accompanied by Dominick, Nino followed Berardelli into a restaurant one day and made a point of saying hello. Berardelli, of course, turned gray.

A few days later, however, Nino told Dominick that ''Paulie's called it off. He thinks Artie boy will listen to reason.''

Dominick began to see that the power of men such as Nino and uncles Carlo and Paul lay in how others perceived them as much as their actual use of power. Though Paul faced prison if convicted, he seemed confident he had been perceived correctly and that the case would fall apart at the end.

Nino began taking Dominick to regular Wednesday afternoon luncheons with Carlo, Paul, and a changing cast of other family members. This was a heady privilege for Dominick, but he was a beneficiary of the personal connections between Carlo and Paul and between Paul and Nino. Roy was never invited to these meetings, which were largely social; Carlo did not even know who he was; Paul knew him only a little and was not especially taken because, the few times they had met, Roy had come on like too much of a brown-noser. In Paul's mind, another problem with Roy was that his ancestors came from Naples, not Sicily. Naples was the crime capital of southern Italy, but Sicilians came to America with chauvinistic baggage—they considered Neapolitans showy, coarse, and unreliable.

Listening to Carlo's stories, Dominick further understood Paul's confidence in the outcome of his loanshark case. Carlo, now seventy-three, had beaten the government so often any new case against him or his men was just a nettlesome fly to swat—the odd loss was just the vig the family had to pay society on occasion. Having failed to convict Carlo, the government was trying to deport him as an undesirable alien, as it had Charles "Lucky" Luciano, Frank Scalise's mentor. He had resisted so far on grounds he was too ill to travel because of a recent heart attack; the government considered its stated effects exaggerated, but Carlo did look like a frail old man in the summer of 1975.

Though he had his country home near Roy's, Carlo lived most of the time in an apartment near Bensonhurst. Shopping in corner stores, he portrayed himself as merely a humble Sicilian whose fate it was to protect and provide for his people. From his men, he demanded unequivocal fealty, as befitting a man of his tradition.

His tradition was tied to Sicily's tortured past. The island was exploited by generations of conquerors. Unable to rule their own land, abused by the fickle laws of other cultures, Sicilians developed the anti-authority attitudes that even law-abiding men like Nino's father, Angelo Gaggi, brought to America. The flip side was belief in family as the only source of protection and justice. The word "*mafia*" derived from Sicilian and Arabic expressions for these concepts.

In Sicily, plundering and feuding over depleted resources caused groups of peasant families to form large

families led by *uomini di rispettu* ("men of respect")—
the first Mafia bosses. By the twentieth century, these
men ruled Sicily, and some became as lawless and tyran-
nical as their former oppressors. Some bosses and their
disciples, like Carlo, fled to the United States when Italian dictator Benito Mussolini ordered his army to eliminate them.

In New York at that time, the large numbers of Sicilian
and Italian immigrants—cut off from English-speaking
society, segregated in ghettos and denied all but the most
menial jobs—created ready-made conditions for men like
Carlo. Although all that had changed by 1975, Carlo had
his Machiavellian justification—a leader must do what he
has to do to hold onto power.

"A lion scares away the wolves; a fox recognizes
traps," Carlo was still fond of saying to Dominick.

Paul's contempt for his daughter Connie's husband was
another frequent topic at the luncheons. After Dominick
came home from Vietnam, Paul had hoped he and Connie
would hit it off, but when it failed to happen, she wound
up marrying a burly Guido Rinaldo–type whose name
was Frank Amato.

Paul had set Amato up in the Italian ices business Nino
had offered Dominick about the same time. The venture
failed, however, and Paul made Amato manager of his
butcher shop chain, known as the Meat Palace. It was a
make-work job because two of Paul's three sons already
managed the chain profitably.

Amato was unhappily married and unhappy living with
Connie in her parents' home on Staten Island. For all the
material advantages of marriage to an important man's
daughter—Connie showered Amato with jewelry and
clothes—there was a price to pay. "I'm a prisoner," he
told a friend. "I have to kowtow to her. I have to kowtow
to him. I have to be available all the time."

With Nino one day at the main Meat Palace office,
Dominick saw Amato being overly friendly with one of
the female employees. "He's already been warned," Nino
said when Dominick mentioned it later. "Paul's
gettin' tired of him foolin' around."

In a few weeks, the female employee was fired and
Amato was transferred to Paul's wholesale meat company, Dial Poultry. In a few months, Amato was caught

cheating on his wife. He was lucky Paul only ordered him out of the house and fired him. Amato then took a job in a clothing store, but Paul's estranged son-in-law also became a lowly burglar.

"The thing that bothers me most is the thought of that fat bastard on top of my daughter," Paul told Dominick.

"I don't know why Paul's acting so crazy about this, the guy's goin' out of his mind," Nino said, after Dominick relayed the remark. "Our life, it's a cuckoo's nest sometimes."

One Flew Over the Cuckoo's Nest was another of Nino's favorite movies. Stuck in Manhattan between appointments recently, he and Dominick had gone to see it. Nino loved the story of a free spirit taking over a mental ward.

When Roy acted friendly, Dominick reciprocated, though he felt every move Roy made was political. An emerging politician himself, however, Dominick went along, so when Roy occasionally asked him to drive him around on errands because he was "tired," he did. This was how he learned, in the fall of 1975, that Roy was involved in a new business—films depicting children, and women and animals, in sexual situations.

Roy directed Dominick to a Bensonhurst bar, where a man came out and transferred several cartons of films from his car to the trunk of Roy's Cadillac. Roy showed Dominick the titles. "It's eleven-year-old kids and people with dogs," he said.

Dominick knew that through a loan Roy had become a partner in a combination peep show and whorehouse in Bricktown, New Jersey, but the child pornography, and the films depicting bestiality, were new. Roy cheerfully said he was buying the "sick shit" for the sex emporium in Bricktown as well as "asshole" customers in Rhode Island, where he had a good connection.

Dominick drove Roy to the Gemini Lounge. The films in the trunk made him feel dirty, but he was learning to justify anything. If anyone should have felt shame for trafficking in such material, it was Roy, the father of three children—two of them were about the age of those in the films—but Roy explained, "My business is just buying and selling." The dollar made everything fair game, or so it seemed until Roy told Nino about the films, and Nino exploded.

"I don't want you selling that shit!"

While shaking down the Manhattan film processor Paul Rothenberg, Nino was in the pornography business himself; currently he profited from Roy's role in the Bricktown whorehouse; his counterfeit movie operation in Manhattan was now distributing copies of X-rated films such as *Behind the Green Door,* so he had no objection to conventional sex films or prostitution.

"But there's a lot of money in this," Roy protested. "It's the way the industry is going. We can't stay competitive if we don't deal in it."

Nino, the father of four children under fourteen, told Roy the subject was closed.

"But Nino . . ."

"I'm telling you, if you don't stop, you're gonna die."

At the time, the ever-industrious Roy also was beginning to deal in larger quantities of drugs, conduct from which Nino was barred under a penalty of death because Carlo feared that the harsh sentences at stake in drug cases might cause a made man to crack and turn informer, which would be ruinous for the family. Ideally, a made man also was not supposed to accept drug profits from an "unmade" associate, but Nino and many others winked at this rule because it was unrealistic given the money to be made. Carlo and Paul must have known what was going on, but their reaction awaited a test case—someone getting arrested.

Roy was financing a major operation that imported Colombian marijuana by the twenty-five-pound bale. The marijuana was unloaded from an offshore freighter and sold out of a body shop in Canarsie.

Roy himself was also selling multiple ounces of cocaine out of the Gemini Lounge. He got into the cocaine business as he got out of the credit union business—after helping push the Boro of Brooklyn Credit Union into insolvency by approving too many uncollected and uncollectible loans. The credit union was merged into another, but the merger drew such scrutiny from police and state banking officials that Roy walked away.

Just in time, Roy also made an indictment-avoiding settlement with his dreaded enemy, the IRS. The deal was based on false affidavits from business friends that helped Roy account for some of his income. One affidavit was filed by Freddy DiNome, Roy's old buddy from his immediate post-high school days. Although he would have done it for friendship, Freddy told people: "It was either lie or die."

Early in 1976, Roy turned his attention to the murder trial of Henry Borelli and Joey Testa, which got underway in Queens on January 5. Roy did not attend the trial, but was spotted outside the courthouse one day having an animated discussion with one of the defense attorneys, his politically connected lawyer, Fred Abrams.

The case was hardly open and shut. Victor Katz was still too terrified to talk. There was no physical evidence linking either Henry or Joey to the devilry inside the Pantry Pride. The main witness was Judy Questal, who had been in protective custody since agreeing to tell her story.

The defense strategy was to put Judy in the dock by poking holes in her credibility, and it worked to perfection. Testifying in disguise, she was destroyed on the stand. Badgering her about her sex life, occasional drug use, and treatment for anxiety, the defense made her seem wanton and unstable. With not much else to go on but her, and she was not at the Pantry Pride, the jury was left with ample reasonable doubt that Henry and Joey, such handsome young men, could commit such a horrible crime. The defendants also benefited from the inability of prosecutors in Queens County to add a kidnapping charge to the indictment; that crime had occurred in a different jurisdiction—New York County (Manhattan). The jury had no lesser charge to fall back on; on January 23, the verdict came in: not guilty.

A celebration was held at the Gemini Lounge. The only mourning was for the six months that Henry and Joey had spent in jail. Andrei Katz had cooperated with the police and gotten what he deserved. Nino, who had avoided the Gemini, returned with Dominick, who saw that the circle of young men orbiting Roy now included a bearded stocky fellow named Peter LaFroscia, whom Chris introduced as "one of the top car guys in New York."

Dominick was also introduced to Henry for the first

time; it was the start of his closest friendship with anyone in the DeMeo crew. Dominick was twenty-eight now, Henry twenty-seven; they were fathers and husbands; both had once wanted to be cops. Like Dominick, Henry had traveled to an exotic country—though Henry's trips to Morocco involved drug deals, not army service, at least he knew a little of life beyond Canarsie.

"I got pinched in Casablanca once," Henry said, "but a few times I didn't."

In the weeks following the party, Dominick and Henry began meeting for drinks. Dominick thought Henry was the only one from the Canarsie crowd whose friendliness was genuine—he suspected the others were courteous only because they wanted him to speak well of them to Nino. Because Nino did not want him around the Gemini unless it was to conduct Nino's business, Dominick began meeting Henry in Manhattan, usually at Pear Tree, a bar and restaurant in midtown on the affluent East Side.

One day, Dominick got a call—"Henry," a voice he recognized said. "Let's go to the Pear Tree. I wanna talk about a little problem that's come up."

The budding friends were familiar faces to the restaurant staff by now. Henry's good looks turned a few female heads—in fact, he drew quite a few male stares too, but he had told Dominick that if a man ever made the wrong approach, he would shoot him. Of course, Dominick had always believed he cut a good figure entering a room; bouncing on the East Side with runaround Henry, he met many attractive women, but out of loyalty to Denise he resisted trying to romance them. Nevertheless, he was struck by how some women were excited by the idea of talking to two cocky young men rumored to be "connected."

Henry's problem was not little. He had dramatically misread the depth of Roy's affection for Chris. "I went to Roy and asked him if I could kill Chris," he began.

"Are you crazy? Why didn't you just ask him if you could kill his son?"

Henry acknowledged his blunder and said Roy had exploded. "Now Roy says even if Chris drops dead of a heart attack, he's going to hold me responsible."

The reason Henry wanted to kill Chris—money—was hardly a surprise. The more Dominick saw of Nino's

world, the more cynical he became. Despite Nino's outburst, Roy was still trafficking in repulsive pornography,
and Nino was taking money from it. Nino just did not
want to know details. Looking back on it, Dominick
thought money, as much as revenge, was the lesson of
the attempt on Vincent Governara's life. If anyone but
Roy abandoned his post during a job they would have
been disciplined, if not killed. But Roy made too much
money; money rationalized everything and was worth
more than loyalty.

"I spent all that time in jail for Chris," Henry said.
"We killed that guy for him and I sat in the can all that
time and Chris didn't take care of my family. He didn't
give my wife or kids any money."

Logically, Henry should have also been angry at Roy—
Andrei Katz was killed for Roy as much as Chris—but
Henry did not dare suggest that Roy was cheap. He was
trying to regain his position in the crew's reactivated
stolen-car operation. While Henry was away, Roy had
moved Patty Testa and one of Patty's friends ahead of
him.

Dominick urged Henry to make peace with Chris. With
Chris's temperament, it was certain Chris would do
something impulsive and thus dig his own grave someday. "Bide your time," the former point man said.

Because of his vantage point, Dominick became a witness to many intrigues. The next came in a few months
when Roy, wearing sunglasses though it was nighttime,
arrived at Nino's house.

"What the fuck are you wearing those for?" Dominick
asked as he led Roy into Nino's basement meeting room.

Roy removed the glasses; his left eye was swollen and
black, the result of a dispute with Joseph Brocchini, a
pornographer who was a made member of another Mafia
family. "Some schmuck sucker-punched me," he said,
"but it's the last important thing he ever did, I'll tell you
that. It'll be a little tricky, that's all." Under explicit
Mafia rules, a made man was not supposed to be killed
without his boss's permission.

Roy said to Nino, "We'll never get permission,
right?"

Nino's reply indicated how selectively he observed
rules: "No, but just make it look like something else."

In a few weeks, on May 20, 1976, Joseph Brocchini, who was identified as a used-car dealer with interests in three X-rated magazine and film stores in Manhattan's Times Square, was shot to death in the office of his used-car dealership. The police said robbery appeared to be the motive because two of Brocchini's employees had first been blindfolded and handcuffed and the office appeared to have been rifled. But in Bath Beach and Canarsie, insiders knew that Roy had accomplished his trick.

In the process, Henry won his way closer to Roy's heart and established that, although he was queasy about dismemberment, he had no qualms about an ordinary murder. "I did that one," he crowed to Dominick a few days later. "I mean, me and Roy did. The other guys took care of the employees, then me and Roy surprised the guy and plugged him five times in the back of the head."

Later, Roy praised Henry's performance, telling Nino: "That Henry, he was ice-cold. He never flinched. He's a natural, like Joe DiMaggio!"

As a reason for revenge, Roy's black eye was equivalent to Nino's broken nose at the hand of Vincent Governara.

Fifteen months after surviving a grenade that destroyed his car, Governara had recovered from his broken leg; he did not know Nino was behind the attempt on his life. He had stayed in Florida until he received assurances that the man he did suspect was not angry at him. In Bensonhurst, on June 12, 1976, this proved to be a fatal misunderstanding.

Governara was driving the same make and model car, only his new Plymouth was silver, according to a tip Nino got from one of Governara's gambling acquaintances. In a virtual replay of his coincidental spotting of Governara the previous year, Dominick, striding home from a trip to a newsstand four blocks away, saw the silver Plymouth parked outside a candy store on Twentieth Avenue, between Eighty-fifth and Eighty-sixth Streets. The store was two blocks from the site of the previous year's crap game. Once again, Governara had come to Nino.

At Nino's house, a birthday party for Denise Montiglio

was underway in Nino's mother's apartment. Birthdays were big events in Nino's house; each family member always got a party, and Roy was one of the guests at this one.

Dominick pulled Nino aside. "Guess who's back in town?"

Nino, Dominick, and Roy all headed toward Nino's basement enclave. "We've got to go out a while," Dominick told Denise.

Denise did not ask where or why. Since coming home from California and not objecting when Dominick went to work for his uncle, she had never asked where or why. Like Rose Gaggi, she read between the lines and that was enough. And like Rose, she was happy being a full-time wife and mother. Her love for her husband, and his for her, was what mattered.

In the basement, Nino and Dominick donned disguises. Nino glued on a fake mustache, put on a fedora and replaced his dark eyeglasses with clear ones. Dominick drew a line of rubber cement across his right cheek—when it dried, it appeared to be a scar; he put on a Navy cap and three jackets to make himself look fat. The former LURP was an expert at subterfuge; in the jungle, for instance, he would cut the soles off his P.F. Flyers, then reattach them in a backward position, so that his footprints in a sandy trail made it appear he was walking in one direction, when in truth he was going the other.

Roy did not bother with a disguise. With his knit shirt dangling outside his chinos, he appeared to be a harmless suburban hardware salesman.

Nino retrieved three handguns—two .38 caliber Smith & Wessons and a .22 caliber, silencer-equipped Ruger—from a false-bottom kitchen cabinet; he also had another secret hiding place in the house, a floor trap in his mother Mary's bedroom closet. Without anyone seeing them, they left the house and drove a few blocks past the candy store and parked. In the car, Nino gave Dominick the handgun with the silencer.

"You get that one because you're going to do the work."

"Fine," Dominick said.

"Hey, Dom," Roy said, "as many people as you

killed in Vietnam, fifty or whatever it was, this ain't like that.''

"You've said that before, Roy."

"You know, it's just like what Michael's brother Sonny said in *The Godfather,* when Michael's going to kill that cop, and Sonny says, 'Hey, Michael, this ain't like war, where you're shootin' people a hundred yards away. Here you walk up and the brains are goin' to fly all over ya.' ''

"You're right, Roy," Dominick snapped. "This ain't war. We are going to shoot this motherfucker down and he doesn't have a fuckin' slingshot.''

The men left the car and walked back to the candy store, where another craps game was underway, and waited in the shadows across the street for Governara to come out. An hour went by; Roy needled Dominick some more.

"This is real war, Dom, real war. Are you ready?''

"Fuck you, Roy. Fuck you and the pig you rode in on.''

"Take it easy, soldier, take it easy. No need for insults.''

"Shut the fuck up," Nino suddenly demanded. "Here he comes.''

Governara walked toward his car. Nino surprised Dominick by countermanding his earlier statement that Dominick "do the work." He told him to stay across the street and back up him and Roy in case Governara was armed; they never talked about it, of course, but Dominick was sure—and thankful—that Nino had deliberately consigned him to a role requiring him to pull a trigger only if Nino was in jeopardy. Pistols out, Nino and Roy walked into the street. Reaching his car door, Governara saw them and started running, but they opened up with their Smith & Wessons and he fell in sight of about twenty bystanders.

The killers began walking toward Roy's car; bystanders began to follow. Roy started to run, but Nino, with Dominick alongside, turned, raised an empty pistol and shouted, "Get down!", and the crowd dived to the street. Nino and Dominick began running too, but Nino, now age fifty-one, slowed to a quick walk halfway to the car.

Dominick stayed behind him—but Roy, who believed in self-preservation more than false heroism, kept on going.

"Where is that fuck Roy?" Nino asked.

"A block ahead."

"How can that cocksucker run so fast?"

"He's a dog, a fucking bunny rabbit."

Roy was behind the wheel of his Cadillac when Nino and Dominick arrived and got inside. As he drove away, he almost collided with another car, whose driver laid on his horn, rolled down his window, and cursed them. Roy yelled out his window—"Sorry!"—and he and Nino began to laugh hysterically. It was comical to them how the driver had no idea who he was yelling at.

"If the cocksucker knew what we just did, I wonder if he'd be laying on the horn!" Nino laughed.

"He don't know how close he was to dyin'!" Roy added.

Just as a man's power sometimes depends on how he is perceived, Nino and Roy sometimes felt as much power in not killing as killing, and so they let the angry driver keep his life and drive away.

They drove toward Manhattan and, while crossing the Brooklyn Bridge, tossed the weapons into the East River. On the Manhattan side, uncle and nephew removed their disguises and gave them to the down-and-outers and junkies who inhabit the Skid Row corner of Delancey Street and the Bowery. Then they drove back to Brooklyn and returned to Denise's birthday party.

Dominick's former classmate would die a week later, unable to identify anyone. Ballistics tests showed that the fatal bullets were .38 caliber, not .22. Dominick had not pulled a trigger that night, but under accomplice theories of the law, he was a murderer. He always wondered what he would have done if the ambush went awry, and usually concluded that out of loyalty to Nino the street outside the candy store would have become Hill 875.

It was a season for revenge. In a couple of weeks, a leader in another Mafia family told Nino that two armed robbers in Florida were overheard bragging that an electrical contractor had told them that a big shot from New York probably kept a lot of cash in his new winter home near Hallandale. The tip was good, but the target was home at the time and they had to smack him down with a pistol.

Nino had vowed to kill the robbers who burst in on him and Rose the year before. Now, however, he judged the contractor's conduct the graver crime. The contractor, George Byrum, had supervised the wiring of his house.

A month after the Governara homicide, Nino and Roy traveled separately to Florida. Roy flew under the name "John Holland"—the surname being the James Madison High School graduate's sly tribute to Dutch-founded Flatlands. In Florida, Roy called Byrum and portrayed himself a potential client; he was building a new home and wanted Byrum to examine the blueprints and make an estimate. After a meeting in Byrum's office, Byrum agreed to a second meeting in the Ocean Shore Motel near Miami. He was immediately shot in the buttocks after walking into Roy's room.

Roy fired several more fatal shots as Nino and a Gambino soldier who lived in Florida, both hiding in the bathroom, came out. They dragged the corpse to the bathtub and waited for its blood to congeal—another Pantry Pride night was in store. Part of Roy's view that cutting up lifeless bodies was psychotically insignificant came from Nino, who had thrown the dead killer of Frank Scalise into a furnace.

Even so, Nino was not keen on dismemberment; he would have preferred another furnace, but with one unavailable and Roy concerned that someone might have seen him with Byrum, they and the Gambino soldier with them agreed they had to make the body disappear Roy's way. The plan was to take the body parts out in suitcases.

As Roy was halfway through sawing off Byrum's head, the Gambino soldier became spooked by the noise of construction workers outside the room and insisted they leave the motel, which they did. On July 14, 1976, a maid who later underwent treatment for psychological trauma came upon the partially decapitated body. The killers had not left any clues, however, and the resulting Dade County police case went nowhere.

In less than two months, a black eye, a broken nose, and a tip to two robbers had caused killings in Queens,

Brooklyn, and Florida. Officially, the Brocchini, Governara, and Byrum murders remained unconnected dots on a map of murder still very much in draft form, so far as Roy DeMeo was concerned.

CHAPTER 7

The Coronation

From appearances in the bicentennial summer of 1976, Dominick Montiglio could have been a traveling salesman, but for the leisurely way he conducted Nino's business. Most days, like Nino, he rose late, took long meals and fit personal errands somewhere into the day's loan pickups. In his subculture, he was achieving status—and much more was just over the horizon. Life was more rewarding than he thought it could possibly be for the average twenty-nine-year-old man with no college degree or professional training apart from silent warfare and the use of light weapons.

The Veterans Administration had ruled that he was not entitled to any disability benefits. Because he did not complain of any problems during his discharge physical examination, no evidence existed that his nightmares and flashbacks were related to his military service—a classic Catch-22 that was used against many Vietnam War veterans, including Agent Orange victims whose symptoms often did not materialize until many years later.

"I knew the government would fuck ya," Nino told his nephew.

The dark visions, however, were appearing less often. Dominick's doctor had prescribed a stronger medication, Thorazine. As Dominick would one day observe in an autobiographical sketch composed during a time of crisis, Thorazine was a form of "pest control" that "tempered the chill of bad thoughts."

At Nino's urging, Dominick kept a hand in the car business—occasionally buying cars at auction for Team Auto Wholesalers, a Bronx firm whose principal owner, Matthew Rega, became involved with the DeMeo crew after meeting Chris Rosenberg and borrowing money from him. Chris turned the "account" over to Roy, and

Rega was now heavily in debt to Roy's book. Rega, the son of a bookmaker for another Mafia family, owned another dealership in New Jersey that had begun fencing dozens of cars stolen in New York by the crew. What he made on cars he spent on clothes, jewelry, extravagant trips, and a developing cocaine habit.

Rega, thirty-three years old, told Dominick he did not like borrowing from Roy because Chris, who sometimes picked up Roy's loans, was so pushy. "Chris has an attitude; he's always in a hurry; you have to stop what you're doing and handle him."

"Chris has a Napoleon complex; he's always trying to prove how tough he is," Dominick said. "But like I once told my friend Henry Borelli, Chris will dig his own grave some day."

In time, Rega began borrowing from Nino as well. When Dominick came to pick up, either in New Jersey or the Bronx, they always had a friendly drink. In New York particularly, in the bars near Rega's dealership on Jerome Avenue in the impoverished South Bronx, Dominick became a familiar presence. The blacks and Hispanics who owned and patronized the shot-and-a-beer bars were not accustomed to socializing with Italians from Brooklyn, especially a seemingly friendly one who might break into a Little Anthony & The Imperials song, if he had enough to drink or—as began to happen the more he was with Matty Rega—had snorted a little cocaine.

At the Gemini Lounge, Dominick also became friendly with a new member of Roy's crew, Edward Daniel Grillo. "Danny" had just got out of prison for hijacking. Like so many others, he knew Roy from the Canarsie junkyard scene. Nearly fifty years old, he was twice the age of anyone in Roy's crew, but up-and-coming Roy was his best prospect, and Roy thought a tough ex-con might come in handy.

One day when Nino was in Florida, Roy telephoned the bunker and told Dominick that Danny needed a place to store some newly acquired merchandise overnight. This was how an arsenal of powerful fifteen-shot Smith & Wesson handguns spent the night on the living room floor of Dominick's and Denise's top-floor apartment. The weapons were bound for a police department in Finland until Danny and other crew members hijacked a truck before it got to John F. Kennedy Airport in Queens.

The use of her home as a hijacking drop violated Denise's unspoken accord with the life Dominick was leading—it was a detail she did not want to see. After Danny arrived in a van and she saw him and Dominick begin to deposit ten crates—each the size of a seaman's trunk—onto her living room floor and saw that they contained handguns, she became furious.

"You can't leave them here! You've got to get them out!"

Dominick tried to placate Denise by saying the situation was only temporary. In a moment, when he and Danny went to the van to retrieve another crate, he said to Danny, "Look, I can't sit here with an armory in the house. Denise will be nutty until they're out of here."

The next day, Roy and Danny came to get the shiny, steel-blue weapons, each in its own gift-like box. "Ain't they beautiful?" Roy said. "You keep one for your trouble."

Dominick hid the gun in the same bedroom trap where he kept the cash he picked up for Nino. Roy and Danny departed with the remainder—one hundred nineteen. Many went into Roy's basement arsenal at the Gemini; the rest were distributed to crew members, sold off in bars and eventually used in many murders.

Although he was beginning to establish his own underworld identity by making friendships with crooks like Henry Borelli, Matty Rega, and Danny Grillo, Dominick's main concern was still Nino's loans and, when Nino was away, a new business Nino had started—R&A Sales, the letters denoting the company's main beneficiaries, Rose and Anthony Gaggi. R&A Sales was a food brokerage. Plugging into the Gambino family's influence in the food industry, Nino began supplying the one hundred sixty stores of the Key Food chain with frozen foods; an executive of the chain was a Gambino capo. With not much work involved, R&A Sales netted Rose and Anthony fifteen hundred dollars a month.

Nino's book was continuing to grow too. Dominick now made pickups from a jeweler in Manhattan's Chinatown and at the Man o' War Room, for highrollers at Aqueduct Raceway in Queens. When Nino was home,

Dominick turned over the cash and Nino kept his own records, but when he was away, Dominick filled out the three-by-five-inch index cards on which payments were recorded. The cards were divided into weekly columns; if someone paid on time, an X was placed in the column; if not, a dash.

Nino's influence and prosperity yielded status dividends for Dominick. For example, at the Westchester Premier Theater, where he had been picking up two thousand dollars a week for two years, Dominick and Denise always got good seats when a headliner like Tom Jones or Dean Martin came to town. They drove there in the new tan Thunderbird he was able to buy on favorable financing terms from another one of Nino's customers.

Other than in the Governara murder, Nino did not ask him to dirty his hands. The one occasion Nino decided a customer needed a physical reminder of his obligation to avoid dashes on his index card, he accompanied Dominick on the pickup and administered the punishment—a slap in the face.

"You can't get too rough with these guys because you want them to be able to pay," Nino explained.

Believing he was shouldering more responsibility for Nino's business, Dominick asked for a raise. In the last two years, he had picked up several hundred thousand dollars for Nino, who was spending more and more time in Florida where he now also owned part of another restaurant, yet he was still making the same salary: two hundred fifty dollars a week.

"Don't you think I've earned a raise?"

"What for?"

"Everything I do. You spend five months in Florida and don't have to worry."

"What I pay you is enough. You're only paying one sixty-five in rent. I don't know why you can't live on two-fifty a week."

"You expect me to look nice—clothes cost money. You expect me to drive a nice car—cars are expensive. Denise and I want to have another baby. I need more money."

"Let's wait and see."

Nino's parsimony was infuriating, but Dominick knew he was not going to win the argument. He felt Nino believed the way to control him was money. Money was Nino's leash and he wanted his nephew on a short one.

"I think I'm worth more to you."

"Let's wait and see."

When Dominick was complaining about his finances one day at the Gemini, Roy said, "Why don't you do what I would do? Go borrow money off a loanshark and kill him the next day."

"Not my style, Roy."

"You won't have to pay him back. It's a way to get a nest egg."

"Okay, Roy, would you loan me a hundred grand?"

It was a well-timed joke, and Dominick smiled and playfully slapped Roy on the back, but he immediately wished he had not tried to be funny at Roy's expense. Especially that way.

Dominick stayed in touch with his stepdad Anthony Montiglio, but never talked about his life with Nino. Now remarried, Anthony did not have to hear details to know that, just as he had predicted, Nino had won Dominick over; all the signs were there. Dominick had money, a car, clothes, and no apparent employment.

As he grew older, Dominick had grown closer to his step-siblings Stephen and Michele, especially Michele. He squired her to fancy restaurants and bought expensive gifts for her birthdays. When Michele was fifteen and fell and injured her foot, he invited her to stay with him and Denise; each day, he changed her bandages and sanitized her stitches.

Michele was fun to be around, a precocious teen who spoke her mind. Because she was four years old when Dominick left for Vietnam, she remembered little of him before that—the main memory was of him and the other Four Directions singing on the back porch. After Vietnam, when she was seven, she remembered the big homecoming party their mother threw and how everyone fussed over the photographs of him that she passed around. Later, she read a story in his old high school newspaper that described him as a "dark and intelligent" man who had won many medals, so she grew up thinking of him as a hero and running to him when frightened or hurt.

After their mom's funeral, Michele had been unable to

fall asleep because she thought she heard noises emanating from the crawl space beneath the house in Levittown. When she was little, Dominick had told her that monsters lived in the crawl space and came out only when people slept. Michele was terrified that the monsters had made a mistake and come out while she was still awake. She ran to his room and asked him to investigate.

Exhausted from four days without much sleep, Dominick got out of bed and went into the crawl space.

"Nothing here," he said.

"Check all the way back," Michele said.

On his hands and knees, Dominick indulged her, checking out each corner with a flashlight. He emerged from the crawl space sweating and covered with dirt and prickly insulation fibers.

"You go to sleep now," he said. No one could ever say anything bad about Dominick in front of Michele.

As with Dominick, no one ever explained to Michele what her Uncle Nino did for a living, but by age sixteen she too was using "that life" to describe his occupation. That summer, Dominick invited her to stay with him and Denise in Bath Beach for part of her vacation. She enjoyed going to Bath Beach. It was the only time she got to see her grandmother, but at the same time, she resented it. Since Marie Montiglio died, Nino had yet to visit the Montiglio family in Levittown; he had never even called.

"It's like he's the king and we're just servants," she complained to Dominick.

"That's Nino."

Michele liked Denise, but was not fond of Rose. "She's like Miss Queen Bee," she said.

"That's Rose," Dominick laughed.

Some longtime loan customers of Nino were permitted to drop payments directly at the bunker. One day, when Denise was away, Dominick told Michele to answer the doorbell if it rang while he showered; someone might be dropping off a package.

"Whoever it is, tell them I say it's okay they give it to you."

The doorbell rang in a few minutes. Hesitatingly, a man eyed Michele up and down.

"Dominick's in the shower. He said to take whatever

it is you have," she said brightly. "I'm his sister, it's okay."

The man handed over a thick envelope. By the size and feel, Michele knew it was money, and from then on she accepted the idea that her hero was some kind of gangster too.

In the fall of 1976, Carlo Gambino's legal and medical team was still forestalling his deportation as an undesirable alien. Carlo had suffered another heart attack, or so said his doctors, who included his son-in-law, Thomas Sinatra, a heart specialist (no relation to the singer). The government was dubious. Carlo fed their doubt by his performance one day when Kenneth McCabe, a police detective assigned to the Brooklyn District Attorney's office, went to Carlo's city apartment to serve a subpoena requiring Carlo's appearance before a grand jury.

McCabe, age twenty-eight, was a tall, strapping detective with a solemn Irish face and controlled manner. He felt a large amount of contempt for the typical "wiseguy," as people in "that life" were sometimes known. Kenny, as he was known, had observed many wiseguys in his seven years on the job. They were his specialty; he believed most were just too indolent to do much else. On the other hand, he grudgingly respected Carlo. He had served subpoenas on the old man before; unlike wiseguys moving up in ranks, Carlo was polite and respectful. He understood Kenny had a job to do; he always invited him into his home for coffee.

When Kenny knocked on the door this time, Dr. Sinatra opened it, then slammed it shut again. Inside, Kenny heard Carlo begin berating the doctor, and then Carlo himself opened the door.

"How are you feeling, Mr. Gambino?" Kenny asked.

Carlo fished in his bathrobe for a vial of pills. "Look at all the pills I'm taking. How good can I feel?"

"I have a subpoena for you."

"You want coffee?"

"No thanks, I have another subpoena to serve. It's for someone in Staten Island. Is it worth my while to go to Staten Island now?" Kenny knew Carlo would understand that he was referring to a Gambino captain who lived there.

"Yes," Carlo said. "He'll be there."

Carlo put out his hand and accepted his subpoena. As Kenny turned to leave, Carlo smiled wryly. He lofted the vial of pills again and began to shake it between his thumb and forefinger like he was playing charades. It was as if he was telling Kenny he was faking it and no one could do anything about it.

Carlo, however, was seventy-four years old, did have a bad heart, and on October 15, in his bed, the Sicilian stowaway who became "the boss of bosses" did die. He passed away "in a state of grace," the Reverend Dominic Sclafani told relatives. Carlo had asked to talk to a priest when the end was near, and Sclafani had administered the Roman Catholic rites of extreme unction.

The body was laid out two days at Cusimano & Russo Funeral Home, the same mortuary where Marie Montiglio was waked. According to custom, the daytime mourners included relatives and close family friends—the Castellanos, the Gaggis, the Montiglios, and some others. Nighttime was when members of Carlo's elaborately extended family and members of other Mafia families paid their respects—and so Paul, Nino, and Dominick all came back without their wives and mingled with an assemblage of criminals exceeded in size only by the city jail population. Roy had urged the importance of the wake on his crew, and all were in attendance.

Naturally, the question of who was to succeed Carlo was on everyone's mind, and the factional consequences of the deal Carlo forged when he took power—naming an Albert Anastasia protégé as his underboss but limiting his authority to certain crews—now came into play. Before dying, Carlo said he wished that cousin Paul succeed him. Nino and the Brooklyn faction naturally agreed and favored a quick vote of family captains. Some captains, however, wanted to wait until Aniello Dellacroce, the leader of the Manhattan faction, got out of prison. Dellacroce was near the end of a year sentence on an income-tax case.

On the other hand, Paul was due to go on trial soon on the loansharking charge for which his nephew, stock swindler Arthur Berardelli, had set him up. Most police and federal agents surveilling the wake were betting that the better-known Dellacroce would become the new boss;

the captains decided to wait. At the wake, no matter what the future held, all the captains made sure to kiss Paul on the cheek, their traditional sign of respect.

At the funeral service, Dominick and Denise were told to sit with Nino and Rose in the second row of mourners, near Paul and his wife, a symbolically important position that in the family hierarchy demonstrated how far they outranked Roy and his crew, who sat in the back.

After the service, Nino and Dominick were also invited to ride with Paul in one of the limousines immediately behind the hearse transporting Carlo's body to the cemetery. That Dominick had such status rankled Chris particularly, but not just because he envied Dominick's proximity to the center of Mafia power. He had complained to Roy recently that Dominick had bad-mouthed him during a conversation with Matty Rega, the Bronx and New Jersey car dealer who was a loan customer of Nino's and Roy's.

"He says I'm always trying to prove how tough I am," Chris said. "Yeah, well, anytime he wants, I'm ready. All his Green Beret bullshit doesn't scare me."

Dominick was unaware that Rega, his supposed new friend, had passed along his observation about Chris's "Napoleon complex"—it was made only in response to Rega's complaints about Chris. Chris never confronted Dominick about the remark, but it festered, and it would not be the last time Rega would play such games.

Chris bit his tongue because Roy ordered him to. Roy had his own status concerns. Nino had always said that the Gambino family would "open the books" and initiate more members after the death of its patriarch, who was wary of expansion in later years. Roy had passed up a chance to become a made man in the Lucchese family on the belief his association with Nino would pay the same dividend in the city's strongest family. That day was closer at hand, and, Roy thought, virtually guaranteed if Paul became boss. So he wanted no confrontation between his and Nino's protégés.

Roy also increased the money he gave Nino each week, so that Nino could increase his weekly tribute to Paul. If he had to, Roy would adjust to life under the Manhattan faction, but now was the time to show the Brooklyn faction what a stalwart he was.

A month later, on November 16, the loansharking case against Paul fell apart in the middle of trial. His nephew, Arthur Berardelli, got on the stand and forgot everything. Artie Boy had no idea what the prosecutor was talking about—what loansharking?

Paul walked out of the courtroom with a smile. The late Carlo could not have pulled off a better one. To a judge who was to sentence Berardelli for contempt for refusing to testify, federal prosecutor Peter Sudler complained: "What happened here is that somebody got to this defendant. There was a setup."

Berardelli, who did testify against another stock swindler, was given five years in prison. He also left the courtroom with a smile, and went off to do his time in peace, pleased to be alive.

On Thanksgiving Day 1976, a few days after Paul's acquittal, Aniello Dellacroce got out of prison. Dellacroce's crews were not all based in Manhattan; his most notorious crew was headquartered in Queens, in fact. His faction was identified with Manhattan because of his social club on Mulberry Street in Little Italy. Dellacroce's rugged Queens crew included the violent Gotti brothers. John Gotti, the former Brownsville-Canarsie resident who was the smartest and most ill-tempered brother, was completing a short prison sentence for a homicide that had been plea-bargained to attempted manslaughter by his connected attorney, Roy Cohn; even so, Dellacroce had a bevy of shooters at his disposal. With Paul backed by, among others, Nino, Roy, and Roy's crew, a bloody showdown was possible if a successor to Carlo could not be agreeably chosen.

A few weeks after Dellacroce was released, he agreed to a summit with Paul. Each contender for power would be allowed to bring two associates to a meeting at Nino's house. On the appointed day, Nino ordered Dominick to see Roy at the Gemini and "pick up a package." After Dominick returned, they would "pack up" Nino's mother Mary, Rose, Denise, and all the children, and send them to Roy Gaggi's house in Staten Island.

"We're gonna make Paul the boss tonight," Nino said.

Outside the Gemini, Roy the gun nut opened his Cadillac's trunk and gave Dominick a package wrapped in newspaper and tied with string. Inside, broken down, was an M-2 automatic rifle and three ''banana clips'' —ammunition magazines containing ninety rounds of highly destructive .72 millimeter shells.

Back in Bath Beach, after the women and children were sent away, Nino issued more orders. As Dominick listened in amazement, it became apparent Paul and Nino intended to eliminate the hierarchy of the Gambino family if the meeting did not go Paul's way. Nino said the meeting would begin early in the evening and he wanted Dominick to assemble the M-2 and station himself by the front window in his upstairs apartment beforehand. The window looked out onto Nino's driveway.

Weapons, Nino said, had been banned from the meeting, ''but I'm going to tape a pistol under the kitchen table just in case.'' If Dominick heard shooting downstairs, he was to shoot anyone who came out the house— if the shooting went Paul's and Nino's way, no one would be leaving. If it did not, they would be dead, and so Dominick should ''shoot anybody who tries to make it out the driveway. Don't let any of the cocksuckers get away alive.''

As darkness fell, Dominick walked up the steps to his apartment. The steps and the M-2 jarred loose memories. He turned off the lights, laid the banana clips on the windowsill, propped the M-2 across two pillows, and assumed a night ambush position. Like stars over a jungle trail, a small porch light illuminated the driveway, his kill zone. Through an opening in the canopy he saw a streetlamp on the corner—it looked like the moon. In its glow, apartment buildings loomed like hills. The only thing missing was the war paint, and Uncle Ben, Bones the radio man, and the rest of his LURP teammates.

A passing car caused Dominick to snap to. This was no time to daydream. Too much reality on the line. If he had to litter the driveway with Gambinos, he would have to race to Staten Island, get Denise and their daughter and flee Brooklyn for a life on the run, wanted by cops and gangsters; what a legacy to leave behind—a massacre to rival the one staged by Frank Scalise and others on St. Valentine's Day in Chicago in 1929.

In a half hour, he saw Paul arrive with two men: Thomas Bilotti, a family captain, or *capo*, and Joe Gallo, an elderly man who was the family's *consigliere*, or in-house lawyer. Dominick had known them since child-hood. He had worked as a landscaper for Bilotti's brother; Joe Gallo attended New Year's parties at Paul's with Carlo. Dominick grew anxious. What if he heard shots and these men came out? Surely, Nino had not meant he should kill them.

In another few minutes, a car containing four men pulled up. Three men he did not recognize came up the driveway and went inside. He had not met Aniello Del-lacroce before but knew this must be the Manhattan fac-tion.

Fifteen minutes passed, without any shooting. The Manhattan faction came out and walked down the drive-way. Dominick looked down the barrel of the M-2 at their backs until they got in the car and drove away. In a few minutes more, Paul and his companions left. Dom-inick waited until Nino tapped on the door. After so much tension, Nino's triumphant announcement was anticli-mactic. "Come on out! They just made Paulie the boss!"

The same deal struck twenty years earlier had been struck again. Rather than risk a fight, Dellacroce would remain underboss with authority over some crews. Dom-inick rejoiced in Nino's jubilation. "Uncle" Paul was the new number one important man. The seat of power would stay in Brooklyn. Dominick felt on the inside of a historic event—a prince at his king's coronation.

He soon threw out the numbing Thorazine his VA doctor had prescribed for his dismemberment flashbacks and nightmares. Sitting by his upstairs window with the M-2, fully prepared to mow down Nino's and Paul's en-emies, he had finally had a flashback worth savoring—him on point, watching out for his buddies.

In his mind, just as he predicted to Denise when he went to work for Nino, the action of "that life" had chased his bad dreams away.

CHAPTER 8

Button Man

Paul issued several decrees after he took over, but none involved Roy, to Roy's utter distress. He promoted soldiers, moved others into different crews, settled old jurisdictional disputes, opened a new social club. He did not, however, make any new members; he told Nino he was against ever admitting Roy. In keeping with a self-image founded on the success of his meat and poultry distributorships, Paul preferred "white collar" rackets such as union manipulation and construction bid-rigging. He looked down his bulky Sicilian nose at "blue collar" crimes like auto theft and hijacking, and thus also Roy. He accepted Roy's money but not Roy, who bitterly protested to Nino and began plotting ways to change Paul's mind.

"I want to be made," Roy complained with more firmness than he normally used with Nino, "and I fucking deserve it."

"I'll speak to Paul; just relax."

Roy felt especially cheated because Nino was one of the men Paul promoted. Nino was now captain, or capo, of Paul's old crew. Most of the soldiers formerly under Paul's command were not very active, however. Most were getting on in years. With his blood relationship to Carlo, and the steady income from his meat business and loanshark book, Paul never needed a strong crew—so his men, apart from Nino, ran errands, smoked cigars, and contented themselves with a little bookmaking and loansharking.

In practical terms, given such a moribund bunch, Nino's promotion meant only a few extra ministerial duties. But in terms of status, it meant everything: Because of his long relationship with Paul, Nino was also the new de facto underboss of the Brooklyn faction. But Roy, who had lined Nino's and Paul's pockets for years, got nothing. He was merely Nino's unmade associate, and he was infuriated that, technically speaking, the cigar-chompers in Nino's crew had more clout than he.

Nino spoke to Paul, but Paul was adamant.

When associates became made men, they got "buttons" or were "straightened out." It was all Roy wanted to talk about in the early days of Paul's reign, Nino complained to Dominick one night.

"Roy wants his button. I'm against it. I told him he doesn't have to get promoted now, he's doing fine. If he gets promoted, Paul ain't gonna stand for half the stuff he's gettin' away with, and he's gonna wind up hurt."

Dominick knew "the stuff" to which Nino referred was drugs and "sick shit" pornography, but these were subjects to be read only between the lines—they were not to be discussed, not with Nino, and it went without saying, never with Paul.

"Does Roy believe he'd get hurt?" he asked.

"He doesn't believe it. He's still pressin'. He wants it."

"What's Paulie say?"

"Paulie doesn't like the way Roy does business; he says he's unpredictable and, you know, Roy is—but Roy still wants it."

At the Bath Beach bunker on another night, Roy kept pressing Nino. "I am bringing a lot of money in every week for the family. I have a real good crew put together. My people do a lot for the family. There are guys straightened out who don't do what I do."

Nino tried a little psychology. Roy actually had more "freedom" as an unmade man. "If you become a member, there are certain restrictions. You have to be more disciplined."

"Nobody turns away the money I bring in."

"Hey, you don't need a button. With me, you don't need it. Any problems you have, I straighten them out."

Owing much of his wealth to Roy, Nino promised to keep talking to Paul on Roy's behalf, which he did again the next time he and Dominick saw Paul at the Meat Palace.

Roy was not just a thief and hijacker, Nino reminded Paul. He had constructed his own sizable loan portfolio, had finagled a credit union right out of business and had assembled a loyal crew of followers who might be useful when any dirty work was necessary.

"Okay, but I just don't trust the guy to do what he is supposed to do," Paul said.

"I'll calm him down, make him do only what I tell him."

"I'm still against it."

On the other hand, Paul was solidly behind the new family social club he ordered Nino to open. Paul wished to consolidate his base of power and establish a presence among the other crews. With his businessman's approach, it made sense to have a sort of conference center, where he could confer with the capos and they with their soldiers and unmade associates. Because it was cheap and available, Nino chose a storefront in Bensonhurst on Eighty-sixth Street, a main thoroughfare.

From a distance, the club appeared to be the Genovese Tile Company, the former tenant. The company's twenty-foot-wide yellow and black marquee, which separated the storefront from the apartments above it, was never removed—just as venetian blinds covering the all-glass facade were rarely opened. Stenciled onto the glass, however, was the club's name, "Veterans and Friends."

Nino enlisted Dominick and other young men to renovate the club. They painted the inside, built a bar, cleaned a kitchen in the back, installed coffee, espresso, and cappuccino machines and brought in tables for card games and meals. Dominick hung a few old moviestar posters—W. C. Fields, Jean Harlow, and Nino's favorite, George Raft. "Your grandmother grew up with him," Nino was always boasting.

Because it would serve drinks and food, a state license was required to operate the club legally. "We're gonna put it in your name because you're the only vet we got that doesn't have a criminal record," Nino told Dominick, who signed the official papers.

The club was wedged between Liberty Post 1073 of the American Legion and Tommaso's Restaurant, which club members came to treat as their private dining room—in fact, off the main floor, they eventually did get a private room, where the restaurant's owner, an opera buff, sang arias for them. Paul and Nino conducted meetings there; so did Roy, but not at the same time.

Mafia etiquette prohibited Roy from making his own approach to Paul. An unmade associate had to seek a meeting with the boss through his capo. Roy did that and was turned down. Among his own crew, he began referring to Paul as "Waterhead," a play on Paul's prominent cranium and a reflection of his growing contempt. "Paul ain't a street guy," Roy would say. "He's just a meat salesman."

Made and unmade members of each crew in the Brooklyn faction were required to "shape up" at the Veterans and Friends on a particular night. Monday was Nino's crew's night. Roy loyally attended the shapeups, to keep on Nino's good side, but he thought they were a waste of his time. None of the others made the money he did and he was never going to do much business with people who sat around complaining about their deadbeat loanshark customers without taking action. If he was not cooking a new deal, Roy preferred to socialize by his pool in Massapequa Park, with Chris, Henry, and Joey and Anthony gathered around, or at the Gemini, where he was the undeniable star of the show.

Nino was not that fond of the club either. It invited surveillance by authorities. With schemes always afoot, several men were certain to be under surveillance at any given time and that meant cops and agents would be hovering around, taking photographs and license plate numbers and trying to figure out who was what. Nino cherished his privacy; he was fifty-two years old now, a potent force, but still practically unknown to the FBI's Mafia experts. There was that notation in a file about "Nino and Roy" shaking down an X-rated distributor and that was it.

The New York City Police Department did not know much more. In 1973, Kenny McCabe, the Brooklyn detective whom Carlo had always offered a cup of coffee, was told by an informant—a woman who patronized the Gemini—that "a guy named Roy DeMeo" was "with a guy named Nino." Kenny's files also contained a notation that a man seen leaving a social club in 1969 in the company of a Genovese Mafia capo had been identified as a loanshark whose name was Anthony Gaggi. In countless surveillances of Mafia hangouts, including the Brooklyn club of the late Carlo's driver, Kenny and other cops had not seen Anthony Gaggi again; only people in certain circles knew that Anthony and Nino were one and the same.

Nino had stayed in the background because he was spending a lot more time in Florida and because, when in Brooklyn, he rarely had to leave the bunker for anything but mundane errands. Most of his illegal business, in the form of Roy, came to him. Otherwise, Nino doted on Rose and their children. As much as possible for someone whom the neighbors never saw working, Nino, as Roy did, tried presenting a civic face. He donated money to the American Legion—though not to the post next to the club—and purchased the uniforms for a local church-sponsored Little League. In his mind, the Veterans and Friends social club threatened to nullify these efforts to keep a low and respectable profile. In a rare moment of misgiving, he told Dominick, "The club's gonna put me in jail someday. It might even be the death of me someday."

Sunday at the club made Nino cringe. Sundays were when Paul considered it good form for everyone in all the crews to shape up and pay homage to their leaders. The club was too small to accommodate so many and inevitably the men spilled onto the main drag of Eighty-sixth Street to find elbowroom, and this created a scene.

It was impossible for passersby to not see that the wiseguys and "good fellows"—as they were also known—were having a meeting. Though Nino stuck to his conservative suits and Roy to his knit shirts and chinos, Roy's crew and Dominick always turned up in their flashiest clothes. They favored flared suits and sportscoats and bright contrasting silk shirts with collars wide enough to cover jacket lapels. The shirts were unbuttoned to mid-chest to show off gold chains. It was a style recently described in a magazine article on the culture of Eighty-sixth Street; the article had led to a movie deal and scenes from *Saturday Night Fever*—the story of Tony Manero, white-suited king of the Brooklyn discos—were being shot in a pizzeria near the club and at other locations in Bensonhurst.

At the time, a familiar topic at the club was all the

newspaper stories quoting law enforcement officials as saying Aniello Dellacroce was now boss of what they continued to refer to as the Gambino crime family. The men mocked authorities for their faulty intelligence and ridiculed "Gambino crime family" as a law enforcement invention for the media. The men referred to their organization as simply "the family" or "the outfit." Older traditionalists spoke of "our thing"—*cosa nostra* in Italian.

In the beginning, Paul, the traditionalist boss, came to the club almost every day. Smoking a cigar, he enjoyed holding court in the kitchen; paranoid about government listening devices since being secretly taped by his nephew the stock swindler, he ran tap water and played a radio when discussing business. Early in 1977, not long after the club opened, the men began noticing suspicious cars passing the club or parked nearby. They began telling each other to smile for the "cop cameras" when coming and going. Nino and Roy figured they had already been captured on film, so they kept going to the club. Paul, however, was alarmed and began avoiding his innovation, the family conference center.

One of the surveillance cars outside Veterans and Friends social club in the early days was unforgettable— a dinky, beat-up blue Ford Pinto with a yellow hood. Detective Kenny McCabe took pride in his private car, which resembled a wounded parakeet. He did not mind that it made him conspicuous—sometimes that was the idea. If he wanted to avoid detection, he used a government car, but if he wanted to be seen, in the hope it might ruin a wiseguy's day, he used the patchwork Pinto. The sight of Kenny in such a car was just as remarkable. A former college basketball player stocky enough to play the line in football, he overwhelmed the driver's seat.

Kenny happened onto the club after he and Anthony Nelson, an FBI special agent who frequently joined him on surveillance, tailed some men from the West Side Civic Center, the social club of Carlo's former driver. Since becoming a detective in 1969, Kenny had conducted much surveillance on his own time—sometimes with other motivated cops or his FBI friend, many times alone. Detecting was his vocation and avocation. Usually, he acquired only bits of information—a new name, or an old face in a new place—but cases were made in bits, so all observable details about a subject—his mannerisms, routine, car, his girlfriend or wife—were recorded. In fact, in 1973, after he was told about a Roy DeMeo who owned a bar in Flatlands, Kenny had driven to the Gemini and waited outside until a man fitting Roy's description got into a Cadillac matching the informant's tip.

The Cadillac, it turned out, was registered to an Eleanor DeMeo, a sixty-six-year-old woman who lived in Massapequa Park, according to a license plate check. Thus, Roy's name, and his mother's, went into a report placed in a stack of files accumulating in the basement of Kenny's home. In truth of course, the widowed Eleanor did not live with her son, but with her friend Mrs. Profaci.

Kenny McCabe's files contained hundreds of names and photographs. By 1977, when it came to "the mob," Kenny was the institutional data bank of the Brooklyn District Attorney's office. It was a fitting accomplishment because Kenneth McCabe, Sr., his father, was the office's former chief deputy—second in power only to the elected district attorney.

Until 1963, Kenneth McCabe, Sr., supervised the office's investigations and its prosecutors, including a better-known lawyer in the office—"Thrill-Kill Case" prosecutor Albert DeMeo—whose blacksheep nephew Roy was then just four years out of James Madison High School. Kenny, Sr., devoted his life to law enforcement until 1963, when he died at the office of a heart attack. Chip-off-the-old-block Kenny, Jr., was a promising fourteen-year-old basketball player at the time.

In 1969, one year after Kenny, Jr., left Loyola University in Maryland and joined the police department, some eyebrows—including his—were raised when he was plucked out of ordinary patrol duty and promoted to detective by officials who admired his father. Fairly soon his ability prevented comment on the favoritism from growing past the raised-eyebrow stage.

When the West Side Civic Center crowd unwittingly led them to the Veterans and Friends, Kenny and FBI Special Agent Tony Nelson were pleased. Surveillance rarely yielded something as important as a new Mafia clubhouse. Returning now and then, on and off duty, they saw soldiers from several different crews—dozens of them; except at funerals and weddings, such congregations were rare. Watching from the Pinto or Tony Nelson's FBI car, they concluded that a new power had risen in the Gambino family.

At the time, the New York City Police Department (NYPD) and the New York offices of the FBI got along like a pair of unmatched shoes. The two crime-fighting agencies stumbled onto each other's investigations with regular acrimony because they rarely shared information. An institutional rivalry was aggravated by differences in style. Most FBI agents—until the recent death of founding patriarch J. Edgar Hoover, they had been required to wear suits while on surveillance—had grown up elsewhere and were more buttoned-up than the average homegrown NYPD detective, who was brash like the city and disdainful of by-the-book federal style.

Tony Nelson was an atypical FBI agent because he was born and raised in Brooklyn; he was the son of an ex-military man who instilled in him the same loathing for lowlifes and wiseguys as Kenny's father had in him. He was twenty-five, of medium height and frame, wore a mustache, and had short black hair. As part of the FBI's Brooklyn-Queens organized crime squad, he had met Kenny the year before when both arrived simultaneously at a hijacking drop. Each was tipped to the stash by an informant trying to collect reward money two ways. It was the kind of situation that historically ruffled feathers, but not those of the Brooklyn natives.

At the scene, Kenny and Tony realized they had the same informant; they agreed to stiff him and stay in touch. Comparing notes the next few months, they saw their interests were mutual. They began going on surveillance together, becoming friends—and unknown to their bosses, unofficial partners.

Among other bits, Tony told Kenny that an informant had told him that a man named Roy DeMeo who hung out at a bar in Flatlands was a ruthless killer. The informant said Roy had killed ''a dozen or so'' people and ''chopped up'' bodies. Undercover, Tony went to the Gemini, got a glance at Roy, and typed a report which did not get much attention. Tony even doubted its legitimacy: A trait of the underworld was the hyperbole of its informants.

It was true, however, that several more car thieves and drug dealers had disappeared in Canarsie. In the wake of Andrei Katz's demise, people in Canarsie credited Roy and his crew anytime anyone in either line of work disappeared without a trace. Short of making admissions, Roy did little to dissuade such rumors.

"I haven't seen that guy and don't expect to," he would say, with a look that discouraged further questions, when someone came to the Gemini inquiring about an acquaintance.

Another time, while with Dominick in a car, he was more direct. "They ought to put a tombstone over there," he said, pointing to a newly constructed gas station. "*Two* tombstones, because we buried two bodies there."

Tony told Kenny about his trip to the Gemini. "I've heard of Roy," Kenny said. "He's supposed to be with a guy named Nino. Might be a Gambino."

"Who's Nino?"

"That one I don't know."

One day, outside the Veterans and Friends, Kenny and Tony saw Roy go inside. This suggested Roy was a Gambino and raised the possibility he was visiting the mysterious Nino.

Later, they saw Roy and others walk out with an older man who became the center of attention as he strolled along Eighty-sixth Street like he owned the sidewalk beneath his shiny loafers. The man stopped beside a Cadillac and waited until someone opened the door. In Kenny's and Tony's experience, this was respect only a capo or boss was accorded. They called in the license plate. The number came back to R&A Sales.

In a few days, a check on R&A Sales revealed it to be a food brokerage, and the name, Anthony Gaggi. Kenny went to his files. Bingo. He could hardly wait, in his low-key way, to telephone Tony. "Nino is Anthony Gaggi, a loanshark; take it to the bank he is the guy we saw and the guy Roy is with."

"All right!"

Kenny and Tony resumed their surveillance of the Veterans and Friends. One night, they spotted Roy across the street from the club, talking to a Gambino soldier who helped run a catering hall when he was not running errands for Nino. Roy spotted them back, and grabbed his crotch and thrust his hips forward—the Brooklyn gesture for "Suck my cock!"

The cop and the agent smiled back at Roy, and Kenny said, "Suck yourself. Asshole."

Continual surveillance of Nino and Roy was impossible and, with no open case against them, unjustifiable. Still, when time allowed, Kenny, Tony, and others picked up their trail frequently enough that they began to disturb Roy.

Outside the Gemini one afternoon, Roy decided to confront Kenny, parked nearby with two other detectives in his battered Pinto, now minus a headlight.

"What are you breakin' my balls for? Can I help you with something?"

"You could help with a lot," Kenny said.

"Every place I go, I see you! I look up and you're there! Why are you wasting your time with me? I don't bother anybody."

"That's not what I hear."

"You're not hearing right. You've never seen me do anything wrong. Why are you wasting your time with me? You know everybody, but nobody knows you."

"Yeah, I'm a big fucking secret, especially in my car."

"I can't believe anyone tells you bad things about me."

"Poor Roy, nobody loves you, that's for sure."

The surveillance annoyed Roy, but not as much as Paul's ill regard and continuing refusal to make him a made man. He simmered over Paul's complaints about his unpredictability. He thought he was predictable as a sunrise, and highly disciplined. He commanded an efficient crew and worked hard; his "discipline" of informants like Andrei Katz was what kept money flowing to Nino and "Waterhead."

In the spring of 1977, he grudgingly concluded that the only way to win Paul over was to make him even more money. That called for a new scheme of some kind, and just as he began casting about, one fell into his lap courtesy of Danny Grillo, the fifty-year-old Smith & Wesson hijacker he had invited into his crew on the belief that a hard-boiled ex-con with no options might come in handy someday.

At one time, Danny had worked as a "sandhog"—a laborer on underground tunnel excavations that typically employed many Irish-Americans. While drinking with co-workers, he had met several members of a gang that plied the underside of Hell's Kitchen, the old neighborhood of Mary Gaggi and George Raft on the West Side of Manhattan. It was an area of tenements, warehouses and small factories stretching from Thirty-fourth to Fifty-seventh Streets and from Eighth Avenue to the Hudson River. The West Side gang was dominated by men of Irish descent—through the years, their ancestors had clashed violently with the Gambino family and other Mafia gangs with gambling, loansharking, and shakedown interests in the area. Among their kind, the West Side gang was called the "Irish Mob," but then a media-wise homicide detective, Joseph Coffey, coined another name that stuck—"Westies."

In prison, Danny Grillo met James Coonan, an ambitious young Westie with a lingering grudge against the long-time boss of the gang. After Danny and Coonan were paroled, they had regular reunions in Gemini Lounge–type bars on the West Side. This was how Danny learned that Coonan and some followers had dreams of becoming the most important Westies. He told Roy the group was ruthless but underfunded.

Where Danny just saw intrigue, Roy saw opportunity; if he bankrolled Coonan and helped him take over, Coonan would have to share underworld power on the West Side with the Gambino family. Roy saw a new vein of riches for Paul—and a button for himself.

"Let's meet this kid," he said. "Maybe we got business."

Several meetings were held in a trailer near a sewage treatment plant on Wards Island, an outcrop in the East River where New York had also placed the Manhattan State Hospital for the Insane. A Westie employed at the plant told Roy that the underwater currents swirling around the island were so swift that if a body was properly "opened up"—stomach and lungs punctured—it would sink and sail past the southern tip of Manhattan and then on out to sea without ever popping to the surface—perpetually and deeply asleep "with the fishes."

Unlike his followers, but like Roy, thirty-year-old Jimmy Coonan came from a respectable middle-class family; his father was a Hell's Kitchen tax accountant. He told Roy that the Westie leadership was in shambles because of the semiretirement of one Mickey Spillane; besides having the same name as the Brooklyn-born writer of cops-and-robbers books, Mickey Spillane was the Irish equivalent of Carlo Gambino in the 1960s and early 1970s.

Coonan hated Spillane because Mickey had slapped his father around when Coonan was nineteen years old. He had vowed to kill Spillane but got caught trying to murder someone else and went to prison. In the interlude, Spillane began slowing down; at age fifty-three, he even moved out of Hell's Kitchen. Many former associates began going their own way; nobody was steering the ship.

Roy saw that it was going to be easy to strike a deal with Coonan. Coonan was still unsure of himself and plainly awed just to be having meetings with associates of the Gambino family. In prison, Coonan was friendly with many Italian inmates and came to the notion that Irish criminals would be a lot more effective if they had a tradition like the Mafia, with its secret oaths, rules, and rituals. With embarrassing reverence, he told his little band that they could dominate the West Side by making an alliance with "the Italians from Brooklyn."

Roy loaned Coonan fifty thousand dollars so Coonan could make some impressive loans in West Side bars. Then they and a few others from each of their crews hijacked a tractor trailer load of newfangled machines—videocassette recorders, at the time worth about a thousand dollars each—and split the profit.

Money paved the way for the alliance; blood sealed it. Just as Roy bound himself to Nino by murdering blue-movie distributor Paul Rothenberg, Roy would bind Coonan to him by murdering the man who slapped the young Westie's father around years before—Mickey Spillane.

The ambush-murder occurred at night on a Friday the 13th in May. Roy hid behind a first-floor staircase in a

Queens apartment building and waited for the old Westie to come down from the second floor to talk to an acquaintance—Danny Grillo, who had just rung Spillane's doorbell. As the victim walked out the door, Roy came from behind and both he and Danny opened up with silencer-equipped pistols. Spillane started running, but they followed him into the street and shot him several more times. Chris and Henry were parked in a nearby car, the Gemini twins in another, in case they were needed, but the second volley did the job.

Spillane was left on the street so everyone would know he was dead and believe that Jimmy Coonan had taken his revenge.

Danny called Coonan. "Congratulations," Danny said, "we got you your birthday present a little early this year."

The present emboldened Coonan; it was now time to make his move. In a West Side bar two days later, he and a few others, including Danny, laid a trap for an elderly loanshark, Ruby Stein, whose expansive book funded discos, restaurants, peepshows and X-rated magazine shops; he also operated a West Side gambling parlor. Several Westies, including Coonan, owed him money; so did Danny, a gambling addict who had kept his addiction a secret from Roy. By murdering Stein, Coonan hoped to make more Westies indebted to him. It was a Roy DeMeo–style move, but Roy—much to his later anger, particularly at Danny—was not consulted.

As soon as Coonan led Stein into the deserted bar, Danny came out of a bathroom and shot him dead. Effectively wiping out several hundred thousand dollars of debt, they confiscated a notebook Stein used to record the status of his loans and which he was known always to carry with him. While Danny sat at the bar and drank, Coonan and some of his most devoted followers took a page out of Roy's Pantry Pride book and dismembered the victim. The body parts were packaged in garbage bags, which were then tossed into the swift East River currents that swirled around Wards Island and the Manhattan State Hospital for the Insane.

In ensuing weeks, Coonan recruited more West Side misfits into "my Mafia" and began dressing in the *Saturday Night Fever* style of the Veterans and Friends social club. He became the undisputed leader of the Westies and let potential rivals know he was backed by the heavy firepower of the Italians from Brooklyn.

"We got this kid on the West Side who will give us ten percent of his action and do whatever we tell him," Roy told Nino, who took the news to Paul.

While Roy was romancing Coonan, Paul had decided to "open the books" and expand the family roster. He had chosen ten men endorsed by his capos, but not Roy, the choice of his top capo, Nino. Given the deal Roy had arranged with the Westies, however, he decided he could no longer credibly dismiss him as an unpredictable blue-collar car thief and hijacker; Roy had brought a historically troublesome gang, an entire new field of plunder, right into the family tent. And so finally, at age thirty-seven, Roy the former weightlifter of Ivory Snow boxes got his button.

For all its meaning for the men involved, the ceremony by which associates became made men was simple. By tradition, the inductees and incumbent made men would have become brothers by pricking each other's fingers and drawing blood. Then Paul would have spoken about how the inductees were now members of a family whose interests were paramount to personal concerns. They would have to unequivocally obey him and the capos and pledge allegiance to *omerta,* a code of noncooperation with all authority that originated in the hills of Sicily. Anyone violating *omerta* would be killed. One never left the family, not while alive.

Apart from the severity of the sanctions, the ritual was not much different from a fraternity initiation or a night at the local Moose Lodge. Only outsiders would say it was a lot of hokum.

A rambunctious dinner in the private family dining room in Tommaso's Restaurant next to the Veterans and Friends followed the ceremony. Sipping wine, Nino toasted Roy, then put salt on his triumph. He said Roy was now part of a great tradition, but would never go higher in the family: "Only Sicilians get to be capos in our family."

Nino's romantic view was not quite accurate. In the Manhattan faction, Aniello Dellacroce was about to name

John Gotti, a Neapolitan like Roy, to be the capo of his tough Queens crew.

"I'm happy with what I got," Roy said.

Jimmy Coonan was more struck by Mafia oaths and rules than Roy was: For Roy, his button was pure ego gratification. The moment he was made he was in direct violation of one of the rules that Carlo initiated and which Paul had reaffirmed—no drug dealing. Roy was still backing an operation that imported Colombian marijuana by the twenty-five pound bale and was still selling multiple ounces of cocaine out of the Gemini. He had no intention of stopping; he would just be more secretive, more alert to potential threats.

One of Roy's frequent cocaine customers was a very successful car thief and chop shop operator named John Quinn, who was yet another graduate of the Canarsie junkyard school. Quinn had a cop in his pocket who tipped him to neighborhood patrol patterns and used police computers to learn, via license plate checks, the addresses of people owning cars Quinn had seen and coveted. Quinn employed two expert thieves who cruised for cars every night. It took them about forty-five seconds to "pop" a locked car, disable its alarm, remove the ignition lock, and drive it away. They stole up to fifteen a night.

The real key to Quinn's success was his ability to "wash" the cars. From break-ins of state offices, he acquired stacks of blank title and registration forms; he also possessed stamping equipment for punching out vehicle identification numbers. This enabled him to replace the dashboard VIN plate with a realistic phony, using serial numbers he knew from cop computers were not already in use in New York State. The numbers were then typed or engraved onto the state documents—presto! the car was "clean."

Quinn's operation was much more sophisticated than the one Anthony Gaggi once had. In Nino's era state-issued titles were not required to show ownership, just a dealer-issued registration. By comparison, the Rosenberg-Katz operation also was amateurish. Chris's VIN plates appeared to be made by a hand-held label-making device of the type commonly sold in Woolworth's.

Quinn was making more money in cars than the DeMeo crew. In fact, for three thousand to thirty-five hundred dollars each, Roy was buying tag jobs from Quinn, mostly luxury Lincolns and Cadillacs; tacking on another thousand or two, he was selling them to customers lined up by him or by Joey Testa's younger brother Patty. At age twenty, Patty, the former boy-wonder mechanic, was owner of his own dealership, Patty Testa Motorcars. Flush with cash like his brother, who had moved out of Canarsie (but only physically), Patty had purchased his father's Canarsie home, and was storing many stolen cars in a lot next door—a situation about which his see-no-evil neighbors were deaf, dumb, and blind.

One reason Quinn and Roy did business was that one of Roy's men, Peter LaFroscia, the bearded lumberjack type whom Chris had introduced to Dominick as "one of the top car guys in New York," actually worked more for Quinn than Roy. LaFroscia was one of the two men who cruised the streets for Quinn each night. He and the other thief, a freelancer more loyal to Quinn, always cruised in a Jaguar because they believed it made them appear more respectable. In the last eighteen months, they had stolen nearly two thousand cars.

Between the DeMeo crew and John Quinn, it had gotten so a new-car customer in Canarsie or Flatlands with no qualms and an informed ear to the ground would never think of paying retail at a legitimate dealer. Quinn also served customers who sought to "steal" their own cars. For fifteen hundred dollars, he sold "kits" containing a VIN plate and the necessary phony paper. The kits, also available through the crew, were known as "Quinn Paper."

Roy and the crew viewed the independent-minded Quinn as an outsider but also as a "stand-up guy." For the last year, pending appeals, he had been awaiting sentencing in an FBI-made case in which he pleaded guilty to conspiring to transport a stolen car across state lines. As cases go, it was not much of a bother; he might have to "go away," but only for a couple of months. When convicted of hijacking years before, he had served his sentence quietly, so the pending sentence did not cause too much worry. What did alarm Roy, however, was that Quinn, a married, thirty-five-year-old father of six children, was having an affair with a nineteen-year-old woman—and had exposed her to details of his operations.

The woman was Cherie Golden, a perky waitress in a Brooklyn restaurant known as The Butcher Shop when she met Quinn. She was a pretty teenager, the winner of a beauty contest in which competitors were judged by their resemblance to a superslim Cockney fashion model Leslie Hornby, otherwise known as Twiggy. Unlike blond, close-cropped Twiggy, Cherie had brown cascading hair, but her willowy profile, big brown eyes, and cherubic smile did evoke Twiggy's "adolescent angel" look. A year out of high school, she lived with her parents in Flatbush, west of Flatlands.

Quinn dazzled Cherie. His luxury oceanfront apartment was not far from her job; he drove two cars, a Cadillac El Dorado and a Lincoln Continental with a then innovative, retractable "moon roof"; he had money, clothes, jewelry, and a charming way. Cherie learned later that he also had a house, wife, and half-dozen kids on Long Island—but by then, she told girlfriends, she was in love and having the time of her life.

Quinn showed Cherie off at restaurants in Little Italy and let her use one of his cars—whichever one he did not want that day. Soon she was sleeping overnight in his city apartment. If her parents knew of his other life, only unsuccessful attempts were made to warn her away.

To his peers' amazement, Quinn began bringing Cherie along when he was conducting business—buying hot cars off freelance thieves, monitoring his chop shops, or settling accounts with his "Jaguar squad." He usually paid LaFroscia and the other thief one hundred fifty dollars for an ordinary car destined for a chop shop, two-fifty for a taggable Cadillac or Lincoln. Quinn added a fifty-dollar bonus if they stole cars with popular colors.

Through LaFroscia, Roy heard about Cherie Golden right away, and told Quinn: "You're nuts." Cherie could not stand up to pressure if the police went after her. Quinn ought to get rid of her. "She's a liability," Roy said.

Quinn viewed Cherie as a rare asset, someone absolutely trustworthy. He had installed a telephone line in her bedroom at her parents' house so she could take his messages and make appointments. He had hidden a handgun there and given her an IBM Selectric typewriter so she could type his bogus titles and registrations.

As the summer of 1977 began, Quinn was socked by consecutive legal problems that made his pending federal sentence potentially ominous. Police raided one of his chop shops; then his name surfaced in an investigation on Long Island into the sale of stolen bonds, and he was subpoenaed to testify before a grand jury.

Quinn's new problems meant the judge about to sentence him in his pending stolen-car case was likely to give him more time in prison. Suddenly, he did not feel like standing up to prison anymore. He saw only one way out: He was just the go-between in the bond sale; if he cooperated, he might impress the sentencing judge. Co-operating might even make his chop shop problem vanish. He decided to testify before the grand jury rather than invoke his right to remain silent. He of all people should have feared the secret would not last long, not with the eyes and ears Roy had in official places.

A few days after Quinn's testimony, Peter LaFroscia called a cousin of Quinn's, Joseph Bennett, an employee of Quinn's retagging division, and asked him to meet Roy. Potentially, this was a disastrous mistake because Bennett—with Quinn headed for prison—had recently become an informer for the FBI, which was still investigating Quinn's interstate reach. Being from Canarsie, however, Bennett was well aware that many men in his business were no longer around. He, like FBI agent Tony Nelson, had heard that Roy "chopped up" bodies; he, unlike Tony, believed it absolutely. So he would not tell the FBI what he was about to hear.

"Johnny went before the grand jury and we know it," Roy told Bennett. "He was told to get rid of Cherie. I told him personally and he didn't do it." Roy offered Bennett ten thousand dollars to lure his cousin Quinn into a trap: "We'll put the bullets in his head, you don't have to worry about that."

Showing he was growing ever more murderous, Roy the newly made man also said he would pay a ten-thousand-dollar bonus if Bennett lured Cherie Golden into the same trap. He had, he said, come to a decision: "We're going to get rid of both of them." He emphasized the urgency of the situation: "You don't have too much time to make a decision. It's a rush deal here."

Bennett, however, neither set up his cousin nor told him of the plot. He was unsure if he was being set up. He continued associating with Quinn as though Roy had not said a word and even accompanied Quinn to the Gemini to inspect a Porsche that Quinn was considering buying for Cherie.

Using "Quinn Paper," the DeMeo crew had begun stealing and retagging foreign luxury cars, Porsches and Mercedes mainly; each member kept one or more for personal use. When they shaped up at the Gemini on Friday nights, the nearby streets came as close as they ever would to Rodeo Drive during a boutique opening.

While Quinn inspected the Porsche, Peter LaFroscia pulled Bennett aside and asked if was going to pass up the twenty thousand dollars Roy had offered for Quinn and his lover.

"I'm not so sure I like it," Bennett said.

"Don't miss a good opportunity," LaFroscia said. Showing he had become more than a car thief since joining the crew, he pulled a pistol from a brown paper bag and added: "Look, we're always ready to take care of this on our own, you know. Don't sleep on this. Decide."

Once again, leaving the Gemini, Bennett did not say anything to Quinn. Ignoring LaFroscia, he kept sleeping on it.

Three days later, on the afternoon of July 20, 1977, Cherie Golden came home in an agitated huff and stayed in her room for several hours. Quinn had told her that he was due to be sentenced the next day and was likely to go to jail for a while, but not as long as he might have if he had not gone before the grand jury.

Near twilight, as Quinn's silver Lincoln with the moon roof pulled up on her street, Cherie came out of her room dressed in an adolescent angel outfit—a white and yellow halter top, blue short shorts, and open-toe sandals revealing toenails painted pink. Her face was not as care-free.

"What's wrong, honey?" her grandmother asked.

"He's going away!" Cherie said angrily. Without

another word, she steamed out of the house and got into Quinn's car.

At twenty minutes past eight o'clock in the evening, Quinn picked up a telephone message from the answering service he used in addition to Cherie. The message was from "Pete." "You know the number, it's important." Quinn and Cherie went to the Gemini soon afterward. Quinn still wanted to buy the Porsche for Cherie; he also was made to think that the crew wanted to buy more of his phony paper and VIN-making tools. With Cherie along, Quinn must have felt safe, the last of his many recent miscalculations.

These days, business at the Gemini Lounge was conducted in an apartment immediately to the rear of the tavern, on the first floor in the same building. A cousin of Roy's, an older man with a deep voice and silver mane whom the younger men called "Dracula," had recently moved in after getting out of jail for bank robbery. The telephone in his apartment was an extension of the telephone in the bar. He cooked Friday night shapeup meals for crew members, and they had begun using his home as a sort of clubhouse. Nowadays, when crew members or associates said they were headed for the Gemini, they meant the apartment more than the bar.

About an hour after picking up the message, Quinn went inside the crew's clubhouse while Cherie stayed in the Lincoln. Because a silencer was used, she did not hear the single shot fired into the back of her lover's head, killing him instantly. In an account of the murder he gave to an acquaintance, Henry Borelli neglected to say who shot Quinn, but said he, Roy, Chris, and La-Froscia were inside and that outside, in the car, Cherie was distracted by Joey Testa and Anthony Senter, standing on either side and leaning through the windows talking to her. When she turned toward Joey, his inseparable buddy Anthony shot her twice in the head, and when her head whipped around from the bullets tearing through her brain, Anthony shot her again in the face.

Neither Quinn nor Cherie would disappear because Roy wanted their bodies found—to send a message about the price of cooperating with official authority when the DeMeo crew was involved.

One team of killers bundled up Quinn's body, drove

to Staten Island and dumped it along a desolate road. Another squad, after rifling Quinn's car and taking away stacks of blank titles, registrations, birth certificates, and the VIN-making equipment, took care of Cherie, whose body was pushed up toward the underside of the dashboard, contorted like a ragdoll, and covered with clothes taken from the car's trunk. Someone pulled down her halter top, just to throw a sexual curve into the police investigation. The Lincoln was then driven to the Gerritsen Beach section of Brooklyn, near Coney Island, and left on a residential block.

Quinn's body was found that night; Cherie's body lay in the sealed-up Lincoln for three sweltering days. On the fourth, Sunday, July 24, 1977, a resident of the block called police to report a possibly stolen car. An officer came and detected the unmistakable rotten-egg odor of human decomposition. Beneath the body, on the floorboard, Detective Joseph Polizzi was intrigued to discover, of all things, a blood-stained set of blank documents for transferring ownership of a car.

Within days, LaFroscia met Joseph Bennett, Quinn's tongue-tied cousin, in a coffee shop. "See, we weren't kidding," he said. "You missed out on an easy twenty thousand. It was easy, although with Cherie it was a little squeemy, a little squirmy."

What he meant, he added, was that Cherie was so young and so pretty it was a shame she had to die.

The night before Cherie's body was found, the police had also been called to break up a fight in a catering hall a short distance away. The fight began when a waiter set a plate a little too carelessly in front of Roy.

"What's wrong with you, don't you know how to serve people?"

"Doin' the best I can, pal."

The catering hall's waiters were as insolent as Roy's crew because many were aspiring soldiers for their boss, who owned the hall and was a captain in another family.

"Do you know who you're talkin' to!"

"Don't know, don't care, buddy."

It was now a situation where Roy wanted to show power and be perceived correctly. He stood and smacked the waiter hard in the face. Other waiters came to their co-worker's aid, and before long the catering hall was turned into a Dodge City saloon. Danny Grillo tossed a waiter through a window. Henry Borelli, however, was badly beaten; his pal Dominick—a few days before, the son of the former Army Air Corps boxing champ had become the father of a baby boy, Dominick, Jr.—came to his aid and punched a waiter so hard, awestruck Roy later told Nino, "I felt the force go by."

The crew had gathered at the catering hall because earlier that day, as Cherie's body waited to be found, the man Henry said shot her in the head and the face—Anthony Senter, the Roman-looking favorite of all the Canarsie women—got married to a Canarsie woman about Cherie's age.

When the case hit the newspapers, Nino instantly suspected Roy and furiously called him to a sitdown at the bunker, where Roy confessed and pleaded his case—just as Cherie's distraught parents offered a ten thousand dollar reward for information.

All too clearly Nino recognized that the murder of Cherie went straight to the core of Paul's concerns about Roy's unpredictability. Cherie was not even given a chance to show that she could stand up to police pressure. The murder made Nino look bad; he could not, as he had promised Paul, control Roy.

"You just can't be runnin' around doin' this cowboy stuff!" he screamed.

To Roy, the murders were just another example of how the underworld had to maintain its law and order. "Quinn already talked, she knew it, she had to go too."

"But you can't go around killing everybody you feel you have to kill without talkin' to me!"

"I'm telling you, she was part of his operation. She could have hurt us bad as him."

"Paulie ain't going to like this."

The next day, accompanied by Dominick, who learned about the murders the same time as Nino, Nino visited Paul at the Meat Palace to give Roy's explanation. Paul also had suspected Roy as he read the newspapers and saw Quinn identified as a leader of a car-theft ring.

"Why did the girl have to be killed?" he asked.

"She was part of his operation," Nino said. "She might have been talking. She had to go."

Dominick was amazed to hear Nino defend Roy, until he mulled the politics of the situation: Nino had vouched for Roy; he had to make it look as though Roy had no choice; otherwise, he would be admitting he was unable to control him.

Paul's low-key reaction would also surprise, but then Paul had no one but himself to blame. Despite all his misgivings, he had second-guessed himself, partly because of Nino's urging and partly because of Roy's success with the Westies, and initiated Roy into the family. "Just talk to Roy," he said wearily. "Make sure people just don't start going who don't have to go."

By the standard of Carlo Gambino, it was a very weak reply. Now a half-year into his reign, Paul was having trouble managing the reins of power. His naive managerial idea for a central club had been proven to be a reckless security risk, and now a man he had personally anointed had murdered a teenage girl without his bosses' permission.

Things could not get much worse, but they would.

CHAPTER 9

Killing Spree

Happy with the Westies alliance Roy conceived and executed, Paul never called him on the carpet for the Cherie Golden murder and eventually even adopted Roy's and Nino's spin on it—"Twiggy" was a threat who had to go. Happy with the thousands a week Roy funneled to the bunker, Nino granted Roy a long leash and never seriously demanded that he clear all murders in advance. Unrebuked and unrestrained, and now with full Gambino cachet, Roy began adding to his barony and expanding his crew, who grew even more quick to kill, feeding a reputation for merciless brutality that led to a new sideline—murder for hire.

Seven victims linked to the crew were found during the next eighteen months. Undoubtedly, some more wound up in a vast landfill the crew began using when they wanted someone to disappear for one reason or another. These would have been dismembered and tossed in with seven thousand tons of garbage deposited daily in the Fountain Avenue dump; the dump was just west of Canarsie at the edge of Jamaica Bay and was then the subject of a neighborhood furor over contaminants leeching into the local water supply. Anthony Senter tipped Roy to the dump's possibilities; his uncle's sanitation company was one of the landfill's principal dumpers.

Proof that Roy and the crew used it was only circumstantial during this period, but incriminating. "I don't know where that guy is," Roy would say now, when people came to the Gemini with questions about their friends or drug connections. "Did you look in Fountain Avenue?" Roy also presented Chris and his would-be brothers, Joey and Anthony, with sets of carving knives that Roy called "tool kits." The boys—all were using more and more cocaine, though not in front of Roy, who only sold it—kept the knives in gym bags they hid in the trunks of their Rodeo Drive tag jobs, in case a quick assignment arose.

While Chris and Joey and Anthony improved their dismemberment skills, Henry emerged as Roy's number-one sharpshooter. The others also grew proficient with guns, because victims slated for dismemberment were always shot first, but they were never as accurate and fast as "Dirty Henry" (as they began to call him, inspired by Clint Eastwood's Dirty Harry character). Henry managed to get along with Chris, and forget Chris's ingratitude for the half-year he spent in jail waiting for the Andrei Katz case to come to trial, but he and Chris were too competitive about Roy's attention to ever be as close as Chris and the Gemini twins were. Henry's friendship with Dominick also set him apart from Chris, still peeved about Dominick's "Napoleon-complex" remark.

After meeting a man with no scruples and a machine shop in his basement, Roy bought several more custom-made silencers and presented one to each crew member. The crew held regular practice sessions with the silencers and their handguns, which Roy told them to be sure always to destroy and toss away after a "piece of work," so they would never get caught with a gun whose barrel matched the rifling marks on a bullet found in a body. "You don't want to get stopped for some stupid fucking speeding ticket and have some cop find a hot piece in your car," Roy explained.

Throughout the rest of 1977 and 1978, the murders came fast and furious. Anyone posing a threat, or foolish enough to get in the crew's way or to try and cheat it, was eliminated.

And so John Costello and Daniel Conti, two men hired to assist in a hijacking, were found shot to death after the hijacking went awry. They were judged to be weak links who could not stand up to the resulting police investigation. Conti was Peter LaFroscia's brother-in-law. He went first, Costello two weeks later.

Patrick Presinzano was next. He made the mistake of stealing jewelry from someone who knew Roy. He proclaimed his innocence to Roy, refused to return the jewelry, and continued wearing it. Roy shot him dead, slit his throat and—as either he or a crew member did in the Cherie Golden murder—threw the police a sexual curve by leaving the victim in the backseat of a car with his trousers and underwear down to his ankles.

Then came Michael Mantellino and Nino Martini. Mantellino was suspected of tipping two robbers that Peter LaFroscia always had a lot of money, jewelry, and cocaine around. After LaFroscia was robbed, the crew caught up with Mantellino at a body shop he operated. They shot him and Martini, a friend who just happened along, then stuffed the bodies into a car and set fire to the body shop.

Kevin Guelli was next. He had bragged to Chris that he knew many people to whom he could sell cocaine, so Chris gave him ten thousand dollars worth on consignment. When Chris came to collect, Guelli said the darndest thing had happened. Someone had broken into his house and stolen the cocaine. Sure, Chris said, shooting him dead.

That anyone in Canarsie would try to cheat Chris "DeMeo" was incredible by now, but Gary Gardine tried. He took three pounds of marijuana and never paid, except with his life. He was shot and stuffed in the trunk of his car, which was then torched.

If mentioned at all, such murders were invariably described in the few paragraphs of newspaper copy they generated as "apparently the work of professional hit men"—words that always tickled Roy and the crew. "Hello and how are you today, Mr. Professional Hit Man?" they would tease each other on the telephone.

In the middle of this killing spree, the deal that Roy made between the Westies and the Gambinos almost blew up in his face, but as before, Paul and Nino were blinded by the color green and Roy would be able to convert trouble to triumph.

The trouble began when the torso of a body washed ashore on a south Brooklyn beach after several months in the water. It was identified by a scar from a recent heart operation as that of Ruby Stein, the elderly loanshark shot by Danny Grillo and dismembered by Jimmy Coonan and a couple of Westies as a way of writing off some loans, theirs and others'.

Coonan had tried to make Stein disappear so there would be no proof he was dead or credible suspicion that he was involved, but young Jimmy forgot to heed the Westies' own grisly folklore when he deposited Stein's packaged remains into the East River. He forgot to puncture the torso's stomach and lungs—so rather than sinking and sailing out to sea with the river's swift underwater currents, the torso stayed afloat and came to rest on a finger of Brooklyn jutting into the sea southeast of Manhattan.

Danny had admitted the murder to Roy soon after the fact. The news angered Roy because he knew that another Mafia family boss was a major investor in Stein's loanshark book. If it got out that the Westies and a member of the DeMeo crew had killed Stein, the other Mafia boss would complain to Paul and demand that the Gambinos reimburse his financial loss.

That is exactly what happened after Stein's body was identified. With good reasons—West Side, dismemberment—the other boss suspected the Irish Italophile, and one or more of his new Gambino friends and complained to Paul. As a new member of the "Commission"—a board of directors–like group composed of the bosses of the city's five families—Paul was obliged to conduct an inquiry and try and resolve the issue equitably.

Paul ordered Nino to tell Roy to summon Coonan to a sitdown at Tommaso's. If the "Irish kids" and Roy or someone in his crew were behind such a reckless murder, he would order them to reimburse the Mafia boss and then end the alliance; the ten percent of the Westie action that he now got was not worth such bother.

Though perturbed at Danny and Coonan, Roy resolved to save the alliance. Before the sitdown, he told Coonan to deny any involvement, to just show deference and talk about other money the Westies and Gambinos might make together. Eventually that would mollify Paul, Roy was sure, even though Paul hardly needed more money. With all the cash pouring in from his legitimate and illegitimate enterprises, Paul had just moved into a palatial new house on Staten Island; neighbors had dubbed it "The White House" because of its resemblance to the real one.

Meanwhile of course, Roy did not admit to Paul or Nino that Danny fired the shots that killed Stein; he did say Coonan had insisted he was not involved and he believed him. But no matter who killed Stein, Roy added, it was a blessing in disguise because the Westies would now get all the big loan action on the West Side, which meant more money for the Gambino family.

The thing to do, Roy proposed, was to take up a collection and compensate the Mafia boss who backed Stein—even though innocent, Coonan would contribute and so would he, in hopes of avoiding trouble and locking up the West Side. With the fifty thousand dollars Roy gave to build a book, Coonan had won some union contacts along the docks and in the sprawling trade-show convention halls on the West Side.

Paul and Nino doubted Roy's proclamations and denials, but were swayed by the potential of greater profit. They liked his plan, so the sitdown between the Westies and the Gambinos became less a forum for the truth than a meeting to strengthen the alliance.

Playing bad cop to Paul's good, Nino did work up a temper and tell Coonan that even if he was not responsible for Stein's death, he could never kill anyone again without authorization: "Anytime there is a problem with somebody, before anybody gets killed, you've got to get our okay so we can make sure it isn't one of our people." Resorting to language he used a year before, when he yelled at Roy for killing Cherie Golden, he added, "You can't go around actin' like cowboys."

In return for Westie influence on the docks and in convention centers, Paul gave the Westies access to Gambino money at one percent interest a week—the same rate charged family members. The ten-percent rule stayed in effect and Paul said that from now on, Roy was the Westies' "official contact" in the Gambino family. Roy reported to Nino, of course, but because Nino was in Florida a lot, Roy was their day-to-day "supervisor."

Dominick, who attended the sitdown as Nino's aide-de-camp, thought that when Roy left the room with Chris he was feeling ten feet tall. Dominick felt tall himself.

He said to Coonan's aide-de-camp, Mickey Feather-stone, who also was a former Green Beret, "With our families together like this, we will fucking take over New York!"

On a typical day, Roy usually departed to Brooklyn from his home in Massapequa Park in the middle of the afternoon. The drive took most people about forty-five minutes; it took heavy-footed Roy about ten minutes less. Frequently, one of his first stops was at a gas station run by an old and devoted pal from teenage days, the oddball dyslexic kid he befriended when no one else would, "Broadway Freddy" DiNome.

After a near fatal accident during a race, Freddy's drag-racing career had floundered during the early 1970s; though he had bought a home with a pool on Long Island, and owned, besides a gas station, a body shop and repair business known as Broadway Freddy's Diagnostic Center, he had frittered away most of his big racetrack pay-days and was usually broke. Desperate for cash, he had for insurance purposes falsely reported the theft of his race car, set fire to two stores for friends who wanted to break their leases, and begun dabbling in the stolen-car business again.

Roy had been loaning him money since 1971, when Freddy, then in the midst of a divorce and custody battle over his son Freddy, Jr., needed three thousand dollars to pay his gasoline supplier. Freddy, who subsequently married another woman and became the father of a sec-ond child he named Freddy, Jr., now owed Roy seventy-five thousand dollars. He was still loosely associated with the junkyard bosses of the Lucchese family, but with his reputation for erratic and infantile behavior, he would never get a button, not from any family.

In Canarsie, Broadway Freddy was now known as "Crazy Freddy." With a similarly inclined friend at the wheel of his Cadillac, he liked to speed up and down streets with his naked posterior hanging out the window. After some dispute with the owner of a live-chicken mar-ket next to his station, he broke into the market, opened the cages, and sent eight hundred birds madly squawking into the streets. At his gas station, he also kept a pet monkey, "Susie," that he trained to pump gas. When a dice game he ran there was busted, he took Susie to court and caused a scene when a judge refused to let her take the stand in his defense.

At age thirty-five, with his gullied face and droopy eyes, Freddy looked like a bottomed-out, burned-out pothead. In fact, he was frequently stoned on marijuana, but he never smoked it in front of Roy, who he knew disapproved.

Freddy was even in more awe of Roy now than when they were teenagers. Roy had made it on his brains—muscle too, but anybody could use muscle. It was an honor just to fill Roy's tank. When Roy arrived for a fill-up, it was the highlight of Freddy's dismal day. "That Roy is the smartest man I know," he told anyone appropriate. "I would do anything for Roy."

So naturally Freddy was elated when Roy asked him to become his chauffeur. Roy hardly needed a chauffeur, but Paul employed one, and Nino used Dominick a lot—a chauffeur was a decoration befitting Roy's new status. He told Freddy he had been promoted by "Mr. Gaggi, my sponsor" and had so many responsibilities he needed the time normally spent driving to relax and concentrate on his business. This service would be necessary only after Roy arrived in Brooklyn from Massapequa Park.

To employ Freddy, Roy had to obtain his "release" from the Luchese family, to which Freddy was nominally responsible. Roy's new stature made this normally delicate negotiation a simple formality.

Roy also told Freddy that occasionally he might be asked to help out in a hijacking and that, if things worked out, Roy might set him up in a money-making venture of his own that would enable him to knock down his seventy-five-thousand debt to Roy. Seeking to improve the impression Freddy made, Roy also gave him cash for clothes and much-needed dental work—Freddy's incisors were all rotted. "Ya know somethin'? Ya gotta stop smoking so much dope too," Roy added.

Freddy never gave up dope, but he did go to a dentist and begin dressing better. "Roy is making a gentleman out of me," he said to his younger stumblebum brother Richard, who was somehow earning a living stealing cars for a chop shop in Staten Island.

Unable to read street signs and other highway information because his dyslexia had gone unnoticed and untreated as a child, illiterate Freddy was nonetheless a capable chauffeur because he never forgot how to get someplace once someone led him there. "I have a good sense of direction," is how he explained it.

As with anyone in the car business in Canarsie, he was well aware of Roy's reputation for violence, but personally had never seen Bad Roy in action. In fact, as Freddy began eating occasional dinners at Roy's house, he was struck by how much of a softie Roy was around his kids and was amazed to hear him recite grace before the meals. Roy, of course, as a few hardeyed waitresses at the Gemini knew, was only a family man at home.

"I think Roy is two people, you know, like Jekyll and Hyde," Freddy later told acquaintances, who were struck by his ability to mount even a trite analogy.

In truth, though it was hardly on the same scale, Freddy had a violent streak of his own. On Long Island, angry at some neighbor, he dognapped the man's pet, chopped off its head, and left it on the porch. His neighbors left Freddy alone after that.

As he was acquiring a chauffeur and new crew member, Roy was also searching for a new home. In February of 1978, he found one. With his famous lawyer uncle, Albert DeMeo, doing the legal chores, Roy and his wife Gladys bought a white house to rival Paul's new home on Staten Island. The new house was also located in Massapequa Park, but on a grander site a mile and a half away on Whitewood Drive, in the part of town where Carlo Gambino once had his country manor. The backyard of Roy's exquisite homestead abutted Jones Creek, a deep inlet offering nautical passage to South Oyster Bay and the Atlantic Ocean, one thousand yards away. The international statesman U Thant had lived in the house next door, when he was secretary-general of the United Nations.

The property and the two-story house with its large columned portico cost nearly a half million dollars. Thirty-eight-year-old Roy immediately commenced a wholesale renovation and hired a uniformed guard to watch the property while workmen installed marble hallways and floors, new lighting, and a security system that included, in the front of the house, a large pole with a rotating camera. Outside, he built a wide terraced walkway of marble leading to the street and added new trees and shrubs; in the backyard, which was adjacent to Jones Creek and the boat dock that came with the house, he rebuilt the pool, patio, and barbecue area.

Soon a speedboat Roy bought more for son Albert than himself was hanging from the dock's twin hoists. Roy's reputation for leaving for his "office" in the middle of the afternoon and carrying his money in a brown paper bag followed him over to the new house, so his family continued to be the subject of neighborhood chatter. Unlike Nino's four children, whose more secretive father had succeeded in minimizing gossip, Roy's son and two daughters were known in their suburban schools as "the gangster's kids."

Although he adored his daughters, both bright and talented, Roy particularly enjoyed twelve-year-old Albert. Once, he brought him to the Little Italy social club of Aniello Dellacroce, leader of the family's Manhattan faction. In front of several men, Roy teasingly asked Albert to tell them what he would do if a bully picked on him. Everyone fell over laughing when little Albert said, "I'd shoot him and cut his fucking head off!"

"That's my boy!" Roy beamed.

Chris Rosenberg, who sometimes passed himself off as Roy's son, was displaying a new level of prosperity in 1978 too. More than other crew members, and only from a business point of view, Chris's relationship to Roy was more like Roy's to Nino. He was answerable to Roy, but did not sit around waiting for orders or ideas. Chris developed schemes on his own and made money for Roy and himself. His partnership with Roy and the qualities they shared—resourcefulness, intelligence, and viciousness—was beginning to make the twenty-nine-year-old dropout fairly wealthy.

He now owned a popular pizzeria and a second body shop and had recently purchased two homes in Florida, one for his parents—not that he wanted to be Jewish any more than before, but it was a way of saying he was sorry for the way he treated them while growing up. He now lived in a plush apartment in Belle Harbor, an exclusive seaside community in Queens, and he and his girlfriend, a college student he would soon marry, frequently jetted off to various Club Meds. When he was not working on his deals, which increasingly involved drugs more than cars, he was taking flying lessons and studying for his pilot's license.

Many times, with Dominick, Chris boasted that he was as valuable an earner and as tough an enforcer as any Sicilian ever made by the family; he still believed that by the sheer force of criminal will, he could overcome the obstacle to being made that his Jewish ancestry presented.

"I don't know, Chris, they never even made Meyer Lansky," Dominick would say.

"Yeah, but he never took people out like I have," Chris would reply. After he married his Italian-American girlfriend, Chris began using her last name, Rosalia, on personal identifications such as his driver's license.

One night at the Gemini, Chris bragged to Dominick that he and Roy were making fifty thousand dollars a week dealing drugs—cocaine, marijuana, and methaqualone. They were making so much it did not even hurt that a ship containing bales of marijuana destined for an offshore unloading by the crew had sunk at sea. "We'd just unloaded another one a few days before, about five minutes before the fucking Coast Guard showed up!"

Because drug-dealing was an infraction of Paul's made-man rules, Roy avoided the topic in front of Dominick, just as Nino did. The hypocrisy was too embarrassing. When Dominick collected Roy's weekly cash testimonials to Nino and Paul on Friday nights at the Gemini, the money was described by category—"This is for the cars," Roy would say, "and this is for porno and this is the loans." Drugs were never mentioned in the boxscore, although Roy would always hand over several thousand more and say, "Tell Nino this is something extra." Roy knew that Dominick knew what Nino knew about the origin of the money, but no one talked for fear Paul might know.

This is why Roy astonished Dominick one Friday night by suggesting that he ask Nino for permission to join the crew's "drug thing." Dominick had been complaining that he was finding it difficult to live on the same two hundred fifty dollars a week—his starting salary in 1973—that Nino was still paying him.

"That's five years without a raise," Dominick said.

In a conspiratorial whisper, Roy said, "If your uncle would go for it, you know, there's our drug thing."

Also perturbed that Nino had not made good on a promise to give him something to do besides loan pick-ups, Dominick decided to needle Nino and float Roy's idea. Sparing Nino some distress, however, he described "drug thing" as "Roy's action with Chris."

"You stay out of that, no way!"

Emphasizing his objection, Nino also angrily reordered Dominick to stop associating with anyone in the crew and to stay out of the Gemini. Except on Friday nights of course.

With Nino in Florida so much, and with the way the crew used his nephew to communicate with him, this was an impractical order that Dominick violated out of necessity and spite—even though he did not particularly enjoy the company of Chris, or Peter LaFroscia, or Joey Testa and Anthony Senter. Despite what he said about Chris to Matty Rega, Dominick grudgingly respected him, and Joey too; he was indifferent about Peter and thought Anthony was just an appendage to Joey.

"Anthony is Joey's robot," he would snicker to Henry.

"Don't ever say that to Joey," Henry would warn.

Dominick did enjoy the company of murderous, but righteous and engaging Henry, who posted him on crew goings-on, and fifty-year-old Danny Grillo, because opportunistic Danny was a grizzly Sergeant Major type who, unlike Chris, or Joey and Anthony, showed some respect for his Army background. At this point, Dominick had only heard goofy stories about new crew member Freddy DiNome.

Despite the emerging cliques, the crew, and Nino's point man Dominick, rambled together outside the Gemini. Dominick, for instance, rode Jet-Skis with Chris and Joey in the surf off Belle Harbor, and there were regular paddleball tournaments with crew members from both sides—as well as another new, but familiar, recruit, Joseph Guglielmo.

Guglielmo was the man whom they first knew as tenant and superintendent of the clubhouse-apartment next to the Gemini, the gravel-voiced, silver-maned cousin of Roy's that they had nicknamed "Dracula." Roy, however, had recently decided to give Guglielmo crew status so that the ex-convict and bankrobber could keep an eye on Roy's small bookmaking business and generally on goings-on at the Gemini.

No one in the crew knew how old Guglielmo was, but it was somewhere over fifty-five. Some crew members regarded him as a kind of mascot. They teased him for being the only man ever imprisoned because he could not drive a standard-shift car. It happened after a team of robbers changed plans in the midst of a job and made him wheelman; he was too embarrassed to admit his shortcoming, and after his confederates came out with the money, all were caught as the car lurched down the street.

Like the rest of the crew, Dominick thought Guglielmo was a docile man until he saw him, during one of the crew's paddleball tournaments, pull a knife and threaten to stab some teenagers who would not relinquish a court.

"What the fuck are you doing, there's three other courts open!" Dominick snapped.

"Someone's gotta teach these little cocksuckers a lesson."

"Don't be fucking ridiculous. Put it away."

Pulling Henry aside, Dominick said, "Dracula's been hanging around Roy too much."

On the night of May 16, 1978, when no one was around to stop Dracula from pulling out his knife, the crew stopped thinking of him as a mascot. He was one of the lead participants when the DeMeo crew—entering a new business—sent their first murder-for-hire victim to the Fountain Avenue dump.

The victim was Michael DiCarlo, a champion bodybuilder known as "Mikey Muscles." He also was a gopher for a Lucchese capo, and—it turned out—a secret pederast who, according to the Lucchese capo, had made the mistake of molesting a boy whose parents knew whom to see for justice. Mikey Muscles was made to disappear because the capo, acting as prosecutor, jury, and judge, decided the crime demanded it. The dismemberment was carried out in an after-hours club in Flatlands that the crew briefly operated. "I shoved a broomstick up his ass!" Dracula Guglielmo boasted many times.

When Roy came to the bunker and admitted the murder, he was like a cat who deposits his mouse on the kitchen floor and then sits there and gloats about it. Telling the story with ghoulish glee, he said, "We thought the guy was dead, but when we went to take off his fucking head, he reaches up and grabs me by the fucking neck, but Anthony finished him off with a hammer."

"Was Henry there?" Dominick asked.

"He got a little sick and left."

Now that his nightmares had ceased, Dominick frequently boasted to Henry that after what he saw in Vietnam nothing bothered him—but this was not altogether true. Shortly after the murder, he was present at the after-hours club where the bodybuilder was slaughtered, when Chris, Joey, and Anthony began teasing Henry about his "weak stomach" and "lack of balls."

"Fuck you!" Henry finally protested, "I'd kill just about anyone, but I just don't like taking 'em apart."

"You never went hunting before? It's just like taking apart a deer," Anthony said, mouthing Roy's philosophy. "Ain't no difference."

"It is different," Dominick said sharply. "That is a person, not an animal, and you're not killin' him for food. It's a lot fucking different. It's sicker than anything I saw in 'Nam."

Dominick warily noted the betrayed looks he saw on the faces of Chris and the Gemini twins. Thereafter, he always felt an anxious twinge each time he went to the Gemini or entered Dracula's clubhouse apartment.

Given their own brutal predilections and the reputation they steeped in the blood of Andrei Katz and Cherie Golden, among many others, a murder-for-hire sideline was a logical step for Roy and the crew. Filled with a new air of invincibility, Roy had recently informed other made men, in the Gambinos and other families,

that he and his ferocious followers were available for
"work."

Roy and his crew had killed so many by now none
were going to lose sleep killing for no motive but money.
The proof was in how cheaply they would do work—five
thousand dollars for Mikey Muscles.

CHAPTER 10

Thin Blue Line

With all their diverse and widespread interests, Paul, Nino, Roy, and all their crews were always playing with fire, but so far they had stayed several steps ahead of the disparate law enforcement groups arrayed against them. Because of continuing surveillance by Detective Kenny McCabe and Special Agent Tony Nelson, it was now known that Paul, not Aniello Dellacroce of the Manhattan faction, was the true boss of the Gambino family, but little else had been accomplished. Slowly and often haphazardly, however, the authorities began making some headway. To his furious dismay, Anthony Gaggi was first to feel the heat.

Nino had taken great pains to insulate himself. He used Dominick to collect his loans and never went to the Gemini anymore. Although he still went to the Veterans and Friends, he was afraid the club was bugged and never discussed business there. Afraid of wiretaps, he never discussed business on the telephone either. He had ordered all of his crew members to be as supercautious. Roy shared Nino's caution and as usual took action. From some of his police contacts, he acquired electronic detectors that he regularly used to sweep the bunker, the club, and the Gemini for the presence of bugs and wiretaps. Nino did not have as much faith in gadgets as Roy and still watched what he said and where.

A new member of Nino's crew, however, was not so prudent. His name was Gregory DePalma; he was the nephew of a retired Gambino capo and the man who four years earlier had talked the late Carlo and Paul and Nino into loaning the Westchester Premier Theater three hundred thousand dollars. All that time, the theater had met its weekly vig, but never made progress on the principal. The nonperforming loan was a constant worry to Nino.

He had already tried and failed to get a bank to loan the theater money so it could pay back him and Paul. "That place has been nothing but a problem for me," he complained to a crooked union contact who was to broker the failed deal. "They paid Diana Ross two hundred and fifty grand a week just to open up. They built a parking lot, and every time it rains it's ninety-five percent under water. It's gettin' to be a bigger and bigger problem."

Besides having led the theater's developers into a financial arrangement with the Mafia, DePalma owned a secret stake in the theater and was involved in day-to-day management. Against Nino's better judgment, Paul had given DePalma a button and assigned him to Nino's crew on the belief that it guaranteed he and Nino would get their money back.

Nino thought DePalma was untrustworthy and inept: DePalma had overseen construction of the underwater parking lot. Nino also suspected that he was skimming too much profit—a little would have been understandable.

Nino was not alone in his suspicion. The FBI had become interested in the theater after an informant displayed pictures of Frank Sinatra backstage with Carlo and Paul and said the theater was being operated like a Havana casino before Castro. A wiretap was placed on DePalma's telephone at the theater just as he began discussing another scheme for getting the Mafia money out of the theater: By filing for bankruptcy, the theater could stop paying its bills, and thus increase the potential skim from concerts.

The wiretap picked up Nino discussing only subjects as innocent as lunch, and then not very often because, as he had told Dominick, "If Gregory DePalma calls, I'm not home. The guy is always shootin' his mouth off all over the lot." Nino the erstwhile used-car salesman attached "all over the lot" to the end of many of his sentences.

From DePalma's mouth, however, the wiretap recorded incriminating evidence about the plot to raise cash to pay off Paul and Nino by the intentional and fraudulent filing of a bankruptcy petition.

On June 6, 1978, a federal grand jury in New York indicted Nino, DePalma, and nine others on charges that they conspired to drive the theater into bankruptcy, thus temporarily shielding it from creditors, and that while it was under a trustee's supervision they skimmed proceeds from concerts and concessions, thus depriving legitimate creditors and shareholders of a chance to recoup some of their losses. Paul escaped indictment because he had turned over to Nino all matters related to the theater, and consequently DePalma never mentioned Paul on the telephone.

Nino was enraged. "That fuckin' DePalma and his cocksucking big fat mouth!" he ranted to Dominick after his arraignment and release on bail. "That fucker! I told him not to talk on the fucking phone! I should whack 'im! The fucking scumbag!"

Nino's prominent neck vein was pulsing more than expected because now, very much against his will, he was about to become a celebrity gangster; he knew that the concerts that Frank Sinatra gave to try and pull the theater out of red ink ensured substantial media coverage of the trial.

In fact, Assistant United States Attorney Nick Akerman intended to allege that DePalma skimmed five thousand dollars from the last of Sinatra's three concerts and gave it to a California gangster who used it to bribe an official of a Catholic fraternal society, the Knights of Malta, into admitting the singer into the group. The government had not accused Sinatra of any wrongdoing, but planned to introduce photographs of him backstage with Carlo, Paul, DePalma, and other gangsters.

Trying to be upbeat, Dominick observed that the indictment did not accuse Nino of loansharking—his uncle's main role all the while. "You didn't have anything to do with the skim—I mean, maybe you did, but you sure as fuck didn't talk about it on the phone. Did you?"

"What am I—*stupido*?"

"Then they ain't got ya."

"Where did you get your law degree? If I had a nickel for every guy in the can who shouldn't be, I could buy a fuckin' federal judge. What a pisser this is. Fuckin' DePalma, that scum."

Though Nino's lawyers also assured him he had a good chance of beating the case, it was a ceaseless pain over the next half year of pretrial motions and hearings. At times, he was untypically melancholy. The families of

Paul Rothenberg, George Byrum, Vincent Governara, and others would never muster much sympathy for him, but family man Nino dreaded the prospect of leaving his wife and children and entering prison at age fifty-three; he could not imagine himself living in a cage either.

"I don't know if I can handle prison," he told Dominick's stepfather during a family gathering after returning from Florida that fall. "Some guys can do time. I don't think I'm one of 'em."

So far, in the car business, Roy and the crew were the beneficiaries of a legal system that did not take car theft seriously. Despite rampant activity, they had enjoyed virtual impunity, but that situation would begin to change.

The NYPD had mounted only a weak effort against auto theft for many years. In 1976, ninety thousand cars had been stolen, the worst year yet, but that year the NYPD citywide Auto Crime Unit was reduced from sixty to forty officers because of the city's near financial collapse.

The Auto Crime Unit was headquartered in Queens. In two-man teams, officers conducted patrols of high-theft areas or responded to service calls from the city's seventy-five precincts, typically when a patrol officer arrested a driver whose license, registration, or title appeared suspicious. Often, only two officers were available per shift to cover sprawling boroughs like Queens and Brooklyn, each with more than two million residents.

The unit was formed only a few years before, after the sudden surge in new-car and replacement-part prices caused the boom in auto theft. Many officers bored with routine patrol volunteered for the new unit, including John Murphy, a Bronx-born and -bred Irish-American who spoke in such a muffled rumble he was hard to hear sometimes. The voice matched his personality, low-key. A devout family man in private life, he was a hard-nosed cynic on the job. Despite feeling the opposition held all the cards, he liked the work. No shift was ever dull; the entire city was his beat.

Murphy joined the NYPD comparatively late, at age thirty-four, after serving in the 1st Marine Division in Korea and with an Air Force civilian security unit in

Vietnam. A medium-size man with fair features, he was forty-three by 1977, a mature, steady sort ready to take on an important job. His opportunity came that year, when he was asked to become the Auto Crime Unit's first intelligence officer. His commanding officer, Frank Hubert, wanted to determine if the auto thieves who were caught now and then were connected to each other, and if they worked for the same chop shops and junkyards.

"I've been saying for years that the Gambinos and Luccheses control all these mutts," Murphy reminded his boss.

Murphy began reviewing arrest records and visiting precinct stationhouses and jails to interview officers, suspects, and informants. He was already familiar with the late John Quinn's operations and the phenomenon of "Quinn Paper" and began connecting Quinn to other names. The name that turned up most was Patty Testa. Joey's younger brother was only twenty-one, but most auto thieves who talked to Murphy said Patty had been Quinn's biggest customer, and Murphy's surveillance of Patty Testa Motorcars did indicate a lot of traffic in late-model luxury cars.

The more he looked, the more Murphy became convinced that Patty was the common denominator of a network of thieves, chop shops, and junkyards. He diagramed charts whose lines came back to Patty from many directions. Some officers thought he was becoming obsessed. They joked that when they called him for advice on a case, he always replied, "Patty Testa. Have you thought of Patty Testa yet? He was moving all of Quinn's cars." Early on Murphy did not know about Patty's connection to Roy.

Two other auto crime officers stopped by Murphy's desk almost every day. John Doherty and Peter Calabro always expressed interest in what patterns Murphy was finding and what chop shops and junkyards he was recommending for raids. Murphy thought they were just being curious cops; of the two, he knew Doherty better. They were assigned to be partners three years earlier, but then Doherty's wife fell ill, and he was temporarily given a desk job, and Murphy was teamed with another officer.

Murphy never got to know Doherty well, however. He did not know the cop was one of the Doherty brothers of

Avenue P in Flatlands or that he grew up three blocks from Roy DeMeo's childhood home and was a Saint Thomas Aquinas School classmate. Murphy did not know that another Doherty brother, Daniel, was a bartender at the Gemini and that yet another, Charles, fronted Roy's ownership of the bar. He did not know John Doherty's current partner, Peter Calabro, became Roy's friend after Doherty made the introduction. He especially did not know that in 1974, Calabro was the cop who appeared in the shadows outside the Gemini and told Roy that Andrei Katz was cooperating against Chris Rosenberg.

With some twenty-six thousand officers, the NYPD is larger than the armies of most countries—and, cops like to say, as bureaucratic as the Pentagon. In addition to the seventy-five individual precincts, the department has dozens of special citywide divisions and units (like the auto unit) and other special squads that investigate specific crimes like robbery and murder and operate according to precinct, borough, or other geographic boundaries.

As Murphy was beginning to penetrate the Canarsie car jungle, a squad of homicide detectives responsible for a "zone" of the city including Flatlands and Canarsie was assigned to investigate the murders of John Costello and Daniel Conti, the part-time hijackers who had been killed because the crew feared they could not stand up to an investigation of a bungled hijacking. The squad did not make much headway, other than turning up the fact Conti was the brother-in-law of Peter LaFroscia.

In the meantime, an informant telephoned an investigator for another special NYPD squad, the one that worked for the Brooklyn District Attorney and included Mafia expert Kenny McCabe. "You ought to check out what's going on in Canarsie," the informant told investigator Joseph Wendling. "People are dropping like flies and nobody's getting locked up for it."

Wendling was the opposite of the Auto Crime Unit's John Murphy. He was high-key, hefty, brash and cocky, and only twenty-seven when chosen for the prestigious District Attorney's squad (he was now thirty-one). He came to departmental notice while assigned to one of the city's most violent and angry precincts, the Seven-Three, a ghetto outpost in central Brooklyn nicknamed Fort Zinderneuf after a French fort in Algiers whose soldiers fought to the end. Wendling was promoted after a homicide squad asked him to help find two murder suspects, and he found them—as he liked to say—one by lunchtime, the other by the next morning.

Wendling met with his Canarsie informant, who said that Peter LaFroscia had discussed the John Quinn murder in a way indicating more than secondhand knowledge and that he hung out with a young but lethal crowd rumored to be involved in many homicides. The informant did not mention Cherie Golden's murder, because La-Froscia was silent about it, but Wendling checked the man's story about other homicides against unsolved murder files and became convinced some were connected.

He then spoke to Inspector John Nevins, commander of the DA's squad: "Except for Cherie Golden, no one cares about these cases; the victims are dirtbags, and the homicide squads have too many good victims. But there's a new kind of group out there."

In time, persuaded that several of the murders were linked, Nevins formed a special task force based out of his office. The homicide squads, whose toes were being stepped on, were reluctant to give up their cases until Nevins arranged to have members of the squads attached to the task force.

Wendling, alone or with different partners also attached to the task force, began surveilling LaFroscia. He learned that he was one of the two thieves who cruised around in a Jaguar while stealing cars for Quinn; he saw him meeting with Patty Testa, then followed him and Patty to the Gemini Lounge.

"Jesus, that's Roy DeMeo's place," Wendling told his partner that day, "and some people will tell you Roy is the most dangerous man in Brooklyn."

Wendling first heard of Roy when he and Kenny Mc-Cabe investigated the merger of the Boro of Brooklyn Credit Union into another and saw Roy, other Mafia gangsters, and men they later identified as major drug dealers from Harlem in Manhattan going into the offices of both credit unions. It was the heat of that investigation that caused Roy to get out of the credit union business.

Following LaFroscia and Patty, Wendling and his partner saw them meeting with a young and lethal-looking crowd; Patty was the only one who appeared to have a seemingly legitimate occupation. With the help of Kenny and others, they identified them as Chris Rosenberg, Joey Testa, Anthony Senter, and Henry Borelli.

"Look at the fucking Porsches and Mercedes these guys have!" Wendling said to Kenny one day. "And they're just fucking kids! What is going on with these guys?"

Kenny had a few ideas: "Cars, drugs, murder. They work for Roy and he works for a guy named Nino."

Meanwhile, in Nassau County, which abuts the borough of Queens, the county police department began an investigation that linked several car thefts in suburban areas to Patty Testa and LaFroscia. On November 18, 1977, a Nassau squad raided LaFroscia's home and found some of John Quinn's record books.

The next day, Norman Blau, an NYPD officer from the Six-Nine precinct in Canarsie, telephoned a Nassau detective and offered to help in the investigation. He invited him to come to his home and meet Willie Kampf, whom Blau identified as an informer well grounded in the car-theft world.

That much was true. Willie Kampf was an adept and prolific car thief. It took him only thirty seconds to enter a locked car, extract the ignition assembly, and start the engine. All he needed was a "slim-jim" to slide into a door to pop the lock and a "slap hammer" to break and extract the ignition. He had developed his technique over ten years, since he was thirteen years old. Chop shops and junkyards often used juvenile thieves because, if caught, they were just sent home to their parents.

Joseph Wendling had heard of Kampf and was trying to locate him. Kampf, Wendling's sources said, was LaFroscia's freelance partner—the second, and more expert, thief in the Jaguar. Soon Wendling also got a telephone call from Norman Blau, offering to produce Kampf.

Wendling then spoke to Kampf by telephone, but Kampf was reluctant to say much. "You have no idea how these guys are," he said. "They're crazy; they'll kill anybody." After a few conversations with Wendling, Kampf fled New York.

Wendling became convinced that Kampf knew La-

Froscia killed, or helped to kill, Quinn and maybe Cherie Golden. What he did not know—just as John Murphy did not know of the rogue cops in the Auto Crime Unit—was that Norman Blau was more interested in discovering what Wendling knew about Kampf and LaFroscia than solving two murders. For years Blau had been giving inside information about police patrol patterns to Kampf and LaFroscia and had used NYPD computers to tell them where to find popular makes and models.

Meanwhile, because their informants told them too many troubling stories about some NYPD officers, agents from the Brooklyn-Queens office of the FBI were not telling outsiders anything too substantial about their continuing investigation of the murdered Quinn and his interstate retagging operation. In a raid at the home of a girlfriend of a minor DeMeo crew functionary, agents had recovered the stacks of blank car documents and VIN-making tools stolen when Quinn and his young lover were murdered.

The corruption was an obvious asset, but the overlapping and uncoordinated rivalries of the city's law enforcement groups were another important part of the reason Paul, Nino, Roy, and the crew had been so successful for so long.

The more Roy turned up in informants' stories, the more Kenny McCabe paid attention, and it intrigued him when he began seeing Freddy DiNome loitering outside the Gemini Lounge during his customary drive-bys on the way home from work—not that the Gemini was directly on Kenny's way home.

Kenny knew Freddy from 1969, his rookie year as a detective, when the NYPD was making a lot of nuisance arrests to inflate its statistics during another periodic crackdown on illegal gambling. The arrests rarely caused much inconvenience, but they did have some intelligence value. Kenny and others from the DA's squad had descended on Freddy's gas station and arrested him and nine others as they stood around a mechanic's bay tossing dice.

This was the arrest that caused Freddy to take his pet monkey Susie to court. Though outwardly treating it as a joke, Freddy had carried a grudge against the detectives for making such a fuss of something so trivial. When Kenny, nine years later, made a pass of the Gemini, and then parked directly opposite, Freddy, whose memory recorded landmarks and large detectives, remembered him immediately.

"You're Kenny McCabe, right?" Freddy yelled from across the street.

"You got a fuckin' good memory, Freddy Boy."

"You're the bastard who arrested me. Why don't you go have an accident!"

Baiting Freddy, Kenny stuck his arm out the window of his battered Pinto and asked, "Come here and say that!"

"Kiss my ass!" Freddy said, walking into the Gemini.

In a few weeks, on another pass-and-park of the Gemini, Kenny was surprised to see Roy come out and approach his car in what appeared to be a friendly manner.

After they exchanged coy hellos, Kenny said to Roy, "You ought to straighten out that friend of yours, Freddy. He's a little excitable. You better watch him."

"What can I do? Freddy is crazy."

Roy seemed in a talkative, easy mood, and Kenny came to believe that as long as Nino and others were not around, Roy actually enjoyed playing Kenny's cat-and-mouse game.

"I went to watch Freddy race once," Roy continued, "and he crashed. He climbs out of the car and he's on fire. He looks like an astronaut who's crash-landed. The firemen are hosin' him down, but he looks up at me in the stands and begins to smile and wave like some kids were just squirtin' him by the pool. Don't tell me Freddy is crazy. I know he's fuckin' nuts."

Armed with a pistol, Freddy sat and waited in Roy's Cadillac when Roy had meetings with Nino or anyone else important. Roy had given him only one standing instruction: "If anyone comes out of a meet and says they want you inside, don't go. Instead, I want you to shoot them and run because I'll already be dead. If I want you, *I'll* come get you."

After the sun set on his racing career, Freddy had done some stolen-car business with both John Quinn and Peter

LaFroscia, the crew member whom investigator Joseph Wendling of the Brooklyn District Attorney's homicide task force had targeted in the Quinn murder.

Without any help from the FBI's informant, Quinn's cousin Joseph Bennett, Wendling was having some success; he had traced master car thief Willie Kampf, LaFroscia's former partner, to a relative's home in Florida and had gone there to interview him. He was accompanied by Norman Blau, the cop who unknown to him had used NYPD computers to help Kampf and LaFroscia steal cars.

Blau had told Wendling and Steven Samuel, an assistant district attorney working on the case, that he might be able to get Kampf to talk. Wendling and Samuel had no reason yet not to trust Blau—and Kampf did talk: LaFroscia, he said, told him days after the murder that he killed Quinn.

"We did it because he was a rat," Kampf quoted LaFroscia.

Kampf could not link LaFroscia nor anyone to Cherie Golden's murder, but hoping to find her killers and make the case against LaFroscia stronger, Wendling and Samuel decided to delay arresting him. Instead, they informed his federal probation officer (LaFroscia was on probation for conspiring to attempt to import marijuana) that LaFroscia was violating his probationary status by "consorting with known criminals." Subsequently, a hearing was held and a judge sent LaFroscia away to prison for a year.

Meanwhile, in a matter that was still departmentally unrelated, NYPD auto crime intelligence officer John Murphy began urging his superiors to authorize an all-out investigation of Mafia domination of the city's stolen-car trade.

Like Wendling with Blau, Murphy was still unaware that fellow auto crime officers John Doherty and Peter Calabro were double agents, but he had learned, without FBI aid, about Roy DeMeo; he told his bosses that Patty Testa and other thieves worked for Roy and were responsible for seven murders, maybe more.

Some of Murphy's information came from a twenty-nine-year-old Nassau County police officer, Charles

Meade, whom Murphy had befriended early in 1978. Meade had come to Queens and asked Murphy to brief him about auto crime. He was preparing himself for a new assignment—responding to an epidemic of thefts, Nassau brass had tripled the size of their Auto Squad—from three to nine officers.

"We believe we're just victims in Nassau," Meade told Murphy. "We believe our cars are stolen and brought to the city."

"Canarsie," Murphy said. "I can show you the places."

Since that first meeting, almost each time Meade made an arrest or recovered a stolen car, Canarsie had figured in the case somehow. Frequently, Meade found the hulks of Nassau cars on the streets of Canarsie, stripped of all valuable parts.

Murphy also began comparing notes with Joseph Wendling and Kenny McCabe, after meeting Wendling while standing in line for admission to a classroom where the department's test for promotion to sergeant was being given. Wendling was as obsessed with John Quinn's murder as Murphy was with Patty Testa. Both passed the test and with McCabe began conducting surveillance of the Flatlands-Canarsie area on their own time.

With help from Meade, Wendling, and McCabe, Murphy believed he had done what his bosses wanted when they made him the auto crime intelligence officer: show that dozens of chop shops and thieves were linked to made members of the Gambino and Lucchese families. Even so, no boss would commit the resources and manpower—the twenty-four-hour surveillance teams and cash for informants—a serious investigation would require. The city's fiscal crisis, which had frozen budget and personnel levels, was a factor, as was the revolving door to the unit commander's office: There had been three in a year, and each new boss wanted to get comfortable before committing to an effort that would test his ability to provide routine patrol and investigative services.

A sympathetic sergeant pulled Murphy aside one day and suggested he turn his files over to the homicide squads. ''The case is gettin' too big, give it to the detectives,'' he said.

''Fuck that,'' said Murphy, who believed the files would then just gather dust. ''I'd throw 'em away before I give 'em away.''

CHAPTER 11

Pet of the Year

Nino's promotion to capo and the drama over Roy's elevation to made man understandably caused Dominick Montiglio to dwell on his future. With his uncle now de facto underboss of the Brooklyn faction, it was hardly unreasonable to imagine Nino succeeding sixty-two-year-old Paul some day. And hardly unreasonable for the ex-Green Beret to see himself becoming a made man, a capo, and like Michael Corleone, even the—Who knew what the future held? At the very party celebrating Roy's button, Nino had fueled such thoughts: "I put you up for a button, but Paulie knocked it down because you're too young. You'll have to wait a while." In the glow of high status derived from his relationships to Nino and Paul, Dominick waited and began living it up.

Picking up Nino's loans and his offerings from Roy, Dominick at age thirty had already spent a lot of time in bars, nightclubs, and restaurants; he had a hard time turning a drink down, and some days it seemed like everyone wanted to buy him one. He was still buying cars at auction for Matty Rega, the auto dealer in debt to both Nino and Roy, and still on friendly terms, unaware that Rega had passed along his private and disparaging remarks about Chris. Rega had been generous with his cocaine before, and after Nino's promotion to capo, he began laying more white lines on the table when Dominick, frequently joined by Henry, came by to pick up a payment—nowadays at the Bottom of the Barrel, a restaurant Rega had since acquired in New Jersey. Between the coke and the drinking, Denise Montiglio had grown accustomed to her husband coming home a bit unsteady sometimes.

Though Dominick had introduced Denise to Henry and to Danny Grillo and their wives, the rest of the DeMeo crew and most other people he met working for Nino never become part of their social whirl. She did not, for example, attend Anthony Senter's wedding, or Chris's, or Joey's when he got married a few years later. She never asked questions about his separate life because it was supposed to be business, not social.

So far, he had not given her a reason to distrust him. But he was contracting an acute case of roving eye, and had told Henry: "Some women, soon as they figure you're a half-assed wiseguy, they're throwing themselves at you."

Dominick had begun using cocaine regularly by the summer of 1977; it was partly why he had begun pestering Nino for a raise—not that he wasn't entitled to one, based purely on inflation. If Rega did not have any cocaine, Henry did, hardly a surprise since Henry's boss, Roy, sold it out of the Gemini. Henry rarely went anywhere anymore without a black leather men's purse, in which he carried a clean handgun and a coke kit—vial, mirror, and straw, all with gold trim.

Dominick loved cocaine. It was so different from the other drugs he had sampled before—marijuana, LSD, mescaline—and so enjoyable compared to Thorazine, the prescription drug he had briefly taken to combat the psychological terrors of Vietnam.

Where Thorazine numbed his mind, cocaine overstimulated it, enhancing his sense of personal well-being and power and making him feel excited when there was no reason to. He quickly discovered these emotions soon went away, and to maintain the high, more coke was needed. Still, like most users at the time, he believed it was not a dangerous drug and was not physically addicting—only expensive because people who did not know much about it controlled drug policy and made it illegal.

In New York, cocaine was wildly popular. The euphoric burst of energy it gave users had even changed the nature of nightlife—clubs where marijuana-mellow crowds listened to live rock bands became discos where coked-up patrons danced to repetitive recorded music. At Studio 54, the Manhattan disco of the moment, dancers snorted cocaine openly against a backdrop that included a large caricature of the man in the moon with a coke spoon up his nose.

Dominick began going to Studio 54 with Rega and Henry. The club controlled the composition of its nightly crowd by a selective admittance policy at the door, but Rega guaranteed that he, Dominick, and Henry never had a problem getting in by giving the doorman a new Mercedes. They might have been waved past the velvet ropes anyway; swarthy and dandy young men were a part of the club's crowd formula, which also was weighted toward celebrities, rich degenerates, and any attractive woman in a particularly daring outfit.

In time, the three men were regulars. Dominick began drinking heavily; his usual drink—double Jack Daniel's, no ice—tempered the speedy effect of cocaine. One night at the bar, he bumped into a woman he had met while a member of the Four Directions—a singer-actress now known simply as Cher. She remembered appearing on the same television show with the group, but not him—at least that was what he recalled about their hazy conversation the following day.

On another night, after Paul Castellano expressed curiosity about all the publicity the club was receiving, Dominick arranged to escort him past the velvet ropes. Paul took a look at the man in the moon and the couples practically fornicating on the dance floor and was gone in five minutes.

Sliding into cocaine and the hedonistic nightlife that went with it, Dominick violated his look-but-don't-touch rule and began cheating on Denise—"the best woman a man ever had," he had frequently boasted to Henry and others. His infidelity began not at Studio 54, but at another place where drugs and women in daring outfits came together—his former 21 Club co-worker Chuck Anderson's penthouse apartment next to the Park Lane Hotel in Manhattan.

On one occasion, when making his weekly pickup, Dominick went to Anderson's apartment rather than the club because "Mr. New York" had been fired earlier that evening. The management disapproved of Anderson, who described himself as a friend of *Penthouse* magazine publisher Bob Guccione, attempting to bring three Penthouse "Pets"—as the magazine's monthly centerfold models were known—into the club. The Pets' slinky attire violated the 21 Club's idea of good taste.

At Anderson's penthouse, Anderson introduced the three Pets, all accompanied by much older men, to Dominick. One of the women was twenty-four-year-old "Anneka di Lorenzo"—Marjorie Lee Thoreson to friends and family in St. Paul, Minnesota. Aggressive Anneka, however, had left St. Paul behind long ago; at fifteen, she was a topless dancer in Hollywood, and she came to New York after seeing publisher Guccione on the Merv Griffin Show talking about his idea of beauty. "I want to become the sexiest woman in the world," she told Guccione, after contacting the magazine.

When Dominick met her, she said she hoped to capitalize on her election the previous year as Penthouse Pet of the Year and return to Hollywood and get her star on Sunset Boulevard. However, as Dominick left with Anderson's payment, blond and tan Anneka, wearing not much of a white dress, had more immediate conquests in mind. She followed him out the door.

"Do you like to do cocaine?" she asked.

"Sure, once in a while."

"Come with me. I like to do lines the size of my finger."

Dominick went back into the penthouse and did not make it to Brooklyn until the following afternoon. Hung over and burned out, he was spared having to tell lies because Denise did not even ask where he was—he had stayed out all night before playing cards at the Veterans and Friends and other social clubs.

Short of making an accusation, loyal husband Nino did not let Dominick off the hook so easy. "Where were you last night?" he asked when his haggard nephew hauled himself out of bed and wandered into the bunker's common kitchen. "You were supposed to come to the club and you never showed up."

"I had to make so many pickups, it just got late. I slept over at Matty's place."

"If you can't make it, you call," Nino said. "You got to learn to treat people with respect."

Trying to extricate himself from further lies and criticism, Dominick said, walking out of the kitchen: "We're still short on a couple pickups, but I'm getting the rest today. I'll definitely bring them to the club tonight. See you there."

Later, trying to rationalize his behavior while talking to Henry, he quoted a passage in a book he had recently read about Lucky Luciano, Frank Scalise's mentor. "Lucky said that people in our life should never get married. He was right."

In the fall of 1977, Dominick became close friends with another man who told him about another book—*The Prince*, by Niccolò Machiavelli. Like Dominick, Emil "Buzzy" Scioli was thirty years old; he was affiliated with another Gambino crew. He was clever, flamboyant, and athletic—and also a college graduate.

Dominick met Buzzy at the Veterans and Friends, but they became friends after both were asked by their bosses to work at a "Las Vegas Night"—one of a series of gambling events sponsored by a consortium of Mafia families and staged at a Brooklyn synagogue. For a thousand dollars each, two orthodox rabbis had acted as fronts and applied for a special waiver allowing tax-exempt organizations to hold gambling events for fund-raising purposes.

Dominick and Buzzy were selected to supervise the action at the dozen or so crap, blackjack, and poker tables arrayed in the synagogue because the event's sponsors were certain they would never cheat the house. Reminiscing about Carlo Gambino, Dominick told Buzzy that Carlo used to lecture him about the importance of being like a lion and a fox.

"That's right out of *The Prince*, you know," Buzzy said.

"Right," Dominick said, so unconvincingly that Buzzy knew his new friend was unaware that for all those years Uncle Carlo was cribbing from Machiavelli.

But Buzzy did not lord his Fordham University degree over Dominick, one of the reasons the pair got along so well. In a few days, however, Buzzy gave Dominick a copy of the book, which he immediately read. For Dominick, who began carrying it around in the Thunderbird he now drove, *The Prince* was an epiphany.

"What's that?" Nino asked when Dominick drove him on an errand one day.

"That is our life."

Nino thumbed a few pages. If he had given the watchdog at his old used-car lot the name "Prince" because

Carlo Gambino had once given him a Machiavellian lecture, he never admitted it.

"Read it," Dominick said. "It helps justify everything. Whatever you have to do to hold onto power, you do."

"Who needs to justify anything? We are what we are."

"Read it, you'll see." Nino took the book and later claimed to have lost it. He promised to buy another copy but never did.

For more than the obvious reasons, Dominick dared not admit his cocaine use or his infidelity to Nino. Because he was trying to get Nino to raise his salary and deliver on a promise made after Paul became boss—a pledge to set Dominick up in some venture of his own—it was no time to give Nino more excuses than he so far had proved capable of producing.

"Just be patient," Nino would say. "I told you I was gonna pass the torch to you some day. Ain't that enough?"

"Yeah, but my family and me, we have to eat now."

"Don't be a smartass."

The more he dwelled on it, the more it infuriated Dominick that, even though he watched over Nino's affairs, including his R&A Sales food brokerage, during the five months a year Nino was in Florida, Nino was still paying him the same salary—two hundred fifty dollars a week—that he had in 1973. There were occasional bonuses—a hundred or so off the bottom of a week's worth of pickups—but he thought he was being cheated, and one evening he used that word when he confronted Nino again.

Nino's reaction to such an insult was to play a family card. "Cheat? Dom, you're like a son to me. You're godfather to one of my sons."

"Give me a break. I have a wife and two kids. I go everywhere for you; you don't have to worry about anything. I really need the money. I deserve five hundred a week."

Nino, although not as much with Rose or their children, was tight with a dollar because he had grown up during the Depression. He genuinely meant it when he replied, "I don't understand why two-fifty isn't enough. I buy the food in this house. You're still only payin' one-sixty-five a month in rent."

"There are chumps working for Roy makin' a thousand a week."

"They may be making it, but nobody in Roy's crew is going anywhere. You are. Someday. Chris will never be made because he's Jewish. Henry will never be made because he took the test to be a cop once. Joey Testa has a little on the ball, but the rest are lightweights."

That same evening, Roy came by Nino's house and was drawn into the argument. He took Dominick's side.

"Nino, a guy can't live on two-fifty a week with two kids and a wife. Tell you what: Let's let Dom take care of our New Jersey porno thing—that'll get him some more money."

That suggestion set Nino off. "No way! If his grandmother ever saw him arrested with porno, it would kill her. No way!"

"What would she say," Dominick said, "if she saw me arrested for helping shoot someone down in the street?"

"It's not the same thing! End of discussion!"

Nino's contorted distinction arose from a desire to shield his family, except for Dominick, from the grimy world that provided them a comfortable life. He did not want his own sons—one was in college and on his way to becoming an optometrist—to take the road he did. He also did not want his daughter dating anyone remotely like his nephew, who was mostly his creation.

Dominick discovered this after Buzzy confided that he was smitten by Nino's nineteen-year-old daughter Regina. He had met her at Nino's house while visiting Dominick and Denise; she was the type of woman he wanted to marry some day, Buzzy said.

"Regina is terrific," Dominick replied, "and that would be great if you two ever got together because that would bring you to our faction of the family. But I'm not sure Nino would think it's a good thing. Since you're my friend, he probably thinks you're a fuckin' wacko."

"What if I asked him if I could ask her out?"

"Do so at your peril."

Thirty-year-old Buzzy put on a coat and tie and made an appointment with Nino at the Veterans and Friends. Nino, to Dominick's amazement, said yes. Buzzy could ask Regina out. Nino soon began to complain, however, that Buzzy had caught him off-guard; as the day of the date neared, he became frantically opposed.

"Maybe you ought to back out," Dominick told Buzzy. "The man is flippin' out. He's saying it's my fault, I didn't warn him."

Buzzy went ahead with his date with Regina, but Nino dispatched one of his sons and several other relatives and friends to accompany them. Buzzy deemed the relationship doomed and never asked her out again.

"You wouldn't have wanted him as a father-in-law anyway," Dominick said. "Believe me."

By the spring of 1978, Dominick was getting more restless being around so much money, none of it his. On occasion, during Nino's longer stays in Florida, the trap in the bedroom where he stored Nino's cash approached a quarter-million dollars, augmented as it was with the ten, twenty, or thirty thousand dollars a week he collected from Roy, plus all Nino's loan pickups.

It began to aggravate him that the clannish Canarsie trio, twenty-nine-year-old Chris and twenty-four-year-old Joey and Anthony were making comparative fortunes. Their successes were due less to ability than freedom from Nino's hypocritical rules, he believed. Ruthlessness aside, he was at least as capable as any; he was particularly aggravated by Chris, who was doing a lot better at Roy's knee than he was at Nino's, and who had a sarcastic habit of reminding him that if only he worked for Roy, and not Nino, he would be doing well too.

It also was irksome that his status with Paul carried no financial reward. When Nino was away, anytime Roy wanted to talk to Paul or send a message or money, he had to go through Dominick. It was galling that the importance of this role was worth nothing extra, as galling for him as it was for Roy to have to communicate with "Waterhead" that way.

A few times, Dominick had made a few dollars buying a few grams of cocaine from Rega and selling it to nightlifers he met in Studio 54. Now, to finance his own consumption and make more money, he began buying and selling larger amounts of Rega's coke and developing a convenient use-and-be-used relationship.

He and Buzzy told Rega, whose thousand-dollar-a-week habit was making him paranoid, that Henry, who sometimes collected for Roy, and Chris were going to hurt him the next time he was late with the vig on the one hundred thousand dollars Rega owed Nino and Roy.

Rega, for more reasons than paranoia and fear, began paying Dominick a couple of hundred dollars just to hang around as installments came due on Roy's half-interest in the loan. He knew Dominick would never side with him against Henry, but felt that investing in Dominick strengthened his relations with Nino and Roy; their loans kept his car business and restaurant afloat and supported his big-spender lifestyle. Of course, with such emergency bankers available, he also never had to worry about funding his coke deals and abuse, which began as soon as he awoke.

The son of a connected New Jersey bookmaker, Rega lived from week to week. He was not as concerned about retiring the principal of his debt as much as meeting the weekly vig and keeping his index card free of dashes. Nino would have appreciated his logic: "As long as I owe money, I will stay alive," Rega told Dominick.

Rega had access to all the cocaine he wanted because he had fostered a relationship with a busy New York cocaine dealer named Pedro Rodriguez, who did business as "Paz." Creating a customer, Paz introduced Rega to cocaine a few years earlier, after buying a car from him on Jerome Avenue in the South Bronx.

Through Rega, Dominick met Paz and got what he needed least: a direct pipeline to an even cheaper source of cocaine. The much-decorated former war hero also began earning a few hundred dollars more as an armed bodyguard during drug deals at Paz's apartment in Queens.

He began staying away from home for more than overnight. All Denise asked was that he telephone each night and let her know he was alive, which he did. A husband who was occasionally away from home a few days at a time became part of her natural order, like that of a traveling salesman's wife. If not always the instant he walked in the door, they usually made love when he returned, and the spark was still there.

While away from home, Dominick always made sure to collect Nino's loans and conduct his business at the

Gemini, but after these errands, he went with Buzzy or
Henry or Rega or his new Westie friend Mickey Feath-
erstone—sometimes all four—to Studio 54, or to a new
Manhattan disco called Xenon. There they became
friendly with the owner, whose late father was Ruby
Stein, the loanshark murdered by Danny Grillo and the
Westies.

"If they're not from Brooklyn, they're farmers!"
Dominick would shout to his coked-up pals as beefcake
waiters in silver lamé hot pants replenished his and the
other connected guests' drinks.

"I'll make us all millions!" Rega would scream beneath the pulsating music.

Sliding downhill fast, Dominick cheated on Denise
again with a waitress he met at the Bottom of the Barrel.
"I told myself I wasn't going to do that again, but, you
know, I got loaded," he said to Henry.

"Stop making excuses and admit you're just as much
a prick as the rest of us."

"You're right."

In a few days more, on July 17, his thirty-first birthday, he accepted a gift from Danny Grillo—a "session"
at an elegant Manhattan massage parlor. It was operated
by a former Swedish beauty queen, his companion for
the evening.

By the end of the summer, moving from a vile life to
a vile and degenerate one, Dominick was snorting a gram
of cocaine and drinking a fifth of Jack Daniel's over the
course of an ordinary day. Such abuse required a prodi-
gious constitution, of which the former Airborne Ranger
and Green Beret was confident and proud.

During college, and with Dominick in California, Denise had seen a lot of casual drug use. She knew of his
increasing taste for cocaine—he, Henry and Danny laid
out lines for everyone at dinner parties—but did not know
to what extent because he was away so much, purport-
edly on business. "Coke ain't like LSD," he told her,
"it's a social drug. I can do coke all day and still function. I'm under control."

Dominick, however, had begun to lose weight in his
face and upper body. Having also cut his hair short and
begun combing the top forward, he was demonstrating a
familiar talent for physical metamorphosis. Oddly, the

less imposing his chest and shoulders became, the more dangerous he appeared because of the Nero-style hair and the harder, slimmer lines of his face; with the mostly all-black clothes he now wore, it was a look that caused people to whisper, after he entered a restaurant, "There goes a gangster."

After Anthony Gaggi returned to Bath Beach in the fall of 1978, and was unable to track his nephew down when he wanted, he accused Dominick of becoming more punk than gangster. He did not know enough about cocaine to detect signs of regular use—runny nose, loss of appetite, abrupt mood swings. He was more alarmed by Dominick's drinking and that he no longer shaped up each day at the Veterans and Friends social club.

"If you keep drinking like you are, you're going to fucking kill yourself," Nino would scream during what became a recurring argument. "Don't be the fucking idiot your old man was!"

"He drank, but he was champ of the Army Air Corps!"

"He was a chump!"

"Everybody don't see things the way you do."

"I ain't everybody—but you better start shaping up at the club. You gotta go there every day."

"So fucking McCabe can take my picture? I thought you said that club was going to be the end of you someday? If I ain't gettin' anything for it, I don't want it to be the end of me."

"Fuck the cops, they don't know shit."

After such a confrontation, Dominick would shape up for a few days, then do what he wanted, which was to run with his own friends, his own "crew." After all the years under Nino's thumb, he decided that his uncle's bark was worse than his bite. Since Nino was not making room for him on even the handle of the torch, he had no right to control his life. However, he would still do what Nino paid him to do: keep an eye on the DeMeo crew and collect Nino's money. That was business; unprofitable as it was, at least it kept his foot in the door. His relationship with Nino was also becoming more of a use-and-be-used arrangement.

These days, however, he did not worry much about the ethics of the situation—or traditional family values, for that matter. One day, as his downward spiral accelerated, he met a woman who actually came to mean something to him, bizarre as the relationship would become.

The affair began as he, Buzzy and Henry were about to leave the apartment of a cocaine dealer they had met in Studio 54. As he walked toward the door, he saw a woman lounging on a bed in another room reading a copy of *Cosmopolitan* magazine.

Feeling enhanced, he said, "Do you want to stay with the scumbag or come with us?"

"Let me get my things," she said.

Cheryl Anderson, it turned out, had seen Dominick and the boys club-hopping before. She was twenty-five years old and the daughter of a wealthy Long Island building contractor; she was slim, attractive, had pale green eyes and long straight hair the color of autumn wheat, and had come to the city to sow her oats. In the process, she became a major dealer of Quāaludes, a prescription drug whose sedating, dreamy effects helped cocaine users decelerate from their highs more comfortably. She obtained thousands of "ludes" from Frank Elman, a seventy-one-year-old Greenwich Village pharmacist with a crush on her, and soon she, Dominick and the rest were selling them at Studio 54, Xenon, and many other clubs and bars. In appreciation, the boys gave her a gold replica of the most popular Quāalude, "Lemon 714."

With Cheryl, Dominick began deceiving himself into believing that it was possible to love two women at once. Where Denise was the perfect wife and mother, Cheryl was the perfect moll. She was an outrageous anomaly, having grown up with every seeming benefit of upper middle-class WASP respectability, yet turning out every bit as self-destructive as he. She was a renegade, a broad and a pal, and she had balls.

In time, so certain of Denise's trust, he introduced Cheryl to her and they and the others went out together. "Cheryl's one of the guys," he told Denise, "our secret weapon. If anyone ever tried to get the drop on us, she'd shoot them." If Denise ever suspected anything, she never said so.

Cheryl tried to talk Dominick and the others into burglarizing Elman's country home in Connecticut—she said he had hidden a million dollars in the basement or under his driveway—but they laughed her off. "You jerks are blowing a big score," she insisted.

"Whatever you say, Ma Barker," teased Dominick.

The nickname stuck, and Ma Barker became a full-fledged member of the Montiglio crew. High on cocaine, and low on ludes and alcohol, the group binged days at a time. Matty Rega, a married man like Dominick and Henry, decided they needed a crash pad and rented a penthouse aerie in a highrise building in Fort Lee, New Jersey, just across the George Washington Bridge from Manhattan. Like children with secret passwords, hideouts, and outlaw fantasies, they nicknamed it "Hole in the Wall" and dubbed themselves "Ma Barker and the Hole in the Wall Gang."

As always, Dominick made sure to telephone Denise each day. "Nino's throwing a fit," she would report. "He keeps asking me when you're coming home."

"Tell him you haven't heard from me."

"When are you coming home?"

"I don't know. Soon. I'm making us some money."

As far as it went, the statement was true, because he was beginning to make more than he spent on drugs. The man known as Stubby in Vietnam now became known as "Cape," thanks to Henry who said Dominick moved in and out of a place where drugs were being bought and sold so quietly and so fast that he was like "Batman, the caped crusader." Batman's creators would find the comparison offensive, but the nickname Cape stuck like Ma Barker.

Eventually, Dominick always made it home, but not always in the best condition. Once, after a weekend of alcohol and cocaine, he came home intoxicated and plopped in front of the television in Nino's den to watch Monday Night Football and drink a beer. In a few minutes, reaching across a table for the bottle, he fell out of his chair and, biting deeply into his tongue as he hit the floor, passed out.

At the sight of blood pouring out of Dominick's mouth, Nino thought he had suffered a convulsion and was in danger of choking to death. He began slapping him on the back, and yelled to Rose Gaggi to call for an ambulance. Just as panic filled the room, Dominick regained consciousness.

"I guess my body was just giving me a warning," he said.

"You're an asshole," Nino said.

"Yeah, yeah, yeah."

For years, Nino would say he saved Dominick from dying that night. For his part, after a few hours sleep, Dominick got up, went straight to New Jersey and began living it up again with Matty Rega at the Bottom of the Barrel—just to show Uncle Nino who was responsible for his life, such as it was.

Between binges, Matty Rega still did automobile business with the DeMeo crew. One deal involving five cars—three Cadillacs and two Corvettes—that he bought from Patrick Testa Motorcars for five thousand dollars each in the fall of 1978 further eroded Dominick's relations with what he regarded—ever since Henry was teased for his aversion to dismemberment—as the DeMeo crew's Chris-Joey-Anthony faction.

One of the Cadillacs was confiscated by the FBI from the man in New Jersey who bought it from Rega; the man had tried to obtain license plates for the car and a clerk had become suspicious of what the FBI eventually determined to be a phony title. The bureau linked the car's equally bogus VIN plate to the same tools used to manufacture the counterfeit VINs of several other cars it had recovered in its investigation of the remains of the murdered John Quinn's retagging operation.

Because a fictitious name was originally used on the title, Rega slithered out of trouble with the FBI by claiming he bought the car from someone who walked in off the street. The man Rega sold it to, however, was out six thousand dollars and demanded a refund. Rega thought Patty should pay it, but Patty refused.

Rega tried to get Roy involved, but Roy did not care if Rega lost money. At another family-sponsored Las Vegas Night, Roy ordered Henry to wave a gun in his Hole in the Wall friend's face, to emphasize how important it was that Rega continued to lie to the FBI about the car. After several fruitless attempts to get Patty to pay, Rega complained to Dominick, who called Patty, who agreed to a sitdown at a Flatlands diner.

"You're not standing behind your work," Dominick began.

"A deal's a deal," Patty said. "Forget about it."

The discussion grew more heated until Patty abruptly got up and left Dominick in midsentence. That afternoon, he telephoned Dominick at home, but only Denise was there. Breaking crew etiquette that wives were to be told nothing, Patty told Denise that her husband had come on like a bully about a car that Rega knew was stolen and was "a fucking asshole."

When Denise relayed the remark, Dominick angrily complained to Nino and wondered aloud how he should respond.

"Clip 'im—what the fuck do I care?" said Nino. "We can do without 'im." He was in a more irascible mood than usual because the Westchester Premier Theater bankruptcy fraud case had finally gone to trial and his name had appeared in *The New York Times*. In the government's opening argument, prosecutor Nick Akerman portrayed him as a major Mafia loanshark. Accompanied by the always groomed Rose, who looked like an investment banker's wife, Nino tried giving jurors another impression as he sauntered into the courtroom. Normally a *Daily News* reader, Nino carried a copy of the *Wall Street Journal* under his arm.

Dominick was so angry that Nino's casual prescription for Patty's disrespectful behavior made momentary sense. He went to the trap in his bedroom and retrieved the Smith & Wesson handgun that Danny Grillo gave him, got into his car, collected Buzzy and Henry, and tailed Patty from his home to a girlfriend's house in Canarsie. The drive, however, cooled him off. Finally, he said to Henry, "This is stupid, let's go."

"You want me to do it?" said ever-accommodating Dirty Henry, uneasy with knives but otherwise a stone-cold killer now.

"Forget it. It's just too fucking minor. He ain't worth it. It'd only get you in deep shit. I'm the one with the okay to do it, not you."

Sometimes, coming down hard from "toot," Dominick did dimly appraise his life; it pained him to recall he was once so naive he regarded himself and Nino as real-life Corleones. During these fitful times, mired in the blue maw of cocaine meltdown, the only positive thing he could say about the way his life turned out was that, when by the perverse rules of Nino's and his world he was entitled to kill Patty, he could not squeeze the trigger. On the other hand, if he remained where he was, someday he would have to kill—not just stand on the sidelines as in the Governara case—but kill, up close where blood got into your eyes, where it really was not like war—or else he would be killed. And for what? Another high? The clever soldier had strayed too far into the jungle, and no one like Uncle Ben was around to lead him back out.

"This life of ours is a losing proposition," he said to Henry one day. "No matter what we do, we can't win."

"Maybe so, but it beats workin'."

"I guess you got a point."

"Here, Cape, have some toot."

CHAPTER 12

The Car Deal

Unaware that the NYPD and the FBI were in their own separate ways beginning to pry loose some secrets in the stolen-car world, Roy still thought it was a no-lose business and had big ideas for expansion. Laying these plans, and feeling ever more invincible, he became less attentive to quality-control, in terms of the recruits he admitted to his expanding crew, and even more violent about people who displeased him, even those in his crew.

"I'm working on something so fuckin' big, you'll be able to get your own driver," Roy told Freddy DiNome, his new boy Friday one day.

"Oh yeah?"

"Can't say too much right now, but it has to do with cars, lots of cars. Lots. You'll see, and I'm goin' give you a piece."

With this idea planted in his dyslexic but more-astute-than-people-imagined mind and therefore suddenly optimistic, Freddy, when he was not driving Roy there and about in Brooklyn, continued to mind his gas station and his tune-up shop, Broadway Freddy's Diagnostic Center with a few young helpers.

One day in 1978, at the tune-up shop, an old acquaintance of Freddy's named Vito Arena stopped by to say hello. Vito was a recent parolee and a former car thief for John Quinn. Until the early 1970s—when he grew too fat to slide beneath dashboards and disable steering-wheel locks and alarms—Vito had by his probably exaggerated but nonetheless revealing count stolen six thousand cars.

He became an armed robber next, specializing in doctors' and dentists' offices but was caught and jailed after the last of a dozen or so ripoffs. Foolishly let out early by his parole board as a good bet for rehabilitation, he began hanging out at his old Brooklyn hangouts, which included Freddy's high-performance tune-up shop in Canarsie.

Vito, who was raised in a foster home, was a rarity in "that life" in that he was openly homosexual. This caused some to keep their distance, but not Freddy, who was heterosexual but adventurously so; Freddy frequently made references to unusual sexual customs and his enjoyment of the deviant films he got from Roy.

Vito's current lover was a boy half his age and weight, a drug-damaged waif who, like Freddy before Roy more or less adopted him, needed dental work badly. Vito would eventually provide the same peridontal service Roy had for Freddy for wandering Joey Lee. Joey, like Vito a product of a broken home, had been picked up by Vito on the Coney Island boardwalk, a formerly popular and elegant esplanade gone to seed.

At the tune-up shop, Freddy asked Vito what he planned to do now.

"I'm looking for something legitimate."

The comment struck Freddy as so preposterous he did not even acknowledge it. "Why don't you get back into cars? You were so good at it."

"I don't want any more problems. I'm tired of jail. I want to go straight."

Freddy must have thought Vito's desire to go straight was a clever pun because he burst out laughing, then added, "Cars are easy for you. There's good money in it now."

Freddy added that he was broke at the moment, but the future looked promising because he was now employed by "a powerful person" who was involved in big deals. Someday, he might introduce Vito to this person, but in the meantime his brother Richie and another man were making decent money stealing cars for a chop shop in Staten Island and might need a hand.

Freddy's brother Richie was not dyslexic, but was considerably less acute. Nevertheless, Richie somehow managed to run a Flatlands body shop around the corner from Freddy's diagnostic center.

Vito was surprised to hear that Richie was apparently doing well. Where Freddy was offbeat but still competent in the clutch, Richie was a whining bumbler. In Vito's mind it was nonsensical that Richie would be doing better

than Freddy until Freddy said that the man stealing cars
with Richie was someone who had learned the trade several years before—from Vito.

"You remember Joey Scorney," Freddy told Vito.
"He says you taught him everything he knows. He talks
about you all the time."

As Vito beamed, Freddy said that Joseph Scorney was
the one who slim-jimmed and slap-hammered the cars;
Richie merely drove them away.

Vito went around the corner to Richie's shop to see
Richie and Joey Scorney, whom Vito remembered as just
a kid who liked to joy-ride and hang out at gas stations.
Now, however, Scorney was another Willie Kampf; he
overcame the typical car's security system and drove it
away within thirty to forty seconds. Like Kampf, he was
a freelancer for whatever chop shop paid the best price.
He had told Richie he would never work for "the Mafia
guys" that Freddy knew in the Canarsie junkyards.

Scorney welcomed ex-con Vito home, but left the impression that Freddy had exaggerated the extent to which
he credited Vito for his criminal knowhow. Scorney, a
foster-home graduate like Vito, acted like he owed nobody any favors.

At twenty-five, even without Mafia sponsorship, Scorney was prosperous beyond his dreams. He and Richie
were making between fifteen and twenty-five hundred
dollars per week. He drove a new thirty-five-thousand-
dollar Porsche Turbo Carrera, owned two more new cars,
and lived in a newly furnished, highrise Bensonhurst
apartment, where he had hidden twenty-five thousand
dollars in the base of an artificial plant—"in case I have
to pay a cop off," he had said; in a bank across the street,
he kept fifty-five thousand more in a safe-deposit box,
which he often visited just to fan the bills.

A month after running into Freddy and becoming reacquainted with Scorney, Vito joined Richie's and Scorney's operation—as a driver only, because of his weight
problem. Richie was more enthusiastic about adding a
new partner than Scorney was because Richie wanted to
please his brother by helping out Freddy's old friend.
Freddy had told Richie that Roy was working on "a big
car deal" that would make everyone who was part of it

very rich. Unlike Scorney, Richie wanted to keep his
Mafia option open.

With two helpers now available to drive away the cars,
Scorney became more productive. Through the summer
of 1978, the trio took between four and seven cars a
night. Though Richie occasionally grumbled that Scorney should let him be the break-and-enter man once in a
while, all was well—until late in August, when Roy told
Freddy that he was finally ready to launch the car deal
and would need Freddy's help.

Roy's plan was as big as promised. As Freddy stood
in admiring awe, Roy said he had reached an agreement
with "some Arab" who wanted to buy all the cars the
crew could steal—"hundreds, thousands, whatever"—
and ship them to Kuwait, which was somewhere in the
desert in the Middle East.

The scheme, Roy said, was perfect. They would get
five thousand dollars per car—the Arab wanted late-model
gas-guzzlers—and their only expense would be the cost
of new ignitions and door and trunk locks and keys. Because the FBI had confiscated most of John Quinn's blank
documents and VIN-making tools, the crew would have
to find its own phony paperwork and tools, but Roy anticipated no problem because he knew so many people in
the car business; besides, making the cars appear legitimate was not as big a worry now because the cars were
going half-a-world away. Even so, his police "hooks"
would give him "good" VIN numbers to use.

Roy's plan was to start small, with just five cars a
month, then expand to a hundred cars a week once the
Arab saw how efficient the crew was and was satisfied
that they could ship stolen cars past federal customs
agents without detection.

"Can you get five a month?" Roy asked Freddy.

Freddy said his brother and his partner were taking that
many a night, so of course he could.

Richie was happy to serve Roy; Vito said okay as long
as they did not have to take Cadillacs, Lincolns, or other
"exotic cars" that attracted more police interest; Scorney said no way. "I told you I ain't working for any
Mafia guys," he told Richie.

Eventually, Richie and Vito would give five different
motives for what happened next—ranging from Richie's

charge that Scorney refused Vito's request for a loan to Vito's charge that Scorney threatened to harm Richie's children if Richie ever laid a hand on his beloved Porsche. The only constant was that at the end of each story Joseph Scorney was dead.

Vito and Richie did agree on some of the facts. Although a few details were overlooked, the murder was a preplanned execution. It began when Vito fired a shot at Scorney's back as Scorney leaned over a workbench in Richie's shop, fine-tuning a slap-hammer on the evening of Thursday, September 28, 1978.

The bullet, however, was a dud. It looped in against Scorney's dungaree jacket and bounced harmlessly away. Startled by the noise, Scorney turned in time to see Vito firing a second shot. This one ripped into his chest, above the heart, and caused him to drop to one knee, too wounded to run. He lifted his head up toward the gun in Vito's hand like a man taking communion.

"Vito, what are you doing?" were his forlorn last words.

Vito lumbered toward the hapless victim and put the pistol into his mouth. "I am killing you, Joey."

Vito squeezed the trigger, but for the second time drew a dud. Scorney was dazed and choking on smoke, but not dead. Vito squeezed again, but now the gun jammed up. Richie then came out of the shadows and now that Scorney was on the floor, incapable of fighting back, picked up a hammer and with a wild show of fury drove it into Scorney's skull.

The killers then removed jewelry and apartment keys— but not a wallet with identification—from the body. Aided by a friend of Richie's, they stuffed the corpse into a fifty-gallon oil barrel and filled it with cement. They had not planned what to do with the barrel, however. But because the cement would not harden for several hours they decided to mull it over the weekend and take care of it Monday morning. They then left and drove into Manhattan and ate dinner in Chinatown.

After a boisterous meal, Vito collected his boyfriend Joey Lee and they ransacked Scorney's apartment. They found the stash of cash hidden in the artificial plant and scavenged about everything of value the pitiful little thief ever owned: more jewelry, clothes—eventually even the fifty-five thousand dollars he kept in a bank vault because they found his safe-deposit key and arranged for a friend to successfully impersonate him at the bank.

On Friday morning, Richie woke in a panic and called Freddy, who was at his home on Long Island preparing for his wedding anniversary party. Richie confessed the murder and said he had just awoke from a dream in which he saw one of Scorney's hands sticking out of the barrel and could not now wait until the weekend was over to remove the barrel—except that he did not know where to put it. Freddy told him to dump it in the ocean, then hung up.

The ocean Richie was most familiar with was near Freddy's house, so in a few hours he and the friend who helped pour the cement surprised Freddy by showing up at his house in a van with the barrel. Agitated, Freddy gave them directions to a fishing pier, but Richie complained that they might get lost, so Freddy sneaked away from his anniversary party, led them to the pier, and—becoming an accomplice to murder—helped roll the barrel out of the van just as they noticed a couple making love in the grass a short distance away. The couple never even looked up.

In a few weeks, Freddy told Vito that he had described the murder to his powerful employer, Roy DeMeo. "But you don't have to worry about him. He's a wiseguy, a connected guy. He's not going to repeat anything. He wants to meet you."

The meeting took place at Freddy's shop, as Roy was updating Freddy on preparations for the Kuwait car deal.

"I have heard a lot about you," Roy told Vito. "Freddy told me about the thing with Joe Scorney. He says that you handled it very well." Freddy did not tell Roy that the killers had gone on a hit with cheap ammunition and a defective weapon, and had not even thought of what to do with the body in the barrel.

"That was something Richie wanted done," Vito said, more than a little self-servingly.

"Well, you and Richie are going to work with us now. We've got a pretty big deal coming up here."

Vito said that sounded good to him. "You are with the most powerful crew in Brooklyn now!" added Freddy, bursting with new self-esteem.

Roy was now selling pornography in New Jersey and Rhode Island, running an Irish gang on the West Side, buying drugs from Central America, arranging to sell stolen cars to Kuwait, loansharking all over New York, and contracting himself and his crew out for murder. He was casting his net farther and farther, and confident that under his direction even people like Vito Arena and the DiNome brothers were worthy additions to his crew.

He began to embroider his reputation too. "I've killed more than fifty guys," he boasted to Dominick during a party held to show off his big new white house in Massapequa Park. The statement was not accurate—yet.

The newest additions to his crew were not the first to cause Roy aggravation. That frightful distinction went to Danny Grillo.

Roy did not know yet that Danny was an addicted gambler and that his addiction was really at the root of his participation in the Ruby Stein murder. Few others in Brooklyn were aware of his addiction either, not until early in November of 1978, when the two Brooklyn rabbis on the Gambino payroll turned over their synagogue for another installment of Las Vegas Night.

The nights were now bigger than ever. Paul, Nino, and capos from different families provided the cash for hot food and complimentary liquor, valet parking, and a half-million dollars in "house" money for thirty-odd gaming tables. Despite the fractious relationships each had with their boss, Dominick and his close buddy Buzzy retained his trust so far as money goes, and so they were in charge of the house the night Danny began losing heavily at craps.

Taking advantage of his friendly relations with Dominick, Danny asked him to "take a few markers"—allow him to continue playing on credit.

"Danny, I can't, this ain't my money."

"Come on, come on, don't worry about it," said Danny, who had given Dominick the degenerate birthday gift of an all-expenses paid night in a whorehouse four months before.

"Dammit, okay, just a few, but don't go crazy."

While Dominick attended to other matters, Danny returned to the craps table and notified the man running the game that "Dom has approved my markers," slips of paper by which Danny promised to pay the face amount. Danny promptly chased the dice down into a deep hole—one hundred thousand dollars. He then pleaded with his friend to make the markers "disappear."

Grudgingly, Dominick talked to Buzzy and, playing with fire, they destroyed half of the markers so that Danny, on paper, owed only fifty thousand.

"You can't do this to me any more because I'm really puttin' my neck out," Dominick said. "You're gonna get me killed. If they find out, they're gonna come after me."

Danny, who survived on the scores Roy cut him in on, was unable to pay even the fifty thousand in markers Dominick and Buzzy did not destroy. The game's benefactors passed the problem on to Roy: As a made man, he was responsible for his crew members' actions. Roy paid the debt and made Danny promise to quit gambling.

A week later, Danny went to a crap game in Manhattan run by a different house and lost one hundred fifty thousand dollars in markers, none of which were made to disappear. In a meeting at the Veterans and Friends, Nino and Roy sought to keep their able hijacker in the fold. They yelled and threatened him, but loaned him the money to pay his newest debt. Danny made another promise to quit gambling, then contacted his old Westies friend Jimmy Coonan and asked him to borrow money for him from Roy, but not tell Roy the money was really for him—a deception so dangerous and desperate Coonan knew Danny was off the deep end.

In a few days more, in the middle of the afternoon, Danny's wife telephoned the bunker in a panic and asked her social friend Dominick to quickly come to the Grillo house. "Danny is locked up in the garage with the car running!"

When Dominick arrived, Danny, in the face of his wife's panic, had left the car and gone into his house. He was wearing a blue bathrobe and trying to shake a black mood with white powder.

"I've reached the end of my rope," he sniffed, inhaling another line. "I lost another fifty grand last night. I am in big trouble with Nino and Roy."

"Hey, Danny," Dominick said. "This ain't the end

of the world. We're gonna figure out some way to break the news.''

''I don't know what I'm gonna do. I feel like I should just end it. I would've if my wife hadn't seen me.''

''Danny, stop being so fucking extreme.''

After Danny artificially brightened his mood, Dominick told him and his wife not to tell anyone what happened. He was afraid that if Nino or Roy found out Danny tried to kill himself, they might kill him. They would see that in his condition, Danny was ''weak'' and thus vulnerable to police pressure.

''If they kill me,'' Danny replied, ''just make sure they find my body because if it ain't found, my wife and kids don't get my insurance money. They get a half-million if my body's found.''

''I ain't going to be able to do that because I'm not going to be there. Just shut up about this.''

In two days, Roy found out about Danny—rushing out the door of his house, Dominick had told Nino that there was some kind of problem at the Grillo house. Roy questioned Dominick, who said he thought Danny had just had a fight with his wife.

Roy already knew better and had already decided what to do. ''Nah, he's cryin' like a baby about his debts. He's gettin' paranoid. We'll have to clip him.''

Dominick pretended to be indifferent. Feeling paranoid himself because he had given away fifty thousand dollars belonging to Paul, Nino, and others, he knew that to maintain Nino's and Roy's confidence, he could not show weakness or sympathy.

''That's your business, not mine,'' he said.

Roy told Nino that Danny was ''cracking up.'' He said that if Danny was arrested, even for running a stop sign, he was bound ''to fall apart'' and begin making deals with the likes of the nagging Kenny McCabe and Tony Nelson. ''We have to do something about it.''

''Do what you have to do,'' said Nino, still more concerned about his fate in the Westchester Premier Theater trial, which was still requiring his presence in a federal courtroom in Manhattan each day.

Dominick considered telling Danny to run away, but if Nino and Roy ever learned he violated their confidence, and had in effect helped steal fifty thousand dollars, he by tradition could be killed—even if he was spared, he would have been branded a thief who stole from his own family. Dominick was unsure what the future held for him, but stealing from the family meant no future at all.

He decided that even if alerted, Danny was unlikely to run away; it was better to try and talk Roy into some other remedy. Two days later, on November 15, 1978, he went to see Roy at the Gemini; he had waited a day too long. Chris and the Gemini twins had already wiped their knives clean and put the dismemberment "tool kits" Roy had given them back into the trunks of their Porsches and Mercedes.

Before talking to Roy, Dominick saw Chris and Joey and Anthony standing outside, examining one of their newest tag jobs. "Have you seen Danny?" he asked Chris, who shrugged, shook his head and smiled in a pointedly ironic way.

"Nobody will see Danny no more."

Dominick heard Joey and Anthony begin to giggle repulsively. The crew was capable of anything, but it was still a shock to imagine them cutting up a supposed friend, rather than just shooting him in the head. He stared at Chris until Chris said: "If you could have seen the way we took Danny. He went like a sucker."

For a moment, Dominick wished he had brought an M-2 like the one he had the night he stood guard over Paul's coronation, but which had since been returned to Roy's basement arsenal at the Gemini. He would have shot Chris first, in his bearded, smirking face, then obliterated Joey and Anthony, just like they were NVA soldiers popping out of a bush. He continued staring at Chris until Joey and Anthony stopped giggling and with Chris fixed him with equally hard glares. Dominick's evolutionary estrangement from the DeMeo crew's dismemberment faction was now complete.

Without a word, he broke away and went inside to ask Roy what happened. Roy was in a smirking mood too: "Danny's car was found on the bridge last night, but if anybody wants to talk to him they'll have to talk to him at the Fountain Avenue dump."

As Danny had feared, his wife and his children were not going to be able to collect on his insurance policy because he was never found. After dismembering and dumping him, his killers had driven his car to the center of the Manhattan Bridge and left it there—with the motor running and the doors open—to make it appear that a despondent Danny had jumped into the East River.

"We committed him suicide," Roy would later joke.

Danny had not gone like a sucker, but like a lamb. The day he disappeared, Roy telephoned his house and told him to come to the Gemini, meaning Joseph Guglielmo's clubhouse-apartment. Suicidal Danny did as commanded. But he told his wife Angellina that he was just going to run an errand, and only later did she think it was significant that he had seemed to make a special effort to say goodbye to her and their two daughters. Only later did she also discover that he had left the house without his wallet or watch, and also his gold rope chain with a cross, which he always wore. Willingly ending his losing streak, Danny the hardboiled ex-convict went right into the lion's den to be slaughtered.

"I wish you would've told me earlier," Roy grunted when his Westie loyalists, Jimmy Coonan and Mickey Featherstone, told him that Danny had tried to secretly borrow from Roy through Coonan. "I would've cut him up in littler pieces."

CHAPTER 13

Sprouting Wings

Even before his uncle was indicted and became preoccupied with his Westchester Premier Theater troubles, Dominick had told his wife he was going to start creating his own "things" because Nino was never going to pay him more money or set him up in some business. He meant to do more than sell drugs at his now familiar post by the ladies' powder room at Studio 54, and he became more determined to sprout his own wings after learning that Nino had arbitrarily nixed a proposal from Paul that Dominick become his new chauffeur.

The driver's job became open when Paul set him up in a concrete business. Unaware of what a party animal Dominick had become, because Nino was too embarrassed to tell him, Paul still thought of Dominick as his reliable and honorary little nephew.

"You did what?" Dominick snapped when Nino informed him. "Paul's driver was making a grand a week!"

"Yeah but you'd practically have to live with the guy. You'd never be home. I didn't think it was a good idea."

"Don't you think you should have asked me first?"

With money and a stronger will, Nino had been controlling Dominick for a long time, but he was also punishing him now for his recent behavior. "What for? You work for me, remember?"

"I'm just your fuckin' mutt."

"That's true."

Rarely was there any more talk in the bunker about a button for Dominick someday other than an occasional remark from Nino whenever Dominick irked him that made men had to demonstrate a responsible nature.

"You mean like Roy?" Dominick would fire back directly.

Technically, Dominick had met one condition of membership—in the Governara homicide, even without pulling a trigger, he had "made his bones"—helped kill someone. Usually only men who had taken part in a murder were made because this made it impossible for undercover cops or agents to infiltrate the family.

"I don't need a button," Dominick would also say to Nino now. "I don't want one." He did not sound as convincing as he wanted to sound.

Telling Denise what Nino had done, Dominick added: "It would be nice having our own house someday, but it ain't gonna happen with me as his slave. I really am gonna have to get my own things together or we're gonna be stuck in this damn bunker forever."

"That would be nice, our own house," agreed Denise, who had long since accepted her situation and was therefore uninterested in a detailed description of the "things" Dominick had in mind.

Having spent the last five years in the company of Nino and the DeMeo crew, it hardly even occurred to Dominick that money was made any way but illicitly. Schemes, scams, ripoffs—these were now the natural order of things. The only unnatural thing was the crew's repellent barbarity, but that had nothing to do with him, he hoped.

Establishing his own order, he returned to the taverns that he formerly patronized in the South Bronx ghetto—when he worked at Matty Rega's car dealership (since shut down) on Jerome Avenue, or went there to pick up payments—and reacquainted himself with the black and Hispanic proprietors, seemingly for a song and old times' sake.

In a few days, however, the bars would get surprise visits from two intruders, who talked and acted like Mafia extortionists—Fordham University graduate Buzzy Scioli and Henry Borelli—and then the owners would complain to the only friendly, connected Italian-American they knew and ask him to intercede.

"I might be able to find out what group's trying to shake ya down, but if it's certain people, I won't be able to do much except maybe get the price a little lower," seemingly sympathetic Dominick would say.

In a few days, he would report that such and such capo usually wanted five hundred dollars a week to assure harmony at his locations, but was willing now to provide the same protection for two or three hundred dollars. Invariably, the grateful owner would say something like: "I'll just give you the money and you give it to them, I don't want those two guys in here."

This classic wiseguy shakedown began netting the co-conspirators a couple of thousand dollars a month—on occasion, more—from bars in the South Bronx and, later on, in New Jersey near Rega's dealership there and the Bottom of the Barrel, his restaurant in Union City. They never had to hurt anyone: The sight of the bulge in Henry's black leather purse and the cold look in his eyes was enough.

Though he never told Nino the details, only that he had a deal in the South Bronx, Dominick was sure Nino would have been proud of the operation; the Mafia captains he named existed only in his imagination, a little Sicilian chicanery Nino would have appreciated.

The money, however, began going out as fast as it came in. As he got even deeper into cocaine, a lot went up his nose, but he also bought expensive jewelry and gifts for his wife and their children Camarie and Dominick, Jr. He treated them and half-siblings Stephen and Michele Montiglio, who were now eighteen and sixteen years old, to elegant meals, concerts, and Broadway tickets. Dominick was many things, but there was one thing he liked everyone to know about him. Unlike Uncle Nino, he was not tight with a dollar.

The shakedown racket was humming nicely along at the time Danny Grillo was murdered by his supposed friends. For a while, Dominick felt partially to blame. By saying to Nino, as he left for the Grillo house after Angellina Grillo's panicky call, that there was "some problem" there, he had inadvertently alerted Nino, and thus Roy, to the possibility of Danny being "weak."

When Roy told him, however, that Danny had wiped out some markers by helping the Westies kill and dismember Ruby Stein, he stopped feeling guilty. Though he and Denise were social friends with Angellina, he never spoke to her again. Many times after the murder, she telephoned the Montiglio apartment to ask if Dominick knew where Danny was, but he told Denise to say he was not home and had no idea where Danny was.

"Let her call the 'Rooster,'" he added, using the

nickname—inspired by Roy's slicked-back hair and double chin—by which he and Henry now sometimes referred to Roy, behind his back of course.

The morning after learning of the murder, Dominick did take a telephone call: "Henry. Did you hear what happened? Am I next?"

"What are you talking about?"

"It looks like Nino and Roy are taking out everybody who uses drugs."

"Get real, they wouldn't have a crew left."

Henry asked Dominick to meet in a small bar they had begun to frequent in SoHo, an artists' colony south of Greenwich Village in Manhattan. Pulling up, Dominick found Henry outside on the street, standing with his hands behind his back in a rigid position.

"What the fuck are you doing? You look like one of those cigar store Indians."

"If I'm next, I'd rather have you do it than anyone else. So go ahead."

"You fuck," Dominick said, with a sadness that Henry failed to detect. "Let's go inside." Dominick was distressed because a special bond he felt with Henry had just snapped. Because Henry believed that Dominick could kill him, it meant Henry did not trust him absolutely and that he could no longer absolutely trust Henry.

Inside the bar, Dominick hid his disappointment. He told Henry that Danny's murder had nothing to do with them "unless Roy ever thinks we're goin' to fall apart."

"No chance of that. I'd die before I'd be a rat. You have my permission to kill me if I ever rat out anybody on anything."

"You have my permission too. But I think my uncle would beat you to it."

In two months, Matty Rega would treat the entire Hole in the Wall Gang to Super Bowl Week in Miami—but Dominick's and Henry's friendship (though each remained a fixture of the other's universe because of their shakedown racket in the South Bronx and New Jersey) would become more of an association.

Running amok, Dominick collected a wondrous assortment of friendships and associations. At the WPA, another bar-restaurant in SoHo, he ran into Richard Emmolo, an old friend from his teenage years in Levittown and at MacArthur High School. Richard was a waiter at the WPA and his girlfriend and eventual wife was a waitress. Her name was Geena Davis; she was outgoing, sharp, and unconventionally pretty, with large lips and eyes and, in those days, black hair. She was studying to be an actress and Richard always said she was going to be a star.

Dominick and Richard renewed their friendship and began seeing one another now and then. Geena was usually working or studying. A couple of times, she and Richard did come out to Bath Beach to babysit Camarie and Dominick, Jr., when Dominick wanted to take Denise to dinner and a jazz club and no one else was around. Understandably, he never told the future Academy Award winner or his old high school friend that when they walked into Camarie's bedroom to check on her, that if they looked beneath her armoire they would find another secret trap he had built that contained an Army-issue machinegun that cocaine dealer Pedro "Paz" Rodriguez had given him, four other weapons, bullets for all, and anything else he was not supposed to have.

He also renewed his acquaintance with the Swedish ex-beauty queen who managed the Spartacus Spa, the swank Manhattan massage parlor where the late Danny Grillo treated him to a birthday session the previous July. This relationship was more of an association, although the woman did invite him to her private apartment several times, and he always accepted.

Though Nino was only suspicious, Roy—because of Henry, who was indiscreet about his and Dominick's romps—was well aware of just how wanton Dominick's philandering had become. But so far he had not told Nino and not only because he occasionally cheated on his wife too. Even with Nino, Roy rarely gave up information until there was a benefit to derive. Besides, not long after Danny was killed, Dominick's association with the Spartacus madam became valuable to Roy.

On one of their visits to Spartacus, the Westies duo, Jimmy Coonan and Mickey Featherstone, had paid with counterfeit one-hundred-dollar bills before they headed home to their wives; when a session attendant went to deposit the bills, a bank officer detected the forgeries and called the United States Treasury Department. The woman promptly gave agents physical descriptions and first names of her customers. The Westies contacted their Gambino family supervisor, Roy, who asked Dominick to ask the woman's boss to ask her employee to rethink her cooperation.

Eventually, the woman's cooperation became unnecessary either way because Secret Service agents and NYPD detectives mounted an undercover sting that linked Coonan and Featherstone to a counterfeiting ring operating in New Jersey and on the West Side; the Italophile and his Green Beret aide-de-camp would be sent to prison more than a year later, a loss for Paul, Nino, and Roy, but by then Roy's Middle Eastern car deal would be churning out money like a printing press, and the Westies duo and their ten-percent honorariums were hardly missed.

That same fall, Dominick came into possession of a firsthand account of the breakup of his deceased parents, Marie and Anthony Santamaria, that helped fortify his increasingly independent attitude toward Nino.

Ironically, the account was provided by an uncle of Roy DeMeo, whom Roy had hired to run a restaurant he had taken over on West Fourth Street in the heart of Greenwich Village in Manhattan. When Dominick and Denise, who frequented jazz clubs in the Village (when his running-around with Cheryl Anderson and others permitted) came to have dinner, the uncle and his wife joined them at their table; it was the first time they had met. The uncle, a former resident of Bath Beach, knew only that Dominick was the nephew of "Nino," an important friend of Roy's.

The men began discussing boxers, which caused Dominick to sail down memory lane: "When I was little, my father, whose nickname was 'The General,' used to take me to a bar and I'd watch him beat people up for money."

"I knew a boxer people called 'The General,' " Roy's uncle said. "What neighborhood was this?"

"Bath Beach."

"The guy's name was Anthony Santamaria. Best fighter I ever saw. Best friend I ever had."

"That was my father!"

"Jesus, you're Anthony Gaggi's nephew!"

For the next hour, Roy DeMeo's uncle described how

Anthony Santamaria and Anthony Gaggi had begun warring because the young boxer would not help the young gangster stage a phony car accident and commit insurance fraud. He described how Marie sided with her brother after her husband began drinking heavily. He described Dominick's dad as the strongest but most gentle man he ever knew, a man who really died the day he left Marie and his boy behind in the bunker. At the end of the story, Roy's uncle began crying.

Dominick had heard fragments of this story before but never the whole narrative and never with as much emotion and sympathy. He and Denise were briefly speechless. "I can see he meant a lot to ya," he finally said.

"Your father hated it when you became like Tony's kid—Tony was what we called your uncle—but Tony had him over a barrel. He ran the house because he made the money. Your dad never had but a few dollars, and he drank that up. It was the saddest situation I ever saw."

"My uncle is a piece of work," was all Dominick could think to say, before turning the conversation toward neutral memories of Bath Beach.

One thing about life now was that it was rarely dull. On December 5, 1978, Dominick beat the reaper one more time; he walked away from a violent head-on collision on an exit ramp of the Belt Parkway, the oceanside expressway rimming the bottom of Brooklyn.

The accident occurred as the sun was rising and he was driving home alone from another night of scamming in the South Bronx. Matty Rega had issued some loans of his own there, and Dominick was his collector. When one customer got a dash beside his name, they became the de facto proprietors of an open-all-night social club catering to the black community; that was where Dominick was most of the evening. In fact, the new Lincoln he was driving at a high rate of speed had been leased for him by the same indebted customer.

The two drivers gave police different versions of the accident, but somehow they ended up in opposite directions of the same lane on the exit ramp leading to Bath Beach. Their cars collided with such force the other driver was propelled through the windshield of his Chevrolet Vega and against the windshield of the Lincoln, whose front end compacted like an accordion as he bounced up and away. The man suffered serious injuries, but eventually recovered; Dominick had a sore neck a few days, but that was it.

"I walked again," he told Buzzy.

"No shit."

"That was the fourth time, forgetting all the battles, just counting crashes and bombs, that I should've been wasted."

"It would've been ridiculous to check out in an accident a few blocks from home."

"That guy upstairs wouldn't ever make it that easy for me. When I go, God has something special planned." The reference to God was about all the religion Dominick or Nino or Roy or any of the other Italian-American crew members took away from their Roman Catholic upbringings. God was in charge of all death, that's all. He either hammered you, or cut you some slack.

Nino was scornful when Dominick finally made it home that morning. "That's what you get for stayin' out all night boozin'. Your luck's gonna run out."

"I didn't have that much to drink."

"Sure, Dom."

Having only spent a few hours in jail, despite a criminal career spanning three decades, Nino had quite a lucky streak of his own going. A few days after the accident, he learned he would no longer have to buy a *Wall Street Journal* before walking into court each day. Before the Westchester Premier Theater case went to the jury, United States District Court Judge Robert Sweet said that the government had failed to prove Anthony Gaggi had sufficient knowledge of the theater's pending bankruptcy and therefore he could not be convicted of fraud.

Nino's voice was on a few recordings played at the trial, but never in a way that proved he knew what was going on. The directed verdict of acquittal (the judge ruled that the ten other defendants did have knowledge) enabled Nino to portray himself as a victim of government oppression. Zealous prosecutors had tried to frame him twice—once for stolen Cadillacs in Brooklyn, then for fraud in Westchester County—but against great odds he had triumphed both times.

"I told you that you'd beat it!" crowed an inebriated Dominick, who momentarily returned to Nino's good graces by showing up for a celebration dinner with Paul and the family's capos at Tommaso's.

"Yeah, okay meathead, so you were right—once. Now we gotta get back to normal, right? You'll come to the club every day and we'll get along, right?"

"Right."

To make Nino feel even better and to demonstrate his respect for tradition, waning as it was, Dominick offered Nino some money from one of his Bronx scores. He had continued to make only vague remarks about his own things; Nino, who had insisted his nephew learn about their life by reading between the lines, did not need details to know Dominick was in his own erratic fashion trying to fashion his own criminal identity, the way Nino himself once had done to demonstrate his ability to his mentor, Frank Scalise. It was a development he welcomed. Even so, locked into his generational framework and personality, he still did not grasp the full destructive degree of Dominick's use of drugs, or women.

"No, no, you keep that, I don't want it, you keep that, you earned it," he said when Dominick offered him the money.

Nino's magnanimity was touching. Dominick and his uncle were on opposites sides of a tug rope, and the younger man was winning the match, he thought. But here was a pull in the opposite direction. "Well, I got a few things goin' on," Dominick said, "if you ever need a little."

"Forget about it, I want you to watch Roy a little closer, that's all. I'm worried about him. I'm wonderin' how much money he's really making."

"I've wondered the same."

"He's got something new and big going with cars, we're gonna have to keep an eye on him."

"Whatever you say, boss."

In a few days of course, Dominick was up and away again, but this time he would bring back business for Nino and Roy; his coke pals Matty Rega and Queens-based Pedro "Paz" Rodriguez asked him if he knew anyone who could loan them ninety-six thousand dollars in a hurry.

"I might," he enjoyed replying. "But, Paz, since my contacts in Brooklyn don't know you, they might want some collateral."

Paz scoured his apartment and began tossing dozens of gold and diamond baubles—rings, watches, bracelets—into a gym bag. Dominick took the bag to Nino, an informed appraiser of jewelry because an old friend and loan customer was a jeweler.

"This gaudy shit is actually worth some money," Nino said. He went to the cash trap he kept in his mother's apartment and gave Dominick half of the ninety-six thousand. "Go see Roy, tell him to give you the other half, but we gotta have a hundred and two grand back tomorrow."

Dominick did not tell his uncle that Rega and Paz wanted the money for a cocaine deal and he never told Paz the names of those who had agreed to front the money. He also stayed shacked up with Cheryl Anderson at the Hole in the Wall for four days because Paz was unable to get the hundred and two thousand together until he sold off the cocaine.

When Paz did collect the money, Dominick said, "I can't go back to Brooklyn with only this because you're late. But if I go back with more, everything will be fine. I guarantee it."

Paz added another six thousand and Dominick caught up with Nino at Tommaso's. Nino glared and refused to speak until Dominick said, "I made ya a little extra, here's one-o-eight."

Dominick savored how the anger melted away from Nino's face, just as he expected.

"Where were ya?" Nino said warmly. "I didn't know if somethin' happened to ya. I was really worried."

In January, 1979, the Westchester trial that the judge had severed Nino from ended in a hung jury, thanks to a single holdout. The government, however, quickly mounted a retrial in which all defendants who did not plead guilty beforehand, such as the talkative Gregory DePalma, were convicted.

After all was said and done, Paul and Nino wound up taking a bath on their investment in the theater—and

DePalma was sent away to do the prison time Nino dreaded: three years.

"That's what he gets for shootin' his mouth off all over the lot," Nino said.

CHAPTER 14

Bay of Pigs

As murderous as it already was, the DeMeo crew's worst days lay ahead. As its tentacles spread far beyond the Gemini, as it began to make fantastic sums, it began weaving a story of infamy not seen in the United States since the era of another Brooklyn-based gang, Murder, Incorporated, four decades before. With more to lose, the crew murdered even more, and as its knife-happy and hair-trigger reputation grew, so did its contract work. In 1979, the DeMeo crew became a murder machine; no one who ran afoul was safe, including, once again, one of its own.

"Those are a favor for someone in Manhattan," Roy casually remarked to new crew member Vito Arena after Vito walked into the Gemini clubhouse one day and pretended not to be startled by the sight of two naked corpses hanging upside down from a shower bar in the bathroom. As with others before and some yet to come, the victims were never identified because they were never found.

With each new murder adding to the foul aura of invincibility Roy already gave off, a collective derangement took hold—and the former little bully fat boy from Flatlands stayed at the feverish center. Young crew members began comparing murder to "getting high," Roy to "having the power of God." Perversely, he was like God now—in charge of death.

The Danny Grillo murder had shown Roy and three of his longest-serving crew members—Chris and the Gemini twins—to be capable of using their tool kits to eliminate problems in the crew itself. But it also showed that over time, and through much experimentation, a ritualistic style of killing had evolved.

From now on, the ritual would be followed whenever possible. Attempts would be made to lure anyone slated for dismemberment to the clubhouse-apartment of Joseph Guglielmo, the man the crew had nicknamed Dracula. The victim would be shot in the head, stabbed in the heart to stop it from pumping blood, then hung upside down over the bathtub to allow the blood to drain and congeal, then laid on a tarpaulin, sawed apart, packaged and dumped.

Roy or Henry normally did the shooting, Chris the stabbing, the others the grisly aftermath—although Roy, Chris, and Dracula always helped with that too. Chris always worked in his underwear so as not to stain the fine and expensive clothes he always wore now. The others thought it was funny, but kept their clothes on and just never rubbed the surgical gloves they wore onto their trousers. The ritual became known as the "Gemini method."

As requested by Nino, Dominick began keeping a closer eye on Roy. And so, early in February of 1979, he witnessed the onset of the rampage. The instigating event occurred in the Gemini Lounge, not the clubhouse beyond its back wall.

That night, as was customary on Fridays, the bar featured a live rock band that drew in ordinary neighborhood residents, including a young, smallish male patron with dirty blond hair who, for reasons Dominick never learned, told a Gemini barmaid that Roy was a "motherfucker."

Most barmaids who worked at the Gemini over the years were as loyal to the secret owner of the bar, Roy, as his crew. More than one had groped with him in the clubhouse, which was a crew lovenest too. The slur was promptly relayed to Roy, who promptly and drunkenly confronted the offender. Departing from his normal practice of never drinking at the Gemini, closet-drinker Roy had been hoisting several Cutty Sarks.

"Come on outside and get in my car," he said, "I want to talk to you."

When the young man hesitated, Roy gently laid an arm on his shoulder. "Come on, what're ya afraid of? The worst that's gonna happen is, you're gonna get smacked."

Concluding his manhood was at stake, the young man stepped outside with Roy. Dominick followed and watched him get into the passenger seat of Roy's Cadillac. He was thinking even Roy would not dare kill someone for and under these circumstances when from about thirty feet, he saw a flash of blue-orange light and a head bounce against the passenger window, and in an amazed moment more Roy driving by, waving and smiling like the slumped body beside him was a drunk buddy to be taken home. The young man was never seen again.

"Roy is fucking out of control," Dominick told Nino.

"You should talk. Anybody else see it?"

"Don't think so." Dominick now had little faith in Nino's desire, even ability, to discipline Roy unless Roy's behavior directly affected Nino or, indirectly, Paul. So Nino's casual reaction did not really surprise: "Okay, I'll talk to him."

Within a week, Peter Waring, a young cocaine dealer who grew up on the same Canarsie street as Joey and Anthony and did business with the crew, was released from jail after a second arrest. His release was too sudden for crew members: They suspected, correctly, that he had agreed to cooperate with narcotics cops—and he too was never seen again by anyone who loved him, such as his wife and child.

Twelve days later, a sixty-year-old man, Frederick Todaro, stepped out of his car and into a wet stinging snow. He walked into the clubhouse, and he too was never seen again. Todaro's misfortune was that while in divorce court, he had placed his film-processing businesses in his nephew's name. The nephew, a patron of the Gemini Lounge, decided he wanted to retain ownership of the companies and enter the pornography business with Roy, whom he had sold some sick films to. So he hired Roy to eliminate the now-divorced uncle who stood in his double-crossing way.

He believed Roy and the crew were available for the job because a story going around in the Gemini Lounge involved a man charged with rape. He beat the case, but lost to Roy and the crew, which was hired by the victim's connected father to ensure that justice denied by the legal system was achieved somehow. That body, Scott Carfaro's, was left to be found, to prove the justice and to illustrate the effectiveness of Roy's court-for-hire.

Freddy DiNome witnessed Todaro's murder—a horrifying demonstration of the Gemini method. Todaro was in the market for a car, and Roy had told Freddy to lure him to the clubhouse on the pretense Roy had a good used one for sale. Freddy knew Todaro's days were numbered, but not how they were to end.

As he walked in behind Todaro, Freddy was dumbfounded to see Chris in his underwear and in possession of a large butcher knife jumping out from behind a door, and then in a scene right out of *Psycho*, Roy gliding in from the kitchen and shooting Todaro in the head and with his other hand wrapping a towel turban-like around the wound as Chris in a frenzy jammed the blade into the old man's heart several times.

Joey and Anthony materialized out of the clubhouse shadows and helped Roy and Chris drag the body to the bathroom. They all waited a while, then laid it on the floor on a blue tarpaulin of the type to cover swimming pools, dismembered it and packaged it in green plastic garbage bags. Freddy was struck by the carefree manner in which Roy and the others went at the work—but he had duped Todaro to his death and did find enough resolve to help them take the packages to the Fountain Avenue dump.

Sometime afterward, Vito Arena visited the clubhouse again to huddle with Roy on the Kuwait stolen-car operation, currently on hold until a way to ship the cars overseas was devised; Vito noticed that the floor by the bathroom had been freshly painted—despite the crew's precautions, some blood always made it to the floor.

"There's a lot of history in that floor," said Dracula.

"What'd ya mean?"

"That floor has had to be painted many times."

The killing went on unabated. A month after Todaro's murder, four more people died, no doubt by the Gemini method. One of the victims was a woman, and perhaps the first female the crew ever sent to the dump. These treacherous murders prompted more treachery and killing, none of it planned, as the crew began careening out of control and running over innocent bystanders. The spectacle, which led to a big command change in the crew, became known as the "Cuban crisis."

The origin of the crisis lay in familiar terrain—cars and loans. In the early 1970s, Roy befriended and loaned money to the owner of a Flatlands body shop, Charles Padnick, whom he hired to install bulletproof windows in one of his Cadillacs. Until 1973, when Padnick left Brooklyn and opened a similar business in Miami Beach, Roy regularly visited his shop. Roy and wife Gladys also attended the bar mitzvah of Padnick's son, Jamie.

Padnick and his wife Muriel also knew Chris, but not as "Christopher Rosalia," as Chris, using his wife's maiden name, had identified himself on his driver's license. The Padnicks knew him as "Harvey Rosenberg" because they had met him and his parents at a Catskill resort years earlier, when six-year-old Harvey was just beginning to hate his name and his Jewishness.

By 1978, Padnick's shop in Florida was floundering; he flew to New York and borrowed twenty thousand dollars from Roy. Business did not get any better, however, and he borrowed ten thousand more from others just to pay the vig on the loan with Roy.

One night in January of 1979, Muriel Padnick was surprised to see Harvey Rosenberg standing in the driveway of her Florida home, talking to her husband. Concluding Harvey was visiting his nearby relatives and had just come by to say hello, she greeted him warmly and gave him a macrame hanging that she had knitted and asked him to give it to his aunt, a friend of hers. She was unaware that to pay Roy off, her husband and her son Jamie, now age twenty and working in his father's shop, had gone into the cocaine business; though amateurs, they began at a professional level—that week, they sold Chris one kilogram (somewhat over two pounds) of cocaine.

Cocaine was so abundant in the Miami area that many otherwise lawful people, tempted by dreams of a score to retire on, became drug dealers. The Padnicks' connection to this white-gold rush was an otherwise legitimate body- and fender-man who worked for them—William Serrano, a Cuban immigrant who saw a chance to help his bosses while making some easy money for himself and his family.

In a former job at a liquor store, Serrano became friendly with a man he introduced to his family only as "Pepon." Pepon was friendly with a dark-skinned Cuban cocaine merchant who permitted himself to be known only as "El Negro"—the black one. Pepon told El Negro that people Serrano worked with, Charles and Jamie Padnick, knew a group of "wealthy Italians" from New York who wanted to buy a lot of cocaine, and thus the one-kilo deal—a dry run to see if everyone involved could be trusted—was arranged. Importantly, Serrano handled the negotiations; Pepon and El Negro remained in the background.

Fresh from the Todaro murder, Chris and Anthony traveled to Florida in February and proposed a large deal—twelve kilos. The amount they agreed to pay never came out, but was likely five to six hundred thousand dollars; whatever the figure promised, they never intended to pay it.

The transaction was set for Saturday, March 17, St. Patrick's Day. The plan was for Charles Padnick and William Serrano to fly to New York with two companions who were actually allied with El Negro: his girlfriend, who had borne him a son, and a cousin, who was his bodyguard. Traveling as a married couple, they would transport the cocaine in a suitcase and turn it over after the "wealthy Italians" paid Padnick and Serrano.

The unlikely quartet made it to New York, and then to the Fountain Avenue dump. At least one of them, probably El Negro's cousin, must have smelled a rip-off and was able to get off some shots before he succumbed to superior firepower, because Chris went to a hospital that night with a superficial bullet wound on the side of his head and another in his left hand—and a bogus story about having been shot by a motorist during a traffic dispute.

The alarm bells sounded in Miami right away because El Negro did not get a reassuring telephone call from his girlfriend. At one o'clock in the morning, Muriel Padnick received the first of many panicky calls from a man she had never spoken to—Pepon. He asked to speak to Jamie Padnick, but she refused to wake him.

The next day, Muriel told Jamie about the calls. He went to a newsstand and returned home with a national edition of the *Daily News*. Without explaining to his mother that he was looking for news of a big cocaine bust in New York, he perused it front-to-back, then made his own phone calls. In a few hours, she left for an errand. When she came back, Jamie was gone—forever, because he flew to New York to investigate what hap-

pened to his father and the others and was subjected to
the Gemini method too.

Two days later, Muriel Padnick telephoned Roy at the
Gemini Lounge; her husband had given her the number
and instructions to call his good friend Roy if she ever
needed anything.

"Something is happening, I don't know what it is,"
she told Roy. "Jamie is missing and Charlie is missing
and I don't know what to do. Charlie went to New York;
I think Jamie did too."

"I'll try my best to find out what's goin' on," Roy
lied. "Don't worry."

In Florida, meanwhile, another of El Negro's men informed the relatives that everyone who went to New York
was probably dead. El Negro himself called Serrano's
brother to a furtive meeting in a darkened room full of
bodyguards and, keeping his face in shadow, vowed: "I
promise you, I will take care of it."

Muriel Padnick never telephoned Roy again, but he
probably would not have taken her call because suddenly
a bigger problem than an anxious wife and mother landed
in his lap.

In Florida negotiating the deal, Chris had made a terrible mistake. It arose from his wishful penchant for
sometimes introducing himself as "Chris DeMeo" and
boasting to strangers that his father, Roy, was a powerful
man in Brooklyn. Portraying himself that way to Serrano
was not the problem, because Serrano was going to be
dead soon anyway; the mistake was in assuming Serrano
was the source of the cocaine, not El Negro, to whom
Serrano had passed along the information before leaving
on the doomed trip to New York.

In the worst of all coincidences for Roy and Chris, El
Negro also knew someone who might know about the
DeMeo family of Brooklyn: Paz Rodriguez, the cocaine
dealer who kept Matty Rega and Dominick Montiglio
happy.

Because Dominick had not identified the "Brooklyn
contacts" who put up the ninety-six thousand dollars Paz
borrowed through him a few months before—money that,
in another twist, probably funded a deal with El Negro—
Paz did not know Nino, Roy, or anyone in the crew. But
he told El Negro that two coke customers of his who

regularly came to his apartment probably would know who in New York was capable of such treachery, especially the one with the Brooklyn contacts.

"Could you find out who this Chris DeMeo is?" Paz said when Dominick, unaware of the slaughter, came with Rega to Paz's apartment later that week. Handing over a slip of paper with the name, Paz added: "He set up a deal, five people weren't heard from no more. Two Jews, three Cubans. One of the Cubans was the mother of the son of my friend, my top supplier. He wants this Chris bad."

From the look Rega gave, Dominick assumed Rega had already told Paz who Chris was; Rega still carried a grudge against Chris for the pushy way Chris collected Roy's loans. Dominick also assumed that because five people were made to disappear in a drug ripoff, Chris had to be involved. Still, until he spoke to Nino, he chose to be coy.

"I don't know a Chris DeMeo, but let me check it out."

He left Paz's apartment astonished that Chris's Roy-worship would result in such reckless talk while setting up such a murderous ripoff. Then, he recalled how Chris smirked over Danny Grillo's murder and his own prediction to Henry that Chris "would dig his own grave someday," and he smiled inside. If the day had come, the world would be better off. Arriving home, he told Anthony Gaggi he was bearing bad news.

"What the fuck have those cowboys done now?"

"It looks like they set a bunch of people up and took them out, and now some Cuban people in Florida are very pissed off."

Nino instructed Dominick to visit Roy and get the details, but Roy was evasive and advised Dominick to "stall" the Cubans until he could learn what happened.

Not for a second did Dominick or Nino doubt that Roy already knew what happened and was personally involved, but Nino told Dominick to attempt to stall the Cubans. The next day, however, Paz told Dominick: "They are very concerned in Florida and they are sending some people up here."

Informed of this implicit threat, Roy now said Chris used his name without his knowledge and that Joey and

Anthony also were involved. "It's a crisis situation with the Cubans now, our own little Bay of Pigs," Dominick replied. "I'm gonna have to tell them something, or they're gonna start shootin'."

Both men spoke to Nino in a diner across from Tommaso's; after hearing Roy's claim and Dominick's warning, he said: "Go tell 'em it was Chris."

Dominick quietly relished the role he was playing, ferrying life and death messages among Nino, Roy, and Paz in an attempt to mollify the mysterious El Negro and preclude a showdown between Gambinos and Cubans. It was diplomacy of the most urgent kind, and a chance to restore relations with Nino and demonstrate his ability. It could even be the episode Nino was waiting for, the test on which he would pass judgment—and pass on the torch! His heroic notions turned inside out by the last six years, his calculating yet still-boyish heart thumped anew with the romantic attraction he felt for "that life" as a child—the daring uniqueness of it!

"I found Chris, his name is Rosenberg," he told Paz. "We know where he is, what do you want?"

Given the precipitating carnage, El Negro's proposal to end the crisis, passed along by Paz, was generous: "We just want him killed and that will end it. But you have to do it in a way that makes the newspapers. We won't take your word for it. It has to be in the papers."

More than fair enough, Nino said. Bolstering his nephew's belief that the situation was a test and he was turning the matter entirely over to him, he added: "Tell Roy to take care of it."

"It's the only way we avoid a big battle," Dominick told a heavily distressed Roy. More than he dared show, he was enjoying seeing Roy twist in the wind. "Nino says to do it."

"I'll take care of it," Roy said solemnly.

All this took place within ten days of the five murders, but the drama—predictably, Paul Castellano was never clued in—would drag on nearly six more weeks. Revealing a heart not yet totally gone to stone, Roy could not muster a murderous attitude toward Chris, his original recruit and would-be son.

"Chris is a hard guy to set up," Roy said after Dominick reported that Paz and El Negro were getting "antsy."

In reality, Chris was an easy target. He was never told anything. Unaware his sacrifice had been demanded and approved, he went about exercising regularly with Roy in a Long Island health club and renovating the new fancy house on the waterfront in Queens that he had recently purchased—in between all his recent murders. The house, he had told the others, was directly across the street from one owned by "that Jew comedian Sam Levenson."

While Roy agonized, Dominick began going to Paz's apartment each day—to monitor the Cuban mood and counsel patience. Soon, he was introduced to two El Negro gunmen, up from Florida. He pulled Paz aside: "Let's don't get carried away here. We'll have bodies all over the place." He had begun going to the apartment "dressed up"—armed with his Smith & Wesson, which was tucked into a girdle-like contraption he wore beneath his trousers.

With the arrival of El Negro's men, Roy began hiding out in his expensive waterfront home. "The Rooster is a nervous wreck," Henry told Dominick after speaking to Roy. "He's seeing Cuban hit men all over the place."

This was about as prophetic a statement as Henry ever made.

Seeking only to make money for college, an eighteen-year-old part-time vacuum cleaner salesman named Dominick A. Ragucci wandered into Roy's paranoid realm shortly after seven o'clock on Thursday evening, April 19, 1979, the fifth day of the fifth week of the Cuban crisis.

Ragucci lived with his parents in Massapequa, which was adjacent to Massapequa Park, where at 159 White-wood Drive nervous wreck Roy was holed up in his security-conscious home with his cousin Joseph Guglielmo and several weapons. Ragucci was a recent honors graduate of a military academy and now a criminal justice student at Nassau Community College: He wanted to be a cop. He had just begun selling vacuum cleaners door-to-door to help pay for his education, dates with the woman he intended to marry, and upkeep on his car, a 1971 Cadillac on its second paint job.

He had already made contacts with two potential customers on Whitewood Drive and had an appointment with one that night at a home down the street from Roy. Afterward, as he drove off in a fateful direction, he pulled over to the curb in front of Roy's house, probably to record notes in the business journal he kept. Several Electrolux vacuum cleaner boxes were visible in his car's backseat, and rosary beads hung from the rearview mirror.

Dominick Ragucci could have passed for a Cuban. His mother was Puerto Rican, his father Italian. He was dark, smallish, and fresh-faced, but had recently grown a thin mustache that made him seem older than eighteen. He was wearing a gray sportscoat and trousers and a flowery white shirt with a gray tie; in the gathering dusk, through the lens of the security camera mounted on a pole outside Roy's home, and especially to the anxious eyes looking at him on the monitor inside, Ragucci could have, and did, pass for a Cuban assassin.

When he saw two men, Roy and Guglielmo, walking toward him with what appeared to be guns, Ragucci slammed his car into gear and sped away—confirmation, in Roy's state of mind, that he was indeed an assassin. Roy and his cousin hustled into Roy's Cadillac and gave chase. Ragucci might have thought they were just a couple of lunatics trying to frighten him until he turned off Whitewood Drive and sped into the nearby community of Amityville, the bucolic setting for a popular horror story.

In Amityville, with Roy behind the wheel, the Cadillac came up behind Ragucci's car. Holding onto the wheel with one hand and leaning out the window with a pistol in the other, Roy fired several shots into Ragucci's car. The young salesman zoomed off again, but over seven more miles of crowded streets—despite running several red lights, weaving perilously through traffic, and barreling across median strips and curbs—he could not shake the wildmen who inexplicably kept firing bullets into his car, shattering three windows.

Nino's "cowboy" references to Roy were never more apt as Roy blazed away, endangering the lives of countless motorists and bystanders, hitting Ragucci's car twenty times. His cousin Dracula kept reloading the pistol, so excited he twice shot holes in the floorboard as the cars raced into neighboring Suffolk County.

Finally at a busy intersection, Ragucci's car crashed into another; despite two flat tires, and with fear only he could describe, he pulled away and drove another five hundred feet before his disabled vehicle came to a halt and Roy's car pulled alongside. Roy jumped out, assumed a combat firing position right out of police training films and kept shooting until his pistol was empty and the teenager was dead from a tight cluster of seven bullet wounds to the upper body. The hapless victim did not even have time to try and run; he was found still buckled in his seatbelt and with his eyes open, as though he had died of fright.

A passerby walked up to Ragucci's car, looked inside, turned off the ignition and then left without ever coming forward again. Hundreds of others saw parts of the fanatical tragedy, but Suffolk County police reported that no one saw enough to help them make much sense of what happened. Some witnesses said only that the shooter returned to his car with executioner-like poise.

"If that guy wasn't a cop, I ain't talkin' to nobody," one added, more astutely than he imagined.

The next day, Roy read a Long Island *Newsday* story and realized, as he later said, that he made a "mistake." He drove into Brooklyn and told Freddy he felt "bad," then asked him to repair his car's bullet-ridden floorboard. He later gave the car to Patty Testa, who quickly sold it through his dealership.

In a few days more, Ragucci's parents emerged from their grief and offered a five thousand dollar reward for information. Ben Ragucci, owner of a local fireplace and garden-supply store Roy had patronized, bitterly complained that the paucity of witnesses to his son's murder reminded him of an infamous murder in Queens, where he lived years before. The victim in that case was Kitty Genovese, whose death became a memorial to urban indifference when her screams for help went unanswered by neighbors.

"I'm heartbroken and sick," Ben Ragucci said. "How the hell could this be?"

In reality, Suffolk County police did have a good lead provided by a witness. John Murphy, intelligence officer of the NYPD Auto Crime Unit, discovered this after reading a followup story in *Newsday* and saying to another cop, "I bet that Canarsie crew has something to do with this. They're the only people who are this wild."

Murphy telephoned a Suffolk detective and asked, "Has the name Patty Testa come up in your investigation?"

The detective's reply showed that Murphy's obsession with Patty was not unwarranted: Indeed, a witness had said the gunmen's car was equipped with special transporter, or automobile dealer, license plates and provided a number that was traced to Patrick Testa Motorcars, which unfortunately had reported to the Secretary of State some time earlier that the plates had been stolen.

"That's what they do all the time, report the plates stolen and put 'em on another car!" Murphy said.

"Well, as far as we're concerned, it doesn't rule him in, or out, of our investigation," the detective said.

Murphy hung up thinking that Suffolk County, which had as many murders the year before as New York City had in an average week, was never going to go anywhere with the case, and he was right.

Portraying himself a victim of circumstances, Roy went to Nino's house to explain his mistake. "The guy looked like a killer and when I tried to talk to him, he took off."

"An eighteen-year-old vacuum cleaner salesman, eh, Roy?"

"Nino, I'm tellin' ya, I thought he was gonna to take out my whole house."

"I told you the Cubans weren't gonna make a move yet, I have that situation under control," Dominick interjected. "For now."

"Ah fuck you, you weren't there."

"Okay, Rooster. Cock-a-doodle-do."

"What did you say? You better watch your smart ass."

"All right, morons," Nino said, "that's it. Roy, take care of this stupid bullshit because there are gonna be other people killed who don't deserve it. Just end it."

In a few days, Nino left for Florida and instructed Dominick to provide regular updates. Dominick kept going to Paz's apartment each day to say the matter would end soon. But Roy still could not bring himself to do what he promised. Instead, as Ben Ragucci kept speaking out about his son's murder, Roy instructed Freddy DiNome to reconnoiter Ragucci's place of business "in case we have to hit him" because he was "puttin' too much heat" on the Suffolk County police.

From the journal found in Ragucci's car, Suffolk detectives did discover he kept an appointment a few doors from Roy's home. They tried to interview Roy, but he ordered them off his property. They did speak to Patty, but he stuck by the story that the plates had been stolen. End of case.

Symbolically, the murder also ended what little marriage Roy had. The bargain Gladys had made with Roy depended on him keeping his crimes out of the house and away from their children; she did not need to know for certain that he actually did it to be acutely embarrassed and angry that during a time of a great community uproar over the death of such an innocent kid, the cops were coming to her home to ask her husband questions about it. Everyone on Whitewood Drive knew Roy was a suspect, even if the case was going nowhere. Although Roy stayed close with his kids, he and Gladys retreated to different corners of the house.

Two weeks after the murder, Paz confronted Dominick about the Chris Rosenberg situation. "Is this gonna happen or what? If it ain't, we're gonna take care of it, and who knows what'll happen."

To buy a little more time, Dominick warned of a bloodbath. "You want to start in? Fine. You ain't scared of them? Fine. But they ain't scared of you either. So lots of people will die. Be patient. Let the Italians straighten out their own problems."

Sure the game was up, Dominick flew to Florida and checked into a hotel near Nino's retreat. He took Cheryl Anderson along for company and Matty Rega for the bill. Alone, he went to see Nino and said war was imminent. Nino then telephoned Roy and told him to stop stalling.

The situation was comparable to a hangman whose own son's neck was in the noose. But Roy was a professional hangman and finally he resolved to open the trap door.

That night, minus Chris, he convened an emergency meeting of his crew to draft a plan for a murder that would make the newspapers. Seeing Roy come to grips with the matter, the crew did too. It was easiest for Henry, who volunteered to do the work, but Roy said he had to; he brought Chris into "that life" and had to be the one to take him out, no matter how much it hurt. And it did hurt. "I loved that kid," he said, in a deliberate past tense, and with glumness the others had never seen before.

The regular Friday-night shapeup of the DeMeo crew occurred two days later, on May 11, 1979. Roy arrived at the clubhouse a little early and put a fresh handgun into a brown paper bag like the one in which he always carried his cash. He laid the bag on the kitchen table where the crew always ate their meals and divvied the week's profits.

Henry and Freddy had been told to make themselves late, but Chris and his would-be brothers Joey and Anthony all arrived at about the usual time, eight o'clock. Chris arrived in a jet-black BMW, his wife's car, because she was using his Mercedes. Inside, as he normally did when greeting Roy, he kissed him on the cheek; he said hello to the others and sat down at the kitchen table, utterly at ease.

Roy smiled, reached into the bag, pulled out the pistol and in one smooth movement shot Chris in the head. Chris fell to the floor—not yet dead, however. Feeling remorse for once, Roy was slow to react when Chris even staggered to one knee, but Anthony rose to the occasion and fired four more bullets into Chris's head, putting an end to his misery and made-man dreams.

After wiping the blood from their old friend's head wounds, Joey and Anthony put an arm under each of Chris's shoulders and walked him out of the clubhouse as if they were taking a drunk buddy home and put him in the passenger seat of his wife's BMW.

To meet the Cubans' demand that the murder make the newspapers, Roy knew that something more unusual than merely leaving Chris and the car on a road somewhere was necessary. Only a handful of the city's average thirty-five murders per week make the newspapers, and though the BMW might stir an editor to decide the murder was unusual enough to be newsworthy, it might well not, particularly on a weekend. So the plan developed two days earlier was put into action.

Anthony drove the BMW with the body propped against the passenger window and abandoned it a couple of miles away on a four-lane stretch of highway dissecting the open grasslands of the Gateway National Recreation Area. The road linked Brooklyn to Belle Harbor and Neponsit, adjacent seaside communities in Queens where Chris and his wife lived and where he was renovating their new home across the street from Sam Levenson.

Freddy DiNome and Henry Borelli followed in a separate car; after Anthony had exited the BMW and joined Roy in yet another car, Freddy drove by and Henry raked the BMW with machinegun fire—even in New York, such an apparent assassination should make news; although the plan was not executed very well, it would.

Perhaps because Henry was too excited by the chance to put even false nails in Chris's coffin, perhaps because Freddy drove by too fast, Henry shot wildly during the first pass-by, and so a second was necessary. This time, using a Thompson submachinegun out of Roy's arsenal, Henry put several bullets into the car and the body.

After patrol officers came upon the scene near midnight, Detective Frank Pergola of the NYPD's 12th Homicide Zone squad was dispatched to investigate. Pergola had been a cop since 1965 and a homicide detective since 1977, when he was drafted from a citywide burglary squad and assigned to the "Son of Sam" serial murder case.

Examining the interior of the BMW, he quickly began to suspect that the murder occurred elsewhere because of the position of the victim—in his haste, Anthony had left the legs of the body straddling the console between the front seats—and because there was hardly any blood in the car even though it appeared the victim had been struck at least a dozen times.

The next clue for Pergola was sitting nearby in a Mercedes Sports Coupe that had pulled off the road—Joey Testa. Joey said he had noticed his friend Chris Rosenberg's car while passing by and, after he stopped to ask the police what was wrong, he was shocked to hear that Chris was apparently dead.

"Then you can identify the body for me?" asked Pergola, who, according to a driver's license in the victim's wallet, thought he was investigating the death of a Christopher Rosalia of Miami.

"I don't think I can do that," said Joey, a good actor. "We were friends all our lives."

Young men, murder, and expensive cars triggered Pergola's memory. In 1977, while investigating the Son of Sam killings, he reviewed many homicide files—among them, the case of Andrei Katz, which was so savage he made a point of studying it carefully. Now he recalled that Joey Testa was charged and acquitted in the Katz homicide and that Chris was an uncharged suspect.

Returning to the BMW, Pergola noticed another Mercedes slow down as it passed the scene. He noted its license-plate number and asked an officer to run a check, which came back to Anthony Senter, whom he remembered as another uncharged suspect in the Katz case. "All we need now is what's-his-name, Henry Borelli!" he said to himself as the name of the second person actually charged in the Katz murder jumped out of his memory.

In another hour, Pergola ran into Henry—at Chris's widow's apartment in Belle Harbor. Joey and Anthony were there too. Joey, who had followed Chris out of Canarsie and with his wife and two daughters moved into an apartment on the same Belle Harbor block, had already broken the news to Stephanie. Anthony and Henry said they had come by to console her, although as Henry later said to Vito Arena, they were really there to make sure she did not say anything "out of the way."

When Pergola walked in, Stephanie was crying; so were Joey and Anthony, but not Henry. Stephanie told Pergola that her husband had been working that night on their Neponsit home, which they bought with wedding gift money. She did not know who might want to kill her husband, who made a good living as a car customizer while she went to school.

Continuing with his disconsolate act, Joey consented to an interview by Pergola, and said he was visiting a brother's hospitalized child earlier that evening. Anthony and Henry each said they knew no one who would want to hurt Chris and then, "Talk to my lawyer." Pergola did not buy what anyone said, and left the apartment thinking he had been in the company of some unusually revolting people.

After Pergola left, Joey and Anthony accompanied Stephanie to a city morgue; Joey and Stephanie could not look at the body, but Anthony, in a mournful performance of his own, identified it as Harvey Rosenberg, aka Chris Rosalia, but not aka Chris DeMeo.

The following afternoon, Roy called Dominick to the Gemini. If Roy was feeling grief or guilt, it no longer showed. "We took care of the problem last night," he said, handing over a newspaper clipping describing how a twenty-nine-year-old car thief with reputed organized crime ties had been found in a luxury car raked by machinegun fire. "Chris kept trying to get up," Roy was compelled to add, "but Anthony shot him and he stayed down."

Getting around now in a black Mercedes 450 SL that Rega had given him to use, Dominick delivered the news clipping to Paz, then with an air of self-satisfaction soon deflated, reported in to Nino: "Paz says it's all over now, but that fucking Roy didn't even say thanks for all the time I spent trying to iron this thing out."

"Thanks? What the fuck did you do?"

"I spent two months with a bunch of crazy fuckin' Cubans!"

"What the fuck you want, another medal? I'll see you at the club when I get back."

"Sure, Nino," came the sarcastic reply. "So long."

Henry was more grateful. He embraced Dominick and kissed him on the cheek. "The cocksucker finally got what he deserved!"

In a few days, someone anonymously called the 12th Homicide Zone squad and informed Detective Frank Pergola that a "gangster named Roy DeMeo was involved with Chris Rosenberg's murder."

Pergola went back to Stephanie several times, but she became evasive and hostile, a perfect standup widow. "We didn't discuss business or school, that was one of our rules," she would eventually say about Chris—after Roy, unknown to Pergola, gave her ten thousand dollars, a measly amount given the hundreds of thousands that began rolling in from the stolen coke.

Following up the anonymous tip, Pergola, unacquainted with any FBI agents, telephoned the bureau blindly and asked if it had any intelligence information on Roy. He placed a similar call to the Brooklyn District Attorney's detective squad, but did not ask for Kenny McCabe or Joseph Wendling, whom he had never met. Both calls produced nothing, and the case, as with the six murders related to it, went nowhere.

As the Cuban crisis played itself out, an old case against a crew member who had been out of circulation for a year did finally go somewhere—but only temporarily.

In March, newly muscled, still bearded Peter LaFroscia was detained on an arrest warrant by police in Memphis, Tennessee, as he departed a federal prison after serving his year for violating probation. Joseph Wendling happily flew to Tennessee and brought LaFroscia back to New York to stand trial for the murder of John Quinn.

Wendling had spent the year persuading LaFroscia's former partner, master car thief Willie Kampf, to testify. First, he forced Kampf back to Brooklyn from his out-of-state hideout with a warrant identifying him as a suspect in an arson case, and then he got him to talk after truthfully informing him that LaFroscia was sleeping with Kampf's girlfriend while the two had been partners.

Try as he could, Wendling could not persuade anyone else to testify against LaFroscia. Quinn's cousin Joseph Bennett, the man asked by Roy and LaFroscia to set up Quinn and Cherie Golden, was still too frightened to admit anything but his name. Another possible witness Wendling found in state prison serving life for a murder Wendling was told LaFroscia helped commit also rejected an offer to boost his chances for early parole by cooperating.

Attempting to influence the inmate's decision, Wendling arranged for the inmate's wife and infant daughter to accompany him to the prison for the interview.

"You're not going to be there when your daughter has her first nightmare," Wendling told him.

"You don't understand," the inmate replied. "You're dealing with people who wouldn't hesitate to kill her and my wife."

Midway through his efforts, Wendling grew suspicious of police officer Norman Blau, the Canarsie cop who introduced him to Kampf and volunteered to accompany him to Florida for his first face-to-face meeting with him. His worries began when a surveillance team saw Blau meeting with some of Kampf's former associates. He confided in his boss, who ordered Blau to keep his nose out of the case.

"I'm worried now about who else knows what we know," Wendling said to Inspector John Nevins.

Still, as the case went to trial in June of 1979, Wendling and Assistant District Attorney Steven Samuel were confident. They had a witness who could testify to a relationship between John Quinn and Peter LaFroscia, to a motive, and to LaFroscia's admission that he helped kill Quinn. They also had the phone message that "Pete" left for Quinn hours before Quinn's body was found.

After Samuel rested the prosecution's case, Fred Abrams, the politically connected Brooklyn defense attorney who was making a nice living representing DeMeo crew members, went to work. He called Kampf's former girlfriend, who said Willie was just angry at LaFroscia because of her affair with him. But Samuel fought back with a tape recording Willie made of a call he received from her instructing him to keep his mouth shut about the case. The tape made her look like a liar.

"Case closed," Wendling said to himself.

Late on a Friday afternoon, Abrams said he would call a surprise defense witness on Monday morning—police officer Norman Blau.

Wendling and other officers spent the weekend trying to locate Blau—police officers are required to notify the NYPD anytime they intend to testify against the state—but Blau made himself scarce. On Monday, he took the stand in his uniform and said that while he was with Wendling and Kampf in Florida, Kampf pulled him aside and said he would do anything to get Peter LaFroscia. Kampf, he added, was not a believable person.

The case *was* closed—not guilty, said the jury.

Samuel and Wendling were devastated. After so much effort, they had been sandbagged by a cop. Strolling out of the courtroom, LaFroscia laughed in their faces.

CHAPTER 15

Body Shop

The terrible thing about 1979, the worst year of the DeMeo crew, was that even with the bloody torrent preceding and including Dominick Ragucci and Chris Rosenberg, the year was less than half over. Bouncing back fast, Roy plunged down a bloody road. He picked Joey Testa to replace Chris as his new right hand, not that he did not like equally capable Henry Borelli, but Roy felt a closer bond to Joey, a former apprentice butcher too, and now, like him, a professional. He fit the last pieces of his car deal together, but did not neglect other deals, all of which led him—and Nino—to yet more heinous murders and one of them, finally, to jail.

Henry was bitterly disappointed when Roy chose younger Joey over him, but Roy quickly sought to soothe his wounded feelings. While Joey and Anthony were given responsibility for moving all the stolen Cuban cocaine, Roy gave Henry a big job in the Kuwait stolen-car operation. Without having to do a lot of work, Henry was made one of the deal's five active partners.

The operation had been in abeyance several months while another partner, a Long Island used-car dealer, concocted a satisfactory scheme for shipping the cars under another man's freight-forwarding company. The dealer was Ronald Ustica, a thirty-four-year-old lifelong resident of Baldwin, Long Island, who met Roy while selling cars for another used-car lot whose owner was perpetually in debt to Roy's book. Ustica was mild-mannered, recently married, and had little in common with Roy and the crew except a larcenous heart.

He and Roy came up with the scheme after he met two Arab importers who came to New York as partners to buy secondhand cars for resale in Kuwait. In discussions, Ustica discovered that one partner, Abdullah Hassan, had the same larcenous flaw as he. Encouraged by Roy, Ustica told the importers he could provide many quality used cars at five thousand dollars each, if they did not mind that they were stolen. Sure he could resell the cars for at least twice as much in Kuwait, Hassan did not mind. His partner, however, did, and they split up with the partner vowing to stay in New York and put his own legitimate deal together. Hassan returned to Kuwait to await the cars.

As he had already indicated he would, Roy also brought Freddy into the deal and, because Freddy's stumblebum brother, Richie, had shown such ambition in the Joey Scorney murder, him also. Roy informed Freddy that a full sixth share of the profit would have to go to Nino and the "hill," meaning Paul Castellano, whose new white house occupied a Staten Island knoll known as Todt Hill (*Todt* meaning "death" in Dutch).

Roy gave the active partners specific roles. Richie, aided by Vito Arena at one hundred dollars per vehicle, would steal the cars; Freddy, in his shop, would replace the locks; together, the brothers would make and install the phony VIN plates, using tool dies Roy had acquired and randomly chosen numbers that Roy would check with his cop pals to prevent the inadvertent invention of a hot VIN number. Henry would create the phony paperwork, a comparatively trifling worry now because a dealer's mere invoice rather than a title would be enough to ship the cars overseas, which Ustica would oversee.

"I want good cars," Ustica said to Freddy the first time Roy introduced them. "Cars with not much mileage on them, possibly velour interiors, and with electric windows and seats."

Velour interiors were desirable, Roy explained, because the Arabs who would buy the cars from Hassan in Kuwait were opposed, for religious reasons, to sitting on leather. They were not opposed, however, to big cars with low gas mileage because gasoline was so cheap in Kuwait. Richie and Vito were told to steal high-end General Motors cars like Chevrolet Caprices, Oldsmobile Regencys and Buick Electras—preferably Caprices and preferably four-door, because some were destined to become taxis.

Beginning in June, Richie and Vito began cruising for

cars each night. Unlike Peter LaFroscia and Willie Kampf who in their heyday drove around in a Jaguar, the Gemini thieves used Richie's homely station wagon, with its stroller, baby seat, and other infant paraphernalia. They began around midnight and usually swept through the predominantly Jewish neighborhood of Borough Park in Brooklyn because, as Vito explained, they would find, for religious reasons, fewer cars with leather seats made from pigskin.

With Joey Scorney out of the way, Richie was finally able to demonstrate he could steal cars too. Bulky Vito was still mainly a getaway driver, but stole on occasion, though he still had difficulty squeezing beneath the dashboards of some cars. The cars were driven to Flatlands and left, with the passenger-side sun visor pulled down, on the streets near Freddy's shop.

"There's four in the bush," Richie would say over the telephone to Freddy each morning, so Freddy and Henry would know, by the sun visors, which four cars to drive into Freddy's shop and begin working on. The shop only had room for four at a time.

After the cars were outfitted with new identities, locks, and transporter plates from Ustica's dealership, they were driven to Nassau County and parked along the streets near his home in Baldwin—around the corner from a police station. Vito's boyfriend Joey Lee, Roy's cousin Joseph Guglielmo, and a few other fringe characters were paid a few dollars to drive the cars to Baldwin, where they sat until they were driven to Ustica's lot and taken by rented car carrier to Pier 292 in Newark, New Jersey, from which they were shipped to al-Shuiaba, Kuwait.

For the first few months, most everything went swimmingly. Freddy did gripe that Henry was hard to work with because he was always showing up late and complaining. In Kuwait, Abdullah Hassan griped that some cars were showing up without their radios, and Roy had to tell Freddy to stop stealing them. The partners, however, were each making seven to nine thousand dollars a week. Roy griped to Freddy they would be hauling in that much more if they did not have to pay Auto Crime Unit cops Peter Calabro and John Doherty fifteen hundred a week to check the VINs and did not also have to cut in Nino and "Waterhead."

Real problems began early in September. Making his arrangements with Hassan, Ustica had failed to consider the persistence of Hassan's former partner, a Jordanian citizen named Khaled Fahd Darwish Daoud. Daoud was a secretary in the chemistry department of the University of Kuwait when Hassan persuaded him they could make money importing cars. Daoud still believed and was trying to do it on his own, and had already written a letter home mentioning Ustica and complaining he was competing against thieves.

That might have been the end of it if Daoud had not begun to notice that rarely were there any more Chevrolet Caprices available at the used-car auctions in New Jersey where new-car dealers dumped trade-ins. Caprices were the cars he wanted most too. Out of curiosity, he stopped by Pier 292 in Newark and found the answer to this riddle—dozens of Caprices lined up for shipment to Kuwait; the reason the dealers and auction lots had so few Caprices was that so many were here, undoubtedly hot. Daoud began writing down the dashboard VINs just as Ustica showed up.

Daoud, a blunt-spoken, defiant man with no appreciation of the deadly nest he had disturbed, began arguing with Ustica and threatened to report him to the police.

At an emergency session of the active Gemini-Kuwait partners, Ustica reported Daoud's remarks to Roy. Of course, this was the same as signing the Jordanian's death warrant. "Then, we'll have to kill him," Roy said to no one's surprise, including ambitious Richie and suddenly prosperous and ruthless Ustica.

"He has to go and I'll pay for it," Ustica volunteered.

Arguing with Daoud, Ustica had learned that Hassan's former partner was living at the Diplomat Hotel in Rockville Centre, in Nassau County, not far from the Gemini. Roy, Henry, Freddy, and Vito promptly staked it out, but discovered that Daoud's room was near the manager's office.

That would not have thrown a wrinkle into the hit if, in an unusual oversight, Roy had not neglected to bring a gun equipped with a silencer and to remind the others. It was a sign that Roy, always the one to worry about armament before departing for work, was getting a bit forgetful as his bloodlust mounted—but then he was drinking a lot, late at night, in his house that was not a home.

"Four guys walkin' in and shootin' the guy, that's gonna be noisy," Vito brilliantly observed as they all regretted the mistake, sitting in Roy's car in the hotel parking lot.

Roy dispatched Henry to telephone Richie DiNome, who lived near the Diplomat Hotel, and tell him to bring the custom silencer Roy had awarded him upon his entry to the crew. Henry did, but an hour went by with no sign of Richie or the spanking new Joey Scorney-type Porsche Turbo Carrera he had purchased. Richie was also dressing like the late Scorney these days—very cool NYPD T-shirts and lots of gold chains under a dungaree jacket.

Henry telephoned Richie's house again and learned that while attaching the silencer to a loaded weapon, Richie—burnishing his reputation for ineptitude—had shot himself in the left hand and was in a hospital. Not knowing how he might have explained away the wound, the assassins abandoned their plan, for the time being.

Making money off cocaine, indirectly or directly, Nino and Roy had been violating Paul's no-drugs policy and thus flirting with personal disaster for many years. So had several other soldiers and crews, including the one led by former Brownsville-Canarsie resident John Gotti, protégé of Manhattan faction leader Aniello Dellacroce. The profit in "going off the record," as the practice was known, was too irresistible. Short of wiping out half of his family, Paul was unable to stop it. Now and then, however, to remind everyone of the rules, someone breaking them in an especially flamboyant way would be sent to the morgue.

Late in September, Nino's and Roy's long flirtation with disaster came home to roost. It began with an intra-family accusation, not the arrest Nino and Roy had always feared. A bookmaker in Nino's crew, Jimmy Eppolito, told Paul that Nino and Roy had been going off the record a long time. Until lately, Eppolito had been the most influential of the elderly cigar chompers in the Bath Beach–Bensonhurst wing of Nino's crew—a feeble bunch, compared to Roy.

Because Paul was his former captain, and because he

was Sicilian and had been made by Carlo Gambino, the sixty-five-year-old Eppolito was still technically Roy's immediate superior when Nino was away. In fact, in Carlo's day, his word alone would have sealed the accused's fate—but these were Paul's days now, and Jimmy's word and life were not worth as much.

In a sign of the times, Eppolito was motivated by his son's off-the-record trouble. In a cocaine deal with Roy's crew, the son, a thirty-four-year-old soldier also known as Jimmy, was swindled out of several thousand dollars. Jimmy, Jr., complained to his father, but Roy—and then Nino—accused Jimmy, Jr., of lying and being a police informer. Dishonored, Jimmy, Sr., went to Paul and made his accusations against Nino and Roy; he even asked for permission to kill them.

His timing was not good. Paul was already angry at Jimmy, Jr., because of his participation in a crooked children's charity that duped several celebrities, including the First Lady of the United States, Rosalynn Carter, and United States Senator Edward Kennedy of Massachusetts. What upset Paul most was that when the scam was uncovered on the CBS television program "60 Minutes" and newspapers published still photographs from the TV footage showing Jimmy, Jr., had conned the First Lady into posing with him at one of the supposed charity's dinners. Paul feared that in retaliation, President Jimmy Carter might send another thousand FBI agents to New York with orders to smash the Gambino family.

Jimmy, Sr., also failed to appreciate the depth of Nino's relationship with Paul, who accepted Nino's version of events and ordered him to resolve the matter however he chose—a de facto death sentence for Jimmy, Sr., and Jimmy, Jr., given how Nino had previously approved and Roy previously carried out executions of closer associates who caused trouble.

One day soon afterward, outside the Veterans and Friends, Dominick saw Roy pointedly refuse to shake Jimmy, Sr.'s extended hand. He later mentioned it to Nino, who, without providing any background, told him to stop speaking to Jimmy, Sr. The next day, again outside the Veterans and Friends, he saw Jimmy, Sr., pacing and madly muttering to himself, "I fucked up. I fucked up."

Nino and Roy chose Monday, October 1, as the day to resolve the matter—employing the Gemini method. Nino had always told Dominick that while he was usually opposed to dismemberment, sometimes it was necessary. This, he now decided, was one of those times. With Jimmy, Sr., so keen about his future, however, Nino and Roy faced a tactical problem: how to get the old man and his son into voluntarily going to the Gemini charnel house. They found a solution in Peter Piacente, another aging soldier Paul had handed off to Nino; they duped Piacente into believing that a sitdown between the Eppolitos and Nino and Roy's crew was to be held at the Gemini and to make everyone feel safe, he was to accompany all of them to the meeting.

Piacente, whom Jimmy, Sr., trusted, would have claimed heart problems and stayed in bed if he had known what Nino and Roy had in mind when, around half-past-eight o'clock in the evening, the five men left for the Gemini in Jimmy, Jr.'s white Thunderbird.

Nino sat in front with Jimmy, Jr.; Roy and Jimmy, Sr., with Piacente between, were in the back. Shortly, Jimmy, Sr.'s wary antennae detected fatal signals. He told his son to pull off the road so he could respond to an emergency bladder problem. Jimmy, Jr., laughed and urged his father to wait until they came upon a gas station. Nino and Roy exchanged wordless, ominous glances.

"Listen to your father!" Jimmy, Sr., screamed. "Pull over!"

As Jimmy, Jr., slowed to a stop on a service road beside the Belt Parkway, Nino and Roy simultaneously drew their weapons. As Nino fired three bullets into Jimmy, Jr.'s head, Roy leaned past Piacente and put four into Jimmy, Sr.'s. Blood splattered in all directions and the driver's window exploded as one bullet exited Jimmy, Jr.'s brain.

The spontaneity of the situation left no time to worry about possible witnesses, such as the three people in a car that happened to pass by at that moment. Behind the wheel of his beatup Buick, twenty-year-old Patrick Penny heard what sounded to him like firecrackers going off, then saw the Thunderbird's window burst, and flashes of light. Two female companions implored him to drive on, but Penny stopped some twenty feet past and looked back. "I think I just saw someone get shot! A woman, I think!"

Ordinarily, Penny might have made a perfect seenothing witness. He was a runty, one-hundred-ten-pound dropout turned burglar in constant trouble with the law and, at the time, was carrying a loaded .25 caliber handgun. However, recently, he had recounted for friends a dream in which he outfoxed a cunning mass murderer and saved the entire city of New York. Against his usual instincts, baby-faced Patrick Penny became civic-minded.

Looking back, he saw three men leave the Thunderbird. First a slender man, Nino, then two squat ones, Piacente and Roy. As a streetlamp lit the scene, it appeared the latter two were stained with blood. One of them wiped his face with a handkerchief and stuck what looked to be a handgun into the belt of his trousers.

As Penny watched, the men talked excitedly, then split up. Roy went one way, Nino and Piacente another. Thinking it uncanny how much the scene resembled his heroic dream, and feeling confident because of the loaded pistol in his pocket, Penny decided to follow the two men who walked away together.

"Let's get out of here!" protested Penny's nineteen-year-old girlfriend.

Undeterred, Penny spotted the two men, Nino and Piacente, a block away. He watched until they turned down another street.

"Let's go!" yelled the other young woman in Penny's car. "Get the cops!"

Penny drove in the direction the men had gone but could not see them. He stopped by a pay phone and got out, only to then see them walking along a sidewalk toward him. He bounded back to his car and stood by it as they ambled by, unaware they were giving a witness another close look at themselves. In a few seconds, Penny saw a car-service driver stop at a nearby intersection and ran over. "Hey cabbie, can you get the cops on your two-way radio?"

Just as Penny was no ordinary passerby, the driver was no ordinary cabbie. He was Police Sergeant Paul Roder, a burly, mustachioed ten-year veteran of the NYPD's Housing Authority division; he was off-duty and moonlighting, without departmental permission, for the Pretty Darn Quick car service. He had just dropped a fare when Penny ran up. Per regulations, he was armed with his service revolver and carrying his badge, and he asked Penny what was wrong.

"I just saw two guys kill a girl in a car over there!" said Penny, pointing toward the scene.

"What guys killed what girl in a car over where?"

"Those two guys just killed a girl in a car!" Now, Penny waved in another direction, to Roder's left, and to Nino and Piacente proceeding farther down the block.

"I'm a policeman, get in the car!"

Penny remembered the gun in his pocket. "I ain't gettin' in your car. I got my own car, I'll follow you."

Roder drifted slowly down the street; twenty-five feet away, he saw that one of the alleged shooters' jackets appeared dark with blood. They were walking quickly and looking about.

Roder rolled on past at about ten miles an hour, to look at their faces. They looked away and kept walking. On the other side of the next intersection, as Nino and Piacente walked past a gas station, Roder decided to act; he turned his car diagonally into the curb, jumped out and stood behind the driver's door with his arms extended, gun in one hand, badge in the other. "Police officer!" he shouted. "Freeze!"

Nino and Piacente were now about twenty feet away, directly in front of two gas pumps. They looked at Roder like they did not understand him.

"Put your hands up!" Roder shouted.

Nino calculated the odds against him—one excited cop—and began walking in a circle around Piacente.

"Police officer!" Roder shouted again. "Put your hands up!"

Suddenly, from behind Piacente, Nino whirled toward Roder and fired three shots, all errant. Roder fired three in return; one struck Nino in the neck and spun him around. Piacente tried to catch him from falling, but was struck in a leg and began hobbling away. Still much alive, Nino fell face first, his palms outstretched. His pistol landed inches away, and he reached out for it with the fingers of his right hand.

Roder told him to stop, but Nino kept reaching—all he

ever wanted, he had always said, was to be like Frank Scalise and die in the street with a pistol in his hand. He had gotten his first wish, and as his fingers now curled around the .38, was on the verge of realizing the second.

"Don't touch it or I'll shoot again!" Roder shouted.

Nino held onto the pistol, but was too weak to lift his arm. Feeling faint, he let the weapon go, rolled his head sideways and lay still. For the first time in his life, Anthony Gaggi gave up.

At the bunker a half-hour later, Nino's twelve-year-old son, Anthony, answered a telephone call from a nurse at Coney Island Hospital, the closest to the scene. Screaming, he ran toward the stairway connecting his and Dominick's and Denise's apartments: "Daddy got shot! Daddy got shot! He's in the hospital!"

Dominick raced downstairs as the Gaggi telephone began ringing again. This time, it was Roy. After separating from Nino and Piacente, he had seen and heard police cars and ambulances shriek past and assumed his accomplices had run into trouble and were in custody or dead. He had tossed his weapon down a sewer and called the clubhouse to have someone come fetch him.

"Where the fuck were you!" Dominick shouted. "My uncle's been shot! He's at Coney Island now!"

"Things got fucked. Meet me at the hospital in ten minutes."

Roy junked his bloody clothes, borrowed a fresh outfit from Freddy and zoomed to the hospital.

Meanwhile, Patrick Penny, after hiding his gun in his car's trunk, had accompanied another police officer who had responded to Sergeant Paul Roder's call for assistance, and helped him locate Peter Piacente, whose leg wound had prevented him from hobbling much more than a block away. Like Nino, Piacente was arrested and taken to Coney Island for emergency treatment.

Neither man was in danger; the outcome would have been different for Nino if the bullet had struck the stressful vein running down the left side of his neck, rather than a muscled area on its right. Stabilized, he was regaining strength rapidly. When an emergency room physician asked what happened, Nino said, "I was walking in the street, and I fucking got shot, that's all."

Dr. Umasanker Paty felt the bullet still burrowed beneath Nino's flesh, then said: "Don't worry, it's super-ficial."

Dominick did not know the wound was superficial. He arrived at the hospital thinking the worst, and that rela-tive to death, even the most serious of his grievances against Nino seemed pathetically petty. He marched past police officers into the emergency room, saw Nino was conscious, but before reaching his bedside, was escorted into a waiting room by officers who said the patient would be all right but was under arrest.

Roy then arrived; saying he was Nino's brother, he also attempted to speak to him, but also was rebuffed. Outside the hospital with Dominick, he tried to explain what happened.

The adrenaline in Dominick's stomach turned to poi-son. His words were fast, deliberate, and contemptuous: "You left him in a bad spot again! Just like with fucking Governara! How come you weren't there! You left him with a fucking old coot! You're one fucking fearless guy. Rooster."

The words hit like a dagger, but Roy let them pass through. "We had to split! It was Nino's idea! We have other things to worry about now. I've got to see Paul. I've got to tell him what happened first, 'cause he ain't gonna like how we used Pete to set them up."

Dominick then went with Roy to Paul's house on Staten Island. Beforehand, they picked up Thomas Bilotti, the Staten Island capo who had accompanied Paul to Nino's house the night Paul was made boss. Since then, Bilotti—a power in the white-collar, labor-manipulating rackets Paul preferred—had almost supplanted Nino in impor-tance because Nino had become so content to hang out in Florida and count his money that he was caring less if someone else got Paul's ear.

At Paul's house, Bilotti told Dominick to wait in the car while he and Roy spoke to Paul. When they returned, Dominick asked Bilotti, "What does Paulie want me to do?"

"For now, we just go home and wait."

Roy was not the waiting type and he immediately be-gan thinking of ways to help out Nino, who in hours would be formally accused of murder, attempted murder, and other charges; so would the deceived Peter Piacente, but Roy and no one but personal family members would give Piacente a thought—so long as he stood up of course.

The next day, Roy and Dominick met at the Gemini. Dominick, so familiar with the signs, thought Roy was so badly hungover that he must have been up all night drinking while thinking. Some of the ideas he began to spew were half-baked, but he also had solid information. From Nino's lawyers, he had already learned that the witnesses in the case were Patrick Penny and Paul Roder; Penny, he said, was bribable—"We give him fifty grand, he'll take it"—but Roder might have to die. He also had already discovered that Roder lived in Flatlands, not far from the Gemini. Unlike most officers, Roder kept his name listed in the telephone directory.

"He practically lives around the corner," Roy said. "We'll just wait outside his house and pop him."

"You're losing it, Roy. You don't know what heat is until you kill a cop. You kill a cop, Nino will kill you."

"Your uncle just tried it! And don't talk to me about heat."

"That was different. That wasn't an assassination."

Roy barely skipped a beat to his next idea. Pending a hearing on a request for bail, Nino had already been transferred to the prison hospital of Rikers Island, a tiny isle in the East River where the city housed most pretrial detainees. "Here's how we bust him out," Roy said. "We'll get some scuba gear and sneak up on Rikers and take the hospital with machineguns."

"That's the stupidest James Bond bullshit I ever heard. If you ever tried a stunt like that, I guarantee it, my uncle would not leave with you. He'd shoot you if he could."

Finally, Roy came up with an idea Dominick found reasonable. Actually, the more he considered it, the idea seemed positively ingenious. On his lawyers' advice, Nino had refused to let doctors extract the bullet that Paul Roder had fired into his neck. In time, the healing process would push it to the surface anyway. If in the meantime however, another bullet was smuggled in to Nino—one that ballistics tests would show was fired by a gun other than Roder's—and Nino could substitute it for the one that would finally pop out of his neck, then, at trial, his lawyers could argue this fantastic, but reasonably plausible scenario: Nino was wounded by the same gunman who had escaped after shooting both Jimmy, Jr., and Jimmy, Sr.; exiting the car, the gunman dropped one of his two weapons; hard-luck Nino grabbed it when he fled on foot—and then pulled it in self-defense when someone who never identified himself as a cop began firing at him.

"A long shot, but I like it," Dominick said. "Only one juror has to buy it."

The plan required retrieval of the gun Roy had tossed in the sewer as he left the scene. So that night, while Dominick, Henry, and Joey stood guard, Roy removed a grating and climbed down into the muck near Bath Beach and recovered the Danny Grillo–type .38 caliber Smith & Wesson he had used. At the Gemini, Roy dipped the weapon into an oil drum filled with water and fired one round, which he then fished out.

"Now, it's your job to smuggle it in," Roy said, handing over the ballistically correct bullet.

On October 8, Rose Gaggi, who was never told about the plot, and Dominick visited Nino in his guarded room at the Rikers Island infirmary. Fearful of metal detectors, Dominick had wrapped the bullet in a condom and concealed it in his mouth. As the visit ended, he coughed into his right hand, then shook Nino's, and kissed him on the cheek, Sicilian to Sicilian. That night, Nino lay awake, hastening nature by gouging at his neck with his fingernails. When the Roder-fired bullet popped out, he flushed it down a toilet; the next day, he gave the smuggled-in round to a corrections officer, who gave the manufactured evidence to police. The fix was on.

With two potential twenty-five-year-to-life prison terms to worry about, however, Nino was not going to rely only on the bullet-switch. He instructed Roy to begin working on another plan—bribing Patrick Penny and/or Paul Roder to forget or alter what they saw and said in the immediate aftermath of the killings.

Penny was targeted first. He was more crucial because he could testify he saw Nino leave the Thunderbird just after the Eppolitos were shot. Penny, however, was proving hard to track down; at the moment, even the police did not know where he was.

After the shooting, detectives had stashed Penny in a motel, to make certain he testified before a grand jury and helped the Brooklyn District Attorney's office obtain

indictments of Nino and Piacente. Afterward, they sought
to keep him in protective custody—to make sure he stayed
alive to testify at trial—but Penny reverted to his anti-
social habits and decided he did not want to hang out
with police anymore. When detectives escorted him home
for fresh clothes, the wiry little burglar went to the bathroom, climbed out a window, and ran away.

Believing Penny would stay in contact with his family,
Nino and Roy decided to send him a message through
his brother Robert. They dispatched Dominick and
Henry, and Joey and Anthony, to the gas station where
Robert worked. Nino paternally told Dominick to go in
disguise; the others did not bother. Joey, Roy's new right
hand, did the talking:

"Your brother is fucking with the wrong people. He
saw what happened to the two guys in the car; if he
testifies, it'll happen to him. Tell him to do the right
thing. We'll give fifty thousand up front and take care of
him the rest of his life."

"I think he'll go along," Robert replied.

"He better," the other Gemini twin said.

Roy's hyperactive imagination in the days following
the Eppolito murders was also due to the unresolved
threat he felt from the Jordanian car exporter, Khaled
Fahd Darwish Daoud. Daoud was still perturbed that car
thieves he believed were led by seemingly mild-mannered
Ronald Ustica were giving his estranged partner in Kuwait, Abdullah Hassan, a distinct competitive advantage.

Unaware the crew had already abandoned one plan to
kill him because Richie DiNome accidentally shot himself in the hand, Daoud had continued grumbling about
Ustica and the shortage of Chevrolet Caprices at the used-
car auctions in New Jersey. As yet, however, he had not
carried out his vow to contact police.

In the month since the plan was aborted, the stakes
had increased. In Kuwait, Abdullah Hassan was ecstatic
with the way the car deal was unfolding and had ordered
more "rentals," as Ustica referred to the stolen cars. To
handle the request, Roy moved the operation out of Freddy's four-car garage and into a former milk company
warehouse where twenty cars at a time were retagged. In
Baldwin, Long Island, now, cars ready for shipment were

stored in a warehouse Hassan had bought for Ustica rather than parked on the streets near Ustica's home.

The five active partners in the car deal, and the inactive tandem of Nino and Paul, were now making up to twenty thousand dollars a week each. The profits were so outrageous even Vito Arena—who got a hundred dollars for every car he helped steal, rather than a full partner's share—was spending thirteen hundred a week just on food.

In the giddy dinners at the Gemini clubhouse before the Eppolito murders, Roy had discussed expanding the operation further and then leveling off at one hundred cars per week—or, based on the five thousand dollars Hassan paid for each car, some eighty-three thousand dollars a week, per partnership.

"No use getting greedy," Roy said to a lot of happy hooting.

In such an avaricious atmosphere, no matter if he never contacted police, Khaled Daoud likely was doomed. But on October 10, two days after Dominick's smuggling trip to Rikers, Roy learned that Daoud had blindly called police and had been told to write a letter outlining his allegations. One more time, Detective Peter Calabro of the Auto Crime Unit provided the tip.

Unusually, because it was Wednesday, Dominick happened to be at the clubhouse that night, updating the Eppolito situation with Roy, when Roy's principal hook came by. As ever, Calabro and Roy talked out of earshot of anyone else, this time in a hallway.

"A lot of guys have got clipped because of that guy," Roy appreciatively said to Dominick after Calabro left.

Because Roy had not discussed Daoud with him, Dominick did not understand the remark's specific implication, only that someone was about to die. He went home depressed and not because of any cocaine letdown. Here Nino was in jail for a double homicide, and Roy was out planning another killing. The murders just never stopped. Roy had recently bragged of being up to a hundred "notches"—and "counting." Was he going for a thousand?

Dominick left and let the Gemini cabal hatch a plan for whoever it was they were set to kill. With all of Roy's experience, a plan was quickly hatched. And because

Daoud was in the market for cars, he decided to lure him to Freddy's engine shop, not the clubhouse. This was not a big step for Freddy to take, because he had always said he would do anything for Roy.

At an auction in New Jersey the next day, Ronald Ustica arranged for a friend to tell Daoud that a man named Freddy DiNome, who happened to be at the auction, had two hard-to-find Caprices for sale at his garage in Brooklyn. Daoud sought out Freddy, who invited him to inspect the cars the following day. That evening, the setup took on a surprise dimension when Daoud telephoned to say he would be coming with a friend.

At a strategy council, Freddy wondered what to do.

It was a silly question, Roy said. "We just shoot them both, and make 'em disappear," he added.

"Disappear?" asked Vito Arena, familiar with the crew's methods, but not its nomenclature.

"Cut them up."

The friend of Daoud's who wandered into this void was Ronald Falcaro, another Long Island used-car dealer who had been assisting Daoud in his efforts to purchase cars legitimately. Leaving home on the morning of October 12, Falcaro, the father of three children, told his wife Donna he had business with his new associate, Khaled Daoud, but would be home in the afternoon to help her prepare for a birthday party for their youngest child.

For his second double homicide in eleven days, Roy arrived at Freddy's shop an hour before the scheduled meeting. The rest arrived within minutes. This time, Roy had distributed clean silencer-equipped weapons beforehand, which he and Dirty Henry began checking and rechecking. The Gemini twins removed a vinyl pool liner and their tool kits from their car trunks and carted everything inside. Although not partners in the car deal, they were helping out "as a favor to me," Roy said to Vito.

With Roy directing, they passed the time rehearsing. A car with its hood up was parked nearly against the door of Freddy's shop. Vito Arena would pretend he was working on the engine and make sure no one not supposed to exited the shop, a windowless building that could be lighted only via a power cord strung from an adjacent building. Roy, Henry, and Joey and Anthony would hide in the darkness and do the work when Freddy led the victims inside. To limit the number of bullets flying around, Roy would take one victim; Henry, his prized stone-cold shooter, the other—with the twins on standby.

Everyone was in position when Falcaro and Daoud arrived on schedule. Freddy led them straight past Vito to the door of the shop and waved them in ahead.

"Christ, your electricity get cut off?" Falcaro said as he stepped into a trap darker than death.

"Fuck, I forgot the lights," Freddy said, so fast that he was able to turn and leave the shop before the victims had any hint of doom, which suddenly announced itself in a series of muffled popping sounds.

Daoud went down quickly; although wounded, Falcaro ran for the door; he pushed against it as Henry kept firing at him, and actually got a single hand around the outside edge, but heavyweight Vito was on the other side; he grunted, pressed against the door, and fed Falcaro to the sharks.

After Freddy turned the lights on and after Roy said it was okay to come in, Vito saw Henry pump be-sure shots into Daoud's head and Roy leaning over Falcaro and deciding nothing more was required there. "Got a little hairy there for a bit," Roy said. "That one guy didn't wanna go down."

"Piece a cake, Roy," Henry said.

Joey and Anthony laid out the pool liner and the knives from their tool kits. Freddy brought in garbage bags and several heavy cardboard boxes the crew used to transport its smut films.

"We've got about forty-five minutes to kill," Roy said to Vito. "Why don't you and Henry go get some hot dogs and pizza?"

By the time Vito and Henry returned with the food, the bodies were stripped of clothes. Roy knowingly redispatched Henry, and Vito, to dispose of Falcaro's car at a local auto shredder.

Then, after making preliminary slices and determining the victims' blood had not yet coagulated, Roy began to have lunch, so cavalier now about this demented work that he never even removed his bloody surgical gloves. The scene was out of some prehistoric time, but Roy calmly snacked as if he was back at Banner Dairy in Flatlands, just eating a Snickers and stocking shelves with Ivory Snow large.

As Chris, Joey, and Anthony once had with Andrei Katz, Freddy proved his toughness to Roy by serving as Roy's apprentice once the ritual butchery got underway. He and Roy began taking apart Falcaro while Joey and Anthony concentrated on Daoud.

"Here's how you do the head," Roy said to Freddy, whose only prior experience was with a neighbor's dog.

Roy then handed Freddy the knife and told him how to make a slice around the shoulders, to detach the arms.

"No, no, no!" he yelled when Freddy mangled the job. "This way!" he said, taking the knife back.

For sheer perversity, however, Freddy outperformed everyone. Vito and Henry returned from disposing of Falcaro's car to witness Freddy cutting off the penis of the beheaded Falcaro, and with a "Fuck you!" sticking it in the victim's mouth.

"Freddy, cut that out!" Roy laughed.

Henry was disturbed that all of this barbarity had not been completed by the time he returned, but he gutted it out, and for the first time, helped out with the packaging, to the extent of holding the garbage bags as the others filled them.

The plastic bags were tied, placed in the smut-film boxes and stacked along a wall. The next day, the boxes would be taken to Richie DiNome's nearby body shop—where Anthony Senter's uncle's sanitation company, a client of the Fountain Avenue dump, picked up the garbage.

In a few hours, everyone reassembled at the Gemini for the regular Friday-evening shapeup. Making his pickup for Nino, Dominick arrived later on, and noticed that everyone seemed unusually euphoric. Vito said he and the boys were all on a "high." Dominick thought they had just killed someone in the clubhouse.

Weary of the crew's relentless killing, Dominick finally verbalized his contempt. "Who checked into the Horror Hotel tonight?" he said sarcastically. "Who didn't check out? A baby?"

Everyone laughed and thought he was only making a joke. He left and felt like never coming back.

At age seven, Anthony "Nino" Gaggi poses for his first Holy Communion portrait. *(Courtesy of Dominick Montiglio)*

After becoming a "Soldier of Christ," Dominick, age ten, poses with his godfather, Uncle Nino. *(Courtesy of Dominick Montiglio)*

In 1949, two-year-old Dominick does the candle thing while his grandfather Angelo and parents Marie and Anthony hold their breath. *(Courtesy of Dominick Montiglio)*

The gang's all there for little Dominick's birthday party, about 1950. That's Uncle Nino showing off his chest hair, and Mary and Angelo Gaggi flanking their grandson. *(Courtesy of Dominick Montiglio)*

Dominick Montiglio,
1965 high school grad.

Dominick the Green Beret,
back home from the war. *(Courtesy of Dominick Montiglio)*

In 1978, nadir of his Studio 54 era, black-shirted, gold-chained, hung-over Dominick gives camera the evil eye.

Acting as the bait, Texas-born model led her pal Dominick into a Big Apple trap. *Right:* Danielle Deneux's jailhouse layout.

The Gemini Lounge was just an ordinary neighborhood bar, but many who entered the side door next to the protruding air conditioner never left—not in one piece anyway.

Joey Testa,
mugging for the camera.

Anthony Senter,
the taller Gemini twin.

Henry Borelli,
dandy and randy.

Chris Rosenberg,
a.k.a. Chris DeMeo.

Roy DeMeo,
the would-be doctor.

Joseph Guglielmo,
a.k.a. Dracula.

Anthony Gaggi, accompanied by devoted wife, Rose, on his way to court in 1984. *(New York Daily News Photo)*

The boss, Paul Castellano, under arrest in 1984 and escorted by Detective Joseph Coffey (left) and Detective Kenneth McCabe. *(New York Daily News Photo)*

In 1982, concrete-filled barrel containing remains of Joseph Scorney is hoisted to dock.

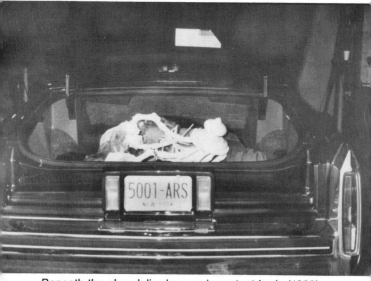

Beneath the chandelier lays an important body (1983).

Roy ordered Henry and Vito to go ransack "the Arab's" hotel room and collect his personal belongings; Freddy had removed the room key from Daoud's trousers. Roy said, "Bring back everything. We wanna make it look like he left town. This way the cops will blame him for the other guy's disappearance."

Although familiar with the Gemini method because of the two naked corpses he saw in the clubhouse bathroom one day, Vito was still taken aback by the afternoon's firsthand illustration. En route to the hotel with Henry, he asked: "Do you always cut 'em into pieces like that?"

"No, but we've done it several times. Not me personally. It just depends. Sometimes you want 'em to be found. Sometimes it's better if they're missing."

Henry asked Vito if he had any qualms and Vito said no.

"Well, don't worry about anything. You're with good people. Roy is good people. He looks out for his people."

Henry continued to ramble on about Roy, then mentioned some of the crew's more notorious murders—Andrei Katz, Cherie Golden, Chris Rosenberg, especially Chris. As he summed up Joey Testa's role in that murder, there was a bitter edge in his voice that Vito mistook for mere irony. "Joey's very good. He even went to ID the body, and he cried. Joey's the best."

Back at the Horror Hotel, Henry and Vito helped Roy inventory Daoud's suitcases; they found Statue of Liberty and Empire State Building souvenirs, family photos, business papers—and a typed letter addressed to various authorities alleging that a gang of thieves was shipping stolen cars to Kuwait.

"We got him just in time," Roy smiled. "Ain't no more problem with the Arab."

The next day, after reporting to police that her husband was missing, a panicky Donna Falcaro discovered that Daoud, whom she had met, had apparently checked out of his room. Because her husband was in the car business, Nassau auto squad officer Charles Meade was among those sent to interview her.

"I don't know much about what he does, but I'm really upset," she said. "All I know is, he was meeting some people in Canarsie or someplace."

Not wanting to upset her further, Meade did not give any indication, when he heard the word "Canarsie," that he was certain her husband was dead.

On her own, Donna Falcaro contacted people she knew her husband had done business with, such as Ronald Ustica. Summoning his best Joey Testa imitation, Ustica appeared to be sympathetic and concerned, and offered this advice: "If I was you, I'd tell your husband not to hang around with that Arab because he's bad news."

The case was assigned to Nassau missing-persons detective Bill O'Laughlin. He interviewed Ustica, but Ustica played dumb, naturally well; as so many times before, the case went nowhere.

CHAPTER 16

Into the Wind

The contempt for Roy and the crew that Dominick began to express during the Eppolito drama—his calling Roy "Rooster" to his face, his sarcastic jab at the clerks of the "Horror Hotel"—did not spring up overnight of course. The root went back to the time the crew equated Henry's aversion to butchery with cowardice; it grew when they made Danny Grillo disappear and when Roy, in a fanatic panic, killed a young vacuum cleaner salesman. Associating with such people, and with his own considerable degeneracy, Dominick was not very entitled to claim to be holier than thou, but he felt that way nonetheless. He was also depressed and anxious, and in the middle of a personal crisis from which he saw no way out; it began months earlier, soon after his do-or-die diplomacy in the Cuban crisis.

One of his favorite haunts was still the Pear Tree, the Manhattan bistro where he and Henry began meeting years before. The Pear Tree usually contained some interesting people. Dominick had met Nino's old childhood pal, former middleweight boxing champ Jake LaMotta there and also the writer Truman Capote, to whom he had introduced himself as "Dominick Santamaria"—a name he sometimes traveled by now, an alias but not really, and therefore another neat Sicilian trick.

At the Pear Tree one evening, Henry brought the news that set Dominick off on another binge. Even though Dominick did not feel close to Henry anymore, because Henry had shown in the wake of Danny Grillo's murder that he believed Dominick had been dispatched to kill him, they still got together. Henry, as always, kept him posted on crew events and politics.

Henry had just begun making easy money in the car deal but was still disappointed that Roy had picked Joey to be his second in command. "That slot ought to be mine," he whined.

"Well, why don't you just whack them both!" Dominick joked.

"Very funny. Even if I wanted to, Roy is a man who can't be killed. I don't know what it is, a sixth sense or something, radar, he just wouldn't let you get 'im.''

"I think Roy thinks the same thing about Nino. Nino's the only guy he's afraid of. Nino would smell ya coming and shoot ya first. That's what keeps them from ever turnin' on each other. It's a wonderful life.''

"I just felt I was entitled to the job. You know how much work I've done?''

"I can imagine. The job should've been yours, but the Rooster thinks you're too friendly with me. Joey's his dog, he knows Joey hates me because Chris hated me. Joey won't spill anything to me, which means he doesn't have to worry about Nino as much.''

"I was there before fuckin' Joey.''

"It's just the way things are. It's the Rooster's crew. My uncle would never get involved in it, if that's what you're driving at.''

"Speaking of Nino, you know that thing with the Cubans? Your uncle got a hundred and fifty grand off the top of that.''

"What?''

"Yep, Roy gave him a hundred and a half of what they made on that.''

Dominick began to boil as he listened to Henry describe how Roy, Joey, and Anthony had sold most of the stolen twelve kilos in lucrative chunks and given Nino maybe the biggest one. In an enraged whisper, he fumed: "The fucking Rooster never said thanks for how I got him out of that situation! And my uncle hollered at me for expecting any! Those fucks! They can't even throw me a lousy ten grand? Sick, greedy fucking miserable fucks!''

"They got balls, that's for sure, but there's no way Roy would try and hide money like that from your uncle; like you said, Nino's the only guy he's afraid of.''

"It's a pacifier, that's what it is! A hundred and fucking fifty grand of pacification! And they don't throw me a dime! Assholes!''

Nino's windfall—he had recently informed Dominick that he and Rose were looking to buy a new, larger house in Bath Beach—was not the only ironic footnote to the miserable Cuban saga.

Soon, big-spender Matty Rega invited several friends to fly with him to Las Vegas for a week's frolic at the MGM Grand Hotel. The group included a Rega girlfriend and the two women in Dominick's life—Cheryl Anderson and Denise, still in the dark about Ma Barker's real relationship with her husband. Cheryl stayed in a room by herself, Dominick stayed with Denise in a fancy suite, until she fell asleep.

Before departing, Rega said he tried to score cocaine for the trip from Paz, but Paz, untypically, was "dry" and wanted Rega to score for him. Dominick called Henry, who came up with five ounces. Rega and Dominick extracted a half-ounce surcharge for themselves, gave the remainder to Paz and left for Nevada.

In Las Vegas, trying to play blackjack while stoned, Rega and Dominick lost thirty-six thousand dollars they had made from drug deals. Coming down, they judged the cocaine as so "harsh" even Lemon 714 Quāaludes failed to ease the crash. They called Paz, who said he liked the coke and could they get some more? They called Henry, who, chuckling licentiously, said sure, and: "Paz should know where this stuff comes from. This is a little stuff that Roy was keeping. It's from the Cuban deal."

Over the summer of 1979, Dominick became a runaway freight train. If his vice were gambling, he would have gambled his way into the Fountain Avenue dump. But his were wine, women, and song—and all the cocaine anyone could ingest and still be alive. With a wife at home who gave him all the rope he wanted and an uncle in Florida who (especially after the way the Cuban cocaine proceeds were dispersed) had as much sway over him as a store owner over his delivery boy, he flew out of control.

Hopping about in his Matty Rega-supplied black Mercedes, he would hook up with Rega—who was still more treacherous than Dominick imagined—at the Bottom of the Barrel; with Henry in the South Bronx after-hours social club they ran; with Cheryl Anderson at the Hole in the Wall; with old high school pal Richard Emmolo in SoHo; and with now best pal Buzzy Scioli everywhere.

After one evening of debauchery and cocaine deals by the women's lounge at Studio 54, he and Buzzy rented an expensive suite at the landmark Plaza Hotel at Central Park and continued drinking themselves silly. "We were born in the wrong century!" Buzzy shouted as they crossed swords into the same toilet. "We would've been great pirates!"

"Fuckin' right, buddy! We're buccaneers!"

At the altitude they were flying, with everything they were up to, it was only a matter of time before someone in the Montiglio orbit crashed. The first to fall were Matty Rega and Cheryl, who were indicted by a federal grand jury in Manhattan for peddling substantial quantities of Quāaludes. Drug agents got onto them while investigating Frank Elman, the elderly Greenwich Village pharmacist who supplied Cheryl, who in turn supplied Rega. Agents also raided a Connecticut country home Elman stayed at and found seven hundred fifty thousand dollars in cash buried beneath the driveway—Ma Barker had known what she was talking about when she urged her friends to rip him off the year before.

Dominick immediately assumed the agents were within striking distance of him and the others, if not already there. As the Hole in the Wall was closed down, all he could hope was that Rega and Cheryl would do the right thing and stand up. Cheryl immediately took herself out of the equation by "getting into the wind" (as the act was known in "that life")—becoming a fugitive.

Against this suddenly uneasy backdrop, Nino came north for business. Informed of Rega's arrest, he and Roy decided to "call" their loan to him—demand immediate payment of what now amounted to about two hundred fifty thousand dollars. A customer about to go to jail was not a good risk.

In a meeting with Nino and Roy, Rega protested that he owed thirty thousand less because he gave that much to Dominick for Nino over the summer. If Nino had not received it, then his nephew must have stolen it and then probably lost it in some scheme with Henry.

"We'll talk to Dom about that and get back with you," Nino said.

Dominick was indignant. He told Nino: "Matty is a fucking liar! I've never stolen any money from you. I've picked up a million or so for you and never lost a penny! Matty, he's a weasel, he's just tryin' to get out from under the loan."

As he spoke, he realized he had lost some of Nino's money—Nino's share of the destroyed Danny Grillo markers—but this was no time to admit that. He was gratified to hear Nino say: "I know that. Don't panic, I believe you. And now, you watch, we're going to grab his restaurant, the little asshole."

Nino's solution to the problem was not going to be as simple a matter as it would be with most of his other customers because Rega was connected through his father to the hierarchy of one of the city's four other Mafia families. Some Rega relatives also owned shares in the Bottom of the Barrel. These factors meant there would have to be sitdowns to sort it all out. It might a take a while, but, Nino vowed, he would take the restaurant.

Dominick drove to New Jersey to see Rega, but Rega had set up house with a new girlfriend and was laying low. He left messages at the Bottom of the Barrel, but Rega never returned them. With much to worry about and Cheryl somewhere in the wind, Dominick laid low too. He began spending more time with Denise and their children. In September, he asked Chuck Anderson, now long gone from the 21 Club and working for *Penthouse* publisher Bob Guccione, if he could borrow his penthouse apartment—the place where he first cheated on Denise, but which he wanted now for a romantic husband-wife evening; that night, the couple's third child was conceived.

Dominick even began shaping up at the Veterans and Friends social club again, and for the first time in a while paid his respects to Paul at the Meat Palace. Paul invited him to lunch and surprised him by spending most of the hour railing against Frank Amato, his daughter's former husband, though the couple had been divorced for several years.

Paul had not forgiven Amato for cheating on Connie Castellano, whom he too belatedly had tried to steer toward Dominick. Amato was still a fixture in Bensonhurst; he had opened his own clothing store, but was still "doing stickups" too—at least he had told Dominick that when their paths crossed at a different social club some months before.

"That part of Connie's life is over now," Dominick said to Paul, not very convincingly.

"It ain't over until that fuck is put away!"

Dominick was startled to hear Paul speak so ruthlessly.

"I only wish I could take care of it myself! Today, tomorrow, they're gonna find that creep dead."

Dominick mentioned the outburst to Nino—"It was almost like he caught a virus from Roy. I never seen him that way."

Nino threw up his hands and said, "I don't know why the guy is talkin' to you about this!" The remark made Dominick believe that Amato's demise was already in the Gemini works.

"It just never ends around here, does it?"

"No, it never does."

A few days later, Nino and Rose found the more stately home they wanted. It was just a few blocks away, still in Bath Beach, but on a more prestigious street and across from a pretty park. Dominick wished the happy buyers well and bought them dinner. He suspected a connection between the house and Nino's windfall in the Cuban crisis, but held his tongue, because during that week—speaking of things that never end—Jimmy Eppolito and his son were murdered and Nino was shot, arrested, and jailed.

During the next month, Dominick did what he could to help Nino out—he slipped him the fake bullet, he joined the crew in the intimidating visit to Patrick Penny's brother—but he also grew anxious and depressed about his own problems.

He was still concerned how much narcotics agents knew or were about to know about him because of their investigation and subsequent arrests of Cheryl Anderson and Matty Rega. It hardly mattered enough while he was doing it, but now he hated the idea of embarrassing Nino and Paul by being arrested on drug charges. Even in Roy's crew, no one had ever been arrested on a drug case, except Peter LaFroscia, who was not significant enough to matter.

Rega's accusation that he had stolen cash from Nino

and Roy also was still unresolved and troubling him more than he let on. Maybe during some coke storm he could not even remember he had confused their money with his own—maybe Rega had evidence. Now, with no guarantee the efforts underway on Nino's behalf would work, Nino might go off to prison, possibly for the rest of his days. Rega's accusation would then become a matter for the master of disappearing acts, Roy. Between the lines, Dominick had a lot to read, all of it bad, and he jumped back into the bottle and the vial.

At the end of October, with the trial several months off, a judge granted Nino bail—a remarkable achievement by Nino's lawyers, considering that their client was charged with two murders and the attempted murder of a police officer. He came home Halloween Night, but not to the bunker.

During his thirty days' confinement, his family had moved into the new Gaggi home in Bath Beach, after his mother Mary and wife Rose wrapped up the purchase and oversaw extensive remodeling. The couple who intended to buy the bunker agreed to continue renting the top floor to Dominick and Denise.

On paper, the bunker had always been solely owned by Dominick's mother Marie—a big secret the Gaggi wing of the family kept from the Montiglio wing when Marie died six years before. Legally, the home could not be sold without her permission, an obvious problem no one in the Gaggi wing was about to admit now to Dominick's stepfather Anthony Montiglio, who would have inherited the house or been entitled to sell it, if only he had known the truth.

The problem was solved on October 5, while Nino was in the Rikers Island hospital. Records of the transfer of the deed to the new owners indicate that on that day, someone signed Marie Gaggi's name.

Dominick was unaware his mother had been the home's actual owner, but did believe she had contributed to the mortgage payments for many years. He telephoned Anthony Montiglio and said the Gaggis should give some of the sale proceeds to Anthony and Marie's children, Stephen and Michele. When Nino's sister died, Nino had promised to help them financially, but he had not. Stephen was now paying his own way to art school, and

Michele had taken an administrative job at the hospital where her mother died.

"They ought to do the right thing," Dominick told his stepdad, "but unless you ask, they won't."

Anthony Montiglio, happy to have the Gaggis out of his life, felt it was useless to make a fuss, and did not.

For two years, Dominick had been thrashing about trying to fashion a life separate from Nino's, but when Nino was freed on bail and began living elsewhere, he began feeling insecure. Including the decade spent with him as a boy, he had lived under the same roof as Nino for sixteen years. For better or worse, they had a history.

The insecurity was heightened by the Matty Rega situation, which Nino, now free on bail, would try to solve. Dominick's underworld integrity was at stake; in his mind, living in separate homes put a new symbolic distance between him and his uncle that could not have come at a worse time. Even just the physical separation had its disadvantages. Communication with Nino was not going to be as convenient now, and it was a bad time not to know when manipulative Roy was dropping by. Roy, Dominick was sure, was carrying a grudge against him from the Chris situation; if Roy wanted, he could burn Nino's ears with tales of Dominick's womanizing—in Nino's book, the most shallow misconduct. Roy could make him look so bad Nino might begin believing Rega.

Of course, this was always possible before Nino moved out, but bouncing up and down on cocaine and alcohol, Dominick was not only feeling insecure and depressed but also paranoid.

In a meeting, Nino told Dominick that Rega, awaiting trial on drug charges, was still holed up in New Jersey, insisting via his father's friends in the Genovese Mafia family that Dominick had stolen thirty thousand dollars.

"I didn't do it, I'm telling ya."

"You're a fuckup, but I believe that. Still, he says he can prove it."

"Let him try!"

Three weeks passed. When asked, Nino indicated he was consulting with Paul about scheduling a sitdown. Then, on Thanksgiving Day, Dominick argued bitterly with the Gemini twins—and then Roy—after, of all things, the Mercedes that Rega had given Dominick to use was stolen while parked outside the bunker.

Dominick telephoned Joey because he believed the thieves had to have come from Canarsie and Joey would know them. He was right on both counts. Joey checked with Anthony and discovered the Mercedes was stolen by two "kids" they knew. They gave the pair five hundred dollars to give the car back, then asked Dominick for reimbursement.

"No way! I'm not payin' to have my car stolen!"

"Hey, look, you take the same chance as anyone else," Joey said. "They didn't know whose car it was."

"Too fucking bad."

"It was our money we paid," Anthony said.

"I didn't tell you to do that. I wouldn't have paid the fucks a dime."

Joey and Anthony complained to Roy, who called Dominick and urged him to pay the money, but Dominick said: "Not in a million years. No fucking way. The punks broke the windows, the ignition, it's gonna cost me five to fix it."

"Joey and Anthony did you a favor."

"Ah, fuck you, Roy, I'm sick of all your Canarsie bullshit. Cock-a-doodle-do, Roy. Goodbye."

Other people had died for less disrespect. But Roy had no choice but to complain to Nino that Dominick was "gettin' out of line." But Nino said: "Forget it, Roy. Those kids fucked up. Don't even talk to me about this. It's too stupid."

Dominick was pleased to see Nino side with him, even if the outcome and his outburst further strained relations with Roy.

Two more weeks passed. Early one afternoon in December, Nino telephoned and finally announced that a sitdown between Paul and the Genovese boss would be held that night at Ruggiero's, a restaurant in Little Italy. Nino and Roy would join Paul; the Genovese boss would be joined by a top aide and Rega's father. Dominick could come to the restaurant, but not sit at the table; he would have to wait at the bar. Matty Rega would not be there.

At the sitdown, Rega's father repeated his son's accusations against Dominick, then got personal. The privileged nephew of Anthony Gaggi, the boy who had eaten at Carlo Gambino's table and grown up with him and Paul Castellano as role models, had become an unreliable junkie. For two years, he had lived so degenerately he embarrassed the Gambino family all over New York; he had been cheating on Denise with hookers and lying to his uncle about everything. The elder Rega knew all this because his son had been that way too, but was straightening out now. His most serious allegation came at the end: Dominick also was a heroin dealer.

On Paul's scale of sins, dealing heroin was still the worst, primarily because it was the drug most associated with the heavy prison terms that could make informers of men accused of trading in it. But Paul had also come to appreciate heroin's destructive effect on users and the social fabric; at the time, cocaine was not seen with the same alarm. So while he might have suspected Roy, and therefore Nino, of trading in cocaine, it was not the same as being told a young man he trusted was dealing heroin.

"Don't worry, though, Paulie stood up for you, he didn't believe the guy," Nino told Dominick during the briefing he gave on the way home. "He thinks you've used drugs, but not that you're a junkie. I tell ya, it's a good thing Paulie likes you so much because otherwise you would be dead on the street."

"Are you saying you believe Matty's bullshit now? The Regas have to keep telling these lies because they started them!"

"I don't believe it about the money, but the women, and the heroin—well, you did spend some time in the South Bronx, right?"

"I never dealt heroin! They're making that up! They'll say anything so they don't lose the restaurant."

Nino no doubt enjoyed the sight of Dominick twisting in the wind and believed a good scare might have positive results, but he also did not realize how sinister he sounded to a suddenly panicky Dominick when he said: "It's a good thing you're my nephew is all I'm gonna say."

The situation had ended without any resolution. Paul and the Genovese boss agreed to make their own inquiries; in the meantime, the parties directly involved would have their own separate sitdown in a week. The accused and the accuser would meet face to face—along with Nino, Roy, and Rega's father.

"We hold onto Matty's Mercedes until this is over," Nino added.

In a few days, Nino told Dominick that he had heard a few "interesting stories" from Roy.

"Roy has a lot of reasons for telling stories. Did he tell you the one about him and all the barmaids at the Gemini?"

Nino still did not realize the paranoia his vague and ominous comments were producing. "I don't know about barmaids, but what about a place called Spartacus? I don't know, Dom, I don't know how this is gonna work out, but you've really screwed up this time."

"I'm being set up," Dominick began saying to himself, as he ran some of Nino's errands in the Rega-model Mercedes and surveyed the landscape for signs of life and death under the influence of too much cocaine and alcohol.

Then, at the Veterans and Friends, Nino made a little joke that landed like a mortar shell in his nephew's overheated mind. As Dominick came into the club, a cigar chomper commented to Nino that he was surprised to see Dominick a third day in a row—but it was great seeing him back where he belonged.

"Yeah, yeah," Nino said, "Lassie came home. Why don't we pet him?"

The remark caused Dominick to say to himself that for all those years that was all he was, a mongrel Santamaria-Gaggi-Montiglio dog, bringing Nino his slippers.

On December 15, the day before the second sitdown, Dominick told Buzzy: "I'm feeling done with this life. I just can't handle it anymore. I feel like a dog in a garbage dump. If I stay around here, I'm gonna flip out, or I'm gonna get whacked, or it's just gonna be more of the same bullshit."

"Lighten up, will ya?"

The next day, coked-up, he became convinced that if he went anywhere in a car with Nino and Roy, it would be to the Fountain Avenue dump. He telephoned Nino and said he had business to conduct first and would make his own way to the sitdown.

That night, he sat in his bunker apartment and pondered what to do. As a baby he had lived with his mother and father on the first floor, as a boy, with his mother on the second floor, as a man, with his wife and his children on the top. The more steps he climbed, the more things had grown worse. The only logical thing to do was to leave—not just the bunker, but Brooklyn.

As the hour of the sitdown came and went, he made his decision. In a general way, he had kept Denise apprised of the Rega situation, and he told her now: "Matty and his dad are telling so many lies; it's like if they tell enough, some stick. If I'm not dead now, I will be. I've had it. Let's go to California."

Denise, four months pregnant, did not object. She was tired of taking angry telephone calls from Nino about Dominick, tired of her husband being away so much chasing his "things." They had started anew in California once before, and they might have made it if Dominick's Brooklyn Back Street Blues Band had gotten a break, if his mother had not been sick, and if *The Godfather* had not been made. Before all that, California was everything they wanted, a fairytale life, and so she was happy to seek it again.

Denise began packing suitcases. Dominick went to the trap in his daughter Camarie's bedroom; he counted his cash—fifteen hundred dollars—and grabbed his weapons, including the machinegun Pedro Rodriguez had given him. He then woke six-year-old Camarie and said they were taking a trip to California.

"What about school tomorrow?"

"They got good schools in California, honey."

After she fully woke, Camarie got excited and could not wait to leave. "We're taking a trip!" she said to two-year-old Dominick, Jr.

Dominick and Denise bundled their children into Rega's Mercedes; the car was worth thirty thousand dollars—the amount he was accused of stealing, now a fee he was charging for aggravation. Just as when they married in 1971, they hit the road for California and got into the wind, believing everything bad was being left behind in Brooklyn. This time for good.

That is what they hoped anyway. But as time would show, the last few months of incremental depression, anxiety and paranoia had only taken the boy out of

Brooklyn, not Brooklyn out of the boy. He would sneak back one day, and at first against his will, then whole-heartedly, he would associate himself with a new crew and begin pounding nails into the coffins of all the good fellows, including those of real and honorary uncles. What goes around comes around; what goes up must come down.

III

THE CHASE

THE CHASE

CHAPTER 17

Travesty of Justice

A lot would happen while Dominick was in the wind, much that was tragically familiar, much that was surprisingly different, and much that was wholly treacherous. The next couple of years would be the long beginning of an end, as the dice began coming up snake-eyes—not always but enough to signal a change in fortunes—for Paul, Nino, Roy, and the DeMeo crew.

For one thing, the forces of law and order arrayed against "that life" began cooperating more and became more effective—not in every example, however, so more victims would die before the cracks in the thin blue line were filled.

Eventually, a man—as unlike anyone in "that life" could be—would step forward and take charge of a historic and monumental effort to smash the evil empire. But all of that was in the future and incapable of occurring to the mind of the likes of Anthony Gaggi, who, as 1980 began, was trying to beat the Eppolito case and deal with the witnesses against him.

In Brooklyn, the prosecutor and detective assigned to the Eppolito murders had labored hard to preserve the case against Nino and Peter Piacente. The prosecutor was Steven Samuel, the assistant district attorney who had been sandbagged by police officer Norman Blau, whose last-minute testimony had enabled Peter LaFroscia to exit the courtroom with a smile on his face and an undeserved acquittal in John Quinn's murder.

Samuel had announced plans to enter private practice when the Eppolitos were murdered, but delayed them to try and avenge his loss in the LaFroscia case by convicting a major Mafia hoodlum such as Nino. The detective was Roland Cadieux, of the 10th Homicide Zone squad;

he had helped Samuel win his first murder case five years before.

One of their two Eppolito witnesses, burglar Patrick Penny, had continued giving Samuel and Cadieux fits—and the other, police officer Paul Roder, was not keen on testifying against two made Mafia men, especially Nino, whose reputation now preceded him, because of the Westchester Premier Theater case and the surveillance intelligence gathered by Kenny McCabe and his unofficial FBI partner, Tony Nelson.

After escaping from protective custody following his grand jury appearance, Penny had been caught—but then had run away again. When he was caught again he was put in jail. He had so embarrassed police that he was transported in chains and leg irons when being brought in for trial preparation. Samuel and Cadieux did not want their witness treated this way, but higher-ups said they could not afford to house Penny and pay officers to guard him.

"What the fuck is going on!" Samuel complained to a superior. "We've got two mobsters redhanded for a double homicide and you're pinching pennies!" Penny was then moved to a motel.

Cadieux tried to make amends with Penny, and reassure fellow cop Paul Roder, who kept saying that testifying in a murder case against a Mafia capo was not the uncomplicated future he imagined when he left the Police Academy ten years before and was assigned to the unorganized crime of the Housing Authority. Still, no one had threatened Roder yet, and Cadieux pointed out several times that it was against Mafia rules to harm a cop acting in the line of duty.

By Mafia tradition, that was true because of the grief it was believed to cause; threaten a cop and every bookmaker, loanshark and made man in the neighborhood starts getting harassed.

However, there was no rule against trying to bribe a cop. So, on January 3, 1980, Joey Testa, who had handled the earlier approach to Penny's brother, was assigned to telephone Roder at his home. Demonstrating that he remained confident of his decision to pick Joey over Henry to replace Chris, Roy told Freddy, "Joey is the only guy I can trust to handle something like this."

Joey told Roder that two friends of his were ready to pay him twenty-five thousand dollars if he lied about a crucial element of the case: "Instead of saying you were a police officer that night, just say you said, 'Hey you, hold it.' Don't say you identified yourself as a police officer."

Regrettably for Roy and Nino, the attempted bribe offended Roder and hardened his attitude. "I am a cop. I'm going to testify the way it happened. I wouldn't take a hundred thousand, and you can tell your friends I'll take a bullet before I'll take their money."

The next day, after he reported the call, the police department moved Roder into hiding—a wise move, because both Nino and Roy had shown they were capable of breaking with Mafia tradition.

With Penny and Roder out of reach and set to testify, the case against Nino remained strong. Even so, as he went into the dock for the third time in his life, on January 30, 1980, the Brooklyn District Attorney's office was still apprehensive. Albert DeMeo, Roy's uncle, had resigned the office many years before to teach law, but the wisdom of his day still applied: The unexpected happens in Mafia cases.

Therefore, prosecutor Samuel and his bosses asked Judge Edward Lentol to sequester the jury for the entire trial—not just during deliberations, as was customary. The risk of jury-tampering was too great, they argued. Judge Lentol, an Italian-American, agreed. This had not happened in Brooklyn since the Murder, Incorporated cases of the 1940s (which were prosecuted by, among others, Kenny McCabe, Sr.).

The judge's order eliminated Nino's last possible ex parte move—bribing a juror—because the jurors would be guarded around the clock. Unable to buy a way out, Nino was reduced to his riskiest option: Make the jury believe his story that he was shot by the same gunman who had shot the Eppolitos, and that he then escaped with one of the assailant's guns and had fired on Roder in self-defense. The phony bullet smuggled in by the departed Dominick made the story plausible, but it was a highly improbable tale; worse yet, it required Nino to testify in his own defense and tell the tale without getting tripped up on cross-examination.

In reality, his dilemma was even worse. Nino was not aware that prosecutor Samuel was ready to ambush the fake bullet evidence. X-rays of Nino's neck shortly after the incident showed that the bullet lodged beneath the surface of his skin was different from the round he turned over later. While the rifling marks on the bullets that killed the Eppolitos and the one that had supposedly come out of Nino's neck were the same, their shapes were different, because they had been fired into different surfaces—flesh and water. The bullet switch was not such a clever idea after all. The X-rays proved that Roder, not the gunman, shot Nino. The question for the jury was reduced to simple terms: Who to believe, the gangster or the cop?

Only a lucky break could save Nino—and on the third day of juror selection, he caught one, as juror number nine was sworn. Her name was Judy May; she was a pretty, doe-eyed paralegal. She was about to be married, and unknown to her, her fiancé's father was one of Anthony Gaggi's oldest loan customers. When her future father-in-law, Sol Hellman, found out from his son that she was a juror in the case, he rushed to tell Roy the serendipitous news.

The search for remaining jurors and two alternates dragged on more than a week. On Valentine's Day, the judge permitted the sequestered jurors to have dinner with their sweethearts, under supervision of court officers. Understandably, no one was suspicious of the way Judy May's fiancé, Wayne Hellman, whispered lovingly into her ear. But a new fix was on. To protect his lawyers, Nino—a savvy client—kept them in the dark.

In the dark too, the prosecution put on its case. Penny and Roder stood by their stories and Samuel introduced his X-ray evidence. Nino took the stand—he had to give Judy May something to work with in the jury room—and told his story. Playing a little joke on his nemesis, Detective McCabe, he said that the gunman in the car with the Eppolitos was a loanshark known to him only as "Kenny." Nino was only there to mediate a dispute between the victims and Kenny, when the loanshark suddenly shot them all. Of course, after he escaped with one of Kenny's guns, he thought Roder was a friend of Kenny's seeking to kill him. The only people in the courtroom who seemed to believe the yarn were Rose Gaggi, who cried, and her and Nino's children.

Roy eschewed the trial, to avoid witness Patrick Penny, who had seen "Kenny" leave the car with Nino and the forgotten man of the case, Peter Piacente.

Besides, Roy had work to attend to—such as, on March 7, the murder of Joseph Coppolino: Another one of the DeMeo crew's offshore marijuana shipments—twenty-three tons, this time—had been waylaid by the authorities, and Roy and the crew fingered Coppolino, a smalltime pot dealer, as the person who tipped police. Coppolino was dealt with in an atypical way—he was stabbed and decapitated, but also left on the street to be found. It was evidence that Roy had confused his two tried and true murder styles while in some ferocious fit of the moment.

Steven Samuel thought his case was a winner as the judge instructed the Eppolito jury. During a break, Piacente's defense attorney told him he feared a quick, devastating verdict. Lawyers on both sides were struck by Nino's calm. Mostly, he stayed seated at the defense table browsing the financial section of a newspaper. Once again, he was a reader of the *Wall Street Journal*, not the *Daily News*.

Once the jury began deliberations, jury foreman Philip Von Esch also expected a quick, devastating verdict of guilty on all counts because the evidence was "so strong." Only Judy May, of course, felt otherwise. In the jury's first vote, only she dissented: "I don't believe anything Patrick Penny said."

Over two days, Von Esch and the other jurors pressed her to further articulate her opinion. "It's just my feeling," she would say.

Rather than declare themselves a hung jury, which would have caused a retrial, Von Esch and others felt compelled to reach a verdict. When the lone dissenter finally conceded there was some evidence Nino had assaulted a policeman, they seized on the compromise and voted to acquit Nino and Piacente of murder, but convict Nino of assault and Piacente of a less serious charge, reckless endangerment. Judy May, a paralegal, knew that a watered-down verdict was better than a hung jury because the defendants would have still been vulnerable to murder charges in a retrial.

The tortured compromise was "a travesty of justice," Von Esch said, after some jurors agreed to discuss the case with lawyers from both sides. "But it was felt it was the only thing we could get because she was not going to budge on the homicide charges."

Because he had a ringer in the jury, and the others did not understand the hung-jury option, Nino was facing five to fifteen years in prison—rather than life. Judge Lentol denied bail pending appeal, but another judge overturned him and Nino went home in a relatively gay mood to await formal sentencing.

A month later, at the sentencing, Nino's lawyer James La Rossa asked for a lenient sentence because his fifty-five-year-old client had lived "an exemplary life," and: "For all intents and purposes, this is his first real brush with the law where someone has found him guilty. He has worked all these years. He has constantly been employed; he has constantly earned money; he has constantly contributed to society." Understandably, all of the cops in the courtroom felt like gagging.

Judge Lentol showed what he felt in the sentence he handed down—the maximum, five to fifteen years. However, because he had already been overturned by an appeals court when he tried to jail Nino after the verdict, Lentol let Nino stay free pending Nino's obligatory appeal of the assault conviction.

Nino, of course, had already decided to punish Patrick Penny, the witness whose testimony made the case, according to what all jurors but Judy May had told lawyers for both sides. In fact, the only reason Penny was not already dead was that Nino dared not act while the sentence was pending, on the off chance La Rossa's pleas for leniency might seduce the judge.

Now, however, the deadly coast was clear. Penny's death was not going to affect the appeal Nino's lawyers were mounting. The appeal was of the conviction, not the sentence, which is almost always legally unassailable.

Much as he wanted to, however, Nino could not do the work himself. Newly convicted, he could not risk another serious arrest; as a two-time loser, he would never leave prison. He would have to get his revenge vicariously, through Roy of course.

Roy was eager to oblige, and not just because Nino assigned him complete responsibility. Roy felt a grudge of his own, however twisted and self-serving it was. It was Penny's fault that for the first time in Roy's indefatigably murderous career that someone on a job with him got caught and convicted—it was doubly embarrassing that this distinction, this chink in his invincible armor, had fallen to his boss, Nino. He also was still smarting over the accusation by Dominick Montiglio, wherever the upstart brat had gone, that he had left Nino in the lurch.

Even before Nino's sentencing, Roy told Vito, "Ya know somethin'? That little cocksucker Penny is gonna pay, soon as we find out where he's hiding and who he hangs with."

From the trial, Roy knew that Penny was a burglar with a police record, because Nino's lawyers had thrown it in Penny's face while trying to discredit his testimony. That meant that the police had to have a mug shot of Penny; Roy wanted the mug shot so he could copy it and distribute it to crew members as they began searching for Penny.

Ordinarily, Roy would have relied on Detective Peter Calabro of the Auto Crime Division for this crooked service, but shortly after Nino was convicted Calabro was murdered in a violent and sudden way—through no fault of the crew, for once.

Driving home to New Jersey after finishing a tour of duty in Queens, Calabro was shotgunned to death by assassins in a passing car. Kenny McCabe and other detectives who investigated the murder never found enough evidence to prosecute, but came to believe that thirty-six-year-old Calabro was murdered by relatives of his wife, who had drowned under suspicious circumstances in 1977.

Calabro had been residing with his young daughter—and with his auto crime partner, John Doherty, the former Flatlands resident and childhood friend of Roy's who introduced Calabro to Roy. Doherty's wife had drowned at home in a bathtub in 1978, after a heart attack, according to the medical examiner's report.

At the time of his partner's murder, Doherty told the

media he was "grief-stricken" and said: "I've had a death in the family."

Leaving Doherty alone, Roy contacted another cop he had befriended during the last three years—another detective, in fact—Thomas Sobota, a ten-year veteran and Canarsie resident who had been drinking heavily at the Gemini since 1977. Sobota also liked to gamble and owed the bar's bookmaker, Joseph Guglielmo, about one thousand dollars. Like all the other officers and firemen who drank and gambled at the Gemini Lounge throughout its history, he never knew what was happening in the clubhouse in the back.

Making his pitch to Sobota, Roy said he needed a mug shot of Penny because a friend wanted to find him and give him an important message. Sobota was not a Mafia expert; he investigated run-of-the-mill crimes in Manhattan's 6th Precinct. He believed Roy was just a loanshark, which was no big deal; he was not principled either. The worst he thought Roy was up to was that Penny had testified against a friend, and Roy or the friend wanted to slap him around—also no big deal.

To cover himself in his Greenwich Village squad room, and make it seem he had reason to request a mug shot of Penny, Sobota began a phony case file claiming that an anonymous tipster had telephoned and claimed that a Pat or Bill Penny of Brooklyn was "ripping off the fags" at the Hudson River docks in the West Village, a traditional gay cruising ground.

After also obtaining Penny's record of arrests, Sobota was even less concerned about providing it and the mug shot to Roy. Penny had been arrested fourteen times in two years; the persistent burglar was, in cop slang, a "skel"—a derivative of *skellum,* an archaic synonym for "rascal."

Unlike the federal government, and like other states, New York did not have a program for protecting and relocating witnesses who risked their lives by testifying. The Brooklyn District Attorney, employing an option that would discourage any witness, tried to keep Penny in protective custody after Nino was convicted—but Penny's Legal Aid lawyer, at his client's urging, filed a motion, and a judge ruled the state did not have authority to detain Penny any longer.

A month passed, then came Nino's sentencing. That day, Detective Roland Cadieux made an urgent visit to Penny's home and delivered a blunt warning. "Up to this point, Patrick, they were not going to kill you, it would have looked bad at Nino's sentencing. But now there's no reason to keep you alive. You have to get out of New York; otherwise, you are a dead man."

"I'm a street guy. I've been around. I can handle myself."

Penny managed to survive two assassination plots: once when Roy and his bookmaking cousin, Dracula, could not find a parking place in time to get him before he got on a bus, and again when he passed himself off to Vito as his brother Robert. He ran away to Florida, but he was soon back—packing a gun—because he missed his girlfriend, the one who urged him to keep on driving the night his sorry fate was entwined with Nino's and Roy's.

Upon his return, police caught him with the loaded gun he was packing, but he was released on a small cash bail after he told the judge: "The mob is looking for me. I needed it for my own protection."

Kenny McCabe told Penny he knew a friendly sheriff in California who would let him hide out in his county, but Penny said, "No thanks. I can handle it."

Though everyone in the crew was carrying mug shots of Penny, Roy assigned Vito to be the principal pursuer. This was because Joey and Anthony—they had already paid an intimidating visit to Penny's brother—had to be careful about the number of times they were seen asking about Penny and because the otherwise gaudy Kuwait stolen-car deal had run into some problems that were keeping Henry and Freddy occupied. In a happy coincidence, Vito's lover, Joey Lee, had attended junior high school with Penny and knew the most about his friends and likely hangouts.

"I spoke with Nino," Roy said, "and Nino says that if you can, take this kid alive and bring him to the clubhouse."

Vito felt especially obliged to accept responsibility; recently, he had complained to Roy that he was worth more to the car deal than the hundred dollars he was receiving for each car he helped Richie DiNome steal.

Roy, saying he had so much money it did not matter to him, gave Vito half of his new, expanded weekly share, fifteen thousand. Vito praised Roy's generosity to the crew, but Freddy, among others, thought Roy charged it to everyone else by taking more off the top for expenses, and in truth, Roy the dealmaker did.

Increasingly uncautious Roy had also welcomed Vito into his home, and at a Christmas party there five months before, gave him a Santa Claus outfit and gifts to pass out to crew members' children.

Vito and Joey searched for Penny every night and finally spotted him at a gas station and learned where he was hiding out by following him. The information was passed to Roy. In another fit of recklessness, Roy decided to kill Penny on the evening of May 12, 1980, a night he could not track down the most loyal and able of his gang, Dirty Henry and the Gemini twins.

The only crew members he was able to reach on short notice were Vito and, pathetically, Richie DiNome. In the aftermath of this, Roy would buy new gadgets, telephone-beepers, for his crew.

The trio waited for Penny outside his hideout and saw him get into a Jeep Scout, then followed him to a bar he stopped at in Sheepshead Bay, near Bensonhurst. They decided to wait until he came back out. They were parked two cars behind his in a black Volkswagen that Richie and Vito had begun using in their Kuwait-deal raids, after deciding it was as inconspicuous as Richie's homely station wagon.

A man walking his dog thought the three men sitting in the Volkswagen were manifestly conspicuous. He telephoned police; two patrol cars responded and parked in front and back of the car; an officer then approached the driver's seat, where Richie was.

"Just be calm," knowing Vito told Richie.

The officer asked for Richie's registration and driver's license. Richie could not find his registration right away and began fumbling papers from the glove compartment and muttering that his wife must have lost it.

Vito asked the officer what the problem was. "Well, you're making somebody nervous," the cop said. "Somebody thinks you're going to break into one of these stores around here."

As Roy, armed and explosively dangerous, sat silently in the backseat, Vito said they were waiting for another friend, who was due to get off a bus at a nearby bus stop; then they all would be going to a card game.

Meanwhile, Richie stumbled onto his registration; the officer called it in, then returned with a smile. "Listen, do me a favor. Wait ten more minutes and if your friend doesn't show, go to the game yourself because the next shift is just going to get called too."

"No problem," Vito said, and the two patrol cars left.

After an encounter with police outside the potential murder scene, prudence dictated that the work be abandoned for another time—but not in the increasingly addled mind of someone anxious to avenge a setback and reclaim his invincible aura.

So Roy told his accomplices they would just have to change their game plan. He told Richie to park the Volkswagen a couple of blocks away and go steal a car—"something that looks good so it doesn't look suspicious, and something with some speed." He and Vito then waited by some telephone booths near a newsstand until Joey Scorney-taught Richie showed up with a sporty blue Chevrolet Malibu.

They parked it in the same spot behind Penny's car, which Roy disabled by disconnecting the battery cables. This time they waited for Penny by stalking the area near the bar on foot. Mildly drunk, Penny came out two hours later and swore when his car would not start. With jolly Vito backing him up, Roy approached, asked Penny if he needed booster cables, and as the baby-faced burglar shouted "Get the fuck away from me!" shot him dead.

The same person who telephoned police once before heard the commotion and called again. From his window, he saw a pudgy man, Roy, getting into a blue Malibu. An even pudgier man, Vito, was behind the wheel as the car roared away. Richie had scooted around a corner to retrieve his Volkswagen.

Later that night, the stolen Malibu was set afire and abandoned. Two days later, after reading about the murder, Detective Thomas Sobota shouted at Roy at the Gemini Lounge: "How the hell could you do this to me! You've really put me in a jackpot!" Roy said, "Tommy, I swear to God on my kids, I had nothing to do with that kid Penny! A thousand guys had to be looking for the kid!'' At that week's shapeup, outside the clubhouse, Freddy gave Joey Lee forty-five hundred dollars. Roy later said the money was a gift to Joey and Vito—''It's from Nino for Patrick Penny.''

That same day, Detective Roland Cadieux had begun a new job in another branch of the NYPD. A detective from his old precinct telephoned him at home with the news. ''Damn it!'' was about all Cadieux could say.

Prosecutor Steven Samuel, now in private practice, learned about it the following day, as he walked to a subway stop in Manhattan and saw the front page of a *New York Post* on display at a newsstand: ''MOB WITNESS RUBBED OUT.'' He was stricken with dread as he opened it to an inside page and saw the victim's mug shot. ''Holy shit!'' he said to himself. ''They can get anyone they want.''

In Penny's case, the NYPD made it easy. The patrol officers who were outside the bar before Penny was shot, checking Richie DiNome's license and registration, gave the detectives assigned to the murder an address in Washingtonville, New York, where for the lower insurance rates, his Volkswagen was registered in his wife's name.

The detectives never linked her to him, a simple investigative chore, and so the patrol officers were not shown any photographs of DeMeo crew members. If they had, the officer who spoke to Richie could have placed him—and maybe Roy—at the murder scene, in suspicious circumstances, a couple of hours beforehand. So, as it was, the case went nowhere.

CHAPTER 18

Empire Boulevard

The reckless fury Roy showed the night he murdered Patrick Penny was partly due to recent setbacks in the Kuwait car deal—problems that were worse than he knew. Along with the arrest and conviction of his patron, these troubles showed that at last he and his crew were losing some of their vaunted invulnerability. In 1980, the winds of decline gathered strength, though by no means were Roy or the crew any less vicious when some poor soul got in their monstrous way, stupidly or otherwise.

All the while Nino was awaiting trial, the car deal had hummed along extravagantly well, but with some adjustments, minor and major. Because Ronald Ustica grew paranoid when a Nassau County missing-persons detective questioned him about Khaled Daoud and Ronald Falcaro, he asked Roy to insulate him from the paperwork involved in the Kuwait shipping arrangements. So the stolen cars were now being shipped through Big A Exporters, a company incorporated by Henry Borelli under a phony name.

The major adjustment involved a move to a still larger warehouse, located next to the Seven-One Precinct on an appropriately named street in Brooklyn—Empire Boulevard. Officers on duty outside the precinct would help direct traffic on those days when the crew was loading the car carrier it rented to transport the cars to the Newark pier. One day, an officer complained to the workers of what he thought was a firm that repossessed automobiles for finance companies that they were leaving too many cars double-parked on the street in front.

"We're short-handed today," Henry responded. "We'll move 'em soon as we can. We're doing the best we can."

On three floors, the warehouse had room for about five

hundred cars. Abdullah Hassan flew in from Kuwait to inspect the facility and was so impressed he ordered more "rentals"; he was expanding into Iraq and Iran, but would continue shipping the cars to Kuwait first because it had the lowest import tax. Each partnership share was now worth thirty thousand dollars a week, and so the partners could afford to employ additional salaried help, such as the back-in-circulation Peter LaFroscia and another Testa brother, Dennis.

Tellingly, however, no one was paying too much attention to quality control. On April 22, four days after Nino was sentenced, a federal customs inspector poking around Pier 292 in Newark saw that the trunk lock was missing on a car destined for shipment to Kuwait.

It was not Joseph Tedeschi's job to determine if cars awaiting shipment were stolen—he was more interested in whether they contained weapons or other contraband—but he had gone to insurance industry seminars on the stolen-car industry, and a missing trunk lock was a flagrant clue that a car was hot. He checked the car further and noticed that a rubber washer was missing from the lock on the driver's door and that the style of lettering on the car's emission sticker was different from what he had seen on a General Motors sticker before. Moreover, the VIN plate numbers were unevenly aligned.

Because the car and others in the same shipment were not to be shipped for several days, Tedeschi delayed checking the others until he could get an expert to help. Two days later, he returned with Anthony Ciardi, an employee of the privately funded National Auto Theft Bureau. In the interim, the Kuwait-bound shipment had swelled to seventy-six cars, mostly Caprices. The dashboard VIN plates of many were checked against a national computer list; no cars with those numbers had been reported stolen.

Tedeschi and Ciardi next began searching for so-called "confidential" VIN plates that as an antitheft device manufacturers emboss on more remote parts of their cars, on engine firewalls or transmissions. When decoded, the numbers and letters on the confidential plates should match the numbers on the "public" dashboard VIN plate. Of the cars Tedeschi and Ciardi checked, none did.

The next day, the cars were confiscated, and in a day

more, following a paper trail, FBI agents from Newark, joined by agents from the Brooklyn-Queens office in New York, took up surveillance positions outside the Empire Boulevard warehouse. They took photographs as men they did not know—Henry, Freddy, and some hired help—loaded two car carriers. Aboard one carrier was an undercover agent.

After loading the carriers, everyone from the crew departed. The agents let them go. They had their photographs and license plate numbers; at the moment, the evidence inside the warehouse was more important. They waited until another agent arrived with a search warrant and then raided the warehouse. They confiscated twelve cars, dozens of discarded license plates, and boxes of material the crew had found in the cars and foolishly, arrogantly, not yet thrown away—strollers, umbrellas, music tapes, and (because many cars came from the mainly Jewish Borough Park area of Brooklyn) Torahs, scrolls, and other religious artifacts. Of all people, Henry Borelli had particularly insisted on not throwing the religious items in the garbage because he thought it would bring bad luck.

After the raid, the warehouse's owner telephoned Henry and said it was best not to come back to work that day, or the next. Henry spread the word to all interested parties. "The joint got busted!" he said to Freddy.

The situation would soon become worse than Freddy and Henry knew. Four days after the Empire Boulevard raid, a man who identified himself only as "Harry" called the FBI in Newark and identified them as the key men in the operation. Furthermore, a year before, they had murdered two people—Ronald Falcaro and Khaled Daoud.

"Harry" called the FBI in Newark twice more in the next few days with other seemingly authentic details. He agreed to a secret meeting but failed to show. Even so, it was a breakthrough: Someone deep inside the Gemini had decided to risk Roy's wrath and look out for himself first. Keeping an interesting card in the hole, however, the caller had not given up the name of the true boss of the operation, Roy.

Because of the Empire Boulevard raid, Roy was in a more wrathful mood than ever. On June 5, 1980, three weeks after Patrick Penny was murdered, he committed his third double homicide in nine months' time. The victims were young body- and fender-men who had taken over one of Chris Rosenberg's old shops, which was next door to Richie DiNome's and across the street from Freddy's. As in the Falcaro-Daoud murders, one victim just happened along at the wrong time.

The plot against the other had unfolded over many months. Outside a Manhattan bar, Charles Mongitore had been in a nasty fight with a nemesis from childhood whose father was a Gambino gangster from Queens; Mongitore was stabbed in the neck and decided to press charges. The defendant's father, Salvatore Mangialino, did not want his son in jail; he asked Roy to intervene.

Roy dispatched Freddy, Richie, and Vito to talk to Mongitore, who knew Roy, but only as a man who was a friend of Freddy's and Richie's. "Roy will give you ten, fifteen thousand," Vito said. "You don't even have to drop the charges. You can wait until you go to court and just make like you can't identify the guy."

Sealing his fate, Mongitore refused to go along despite several more meetings and pointed messages. He had almost died from the stab wound. He wanted some measure of revenge and could not fathom why Roy did not understand. He complained to a friend, "I can't believe it, I get in a fight in Manhattan with a guy from Queens, and now I'm getting static from a guy in Brooklyn."

Underestimating the guy from Brooklyn, Mongitore agreed when Richie asked him to come to his body shop and help him work on a Porsche the crew had recently stolen from designer Pierre Cardin. Inside, Roy had convened his underworld court-for-hire. Without offering a last-minute plea bargain, Judge Roy and his clerk Dirty Henry immediately shot Mongitore more than a dozen times.

With Mongitore, Roy at least had a motive—the young man had refused to listen to reason. With Mongitore's partner and friend, Daniel Scutaro, Roy had no motive at all; it was pure evil bloodlust. He could have spared Scutaro when in a little while Scutaro knocked on the door of Richie's shop and asked if Mongitore was there. He could have told Richie to tell Scutaro he had no idea where Mongitore was.

But no. He told Richie to stall Scutaro while he and Henry reloaded and then wave him inside. Idiotic Richie did as ordered, and Scutaro walked right into a sick hail of thrill-killing fire. The bodies were piled in the trunk of another stolen car, which was then parked and abandoned by a nearby cemetery. Hours later, Richie telephoned Vito and asked him to help cleanse the shop of blood. Roy no longer helped out with such details, which were for peons like Richie.

After Vito arrived, Richie realized his wallet was missing and began worrying it had fallen out of his jacket pocket as he was leaning over and helping Roy and Henry put the bodies into the car trunk. Desperate, he pleaded with Vito to go with him to the cemetery and drive the car back inside the shop, which they did. Inside the trunk, they did indeed find hapless Richie's wallet beside one of the victims; they then reabandoned the car in the same spot by the cemetery.

"Imagine if the police found the bodies with your wallet," Vito said. "You know what happens to you."

"Don't tell Roy! He'll kill me!"

When the bodies were discovered a day later, Frank Pergola, the same detective who drew the Chris Rosenberg murder, was assigned to investigate. Within days, from the distraught families and girlfriends of Mongitore and Scutaro, he learned the probable motive and was certain the same people who killed Chris were involved. But without any witnesses, and with suspects who would tell him to take a hike and talk to their lawyers, there was not much else he could do.

The Scutaro murder showed that Roy was following old friend Danny Grillo off the deep end. Where Danny was in love with dice, Roy was now clearly in love with murder. "It is like having the power of God," he told Vito. "Deciding who lives, who dies."

The fat boy from Flatlands might have achieved the power of God, but as he finally, totally succumbed to the beast inside, he was not happy. His bloodletting had not prevented his mentor Nino from getting jammed up, or his car deal from getting busted—or him from having to kill his equally tortured protégé, Harvey Rosenberg. Roy had made it to the top of the heap, only to feel it begin to collapse. He would never admit it, but the bully felt the ground beneath his feet trembling. He was getting scared.

A month after the murders, Roy and Gladys pretended (not very well) that they were a happy couple and hosted a lavishly catered Fourth of July bash at their splendid waterfront home in Massapequa Park. Of Roy's principal associates, only Nino—who was free on bail while appealing his assault conviction—did not attend; some of the event was videotaped by Freddy, who expended much footage following Roy around like the faithful puppy he was.

"Freddy, if you don't stop, I'm going to shoot you!" camera-shy Roy shouted at one point, to the delight of several children.

Wearing jeans belted too high and a too-tight red pullover, thirty-nine-year-old Roy looked more fat and dumpy than ever; his most dangerous, loyal, and handsome followers—Henry and Joey and Anthony—looked as silky and sleek as ever.

"Look at him," some male guest said as Freddy focused in on Henry Borelli. "He'd like being on television. He's so photogenic Barbara Walters is going to interview him."

Richie took Roy, Roy's son Albert, Freddy, Vito, and Joey Lee for a ride on his newest toy, a cabin cruiser he sailed up to the party on; by the dock area of one particular home along the inlet leading to the ocean, Roy ordered him to cut the engine and spoke familiarly of the home's former occupant, Carlo Gambino, a man he had never met. Back at his refuge, as the day wore on and many empty bottles of Dom Perignon piled up, Roy grew somber.

After Roy's son Albert and some young friends shot off hundreds of large fireworks, Vito saw Roy sitting alone in his living room and asked what was wrong. Roy said he was depressed because one of his usual guests was not there this year.

"I miss the kid Chris," he said, with emotion Vito took as absolutely genuine. "I really loved that kid. Some things you don't like doing and I really didn't like doing that."

Later, after more Dom Perignon, Roy told Freddy

maybe they should do what Dominick Montiglio had done. "You know, just run away from all of this."

Freddy was shocked too. He had never seen all-powerful Roy have a weak moment. Although in emotional turmoil, Roy was hardly immobilized. Two months later, he played God again. At the clubhouse, he machine-gunned Paul Castellano's former son-in-law Frank Amato to death. He told Freddy that Paul had contracted the work; others believed Roy had volunteered, knowing about Paul's rage at the man who cheated on his daughter and wanting, unrealistically, to improve his standing with Paul in the wake of the Eppolito debacle. No matter what, Paul was never going to like Roy—just his money.

The Gemini method was employed on Amato, who was lured to the clubhouse with talk of a business deal. Departing from their normal abnormalities, the crew did not take the packaged remains to the Fountain Avenue dump. Roy, Henry, the Gemini twins, and the DiNome brothers all took a moonlit ride on Richie's cabin cruiser and tossed them overboard many miles out to sea. They joked about using the pieces for bait, and "chumming for man-eating sharks."

Little by little, the authorities made headway against the crew—and further rattled Roy. A federal prosecutor in Brooklyn tied Patty Testa to stolen cars transported across state lines, and rather than face trial, Patty pleaded guilty to interstate transportation of the proceeds from one stolen car and to altering another car's odometer. This would not have caused Roy much stress had not Detective Kenny McCabe shown up at Patty's sentencing hearing.

As an organized crime authority, Kenny was regularly asked by prosecutors in federal and state courts to testify at proceedings involving defendants with Mafia ties. As to Patty, he said that four informants had linked him to Roy, Freddy DiNome, and Peter LaFroscia and to illegal firearms and drug-dealing. Although Patty was just twenty-three years old, he "was an up-and-coming wise-guy in the Canarsie area," Kenny testified.

For his part, Patty—represented by crew stalwart Fred Abrams—filed an affidavit in which he personally asked the judge not to send him to prison. He now employed six people, including youngest Testa brother Michael, at Patty Testa Motorcars. "All the effort that was expended by me in building up my business will have been for naught. I will lose all my business contacts I have built up over these past four years."

Judge Jacob Mishler gave the defendant a break—one year as opposed to ten—because of Patty's age. "Now, if that straightens you out," he told him, "I will have done a good job. If it doesn't, then I took a chance and lost, and society lost."

Naturally, society lost. That night, with Fred Abrams in attendance, the crew held an urgent meeting at Roy's house to discuss Kenny's worrisome testimony: Who were the informants? Kenny soon learned of the meeting and more—courtesy of, indirectly, Freddy DiNome.

While still unknowingly under investigation by FBI agents in Newark and New York because of the telephone tips from "Harry," Freddy had unwittingly stumbled into a Suffolk County sting operation. It began when two auto-crime officers visited his home in Shirley, Long Island, and asked about two motorcycles found in woods nearby. In another of his insurance scams, Freddy had recently reported that the motorcycles, which were his, had been stolen. When the cops more or less suggested this, Freddy got in a heated argument with one of them and ordered both to get off his property, just like Roy would have.

The officers suggested to their bosses that Freddy might be an ideal foil for learning more about organized crime in Suffolk County. The following day, Robert Gately, the officer who had not argued with Freddy, came back alone and, pretending to be corrupt, began cultivating a relationship. That first day, Gately accepted a hundred-dollar goodwill gesture from Freddy, and over time took eleven hundred dollars more, a chainsaw, and a Rolex watch. In return, Gately drank with Freddy, gave him meaningless police gossip and helped him out with a driver's license problem.

Freddy was vulnerable to a police sting because his mentor Roy was so good at collecting cops. Nowadays, Freddy was feeling more on top of his game than his boss was. With money made from the car deal, he had mounted surveillance cameras like Roy's at his house, which he also was renovating in a deluxe way. He had one hundred thousand dollars in loans on the street, and once while drinking with Gately, he pulled forty thousand in hundred-dollar bills from his pockets and ostentatiously tossed them on the bar.

"Put that away, before we have a problem in here," Gately told him.

"Fuck it," said Freddy, all powerfully.

By the time Kenny testified at Patty Testa's sentencing hearing, Freddy believed he and Gately were fast friends. After the emergency crew meeting in which Roy wondered who Kenny's informants were, Freddy told Gately about the pesty Brooklyn detective and asked him to find out who was talking.

Gately then told Kenny of his undercover relationship with Freddy. Happy to string Freddy along, and seeking to unnerve Roy, Kenny gave Gately official-looking documents describing in broad terms what he knew of Nino, Roy, the crew, and a few of their murders—but not mentioning any informants.

The documents fell short of what Freddy wanted, but he was impressed when Gately produced them. Later, he handed them to Roy as they drove to the pornography parlor Roy still owned in Bricktown, New Jersey; although he had launched another car deal, it was not on the same scale as before, and so Roy, trying to compensate for the drop in income, was now planning to import prostitutes from Manhattan to provide onsite services to his peep-show and magazine and film customers.

Freddy told Gately that Roy was shocked by the accuracy of the documents and so angry he ripped them apart and threw them out the windows of his car.

Kenny knew all of this when he and Tony Nelson had a long encounter with Roy in March 1981, on the eve of the day that Nino (an appeals court having finally upheld his conviction) was to surrender to corrections officers and begin serving his five-to-fifteen-year hitch in the Eppolito case.

Nino had already set in motion one more desperate attempt to challenge the conviction on new grounds, by encouraging his ringer on the jury, Judy May, to make some outlandish charges about sexual misconduct by court personnel during the sequestered jury deliberations.

But the legal process would take many months, and for the last two weeks he had come to terms with what he always dreaded, prison, and had been putting his affairs in order.

His and Roy's manipulation of Peter Piacente in the Eppolito murders had strained his relationship with Paul. Even so, he designated Roy as his stand-in with Paul while he, as wiseguys liked to say, went "away to college." A year earlier, the job would have been the elder Jimmy Eppolito's.

Nino had not seen or heard from his mercurial nephew Dominick since December 1979. Nobody from New York had except Buzzy Scioli, who had received a few telephone calls, but he was not about to admit it—except to Quāalude fugitive Cheryl Anderson, who had telephoned from her hideaway somewhere to ask how Dominick was. Denise Montiglio, now mother of her third child, a girl, had not told anyone where she and her family were hiding out and, after a rough start, living well if not normally.

Kenny and Tony ran into Roy outside a pre-"college" sendoff that was held for Nino at Tommaso's; many capos, made men and DeMeo crew members came by—but not Paul. Paul's neighbor Thomas Bilotti, now the new de facto underboss of the Brooklyn faction, did attend.

Anticipating such an event, Kenny and Tony had staked the restaurant out and were sitting in Tony's FBI car. As the party ended, Roy came out and waved at them, then got into his Cadillac, made a U-turn, and pulled alongside. In an agitated way, he yelled through his open window, "I got a bone to pick with you, McCabe! You are gonna get me killed! You've put me in dope! If you can prove I'm in dope, you can shoot me here in the street because I'm a dead man if I deal drugs and you know it!"

"What are you babbling about?" Kenny asked, but well knew.

"You testified I was involved in narcotics. You're gonna get me killed! You can accuse me of killing little babies, but don't say I'm involved in drugs."

"I said four of your friends said you were involved."

"You want to be a rich man, just give me one name."

Kenny laughed, and as the banter continued Roy

seemed to relax, as if the cops were just potential business partners. "You guys have been sitting out here three hours," he said pleasantly. "You should've just come in and had a drink."

For several years now, Kenny, Tony, and others had had Roy, Nino, and others in the crew under surveillance, but Roy was the only one who ever, as he did now by getting out of his car and standing alongside theirs, talked to them at any length.

The conversation lasted forty-five minutes. Roy talked about his uncle the famous lawyer and his cousin the famous medical examiner. He discussed his son and his two daughters and how proud they made him. He talked about how his mother always said he was smart enough to be a doctor.

"But I'm just our family's black sheep," he said, almost remorsefully, Kenny and Tony thought.

"You seem to have done all right for yourself," Tony said. "In a way."

"I'm a legitimate guy! I just buy and sell, that's all."

Roy also wanted Tony to know he was always on the ball. "I know you were in my bar once peeping around. I know it, but so what? Nothin' goes on there."

The detective, the agent, and the gangster continued to play a coy game. They were trying to determine if Roy was a potential informant. He was trying to gauge whether they were straight and narrow as they seemed. Well, a legitimate salesman like you could help us a lot and maybe help yourself, they would say; it would be nice to have friends like you, and maybe you would find the friendship profitable, he would say.

The three men were set in their ways, however, and the game ended with everyone firmly on their own side of the field. As Roy was about to depart, Kenny saw Nino leave Tommaso's, hesitate, then begin walking away from where his car was parked, seemingly because he did not want to pass the FBI car stationed between Tommaso's and his Cadillac.

Kenny was pleased that Nino found him and Tony so irritating. "Where the fuck is he going?" he asked Roy with mock alarm. "You better go tell him he doesn't have to walk home. It's late, you never know who you're going to run into, even in this neighborhood. The streets aren't safe anymore.''

"You know how Nino is," Roy said. "Unlike me, he has a thing about cops."

Roy let Nino go; on March 26, 1981, his last night of freedom, Nino left his car on the street and walked home alone. After orientation and transfers, he was incarcerated at Attica State Prison, the toughest "university" in New York State.

By now, Roy had accurately reasoned that the police suspected someone else, not him, was with Nino and Piacente when the Eppolitos were murdered. Leaving Kenny and Tony, he sarcastically said that he had no idea why anyone would want to harm such a pair of underachievers as the Eppolitos. "It totally beats me, I just can't understand it.''

Kenny accurately sized it up as fake bravado. "Roy's not as strong as he wants you to believe," he said to Tony after Roy left. "I'm not sure if Roy can stand up to pressure.''

Nino had made the same observation to Dominick years earlier, when Roy began gulping Valium after the IRS began investigating his returns. He offered it again during the Cuban crisis, when Roy panicked and an eighteen-year-old college student and vacuum cleaner salesman died. Obviously, Kenny was unaware he and Nino shared this insight of Roy. There was still so much he and the other cops interested in the crew did not know, but this would begin to change soon. In fact, some pivotal groundwork had already been laid by other cops.

John Murphy, the low-key intelligence officer of the NYPD's Auto Crime Unit, was deeply frustrated as the summer of 1980 began. For three years, he had been unable to persuade the NYPD to mount a serious investigation of Mafia influence in the stolen-car rackets. Then, out of the blue, as his undermanned unit underwent another upheaval and was reconstituted as a division of a new Organized Crime Control Bureau, people with power began to listen.

Joseph Harding, the division's first commander, called Murphy to a meeting and announced that the new United States Attorney for the Southern District of New York—

seeking to shore up local–federal relations—wanted to jointly investigate and prosecute a case with the NYPD. The Southern District, the local wing of the United States Justice Department, prosecuted violations of federal law in Manhattan, the Bronx, and several upstate counties; its prosecutors had won convictions in the Westchester Premier Theater case against all defendants but Anthony Gaggi. They could tap into the resources of numerous federal agencies, such as the FBI, the IRS, and the Drug Enforcement Administration (DEA).

The new boss of this well-funded seat of official power was John Martin, who had vowed an assault on organized criminal conspiracies, such as the city's five Mafia families. A friend of his, Robert McGuire, a former assistant U.S. attorney, was currently the "PC," police commissioner of the NYPD.

"We've been asked to give a presentation to Martin's people for a case that could be worked jointly," new auto crimes commander Harding said to Murphy. "Have you got anything?"

Murphy felt like a broken record by now, but Harding—new to auto crimes—was hearing his song the first time: "Sure, I got a great case," Murphy said. "Patty Testa."

The case, of course, was much greater than Murphy or anyone outside the crew realized. But after hearing Murphy and Murphy's friend on the Nassau County Auto Squad, Charles Meade, describe what they knew of Patty's operations, Harding ordered Murphy to prepare a formal presentation.

Over the next month, Murphy updated his charts and files and then briefed the case for Dominick Amorosa, chief of the Southern District organized crime unit, and other prosecutors at a series of meetings held over the summer. The list of homicides that Murphy believed were related to the stolen-car business in Brooklyn now included seventeen names. The DeMeo crew's toll was already much higher, but Murphy yet had no way of knowing that because he was focusing on cars—not drugs, contract hits, intra-crew discipline, and all the rest.

Murphy believed other victims belonged on the list, such as Ronald Falcaro and Khaled Daoud, just because Charles Meade had told him the missing men were in the car business and disappeared en route to Canarsie. Decorous Murphy did not mention that when he began urging action three years before the list contained only seven names.

Because stolen cars appeared to have been transported across state boundaries, the federal government had reason to prosecute; whether the Southern District had geographical jurisdiction was another matter. It appeared the cars had been stolen in Brooklyn, Queens and Long Island—the geographic province of another local arm of the Justice Department, the Eastern District of New York. Murphy was ready with an answer to this question that was more crucial than he imagined—Matty Rega.

After Dominick fled Brooklyn late the year before, Rega was free to be himself again. The flight—Nino was telling Buzzy and others that Dominick had run off with a quarter million dollars of his money—was the proof Rega needed to make it appear he was telling the truth about the disputed thirty thousand dollars. He still owed Nino and Roy other money, however, and was hardly (as his father had claimed at the sitdown over his restaurant) straightening himself out.

Instead, Rega was using drugs again and dealing cocaine with Pedro Rodriguez while still awaiting trial on the Quāalude charge that caused him to shut down the Hole in the Wall and made Cheryl Anderson a fugitive. Rega and Rodriguez had set up shop in a Manhattan apartment, down the street from the New York office of the DEA. In April, agents raided the stash pad and arrested Rega, Rodriguez, and their girlfriends.

About the same time, at his old car dealership in the Bronx, Rega had conferred with Rodriguez and Patty Testa on a scheme to ship twenty stolen cars to Puerto Rico, according to a car thief Charles Meade had arrested in Canarsie. The thief and his accomplices had stolen three Porsche Turbo Carreras right out of dealerships in Great Neck and Amityville. The thief was now Meade's informant, and he said he and two others stole the cars for Patty; one of the Porsches was then confiscated from Rega in New Jersey after he was arrested.

Rega's Manhattan address and the Bronx allegation gave the Southern District jurisdiction. Even the Porsche was enough; it could not have been driven to New Jersey from New York without crossing some highway or bridge in the domain of the Southern District, including the Verrazano-Narrows Bridge. While it connected Brooklyn to Staten Island, where another bridge led to New Jersey, it still was, jurisdictionally speaking, in the domain of the Southern District because the water beneath it was. As the last meeting ended, prosecutors told new auto crimes boss Joseph Harding and John Murphy that they would give them an answer soon.

"I know how these guys work," Harding said afterward. "They'll wait until next year to make a decision."

Instead, in two weeks, in September 1980, the prosecutors committed the government to an investigation. The primary target was Patty; secondary targets included Roy, Joey, Anthony, Henry, Freddy, and Peter LaFroscia—and several junkyards and chop shops. Prosecutors hoped to "turn" Rega—in the meantime, he had pleaded guilty in his drug cases—and persuade him to testify against the others for time off his prison sentence.

That summer, Murphy had also begun to hear that while Patty Testa was important, brother Joey might be more so. One night, he went to the Six-Nine precinct in Canarsie after two officers arrested two car thieves and recovered a Mercedes reported stolen from Reggie Jackson, the all-star rightfielder of the New York Yankees. Murphy asked the officers if the thieves were working for Patty. They were not sure.

"But Patty isn't the guy you should be worried about," one said. "His brother Joey is the boss."

The Testa brothers were the most infamous men in Canarsie, the officer added. Only the oldest one, Salvatore, was living an apparently legitimate life. He was a city police officer.

Murphy and other auto crime officers began working a few days a week at the Southern District offices on Foley Square in Manhattan, preparing reports for an assistant U.S. attorney assigned to the case. Much to Murphy's dismay, however, the prosecutor was occupied with other cases and not much was done with their reports.

To pass the frustrating time, Murphy began going on surveillance with Kenny and Tony and with Joseph Wendling, the DA's investigator he met while waiting to take the NYPD test for promotion to sergeant. Murphy and

Wendling had both passed, but they were not sergeants yet because the NYPD was under pressure to promote minorities first.

By spring of 1981, like Kenny and Tony, Murphy and Wendling had become unofficial partners too. Just as Murphy was kidded by fellow officers for his obsession with Patty Testa, Wendling was ribbed for his desire to get even with Peter LaFroscia, who had taunted him as he walked out of the courtroom with an acquittal in the John Quinn murder case.

With more officers, detectives, and agents outside the Gemini all the time, younger members of the crew began meeting elsewhere when they wanted to get together socially. The Friday night business meetings at the clubhouse continued, but the crew hung out more at a Canarsie body shop, R-Twice Collision, that was run by a friend of Joey Testa's who was involved in a big way in the drug business. When R-Twice became hot, the crew moved on to another bar, the 19th Hole, and then a disco, Scandals.

Wendling "sat" on R-Twice a lot, with Murphy, or Kenny, or by himself. He tailed Peter LaFroscia whenever he could, and began seeing him with known drug dealers. One day, LaFroscia pulled over and waited for Wendling to come up behind, then got out to complain that Wendling was harassing him for no reason.

It was the moment Wendling was waiting for; the aggressive, former Seven-Three cop did not lose many when he served at Fort Zinderneuf. "Remember that day in court when you laughed at me? It was the biggest mistake of your life, pal."

Meanwhile, Murphy grew impatient with the Southern District. So did his police bosses. After all the enthusiasm of the previous fall, the case against Patty Testa and the rest was in repose; the prosecutor assigned to it was busy with other cases and trials, and his superiors had not provided any help. He had met with a few informants and potential cooperating witnesses such as imprisoned Matty Rega, but made no deals; no one had talked to a grand jury, with or without immunity.

Despite the disappointing Southern District effort, a new spirit of federal–local cooperation was in the air—at least insofar as the FBI's investigation of Freddy, Henry, and the Empire Boulevard operation. Unlike 1977, when the NYPD and the FBI were at cross-purposes while investigating Quinn and LaFroscia, they were now sharing information. While on surveillance with Wendling and Kenny, and while attempting to prod the Southern District, Murphy also was assisting the FBI probe on an official basis.

Because of the surveillance photographs shot the day of the Empire Boulevard raid and the anonymous tips from "Harry" right afterward, agents had quickly identified Freddy and Henry. It took about a year more to reach dead ends on the other suspects and Harry's additional tip that Freddy and Henry had murdered Ronald Falcaro and Khaled Daoud. As to interstate shipment of stolen cars, however, the FBI linked Freddy and Henry through their fingerprints to evidence found at the warehouse, and with Murphy's help, tied them to the phony company Henry set up, Big A Exporters.

By late May 1981, the FBI was set to arrest them: A grand jury in Newark had returned sealed indictments. Because so many of their acquaintances in the car world had been questioned by agents, Freddy and Henry suspected their arrests were imminent. On the evening of May 21, when he saw Kenny in a car outside his new house in Queens, Henry thoughtfully notified him: "I'm going to be home all night." In the new spirit of cooperation, Kenny had been asked to assist with Henry's arrest.

At four-thirty a.m. the next day, as another team woke Freddy at home and took him into custody, Henry was shaken from sleep and arrested. They were taken to the FBI's Brooklyn-Queens office for new fingerprints and photographs. John Murphy was telephoned at home on Long Island so he could come in and have the pleasure of helping with the processing.

Once advised of his right to remain silent, Henry snarled and asked to call his lawyer, Fred Abrams. Freddy DiNome was more congenial. He also spelled his name one way, but wrote it another—D-I-N-A-M-E, although this may have been unintentional because he had never learned how to write anything but his name, and he did that in more of a scrawl.

Kenny McCabe suggested to Bruce Mouw, boss of the

FBI's Gambino family squad, that he interview Freddy outside Henry's presence. "Freddy is weak; he could be a witness for us."

Mouw met with Freddy for half an hour, dangling the idea he could help himself by cooperating. Freddy did not bite, although by the questions he asked about Mouw's duties he appeared to enjoy being in the presence of an important person. "But I don't think he's a nut that can be cracked," Mouw told Kenny.

After processing, Freddy and Henry were taken to the federal courthouse in Brooklyn so that they could be legally transferred to the custody of Newark officials. Murphy rode in the car containing Henry, who had relaxed and even decided to be cordial.

Joshing, Henry said he was just a self-employed salesman and a former carpenter with a wife and two daughters, ages twelve and thirteen. He hoped to send the children to college some day, but with inflation he did not know if he could ever afford it.

"Forget about it, Henry," Murphy could not resist replying. "Where you're going, you don't have to worry about it. Tuition, interest rates, inflation, nothing. You're out of the rat race, Henry."

CHAPTER 19

Harry

Even without knowing that he and his crew had attracted federal interest (lame though it still was), Roy felt pressure mounting from other directions in June 1981. Only briefly into his new role as acting captain of Nino's crew, he was worried about the Empire Boulevard arrests and whether the case would reach to him. He also found out about Suffolk County's undercover sting of Freddy, because Freddy made an ominous remark about Kenny McCabe's wife to his supposed dirty cop friend, Robert Gately, who had to warn Kenny, who then told Freddy that if he ever came near his wife, Kenny would forget he was a cop. That warning told Freddy he had been suckered by Gately, and when Freddy admitted it to Roy, Roy could only suppose what secrets his pot-smoking gopher had given Gately.

He also was wondering about another crew member he had admitted during his expanionist heyday—Vito Arena. Vito had stopped coming by the Gemini a few months after the downbeat Fourth of July party at Roy's house and was rumored to have flown the coop to Florida with Joey Lee. It unnerved Roy that someone in his crew had disappeared without his knowledge.

On top of it all, Nino had gone to prison furious at Roy. Leaving his going-away party at Tommaso's, he had seen Roy talking to Kenny and Tony and had felt forced to leave his car on the street and walk home. He mentioned the incident in a farewell chat with Paul, who dispatched a family capo to berate Roy, telling him it was impossible to spend forty-five minutes talking to cops and not give up some information of value.

"Stop being stupid," the capo told Roy, who felt that was the last thing he was.

Since Nino's departure, Roy had handed cash to Paul

a few times, but only at the Meat Palace, never Paul's majestic white house. Paul did not know half of what he should have about Roy, but the Eppolito disaster reaffirmed his negative notions; only because he had such a history with his disappointing friend Nino had he let him put Roy in charge while Nino was at "college."

Roy, on the other hand, hated being treated like a second-class captain. He deserved better treatment because he earned Paul so much money. Roy began having murderous fantasies about Paul. He indulged them after Freddy arrived home from the Newark federal courthouse on bail. He told Freddy that it might become necessary to "whack Waterhead," so they better devise a plan.

It would be difficult to get close enough to kill Paul without getting killed themselves; he had too much security. The plan they settled on was to assassinate Paul, and maybe his driver and now customary companion Thomas Bilotti, along some highway. While doubled up on one of Freddy's motorcycles, they would pull alongside and fill Paul's Lincoln with machinegun fire. Because Freddy was an expert motorcyclist, they would get away quickly and safely, and because of their helmets with dark visors, no one could identify them. Several times in the wooded area around Freddy's home in Shirley, Long Island, they practiced mock assaults.

The drills helped vent the pressure Roy felt, but never for long because the pressure kept mounting—more than he knew sometimes.

On June 10, a made man from another family accused a friend of Patty Testa's of being an informer. Because Roy was responsible for Patty, the accusation was brought to him. A sitdown was held at the Arch Diner, an urban truck stop on the Flatlands–Canarsie border. Roy, his top crew members, and the alleged informer's accusers were all inside arguing when a meter maid arrived outside and began ticketing illegally parked crew cars. Everyone spilled to the street.

After moving their cars, everyone continued arguing outside for most of an hour. Roy was so agitated someone might have died if they were not all in the open. Finally, it ended without resolution, but not without benefit to John Murphy and Harry Brady, another auto crimes cop assigned to the Southern District case. They were shooting photographs through the one-way glass of an undercover NYPD van parked across the street, and had just obtained photos of Roy, his inner circle, and an outer circle not yet well known.

However circumstantial, the photographs were damaging. Murphy gave copies to Gerald Fornino, an agent from the Brooklyn-Queens office working on the Newark FBI's continuing Empire Boulevard investigation, because they showed Roy meeting with the two men under indictment in the case, Henry and Freddy.

On June 13, more pressure. Anthony Senter was arrested and caught with a loaded handgun, cocaine, and loansharking records. Responding to a Canarsie friend's early morning telephone call that some drunk neighborhood punks were urinating on his lawn, Anthony had raced over in another friend's car that he was using at the time—without much ado about what he had inside, or his speed, a probable function of the cocaine. Lately, Anthony was looking more gaunt than sleek.

Just as two highly active officers from the Six-Nine precinct were approaching an intersection in their squad car, Anthony roared through from another direction. Between them, Paul Wuerth and Michael Signorelli had logged more than two thousand arrests. They were Fort Zenderneuf types, and now they turned on their siren and raced after Anthony; they caught up as he pulled into his friend's driveway. On demand, he produced a driver's license giving his real name and age of twenty-six years, but purporting that he was a resident of Nevada.

Having plied Canarsie a few years, Wuerth knew better. "I know the name Anthony Senter and I know he lives in Brooklyn."

"What's your hurry?" added Signorelli.

Just then, Anthony's friend came up. He began to explain why he had called Anthony as Signorelli had the precinct check Anthony's name for outstanding arrest warrants, a standard procedure.

Back came a bulletin that Anthony was wanted in New Jersey for failing to pay a fine for trying in 1976 to register a car with a bogus title. "You're under arrest, pal," Wuerth said.

Searching Anthony, Wuerth found a vial of cocaine in one of his socks. On the front seat of Anthony's friend's car, which had Patty Testa transporter plates, Wuerth found a .38 caliber Smith & Wesson, and in a maroon pouch, five more grams of cocaine—a lot, but in Anthony's case, for personal use.

At this point, Anthony's Canarsie friend panicked; his telephone call had led a connected man right into trouble. He shouted to Wuerth, "It's my gun, it's my pouch! Arrest me! I'll even pay you to arrest me!"

"You better shut the fuck up or I will arrest you, for bribery."

Anthony's friend kept insisting he wanted to be arrested—"I'm telling ya, it's my coke, my gun!"—and finally he was.

At the Canarsie stationhouse, Wuerth and Signorelli vouchered other property seized from Anthony: three thousand dollars in cash, an address book and a small spiral notebook containing the names of several individuals—each with a dollar amount beside, a tipoff the notebook was a loanshark diary.

For what began as a traffic case, it was an unusually productive arrest—but it was not without another demonstration of why the crew had flourished so long in Canarsie. A sergeant approached the officers and said Anthony and his friend were his friends. He did not squash the arrest, but did order them to remove the pair's handcuffs and to return their property: "I know them, I'll be responsible."

Wuerth and Signorelli were furious, and before giving back the loanshark records, secretly copied them. The sergeant, meanwhile, continued having an upsetting shift. In a matter related to Anthony's only by his show of sympathy for suspects, another pair of officers arrived with another handcuffed denizen of Canarsie. "What the fuck is going on here?" the sergeant shouted. "You're lockin' up all my friends in the fuckin' precinct!"

Anthony would make bail, and his case would drag on nearly two years. On the other hand, in a few months, Wuerth would be promoted to detective—and the NYPD's Internal Affairs Division began investigating the sergeant, who was forced to retire.

On June 28, two weeks after Anthony's arrest, another arrest made Anthony's seem almost insignificant. In Brooklyn, two undercover auto crime officers staking out a suspected chop shop saw a car with three furtive men circle the block many times. They decided to pull the car over, but it bolted recklessly away, and a chase down busy streets and across a crowded parking lot was on.

The trio had been stalking a woman eating lunch with friends at a sidewalk café, after deeming her a potentially wealthy robbery victim when she pulled up to the café in a Mercedes. Their pursuers did not know that, but—on the Belt Parkway, after tossing a pistol away—the pursued decided they were the chase's lucky losers. Their main worries were the car, stolen, and its license plates, also hot—small fries next to armed robbery, so they pulled over; Vito Arena, Joey Lee and another man gave up without further resistance.

Unknown to Roy and the crew, Vito had been back in New York for some time. After telling Joey Lee that he believed Dominick Montiglio had "ratted out" and it was best to lie low a while, he and Joey had gone to Florida, but just to hang out at Disneyworld a few weeks. Since then, they had been living in a motel in Suffolk County and plying Vito's pre-car-deal trade—armed robberies of dentists' and doctors' offices. The contemplated robbery of the woman in the Mercedes was a spur-of-the-moment crime concocted with a friend of Vito's.

Vito and Joey had been calling on dentists and doctors late in the afternoon as the victims were about to close their suites. Joey went in alone and complained of a toothache or other malady requiring emergency treatment. Slight, drug-ravaged Joey looked sick all the time, so it was a good setup for Vito, who would then go in, pose as Joey's distraught dad, but pull a gun, tie up the doctors, nurses, and patients and take everyone's money—and sometimes keys to their cars.

Vito never came back to Roy and the crew because he thought they were a literal dead-end street. The signs were plentiful. Roy had told crew members to get phony jobs because they were all under investigation and needed a plausible way to account for their high standard of living. Freddy had said he wanted to kill Detective Kenny McCabe, or maybe his wife. Then Roy and Henry had murdered young body-and-fender man Daniel Scutaro in Richie's shop merely because he came looking for his friend and partner Charles Mongitore.

Although Vito himself was brutally calculating when he executed Joey Scorney and won a position in the crew, the Scutaro murder was beyond his large threshold. He came to believe that the crew might just kill him for fun someday. Near the end, his paranoia became so keen he shook inside when business took him to the Horror Hotel, or whenever he was in a room alone with Roy, or Henry, or Joey and Anthony.

Then there was Vito's homosexuality; though Roy and sexually adventurous Freddy did not care, it was a hurdle other crew members never jumped. They treated him as an outsider; somehow, he was less reliable. Though their reasoning was homophobic, their conclusions were on the money. A few days after the Empire Boulevard raid, Vito had telephoned the FBI in Newark and introduced himself to Special Agent Frank Barletto as "Harry."

By giving the FBI some details and the names of Freddy and Henry, Vito was making a down payment on an insurance policy; if the Empire Boulevard investigation led to him, he could surface as Harry and already be on his way to making a deal with the government that might keep him out of prison, or at least shorten his incarceration.

Now, after his arrest in Brooklyn, opportunistic Vito telephoned Special Agent Barletto again and gave his real name. "I can tell you things you haven't even dreamed about," Vito said.

Hoping the FBI would extricate him from his current jam, he agreed to a meeting, but in the meantime, in the stolen car Vito was using, his arresting officer, Jerry Friedman, found an album containing photographs of Vito, Joey Lee, and other men engaging in sexual acts. Vito then assumed that unless he cooperated with police, they would blackmail him with the photographs, maybe even share them with Roy—a definite turn down a dead-end road, because Roy would solve the potential blackmail problem by killing the potential victim.

Vito decided to become an NYPD informant. He told Friedman he could reveal information about stolen cars—and so many murders they amounted to a "mob graveyard." He wanted to make a deal right away. Friedman's superiors, under pressure to keep overtime down, told Friedman to wait until the next day to begin talking to

Vito. Incredibly, no one thought to tell prosecutors how important it was to keep Vito in jail by asking for a high bail at his arraignment because he was such a potentially important witness.

So, some twenty-four hours later, Friedman was shocked to learn that his potentially important witness had been released from jail on a small bail. So had been Joey. Utterly surprised by the system's ineptness, Vito changed his mind about becoming an informant, and he and Joey ran away again. "Harry" also did not keep his FBI date. No use cashing in the insurance policy if it was not needed.

When all the cops and agents interested in the DeMeo crew heard that Vito had slipped through the cracks, they were naturally furious. Still, learning the identity of "Harry" was a major breakthrough. Vito had given the FBI enough details to establish his authenticity, and was obviously someone who could be pressured into becoming not just an informant but a cooperating witness at a trial. He was a gift, if he could be found. A search for Vito began.

On and off duty, and without much help or guidance from the still too busy Southern District prosecutors, the cops staked out his mother's home and gay bars and hustler hangouts in Greenwich Village—but neither she nor anyone else admitted to having seen Vito or Joey Lee in some time.

The cops also applied new pressure on Roy and the crew. They asked inspector-friends in city and state agencies to visit crew hangouts to examine fire-safety compliance and building and liquor permits. They kept up their annoying surveillance—and soon began to see signs it was producing the desired paranoia. When they pulled up outside bars and discos, crew members began grabbing wives, girlfriends, and barmaids and roaring away. Some replaced the windows in their Mercedes and Porsches with tinted glass so prying eyes could not see inside.

"No matter where I am, when I turn around, you're there," Roy snapped at Murphy one day.

Another time he told Kenny, "Freddy said he saw you by the club last night."

"Freddy's losing it, Roy, he's fucked up. I was in the Bronx last night."

"Yeah, Freddy is losing it." It was such a downcast admission that Kenny thought Roy might be losing it too.

"We've got to keep the pressure on Roy," he told the others.

Though he had remained in the background and left no hard evidence against himself, Roy was a legitimate suspect in the FBI's Empire Boulevard investigation, so a subpoena was obtained in Newark requiring him to give his fingerprints and sit for a photograph—a novel experience in his incorrigible career.

The subpoena was served on Roy by Kenny and Tony, and they decided to let him know they knew about Vito. "We have a subpoena for Vito Arena too," Kenny said. "Can you tell us where he is? We heard he wants to talk to us, but he's just a little bashful."

This was grave news for Roy, and not just because Vito could put him at the top of the car deal: Vito also was an eyewitness to the Falcaro-Daoud murders; he had helped with the cleanup on the Mongitore-Scutaro murders; he had seen naked corpses in the Gemini. Vito knew more than enough to give Roy a lifetime ticket to prison.

While inwardly realizing that he was going to have to find Vito before the cops did, Roy said to Kenny: "I don't know any Vito. Sorry."

"That's not what we hear."

"Quit bustin' my balls, will ya?"

Wendling got under Roy's skin next by stopping at the Gemini to tell him, "An old friend of yours, Peter LaFroscia, led me right to this drug connection in New Jersey."

"What the fuck are you talkin' about?"

"I know how it's flown in, who ships it."

"If you ever put me in drugs, I am a dead man."

"I know, Roy. I also hope."

Hoping it might reduce the pressure, Roy ordered Freddy and Henry to plead guilty in the Empire Boulevard case. Except for a minor case against Patty Testa, crew members had always gone to trial before—and always won—but Roy was betting the Newark FBI and maybe everyone else would take the two scalps and go away.

"It's best for everybody," he told Freddy and Henry.

Most of all (no surprise), it was best for Roy. Trusty lawyer Fred Abrams had reported that the FBI had interviewed more than one hundred witnesses. If they were called to testify, a lot of dirt would fly—a lot in Roy's direction.

Neither Freddy nor Henry wanted to relinquish his right to a trial, but only Henry complained. Ferocious as he was, however, Henry would not cross Roy. As he had often said to estranged pal Dominick, Roy could not be killed. So now, at thirty-three, Henry would give up a few years of freedom without a fight; based on the plea offer the Newark prosecutors had discussed with Fred Abrams, Henry might be sentenced to five years in prison, and would probably have to serve half.

Freddy, whose prison exposure was the same, was sanguine. He was absolutely faithful to Roy, who had rescued him from the ashes of his drag-racing career and a low-prestige association with the Lucchese Mafia family. As Freddy had often said, Roy made him a gentleman, made him rich, and even paid to get his teeth fixed.

On August 4, 1981, Henry and Freddy went to the federal courthouse in Newark and pleaded guilty. They told Federal District Court Judge Vincent P. Biunno that the Empire Boulevard operation was their idea, their fault, and had lasted only a month.

Two months later, in light of the sharply reduced charges the defendants had pleaded to, Judge Biunno gave sentences that were reasonable and expected: five years each. He ordered them taken into custody immediately.

In ordering the guilty pleas, anxious Roy overplayed his hand. His opponents were not holding as many high cards as he thought. The Empire Boulevard investigation had stalled at Henry and Freddy. Vito was still "in the wind," and the Suffolk County sting had ended before Freddy divulged anything seriously damaging. Roy did not know about the nascent Southern District investigation, but it hardly mattered; a year after its inception, it was still in a holding pattern. At a time when it was really unnecessary, Roy deprived himself of his best assassin, Henry, and his utterly devoted valet, Freddy.

That fall, Roy for a change got some good news. A judge ordered a hearing into whether imprisoned Anthony Gaggi should get a retrial in the Eppolito case. The judge acted after Judy May, Nino's secret ringer on the jury, claimed in an affidavit that another juror and a court employee had engaged in sexual relations while the jury was sequestered and mulling a verdict—and that other court personnel had told the jurors the case involved "Mafia people." In the Eppolito case, as in most cases anywhere with defendants like Nino, those words were banished from the trial because of their presumed prejudicial effect.

Under constant harassment from cops, feeling abandoned and ostracized by Paul and the other capos, Roy wanted Nino home badly. Just by being his steely self, Nino would lighten the pressure Roy felt. So he was happy to pay the legal costs associated with Nino's fraudulent new attempt to undermine justice in the Eppolito case, according to what he told Freddy one night, just before Freddy left for "college."

The cost, Roy told Freddy, was one hundred thousand dollars. Carrying the cash in a brown paper bag, Roy personally delivered it to a new lawyer in the case. After meeting the lawyer privately, Roy turned to his driver in mock pain and complained, "These fucking lawyers are breakin' me!"

It was a good investment. In a few months more, after the hearing on Judy May's specious claims, Nino's assault conviction was thrown out and he was released from prison, having only served a little more than a year for a case involving two murders and the attempted murder of a cop. Nino had not exactly lost his touch, and he came home from Attica State Prison to a big victory party at Tommaso's.

By that time, something major had happened at the Southern District. And Roy would begin having reason to wish Nino had stayed in school.

CHAPTER 20

Semper Fidelis

What the moribund Southern District case needed was a prosecutor to take command and devise an orchestrated plan of attack. In December 1981, such a person appeared to step forward at a Christmas party at the Southern District offices in Manhattan; he was a tall thirty-eight-year-old assistant U.S. attorney with sandy hair and a confident bearing, and he strode up to John Murphy and introduced himself.

"Hi, I'm Walter Mack." The voice was crackling and authoritative, the manner crisp yet pleasant. "I'm going to take over that car case."

Murphy suppressed an impulse to respond skeptically. This was a Christmas party and strapping Walter Mack seemed sincere, but he knew that a month before, Walter had been promoted to a big job, chief of the Southern District's organized crime unit. As supervisor of the fifteen assistant U.S. attorneys working on "OC" cases, how would he have any more time than his predecessor?

While Murphy measured his words, Walter read his face. "No, really, I am going to personally handle the case."

Murphy, in his low rumble of a voice, surrendered to his initial impulse, but with a smile—"Yeah, sure you are."

"Apparently, you do not believe me."

"Well, we had this other guy and we've just been walkin' around down here for more than a year."

"If I tell you I am going to take the case, I am going to take it and I will take it to the end."

The statement was disarming. It contained no false or belligerent edge, no hint the speaker was affected by holiday cocktails (a condition that Murphy, a teetotaler, instantly recognized). It was just straightforward matter-of-factness. Still, he would wait to see if words led to action. "Okay, great," he said, raising his tonic water with lime. "Happy holidays."

Walter Mack continued working the room; the Southern District Christmas party was always a spectrum of the city's law-enforcement community and therefore a chance to widen his contacts. Like his boss, United States Attorney John Martin, Walter wanted to demonstrate the effectiveness of the "task force" model of prosecution in which federal, state, and local agencies bring resources to bear in a coordinated attack supervised by the prosecutor who would try the case in court, once a grand jury voted to indict.

Martin had been promoting the idea for a year. John Murphy's car case was to be the prototype, but because it was permitted to languish for so long, Walter had fences to mend, particularly with the NYPD: Murphy's boss, Joseph Harding, was even ready to take the case out of the Southern District and ask the Brooklyn District Attorney to prosecute.

One reason Walter was promoted was his ability to get people to work together. He possessed qualities people want in a doctor—serious, intelligent and, above all, concerned. He had been an assistant U.S. attorney since 1974 and won many types of criminal cases. In the courtroom, he was proper and conservative, methodical and business-like—all outcomes of his upbringing and personality but also the favored federal style.

Few people knew much of Walter's personal history; he rarely spoke about himself, and then only with trepidation, as if he was concerned about misinterpretation. Some of the details, by themselves, suggested a life of genteel privilege. He was raised well and comfortably in a close-knit family on the Upper East Side of Manhattan. His father was an entrepreneur and philanthropist, and a former president of the Pepsi-Cola Company. He was educated in private boarding schools and was a graduate of Harvard College. While an adolescent, he once said, he had been "a pretty spoiled kid."

If so, he was also self-aware. After college, as the Vietnam War heated up, he told his father he wanted to learn more about the world and himself. He also wanted a challenge and so he intended to enlist in the United

States Marine Corps. "The Marines will toughen me up," he said.

His father was a Navy veteran and believed in public service, but knew that during war most Marines saw combat. "Do you have to be in the Marines? Do you have to do it the hardest way?"

Walter had thought it out carefully. He was in the Reserve Officer Training Corps at Harvard. He believed combat asked more of a human being—more intelligence, ability, and determination—than any other endeavor. He believed, as General George S. Patton once said, that next to war, all human endeavor shrinks in significance. Walter wanted to know: Was he up to it? Could he lead men into battle? Walter also believed in linear thinking: Every problem, even the chaos of combat, was susceptible to analysis; all risks could be minimized through rational planning. Was he a rational planner? After the war, he would begin doubting the United States role in Vietnam, but at the time it was where he wanted to be.

"I know I'm being stubborn and selfish, but I want to do this," he told his father shortly before he enlisted in 1965. "It's important to me."

In Vietnam in late 1967, while Dominick Montiglio was conducting LURP patrols on Hill 875 near Dak To for the Army's 173d Airborne Brigade, Marine Corps Captain Walter Mack took command of a rifle company. It was stationed near the allegedly demilitarized zone between the warring northern and southern halves of the country. Its job was to guard against infiltration from the north.

As a company commander, Walter was a relentless cajoler and taskmaster. He wanted every advantage he could seize. He hounded superiors for more and better firepower and scavenged spare parts and supplies from other units. When not on patrol, his men were drilling and cleaning equipment; they had to obey rules—no smoking while on patrol, camouflage gear on at all times. The greatest enemy, Walter said, was habit—always patrolling at the same time, always moving in the same formation, always returning to base along the same route. Anything predictable was bad.

In time, Walter's company became the main "reaction" company when an enemy force penetrated the zone.

Applying his theory that warfare was susceptible to analysis, Walter never let his company move without first studying his maps and intelligence reports and determining where along a trail an ambush might occur. Many hours of preparation preceded a major movement; he worked while others slept. His endurance and devotion impressed his troops. Because they rarely suffered casualties and were never ambushed, morale soared. They and Walter achieved the group loyalty and commitment to duty implicit in the Marine motto—*semper fidelis* ("always faithful"). Even-keeled Walter was never corny or trite about it; neither trait was part of his style.

After eleven months, it came Walter's turn to take a rest and relaxation trip to Hong Kong, but he notified his superior officer that he was going to pass up the R and R. His superior ordered him to go; one vacation a year was Marine policy.

"I'm not going while my company is in the field," Walter said, "I don't give a shit."

Wishing all his officers were as committed, the superior ordered Walter's company in from the field to a secure camp, and then Captain Mack's own troops urged him to go—so he did.

While he was away, an American supply convoy was ambushed on a road near the camp. Because of its reputation, Walter's company was ordered to rescue the convoy. The company's intelligence officer, a Yale man, was next in command. He sent a platoon of forty men ahead to check on the convoy's condition. They were pinned down by a seemingly small enemy force. He then ordered the rest of the company to rush in and help—exactly what the enemy wanted. In the ambush, Walter's company walked into a kill zone. Fifty percent of some two hundred men were either killed or wounded.

On his return from Hong Kong, all Walter could do was write letters to the families of the dead and comfort the wounded. He apologized to them for not being there. He wanted to confront the intelligence officer who ordered troops into ambush, but the man was emotionally devastated and already had been relieved of duties and sent to the rear.

In another month, Walter's tour ended. He came home to New York at a time of mounting domestic turbulence.

He joined Vietnam Veterans Against the War—more for the healing effect of being among other veterans than the radical politics of some of its members. He had serious questions about whether politicians had deceived soldiers about the war's merits but hardly identified with veterans who wanted to wage war against the government or those who fell deep into drugs and negativism. Politically, he was a liberal Republican, and so he took a job as a Nelson Rockefeller advance man in the 1968 presidential primary races.

After that, law school at Columbia University in New York. Then, two years in a private firm. Then, the Southern District. He bought a motorcycle, got his pilot's license and fell in love with a Sarah Lawrence graduate who became a television reporter and his wife. By December 1981, Vietnam was mainly a buried memory, but some of the traits he took to war—and some of the lessons he brought home—were now part of his investigative and prosecutorial approach.

Walter meant it when he told John Murphy that once he took personal command of the car case he would stay with it "to the end"—but he did not believe, as Murphy did, that the case was significant. Having reviewed his predecessor's files, he did not see Patty Testa as a major organized crime figure; the case was just a simple one of interstate shipment of stolen cars involving Patty, with the key witness being Matty Rega, who had in the interim agreed to become a cooperating witness in order to win time off his prison sentence. In Walter's mind, Murphy's claim that as many as seventeen homicides were related to the car-theft business in Brooklyn was interesting, but just an allegation.

Indeed, the case's appeal was its simplicity; it was one Walter could manage while concentrating on his new job—being administrator of the Southern District's organized crime unit and supervising its fifteen other prosecutors. His other motivation was proving to dubious NYPD brass that the Southern District was sincere and that law enforcement agencies could lay turf issues aside and work together under the task force model.

Early in 1982, Walter set about building a team. He already had John Murphy, Harry Brady, and a few other auto crime officers. He called on the FBI first, and discovered that their organized-crime experts also rated the Patty Testa case a minor one. Patty had not turned up in the bureau's Empire Boulevard investigation. The Brooklyn-Queens office was on to other matters—namely, a major heroin investigation involving the Queens-based crew led by former Brownsville-Canarsie resident John Gotti, protégé of Aniello Dellacroce, boss of the Gambino family's Manhattan faction. Unknown to Paul Castellano, Gotti's cronies—including brother Gene—were going way off record and dealing heroin in large quantities, according to a wiretap that had recently been installed on the telephone of Gotti's top aide.

Seeking to increase his firepower, Walter asked Bruce Mouw, supervisor of the bureau's "Gambino squad," to assign six agents to the "Testa task force." From his vantage point, Mouw could not justify the request. Patty was on the Mafia fringe; Gotti was at the center. "Out of the question," he said. "I've got something good going on the Gotti crew. I have to put my resources there."

Walter kept cajoling. Mouw said no; then maybe; then okay, but only one agent would be assigned—"my best agent"—and "only on a very part-time basis." Consequently, Special Agent Arthur Ruffels joined the Testa task force.

Like Kenny McCabe's unofficial partner Tony Nelson, who was busy on another case, "Artie" Ruffels was atypical. Unlike most agents, who are trained as accountants or lawyers, Artie was a former high school art teacher. He also was a Navy veteran, a former amateur boxer, and a champion sailboat captain. With his gold wire-rim spectacles, close-cropped silver hair, and sportscoats with turtleneck sweaters, he still looked like a member of some faculty. He had joined the bureau twelve years earlier, at age thirty-five, after an FBI man came to his school in Connecticut to give a Law Day speech at a time Artie was tired of teaching.

A year later, he was, in FBI parlance, a "brick agent"—a street agent in the New York office, assigned to every manner of federal situation, from bank robbery to surveillance of suspected foreign spies on Manhattan's East Side. He and another agent, Bruce Mouw, became friends, and years later Mouw asked him to seek assignment to the Gambino squad. When the assignment was made in 1981, he was required to write a report listing his "performance objectives." Artie wrote, "One of my objectives is to destroy the Robin Hood image of the Mafia and let the public know what members of the Mafia are really like."

When Artie joined the Testa task force in 1982, he was forty-seven, older than anyone on the team but John Murphy. He had an outdoorsman's weathered face, an aging athlete's still-solid frame, and a professor's gently circumspect manner. Murphy and others on the task force began referring to him as "Mr. FBI."

Artie already knew some aspects of the case because he was a long-time friend of Kenny McCabe's, whom he had met on a previous case. Since joining the Gambino squad, he had sat on surveillance of the crew with Kenny and Tony Nelson. He knew of Vito Arena's aborted attempts to cooperate and urged Walter to launch an all-out hunt for Vito. "Of course, with this crew, he might already be dead," he added.

Artie also gave Walter some feel for the geography of the case, the neighborhood of Canarsie in particular: "A natural death there is defined as six bullets to the head."

Readying for battle, Walter had already picked the brain of Kenny McCabe. Murphy had told him that Kenny and Joseph Wendling knew the most about Patty and company. Listening to the Brooklyn DA's experts, Walter began to appreciate why Murphy kept insisting the case was important. The power behind Patty was Roy DeMeo, a Gambino soldier, and the power behind DeMeo was Anthony Gaggi, a Gambino capo and ally of Paul Castellano himself. "The people who work for them are all killers," Kenny added. "They are the most vicious gang we've seen, and what makes them so unusual is that they are all killers. They are a whole crew of killers."

As Walter heard Kenny and Wendling describe how Joey Testa and Henry Borelli beat the Andrei Katz case and how Peter LaFroscia beat the John Quinn case and how the DeMeo crew had operated with virtual impunity for a decade, he began to believe that despite what the FBI thought, more deserving targets did not exist.

"This is a group that is undervalued as far as law enforcement is concerned," he told his boss, John Martin. "In essence, they have never been touched."

Walter added that it now seemed to him that the simple car case could evolve into a major racketeering and conspiracy case involving numerous defendants—in other words, a lot of time and money.

"Whatever you need, do it," Martin said.

Walter's predecessor had told him he did not believe that cooperating witness Matty Rega had told all he knew, so Walter stepped up the pressure on the former high-flying owner of the Bottom of the Barrel. After acquiring more of Rega's business records, he discovered canceled checks Rega had written to Roy DeMeo; Rega, who had not mentioned Roy's name in previous debriefings, was brought from his prison cell to a meeting.

"What about these?" Walter said. "And we know Roy DeMeo isn't just a guy who hangs out around cars."

Matty was in no position to resist; he had signed an agreement requiring his candor about everything—if he held back, anything he had already said could be used against him. "You are in the worst of worlds," Walter said. "You have given up information, yet you get no credit for cooperating because you haven't done so fully."

Walter had given this speech before. Almost every co-operating witness tries to hold something back—until the noose around the neck tightens and the mouth starts working, as Rega's began to do now. Suddenly, Walter had a witness able to testify about heretofore unknown elements of the case—large-scale loansharking by Roy and, most dramatic of all, a murder: Rega had heard Patty Testa talk about how Roy had gunned down a teenager who worked part-time as a vacuum cleaner salesman. The murder had something to do with a cocaine ripoff in which the victim was mistaken for a Cuban assassin.

Rega also gave up the identity of an individual no one had identified yet, even though he appeared in many surveillance photographs Walter reviewed: Dominick Montiglio. Rega said that except for Gaggi and DeMeo, Montiglio knew more about the crew than anyone because he looked after Gaggi's business with the crew.

As the case grew, Walter began researching the applicable federal statute under which the defendants could be charged if the task force obtained enough evidence to ask a grand jury to return indictments. The Racketeer-

Influenced and Corrupt Organizations Act—or "RICO," as it was commonly referred to—was the centerpiece of a sweeping crime bill approved by Congress some dozen years before with the Mafia specifically in mind.

The package of laws funded a program to protect and relocate witnesses, eased restrictions on wiretapping and electronic surveillance, gave prosecutors more leeway in immunizing balky witnesses, and gave the executive arm of government, rather than the judicial, authority to empanel grand juries. On paper, RICO was the most potent weapon in the government arsenal, a hammer especially molded for incorrigible career criminals such as Paul, Nino, Roy, and the DeMeo crew.

Under certain circumstances, RICO made just the fact of membership in a criminal "enterprise" a separate federal crime punishable by up to twenty years in prison. Under RICO, it was even possible to take another shot at trying defendants for crimes they had already been acquitted of in state court by charging the crime was committed to aid the enterprise. So Walter would now take another look at the Andrei Katz and John Quinn cases.

RICO also made it possible to use a defendant's guilty plea against him—again on the theory that the admitted crime was part of "a pattern of racketeering" in support of the enterprise. Only two crimes, or "predicate acts," were required to show a pattern. A guilty plea to an enterprise crime meant that a prosecutor in a RICO case was halfway home—free of charge. So Walter began taking another look at the case in which Henry and Freddy had pleaded guilty, the FBI's Empire Boulevard case.

Reviewing the John Quinn case, Walter learned about Quinn's cousin Joseph Bennett—the car thief who had kept his mouth shut when Roy and Peter LaFroscia offered him money to lead Quinn and Cherie Golden to their deaths. Walter learned that when the murders occurred, Bennett was an FBI informer, and even though Bennett had not informed the FBI of the plot, he was now sitting in federal prison on an unrelated case; maybe his tongue was looser now.

Walter, John Murphy, and others worked on Bennett during several meetings, but Bennett was a scared, bitter convict. Finally, Murphy told him: "You've been living with the ghost of John Quinn for five years. Why don't you put it to rest?''

''You're right,'' Bennett said.

With cooperating witness number two in the fold, Roy DeMeo became the case's primary target. Freddy, Henry, Joey and Anthony, and LaFroscia all moved ahead of Patty Testa in importance; except possibly with loan-sharking, Walter did not see the case reaching to Anthony Gaggi or his nephew, who appeared too far removed from the crew's actual crimes.

Walter's confidence in the value of the case was increasing, but he was realistic too. The case was going to take time. Getting Matty Rega and Joseph Bennett into the fold were big successes, but just pieces of what was now a much larger puzzle.

Murphy's Auto Crime Division boss, Joseph Harding, visited Walter regularly for updates. Harding wanted to move as quickly as possible against some crew members. ''Let's wait,'' Walter replied. ''It's a big jumble; I'm getting a piece here, a piece there, but let's see how far we can take it.''

''How much more time do you need?''

''Sixty, ninety days.'' Careful, methodical Walter knew this prediction was overly optimistic. As time wore on, his comment became the case mantra and inside joke: ''Sixty-ninety days.''

The Brooklyn District Attorney's office permitted Kenny McCabe to begin spending time with what was now the ''DeMeo task force''— but each time Walter was required to submit an official request. The DA, however, rejected similar requests for Joseph Wendling's help, much to Wendling's chagrin. Wendling was a terrific cop, but not the best politician. Many years before, he had complained about the inability of the homicide squads to make much headway in Canarsie and had offended too many departmental egos. His aggressive nature did not suit his immediate boss either; they had an uneasy acquaintance going back to their days as kids in the same neighborhood.

The Nassau County Police Department also assigned an officer to the task force but not Charlie Meade, the auto crime cop who had helped John Murphy so much when Murphy was first pitching the case to the Southern

District. Meade had since furnished his informant to Walter, and the informant was shoring up the now less important thread of the case involving Patty Testa's interstate shipment of stolen cars with Matty Rega.

Meade was chagrined too. Walter had asked for him, but the Nassau detective assigned to the Falcaro-Daoud missing-persons case successfully argued to Nassau brass that he should be assigned.

"Since I'm just a cop, and he's a detective," a disappointed Meade told Murphy, "I can't plead my case to the level he can."

Murphy tried to be upbeat. "Yeah, well, you don't want the glory. The glory we're getting is sixteen- or eighteen-hour days, six or seven days a week. This guy Walter Mack is amazing."

Walter pushed hard for the people he wanted but placed a greater value on forging the alliance and moving the case ahead. It was one thing to get people to cooperate, another to step on toes. If any end runs would have to be made, Walter would save them for bigger moments.

The first formal meeting of the task force took place in Walter's large ninth-floor office on Foley Square in lower Manhattan. Windows on one side afforded a view of the entranceway to the Brooklyn Bridge, across which lay enemy territory. People were surprised that a man like Walter would have such a cluttered office: It was a confusion of half-open file drawers covered with "I Love NY" stickers; papers and law briefs piled haphazardly on work tables and desk chairs; books, knickknacks, and cartons strewn across shelves and the floor. In the corners, baseball bats, umbrellas, and tennis rackets leaned against poster-size crime-scene exhibits from old cases or were potted in a large Civil Defense emergency potable-water container. The two most unsurprising details hung on one wall and sat on his credenza—a watercolor of Marines on the move from the Corps' Combat Art Collection and a replica of the sculpture of Marines raising the flag at Iwo Jima.

"Don't worry, I can put my finger on anything in a second," Walter would tell first-time visitors.

Everyone at the meeting was optimistic. Because Rega and Bennett had opened up, the beast of Brooklyn, Roy

DeMeo, was within their sights—especially if Vito Arena could be found.

"And I know Roy," Kenny said. "He can't take pressure. He'll crack. So when the time comes he's either going to roll and come on board with us, or his own friends are going to kill him."

CHAPTER 21

Retirement Party

During the first half of 1982, the newly invigorated members of Walter Mack's team chased Vito Arena tips all across the country, even though they believed it was more likely he and Joey Lee were in the New York area—because some more doctors and dentists had been robbed by men fitting their description and ways and means. Because they were questioning so many lowlifes, the intensity of the hunt and the new federal momentum behind it became apparent to Roy, who stepped up his own efforts to find Vito. Roy felt that time was running out—and it was.

While looking for Vito, the task force kept pestering Roy. In May, at the Gemini, Roy again denied to Kenny McCabe that he knew any Vito, but asked: "Have you got a picture?" At the time, Kenny did not.

Two weeks later while at home, Kenny got a tip that Vito was with Roy in a restaurant nearby. Two auto crimes cops on the task force, John Murphy and Harry Brady, happened to be at Kenny's home, paying a get-well call. Days before, in a freak accident at a neighbor's home, Kenny had injured a leg, but he and the others went to the restaurant to check out the tip. He was wearing bermuda shorts, because of a cast on the injured leg.

Roy was with Joey and Anthony and a beefy man the tipster had mistaken for Vito. Roy, greeting the officers gregariously, was about to make a mistake too.

"Hi, Kenny! You guys want to join us? What the fuck happened to your leg?"

"This is not a social call. We're looking for Vito."

"Vito's not here."

"Oh, you do know who he is. I thought you needed a picture."

Embarrassed, Roy tried to recover as best he could.

"Look," he said, now all defiant, "I do know who he is, and he's not here!"

"Where is he?" Murphy asked.

"Haven't seen him in ten months."

The officers searched the restaurant, then left, confident that in Roy's effort to salvage his ego he had actually told the truth. If Roy had not seen Vito in ten months, Vito was probably alive.

He was not just alive, it soon turned out, but nearby.

Early on the evening of June 4, 1982, as a ferocious spring storm pelted Suffolk County, a stolen car with two hungry men inside pulled into the parking lot of the Good Earth Restaurant in Terryville. Vito Arena and Joey Lee got out and went inside for a Chinese meal.

Since slipping through the cracks a year earlier, Vito and Joey had discussed a preemptive strike against Roy, but decided, as Henry Borelli always said, that Roy could not be killed. They had been living in a motel near the restaurant and taking their phony father-son act to dentists' and doctors' offices whenever they ran out of money. They were wanted not just by the task force but by robbery squads in Nassau County and Brooklyn.

Hefty Vito and wispy Joey were a memorable odd couple, and nearly every policeman in the metropolitan region had seen their wanted posters—including Steve Marks, an off-duty NYPD sergeant who recognized them as they walked into the Good Earth and sat at a table some thirty feet from him and his family.

Marks, a robbery squad supervisor in Brooklyn, was en route to a baseball game at Yankee Stadium in the Bronx when the violent rain drove him, his wife, and three sons into the restaurant. He was unarmed and wearing sandals, a short-sleeve shirt, and bermuda shorts.

"Dad, look at that big guy!" whispered Marks' son Philip, whose thirteenth birthday had occasioned the baseball outing.

Marks smiled and reminded his son it was impolite to stare at strangers. Without his weapon, it would have been foolish for Marks to attempt to arrest two probably armed men, and more ill advised to try it in a restaurant. Not wanting to alarm his family, Marks did not explain why he abruptly had to make a telephone call.

Because it was Friday night and the appropriate people

were hard to track down, it took a dozen telephone calls—
and a couple of return calls to him at the restaurant—for
Marks to make all the necessary arrangements and noti-
fications. Fortunately, Vito and Joey were making a meal
of it.

"Dad, look at that big guy eat!"

"Philip!"

Finally, Marks saw the car of a Brooklyn detective—
Bill Behrens, who was leading the robbery squad's hunt
for Vito and Joey—pull into the parking lot. He excused
himself and went outside, leaving his still unaware but
befuddled family inside.

Outside, Marks told Behrens, "They're still eating;
we'll grab them when they come out. But let me go back
in and get my family out first."

Just then, however, the officers saw Vito and Joey rising to pay their dinner check. They waited in the rain for
them to come out. "Police!" Behrens shouted. "Get your
hands up! Faces against the wall!"

Joey was carrying a .45 caliber pistol, but he and the
most wanted man in New York quietly complied. More
police from Suffolk and Brooklyn arrived almost simultaneously. One ran up and teased Marks for his attire as
he handed over a weapon Marks had asked him to bring.
Hearing this, Vito turned and wanly shook his head at
Marks, as if in despair that he had surrendered to an
unarmed cop in bermuda shorts.

"Face against the wall!"

One of the other officers had already notified John
Murphy, who sped from his Long Island home and caught
up with the arrest at the 6th Precinct in Suffolk County.
So far, Vito had refused to speak.

"Who are you?" Vito asked when Murphy approached him in the squad room.

"Murphy, auto crimes."

"I don't want to talk to you."

"You're in a lot of trouble; maybe you should talk to
me."

"You're a cop from auto crimes. What can you do for
me?"

Murphy told Vito that the Suffolk officers would keep
Joey because of the illegal weapon he was carrying, but
the New York cops would take him to the Six-Seven pre-

cinct in Brooklyn and arrange for his robbery victims to view him in a lineup. Maybe then Vito would rethink his position.

From the Six-Seven, Murphy telephoned Walter Mack at home. "Would you like to talk to Vito Arena?" he dryly said. "We're having coffee with him now."

"Fantastic, John!"

Hearing the details, Walter added, "We've got to move fast. If it looks like he wants to talk, we've got to get him transferred to our custody before he has any second thoughts."

Murphy next telephoned his wife, a devout person like him, and active in their parish church and children's charities. They grew up a block apart in the South Bronx, and had been together since their teens. "We got Vito," he said. "I'm gonna be stuck all night and day."

Mary Murphy was upset, but not only because their weekend was ruined. She was worried about the long hours he was logging lately. He looked tired, and two months before, his barber had said his hair was falling out in clumps. She urged him to see a dermatologist, who advised nothing was wrong that he could find. "But something is wrong in your life and you ought to figure out what it is," the doctor said. Mary diagnosed the problem as job-related stress but understood this was no time to remind her husband. "Just tell Vito I'll pray for him," she said.

Murphy hung up and spoke to Vito again. "Can you imagine that? I'm married to my wife twenty-five years. I get spit, but she tells me she's gonna pray for you."

"What is she praying for me for?"

"She thinks you need a friend."

"Maybe I do—what do you want to know?"

"First, you've got to give me something that says you're a credible witness. Something I can bring to the U.S. Attorney's office. I'm working for an important guy, Walter Mack, and he could do something for you if you come around."

"I've got stolen cars all over the place."

"Big deal. I've got all the stolen cars I want. I want something better than that."

Vito squirmed, calculated, then tossed a high card on

the table—the location of the victim whose murder won him a job in the crew. "I'll give you Joey Scorney."

Murphy recognized the name as that of a missing car thief; it was on one of his charts. "Where is he?"

"I can't remember exactly, but he's in a barrel out on the island."

"How do you know it's Joe Scorney?"

"Because I put him there."

Murphy asked what other murders Vito knew about. Vito said plenty, but first he wanted one assurance. "This Walter Mack, if he is so powerful, can he get Joey Lee out of Suffolk County and in jail with me?"

Probably, Murphy said, producing a list of murder victims. Vito began pointing at some of the names. "I was there when they did that one. I know about that one. I heard about that one."

It took all night to process Vito on the robberies and to conduct lineups in which each victim identified him as their oppressor. Early Saturday, Murphy informed Walter of Vito's single demand; moving fast, Walter visited a judge at home and secured a writ requiring Suffolk to release Joey Lee to the Southern District.

With Harry Brady, Murphy returned to Suffolk and picked up Joey Lee. At thirty-three, Brady, a detective's son, was on his way to his detective's shield too. He was fifteen years younger than Murphy, but they had become friends since joining the task force. En route to the Metropolitan Correctional Center, a federal jail adjacent to the Southern District offices, they turned off the highway onto a side road. They were headed to a restaurant.

Joey Lee thought otherwise and began to tremble. "Don't kill me!" he pleaded.

"All we had in mind was coffee and donuts," Brady said.

Vito, meanwhile, agreed to meet with Walter. The paperwork for his transfer to federal custody took until Sunday. Walter met him for the first time that evening. He was joined by Murphy and Brady and by Detective Joseph Coffey, chief of another special NYPD unit, the organized crime homicide task force. Coffey was the detective who had coined the term "Westies" for the press.

None had ever met anyone like Vito, a killer giant with

a seeming soft spot for a comparative midget half his age.

"What do you want in return for your cooperation?" Walter asked.

"All I want is to be in jail with my friend, Joey Lee."

Coffey asked, "Apart from the obvious reason, Vito, why?"

"I have to protect him. They'll rape him and beat him up if I'm not there to take care of him."

Vito would prove more selfless than he appeared and as conniving as he was while in the crew—but by then he would be indispensable to the case and Walter would have to endure him.

That first night, Vito rambled on until three a.m. Walter and the others mainly listened. They were trying to evaluate the man and his credibility and lead him past a point where he had given so much information implicating himself that it would be impossible to back out of a cooperation deal.

A clear sign the task force had struck pay dirt came the very next day. A lawyer telephoned Walter and said a friend of Vito's had hired him to check into Vito's well-being and determine if he wanted legal representation. Unsurprisingly, Vito's friend's name was Roy DeMeo, who was tipped to the arrest by relatives of Vito and Joey Lee, after they made their allowed one telephone call.

After interviewing Vito, and after a separate conversation with Walter, the lawyer gave Roy the pressurizing news: Vito did not want representation and was a witness for the government.

The report was accurate, but premature. Before striking a deal with Vito and putting him in front of a grand jury, the task force had to begin verifying his truthfulness. The natural place to start was Vito's account of Joseph Scorney's unnatural death.

A couple of days later, Vito led Joseph Coffey and other task force members to a pier near Center Moriches on Long Island and pointed out the general area of Scorney's underwater grave.

Scuba divers searched a couple of hours before locating a concrete-filled barrel. They attached chains and it was hoisted to the pier and firemen began tearing at the steel and concrete with large saws. Inevitably, the eerie work yielded dark humor. "First time I ever seen firemen do an autopsy," Harry Brady said.

Joseph Coffey, a tall swashbuckling type whose glibness with reporters made him one of the city's better-known detectives, had waited out the search in a nearby restaurant. Once the sawing began, he came out with a few cocktails under his belt. A Scuba diver then surfaced and gave a medical examiner a piece of concrete that had fallen off the decaying barrel as it was hoisted. It appeared to encase a human bone.

"This is the hip bone," the medical examiner told Coffey.

A few cops nearly fell in the water as Coffey began singing, "The *hip* bone's connected to the *thigh* bone . . . ."

It was no problem identifying the body as Scorney's. He had been entombed with his hands across his chest. Beneath one skeletal hand, in a dungaree jacket pocket, was a wallet; it contained several still intact identification cards. Some cops began thinking that opportunistic Vito had intentionally left it on the body so that some day, if needed, people would have proof they should listen to what he had to say. The wallet was another insurance policy, like the one "Harry" wrote for himself with the FBI.

Vito's arrest was a sudden light in a dark moldy room that sends the vermin scurrying for their holes. Believing, incorrectly, that they would be arrested immediately, Roy and most of the crew suddenly vanished from the Gemini and other feeding grounds. Roy even stayed away from his home in Massapequa Park. His disappearing act, particularly, bolstered the task force's confidence in Vito's credibility.

Hoping to intensify the pressure on Roy at home, Kenny McCabe telephoned Gladys DeMeo and said he was worried about her husband because he had not been seen lately.

"I'll be sure to tell him that," she said, with indifference that struck Kenny as unwifely. Days later, with Roy still in the wind, he went to her house to deliver a grand jury subpoena for him. She would not come to the door. "Just put it in the mailbox," she wearily said from a second-floor window.

These encounters made Kenny feel he had uncovered

another of Roy's secrets, an unhappy home life. In similar situations, Rose Gaggi had exhibited far more concern and defiance: A few times, leaving her house, Rose had seen surveillance cars sitting across the street; she would smile and wave sarcastically, then go back inside and tell Nino. Once, in her car, she saw Kenny and Artie Ruffels approaching from the opposite way; she U-turned and raced back home to warn Nino, honking and waving as she flew by their car.

Roy's home life was worse than Kenny imagined, but Gladys's failure to be like Rose, Kenny concluded, could only help the case. If Roy did not get much support at home, he might become even more out of sorts as the pressure mounted.

Trying to be a good soldier while laying low, Roy did tell Nino and Paul that Vito had "rolled over." Nino and Paul did not show as much concern as they felt. Paul was especially disturbed; Vito knew that Roy had reported to Paul while Nino was away. As Roy had for him, Paul began harboring murderous thoughts about Roy.

The FBI's Gambino squad was aware of Paul's reaction because of the electronic surveillance agents were conducting against the John Gotti crew in Queens. A week after Vito's arrest, they taped Gotti's brother Gene telling another crew member that Paul called John to a meeting and "put out feelers" about killing Roy if he began to crack. Gene added that John was wary of accepting a contract on Roy because Roy had such a violent "army" around him.

Many times while away, Roy telephoned Frank Foronjy, his old childhood friend from Avenue P in Flatlands—the one who taught him so much about weapons—and complained that he was being persecuted by the government. Foronjy was now a successful electrical contractor on Long Island and lived near Roy. They were still close personal friends; between marriages in the late 1970s, Foronjy drank at the Gemini Lounge and bedded women at Dracula's apartment, on those evenings it was not otherwise in use. In 1980, he borrowed twenty thousand dollars from Roy, who told him to repay when he could.

Now, Roy told Foronjy to start making payments on the loan through Roy's sixteen-year-old son Albert because he had to ''keep the cash flow going'' at home while he was in the wind.

The debriefing of Vito continued many weeks. The big man was no dummy and wanted everyone to know it. He enjoyed hearing himself talk, and some of his talk was straight out of Roy's mouth. ''No one understands what it's like to kill,'' he told Artie. ''The power you possess when you kill someone, it's like being God. Do I want this guy to continue living, or should I kill him? No one can understand it unless you do it.''

Vito also was a blatant self-promoter; describing crimes he committed during his limited time with the crew, it was always he who was most calm, brave, and resourceful. ''You know that time you guys came to my mom's house?'' he told Harry Brady. ''I was hiding in the closet with a .45 ready to blow you away.''

Nonetheless, Vito was a valuable witness. He disclosed the stages of the car deal preceding Empire Boulevard and provided names new to the task force—Ronald Ustica and Joseph Guglielmo, manager of the Horror Hotel. Then, Vito talked about murders—some he took part in, others that Henry or Roy had described: Andrei Katz, Chris Rosenberg, Ronald Falcaro, Khaled Daoud, Charles Mongitore, Daniel Scutaro, and the father-son victims, Jimmy Eppolito, Sr. and Jr.

On those he knew the most about, Vito enjoyed reciting the lurid details—and morbidly making light of his own contributions. Describing how he had helped dispose of the packaged remains of Falcaro and Daoud, he joked to John Murphy: ''I just delivered the heads to the garbageman. I was only responsible for the homicides from the neck up.''

His Eppolito revelations were particularly crucial. The gunman in the murder car who got away was Roy DeMeo, not mysterious ''Kenny,'' as Anthony Gaggi had testified. Furthermore, Vito said, through Roy Nino paid him and Joey Lee forty-five hundred dollars for helping Roy and Nino gain their revenge against the Eppolito witness, Patrick Penny. These disclosures hooked a big Mafia fish to Roy and the crew—and to an ongoing criminal enterprise. The DeMeo task force became the Gaggi task force.

Walter Mack asked the NYPD for more help, and so

two men acquainted with parts of the story, homicide detectives Frank Pergola and Roland Cadieux, joined the team full-time. Pergola had investigated the Chris Rosenberg murder and the Mongitore-Scutaro double homicide in Richie DiNome's shop; Cadieux had investigated the Eppolito double. The detectives, both Brooklyn-born and -bred, were excited about their new assignment. With Vito as a witness and federal resources such as Walter and the powers of RICO, maybe they would finally learn the truth of those murders.

From the outset, murder had been a major element of the case, but more as an undertone of the Canarsie stolen-car culture, a thread running through Murphy's files. Now it emerged as the case's dominant and more complicated theme. Not yet knowing it was actually true, task force members began saying to one another that Roy had probably murdered more than any serial killer yet known. The task force currently had him linked to twenty murders. Roy had bragged of a hundred, and eventually the task force would credit him and the crew with seventy-five, many of which could never be proven in court. The worst serial killers in United States history had all been caught somewhere around their thirtieth victim.

Roy, in fact, continued to murder even as his problems grew worse. However briefly, it helped ease the pressure and reaffirm his power. That summer, on July 4—in the uncomplicated past, a day of fireworks and festive parties with Chris and the boys—he came out of hiding long enough to shoot down another father-son pair, Anthony and John Romano. Their mistake was in still being around when Roy, no doubt in an alcohol funk, decided to act on a four-year-old suspicion that they (with two others already dead) had set up someone he did not care much for, Peter LaFroscia, for a robbery.

Two months later, as the summer of 1982 ended, Roy and most of his crew came out of full-time hiding. Anthony Senter, who had the added problem of pending gun and coke charges from his arrest in Canarsie the year before, was an exception. Unless they wanted to leave New York and start over somewhere anonymously, there was not much point in hiding out anyway. If the cops wanted to find them, eventually they would. The better course, Roy decided in consultation with Nino, was to surface and fight in court whatever ill tide Vito was bringing ashore.

Consulting with lawyers about the Southern District investigation, Roy now began seeing his decision to order Freddy and Henry to plead guilty in the Empire Boulevard case as a colossal blunder; all the government had to do was prove that the operation was part of the crew's criminal enterprise and Freddy and Henry would have to pay twice for the same crime. Roy would order no more guilty pleas if anyone was indicted.

"I'm going to fight the government with lawyers," he told his friend from childhood, Frank Foronjy.

Meanwhile, agents from the IRS joined the Gaggi task force—to determine if crew members were vulnerable to income-tax charges. U.S. postal inspectors also came aboard—to investigate whether the crew had used the mail or interstate communications in their phony insurance-claim schemes. The grand jury Walter had impaneled also began issuing subpoenas requiring crew members—and their wives and other relatives—to testify or provide handwriting samples and fingerprints; he was trying to identify who else had a hand in the Empire Boulevard operation and its predecessors.

"We have no beef with you," Harry Brady politely said when Joey Testa's wife Joanne complied with her subpoena for handwriting and fingerprints. Such evidence was evaluated, then stored in a rapidly filling office at the Southern District that was dubbed the "war room."

In telephone switching boxes near crew members' homes, the task force also installed devices that listed the outgoing numbers crew members dialed from their private phones. The so-called "pen registers" were not as potent a weapon as telephone taps and hidden recording devices likely would have been—but actual eavesdropping requires more than mere suspicion; court authorization, which is granted only when there is evidence the target is actually committing a crime, or is about to, is presented. That burden usually requires an informant still on the inside, as was the case in the FBI's ongoing electronic surveillance of the John Gotti crew.

Still, the pen registers helped the task force identify the crew's relatives and friends—all possible interview subjects, or witnesses—and provided insights into the daily rhythms of crew members' lives, which were under surveillance whenever possible.

That fall, Artie Ruffels, Bruce Mouw, and other cops and agents were uninvited guests at an elegant wedding reception for Nino's daughter Regina—the young woman Buzzy Scioli swooned for years before—at the Plaza Hotel in Manhattan. With the hotel's permission, they videotaped the guests from a small room built into the ceiling high above the ballroom. (Normally, Secret Service agents hid there while protecting the President or other dignitaries.)

"There comes Roy with John Gotti," Mouw pointed out. "John's just getting friendly with him so he can kill him."

About ninety minutes into the reception, someone on the hotel's kitchen staff—probably a member of a connected union—informed Nino that the ceiling had eyes. Nino and another family capo, Danny Marino, wound their way to the room and stormed inside. Nino looked on the verge of a heart attack.

"You are ruining my daughter's wedding!" he shouted at Kenny. "These fucking rats at this hotel! They let you in here! I'm not paying them a fucking dime!"

Kenny tried to calm him, but Nino kept ranting. Turning to Marino, Kenny said, "I can't talk to this guy, Danny. He's irrational. Get him out of here, and we can discuss this."

"How would you like it if we came to your daughter's wedding!" Nino screamed.

Six-foot-five, tough-talking Kenny relished his own next words: "You come to my daughter's wedding, and I will shoot you."

James La Rossa, Nino's lawyer in the Eppolito case, then entered the room and politely asked the interlopers to leave, which they did, having ruined Nino's evening and caused his blood pressure to soar—and having recorded it all on videotape.

Evidence in the task force war room piled up. The list of targets now included twenty-four major and minor crew members. The task force was investigating hundreds of alleged new crimes and re-investigating dozens of old cases and arrests. Walter was turning over every stone in the crew history—and so he obtained the Anthony Senter loanshark records the two straight-arrow Canarsie cops had secretly copied, the Westchester Premier Theater files on Anthony Gaggi, the records of Roy's presidency of the Boro of Brooklyn Credit Union, and thousands more documents tracking the crew's bloody march across New York.

Though Nino was the top target, the task force zeroed in on Roy, hoping he might fold. The grand jury subpoenaed Roy's friend Frank Foronjy; he was not a crew member, but had helpful information. He testified that he once took Roy, Roy's son Albert, Freddy, Henry, and others target-shooting on land he owned in upstate New York, and so Walter made plans to search the property for shells and bullets that might be matched to murder weapons.

Hoping his friend would not remember many such stories, Roy told him to deduct from the twenty thousand dollars he owed Roy the seven-thousand-dollar legal tab he ran up trying to minimize his cooperation with the grand jury.

Roy was served his second grand jury subpoena a few weeks before Christmas 1982. The lawyer Roy was fighting the government with now was Gerald Shargel, the one who had taken over the appeal of Nino's assault conviction in the Eppolito case and won a reversal—after, as Roy complained to Freddy, Roy gave Shargel one hundred thousand dollars in a brown paper bag. After a life spent representing the oppressors, the crew's favorite lawyer, Fred Abrams, had peacefully passed away.

Shargel told Walter Mack that Roy would exercise his Fifth Amendment right against self-incrimination before the grand jury, but would come to the Southern District offices and comply with a legal obligation to provide his fingerprints and handwriting samples and to pose for a photograph. Consequently, Walter and Roy had a brief meeting. Roy put on his best salesman's suit and face and acted like a gentleman; even so, he also subtly tried to intimidate Walter by showing he had conducted some research on Walter and learned about one of his hobbies.

"I've heard a lot about you, Mr. Mack. I've heard you like horseback riding. I like to ride too. Maybe we'll run into each other on some trail some day."

Walter interpreted Roy's remark for what it was—an

attempt to make him wonder if he was a candidate for the Fountain Avenue dump. But Walter only smiled and gave Roy more to wonder about. "I've heard quite a lot about you, Mr. DeMeo, and am constantly learning more and more. Every day, I find out some fascinating detail about you that I didn't know before."

Walter's policy was to invite grand jury targets, in the presence of their attorneys, to provide any information they wished the grand jury to know. Roy demurred. "But if there is anything else I could do for you, let me know."

Later, at the Gemini, Kenny McCabe taunted Roy about going away to college soon, like his buddies Henry and Freddy.

"I can do the time," Roy said. "I could do thirty years standing on my head."

Kenny laughed in Roy's face. "No way, Roy, but don't worry about it. On second thought, your friends aren't going to give you the chance."

"No problem, I'm with good people."

"They're gonna put you in the trunk of your Caddy, Roy."

Roy's bravura performance in Walter Mack's office and with Kenny was remarkable because, elsewhere, he was acting more like a man walking up the gallows steps.

He probably now knew that Paul Castellano had spoken murderously about him to John Gotti, and that could only have caused him to worry about Nino, who had not been spending too much time with Roy since getting out of prison. Nino had told him it was wise to limit contact under the circumstances. Besieged by cops everywhere, Roy also was not spending much time with Joey or with Anthony, who had finally decided to come out of hiding and face the music in his pending gun and coke case.

Whatever he was thinking about Paul and Nino as 1983 began, he gave outward signs that he was collapsing emotionally, as predicted. He was frantic and full of foreboding, and increasingly, he turned to relatives and friends for advice and solace.

On January 5, he telephoned his family's white sheep, the man he named his son after, his seventy-one-year-old uncle, Albert DeMeo, the former star prosecutor in the Brooklyn District Attorney's office who now taught at Brooklyn Law School. He told his uncle he was under investigation and requested a meeting because he valued his judgment. Professor DeMeo, a small man with an elfin face and brilliant shock of white hair, lived privately with his wife in Brooklyn. He had not seen Roy in two years; before then, usually at extended family events, or when he served as Roy's real estate lawyer when Roy bought his old and new Massapequa Park homes. He knew enough about his nephew to want to keep his distance.

That afternoon, driving his latest new car, a maroon Cadillac, Roy picked up his uncle outside the law school and drove to a diner. The professor commented on a small microphone, equipped with an on-off switch, that he saw wedged between the backrest and seat on Roy's side of the car. Roy said he was recording his conversations now because he feared "entrapment"—being lured by secret government operatives into committing a crime. A wire connected the microphone to a tape-recorder in the trunk.

At the diner, Roy attributed the grand jury investigation to "a homo" telling "a pack of lies." Even though he knew Vito had raised a curtain on some of his murders, Roy pretended to be most alarmed, as always, about his cooked tax returns and his vulnerability to charges of tax fraud. Just as sixteen years before, when he sought advice from a former classmate who had become an IRS agent, he wanted Uncle Albert to explain how the government assembled a "net-worth case"—how it proved a taxpayer spent more than he claimed to earn.

The preoccupation with money rather than murder showed that Roy was trying to deny reality even as reality was rising up and slapping him in the face. "I think I can show every penny," Roy said.

Mainly, Professor DeMeo listened, but did tell Roy he should not underestimate his problems: "If the government has you right, you could go away many years." As to the government's "homo" witness, the former prosecutor added, "The credibility of a witness is in the eyes of the beholder."

The next day, January 6, Roy visited the office of his target-shooting friend, Frank Foronjy. He was clearly in distress and for reasons Foronjy soon grasped never removed his overcoat. Roy said a "police source" had told him that the government had issued a murder contract on him.

"You're crazy—those things don't happen," Foronjy said.

"If anything happens, just take care of my son and my family."

Foronjy went all the way back to Avenue P in Flat-lands with Roy. The Roy he knew had suffered terribly when Chubby DeMeo was killed in Korea; the Roy he knew doted on children, helped neighbors, and was generous with friends. His lifelong friend may have dabbled on the other side of the law, but just as a loanshark; he was worthy of respect and compassion. He stood, walked from behind his desk and embraced Roy.

His arms around Roy, Foronjy, still an avid gun collector, felt what he believed was a sawed-off shotgun rising out of a deep inside pocket of Roy's overcoat.

"Why are you carryin' that?"

"I told you, the government has a contract on me."

"I told you, that's nonsense."

Roy gave an odd smile. "My mother always said I should have been a doctor."

Roy said he had to go. He invited Foronjy to his house on Monday, January 10, for a nineteenth birthday party for his eldest daughter Dione, a student at the Fashion Institute of Technology. As in Nino Gaggi's house, everyone in Roy's house always got a party for their birthday.

On January 8, Roy visited his lawyer Gerald Shargel's country home in Quogue, Long Island, and gave him a Christmas gift—a .12 gauge, double-barreled shotgun that Roy bought under his own name. He had told the gun store clerk that Quogue in the dark of winter was scary as Times Square after midnight, so he was buying a friend protection against home invaders. "I'll tell him to be careful with the shotgun, though, because if anything ever happened to him or his family, I couldn't live with myself."

That same day, in the parking lot of a shopping center near their homes, Foronjy saw Roy walking to his car. He began walking toward him to say hello, but Roy pointed toward the inside of his overcoat and waved Foronjy away like he expected to be set upon by Cuban assassins at any moment.

In the meantime, Roy became concerned about the state of his personal affairs. He telephoned Professor DeMeo to ask him to get some legal papers together involving his Massapequa Park property transactions. They made an appointment to meet outside the law school at three p.m. on January 10.

On January 10, Roy left home at nine-thirty in the morning. He told Gladys he would be home early for Dione's birthday party. By seven p.m., he had not arrived; he had not kept his appointment with Professor DeMeo either. His son Albert, soon to be a freshman at St. John's University in Queens, began to worry; he telephoned Frank Foronjy, who was finishing paperwork at his office. Foronjy told Albert to relax, Roy would be home soon.

Albert then telephoned his father's attorney and asked Shargel, a former student of Professor DeMeo, if his father had been arrested. After telephoning Walter Mack, Shargel reported to Albert that it did not appear so.

By ten p.m., when Foronjy arrived at Roy's house for Dione's party, Albert, who met him at the door, was panicky. "My father is missing again!" he said.

"Calm down, he probably just got stuck someplace."

"This is not like him. He doesn't miss cake, you know how he is with birthdays, he doesn't miss the cake."

Foronjy conceded it was unlike Roy to be tardy, especially for a daughter's birthday. He said Albert's father might have decided to "disappear" a while, like before. He also noticed that if Gladys DeMeo was concerned she did not show it.

Gladys probably sensed her husband's miserable journey had finally come full circle, and she was right of course. Roy was not found for a week but was dead that day. The fat little bully who became a hardworking, brown-nosing teenager, the high school loanshark and former butcher's apprentice who became one of the most infamous gangsters anywhere, the man who murdered more often than any serial killer yet known to United States history went the way of many of his victims—a volley of head shots at close range.

No one was ever convicted of the crime, but based on

some admissions, an autopsy, other evidence, and their insights into Roy and the situation he was in, the task force developed a theory that is highly plausible, if unprovable.

Under this scenario, Roy was set up just as he once set up Chris Rosenberg. And just as he had to be the one to do the work on Chris, Nino was the one who had to kill Roy, on an order from his superior, Paul, who feared Roy might become a cooperating witness. Just as Chris's recklessness had caused the family grave problems, so had Roy's recklessness in allowing an unreliable person like Vito Arena to get so far inside his crew. Paul had reason to fear the task force investigation might reach to him; Vito would have known he was the ultimate boss of the enterprise.

Because Paul hardly cared for Roy, and because Nino had amply demonstrated his way of solving intrafamily problems, and because he was obligated to obey Paul and had his own interests at stake besides, the scenario makes sense. But, in the details, there is even more treachery and irony—because, like Danny Grillo, forty-two-year-old Roy went right into the lion's den to be killed—not butchered, however, because his killers wanted the government to know he was dead.

On the day of the murder, Nino summoned Roy to a meeting at one of Patty Testa's garages. Patty was not there, but the Gemini twins were, along with Nino. Roy's long-time sponsor and his long-time followers—the only two of his original crew not dead or in jail—were the only people in Brooklyn who could have caused him, in his paranoid state, to let his guard down for a second or two, which was all it took.

After Roy took off the black leather jacket he was wearing, Nino pulled out a handgun and began firing at his head. Roy threw up his hands in defensive surprise at the final moment of reckoning, but the bullets tore through his hands into his face. He was hit seven times in all, and was already dead when he was shot once behind each ear, which suggested to some that Joey and Anthony symbolically demonstrated to Nino that they accepted the necessity of the work by firing their own besures into the contorted brain of their ex-leader. Having helped Roy murder their childhood buddy Chris, such betrayal was nothing new.

As Kenny McCabe predicted, Roy wound up in the trunk of his Cadillac. The killers abandoned the car in the parking lot of the Varuna Boat Club in Sheepshead Bay, in Brooklyn, near where Roy murdered Patrick Penny as Vito Arena watched.

The club's manager noticed the unfamiliar car soon after it was deposited there and telephoned police to complain; precinct officers came, then left after determining the car was not stolen. No telltale rotten-egg odor emanated from the trunk because it was wintertime and Roy's body was frozen.

The car sat in the parking lot until January 20, when the club manager telephoned the local precinct again. By this time, Gladys DeMeo had filed a missing person report and the task force had issued an alert for the car. When he arrived, Kenny McCabe jumped up and down on the Cadillac's rear bumper, trying to determine if anything inside bounced around.

"He ain't in there," Kenny bet.

The car was towed to a nearby police garage. Because the car had sat in the cold so long, NYPD crime-scene experts recommended waiting for two hours before dusting it for fingerprints and popping the trunk.

With most of the victim's police antagonists assembled, Detective Harry Brady of auto crimes, an expert in such matters, easily popped the trunk to Roy's car. The sight inside was bizarre: His body, his leather jacket wrapped around his head like a Gemini-style turban and frozen to a spare tire, lying beneath an ornate chandelier. Roy had put the chandelier in the trunk a few days before, after taking it out of his home for repairs, and his killers had placed it like a shroud over his body.

Poking around in the backseat, Brady and others found a *New York* magazine—the cover story was about drug dealing; they also found a wire leading into the trunk from the car's interior—but no tape recorder, meaning that the killers confiscated the tape Roy had been making and that whatever he said on it was lost to posterity.

Predictably, a macabre mood filled the garage. "Think we should take the chandelier to Gladys, as is?" a cop said.

Someone else said they better get the crime-scene pictures taken before the body thawed. "He looks like a drunk lost in a snowstorm. Hurry, before he melts!"

"Yeah, a retirement party picture!" another cracked.

"I'll bet my badge Nino did it," Kenny later advised Walter, after Patty Testa got confused in an encounter with Kenny and admitted Roy was to come to his shop that day. "I bet Paul ordered him to. I bet Joey and Anthony were there. They all thought Roy was going to cooperate."

To the task force's surprise, the autopsy of Roy, who they had never seen with a drink in his hand, showed his liver to be in the same condition as those of alcoholic bums found on the street.

The night of the recovery, Kenny and others went to Massapequa Park to inform the family. After he rang the bell, an irritated Gladys called out from an upstairs window. She had a drink in her hand. "What is it? Can't you just tell me what it is?"

"It's about Roy, it's freezing out here. Can't you open the door?"

Gladys finally came to the door, with Albert. "My father in the trunk?" Albert said.

"Yes. Shot to death. In Brooklyn."

Young Albert started crying. Gladys did not. She just sat down and silently listened to the details with a blank face.

The next day, Albert had to go to the stationhouse of the Six-One precinct, in which the murder had occurred, to give some biographical details for the local detectives' reports. Hoping Albert might provide information about his father's associates, Kenny was there waiting.

"Your father was smart," Kenny told Albert, "too smart to let a stranger get the drop on him. He was comfortable when he was killed. Inside somewhere. His coat off. His friends killed him. When you realize that, give me a call."

Albert began to respond, then just shrugged, as if his father had taught him that just as an ironworker might fall from a skyscraper, ending up in a trunk was an occupational hazard of that life. Albert never telephoned.

Albert's father was buried in St. John's Cemetery in Middle Village, Long Island, after a one-day wake at a funeral home in Massapequa. No one from the crew attended either ceremony—more evidence that Roy, like Chris, was sacrificed for the presumably greater good of the family. His casket was carried by hired pallbearers. At the funeral home, the mortician asked Gladys to provide some information for a death certificate, so Roy went down in official history as a self-employed business consultant.

Gladys was administrator of Roy's estate; reading the public probate records, a stranger to his life might conclude he was a hermit. He died owning nothing and owing nothing. But Roy had set his unhappily accommodating wife and other family members up for life by placing all his life's bloody spoils in their names—so everything passed on to them without court scrutiny. They received nearly one million dollars in life insurance, several expensive cars, a speedboat, the million-dollar-plus home in Massapequa Park—and any brown bags he might have left around.

In time, the family would sell the house. Gladys would move to a nearby town. Albert would graduate from St. John's; his older sister Dione would marry; and his younger sister, Dawn, would enroll at Yale College—to begin becoming the doctor her grandmother always said her father should have been.

CHAPTER 22

California Schemin'

Although no one lost any sleep over it, the Gaggi task force would have rather beat Roy DeMeo in court than lose him as a target. Just as Vito Arena coming on board had, the murder actually energized them. They were not as far along as their foes feared, but clearly Nino and the remnants of the DeMeo crew—and even Paul—were running scared. Their foes had also miscalculated. Because Roy had murdered so often, the task force never intended to cut him a cooperation deal. Giving Vito Arena one was bad enough.

"Now, we just figure out how to turn this to our advantage, that's all," Walter Mack said at a strategy session after Roy was murdered. In the updated game plan, hundreds more people would be interviewed—crime witnesses; friends and relatives of victims; cops, FBI agents, lawyers, anyone with a history with the crew.

"We're going to do all this in just sixty–ninety more days, right Walter?" someone in the room teased.

"Right, sixty–ninety more days."

With the expanded effort, the case would become massive, but the aggressive patrolling and marshaling of firepower had to be done. Walter was not going to trial with a clever self-promoting murderer like Vito as his key witness without trying to corroborate everything Vito said, and without trying to learn what else was to know. If and when the main battle arose, Captain Mack was not going to walk into any legal ambush because he had failed to prepare well.

So he implored his troops to keep their eyes and ears open for any illuminating details, including those about a character who, from his perspective, was obscure but intriguing, assuming he was still alive. It was someone he knew only by some remarks Matty Rega had made and by surveillance photographs—Dominick Montiglio.

Unknown to anyone in New York but Buzzy Scioli, still in-the-wind Cheryl Anderson, and also Denise Montiglio's suffering parents, Dominick was still alive. Nobody knew many details, out of concern for their personal safety. But the ex-LURP point man was not only alive, but reasonably prosperous, in a Brooklyn sort of way.

His second try at making a go at life in California had begun a few days before Christmas 1979, when he bundled his family into the thirty-thousand-dollar Mercedes that he was revengefully stealing from his accuser and ex-drug partner, Matty Rega. After a paranoid, desperate coast-to-coast drive, the Montiglio crew—now personal family members only—wound up in Sacramento.

Hightailing it across country, Dominick and Denise had reluctantly decided they could not start a new life in their old fantasy playground, the San Francisco–Berkeley area; that was where anyone who wanted to find him—Nino, Roy, or Matty Rega's father's friends—would look.

An old friend of theirs had since moved a few hours east of San Francisco, to Sacramento, so it seemed the next best choice. As former residents of the northern part of the state, they inherited the northern Californian's uppity attitude about the supposed tinselly qualities of the southern part. Sacramento, a farming, textile, and military manufacturing center on a plain between mountain ranges, was also the state capital and home to a quarter-million people. It was a place to prosper and stay anonymous. As a couple, they had time to grow strong new roots. He was thirty-two, she twenty-eight.

They arrived with their clothes and about a thousand dollars in cash. They rented a rundown apartment in a tired neighborhood; Matty Rega's Mercedes, which Dominick intended to sell when their money ran out, was easily the most conspicuous car on the block. Happily for him, unfortunately for taxpayers, he did not have to because to his surprise the family was able to apply for and receive public assistance—enough to cover the rent, feed Camarie and Dominick, Jr., and keep Dominick in Camels. Denise, now in her second trimester, also got free prenatal care.

It was easy to get welfare in California in those days,

so easy Dominick just produced some old letters from a Veterans Administration doctor who treated him for delayed stress syndrome in 1974 and said that for emotional reasons he was still unable to work or relate well with people. Indeed, he told welfare officials, he had not been employed since 1973, when his uncle folded a car service he managed—a job he was able to cope with because it was indoors and did not involve much human interaction.

The irony of this devious fiction was that the war's ill effects, the dismemberment flashbacks, and the nightmares in which artillery shells drilled holes in his chest, subsided two years after he quit the car service and was working full-time for Uncle Nino in a job requiring much interaction, human and inhuman. He still attributed this to the "action of 'that life.' "

Getting away with a fast one a few days after arriving in California was the worst that could have happened. Rather than have to work and possibly find a job he could enjoy and build on, he was back being a wiseguy—though he looked upon the welfare as compensation for the Veterans Administration's Catch-22 finding that his nightmares were not combat-related, because he did not complain about them when he was discharged.

With not much to do, and no money for cocaine, girlfriends, or nightlife, he began hanging out at a Vietnam veterans center in Sacramento and learned that Vietnam veterans were committing suicide at a higher rate than veterans of other wars. He volunteered to become a counselor for men who, unlike him, were still troubled. His clients had similar complaints. They were called to war with grand deceptions, maimed in often meaningless battles, then branded losers; they felt like the butts of a sick national joke. He tried to make them see the war the way he did: no shame in having served or lost; shame was on generals and politicians who sent them to fight with one hand tied behind their backs.

"Easy for you to say," one veteran told him once. "You came home a hero, with all those fucking medals."

Dominick did feel like a hero, a war hero at least, but did not ever admit it. "I never tried for a medal," he said. "Nobody who ever tried for a medal ever got one.

It was all instinct and survival. That's all life is. Watching your back."

Dominick became active in a campaign to force the government to recognize the cancer-causing effects of Agent Orange, a defoliant used in the war, and compensate veterans exposed to it, as he was on Hill 875. In time, his center collected ten thousand signatures on a petition that led to a class-action lawsuit against the government, which insisted—despite substantial evidence—that Agent Orange could not be linked to high cancer rates among Vietnam veterans.

With other veterans on the Agent Orange committee, Dominick built a wooden shack high in the Sierra Nevada mountains. It was a treehouse for men—an actual, legitimate Veterans and Friends social club. The only deals involved marijuana joints. Up in the mountains, he felt removed from the tremors of Brooklyn but not really at peace. Sacramento felt transitional. His welfare scam was cute but damaging to him and his family's self-esteem.

In May of 1980, Denise gave birth to a daughter they named Marina—like Camarie, it was an indirect tribute to his mother Marie. Marina's birth spurred him to action. He told Denise he had to get his own "things" going again. "But not around here, I'm going to start checking out LA."

"Do you have to get back into 'that life' again?"

"What should I do, sell shoes? It's not like I'm going back to Brooklyn. The people down there dress nice, but as someone always said, 'If they're not from Brooklyn, they're farmers.' "

Dominick laughed, and so did Denise. The Uncle Nino in her husband was an amusing trait to see, now that Nino was safely in the past. Even so, she did not like the idea of Dominick going to Los Angeles alone and, rightly provoked into self-analysis by all the current women's liberation debates, was frustrated by him always setting their agenda without consulting her much. She was, however, also tired of poverty—and, after an almost decade-long marriage, convinced he was not going to change. Much as she was beginning to rankle privately at his domineering will and way, family security came first, and so she still passed her husband off as someone who was just a rogue, not a criminal.

That summer, once a month, Dominick deducted fifty dollars from each welfare check and cruised to Los Angeles for the weekend. Unable to afford more expensive bars and discos in Beverly Hills, Hollywood, Westwood, and Santa Monica, he decided to hang out "over the mountain"—at still glitzy but accessible clubs on the north side of Sunset Boulevard and the Hollywood Hills, in the San Fernando Valley area. His Rega-model Mercedes, although not an uncommon sight, made more of an impression, and he introduced himself to people, once again, as Dominick Santamaria.

After a few weekends, at the La Hot Club, someone he got to know at the bar introduced him to a cocaine dealer from Colombia. Dominick turned on the ex-commando charm and soon the Colombian, a much bigger dealer than Paz Rodriguez ever was, was offering him a Brooklyn-type job: collecting a debt—in this case, sixty thousand dollars from another cocaine dealer. It was the break Dominick was surveying for, and he collected that weekend by going to the other dealer's home, pointing a borrowed pistol and saying he was not leaving until he was paid, which was quickly.

The Colombian gave Dominick a fifty-percent collection fee, thirty thousand dollars, and offered a full-time job. Dominick declined; he did not want to work for people he assumed the Colombian worked for, some cartel in his native country. The next weekend he was in Los Angeles, he strode to the entrance of The Daisy—a private, Studio 54–type club on the south side of the mountain, in Beverly Hills—and greased the impressed doorman's palm with a hundred-dollar bill and walked past the velvet rope like he put it there. He was astounded that his act played—and then, in The Daisy, that the cocaine dealer he threatened a month before was seated at the bar and, after their wandering eyes met, the man came over and offered to buy a no-harm-done drink. Talk about farmers, he smiled to himself.

The dealer, Glen Gorio, was short, slim, only twenty-three years old, but already a cocaine millionaire. He operated out of a phony movie-production company. His customers included prominent names in the movie and record businesses; he threw big parties at his house in Chatsworth and gave away ounces of good will. He told

Dominick his uncle was a one-time boss of the Los Angeles Mafia family, but Dominick was hardly impressed; the LA family had fewer made members than Roy DeMeo had killers.

After the second no-harm-done drink, Gorio said, "I could use good security like you. How about it?"

"I don't know, my family's up in Sacramento."

"Forget about it, I'll rent you a place down here, a car, whatever you need."

Back in Sacramento, to disappointed but unsurprised Denise, Dominick described the job with Gorio as a cakewalk, not far off the truth by his standard. "He just wants me there when he's got business. With his customers, all I have do is look scary."

Gorio tossed in moving expenses and before long the Montiglio family left Sacramento for the tinsel life. They moved into a condominium in Calabasas, in the valley; Gorio leased them another car, a Maserati. As Gorio's bodyguard, Dominick jumped back into cocaine; he became a regular at The Daisy, other clubs, and Hollywood parties. The little black book he carried—a made-in-Italy diary purchased years ago during an Italian-week marketing ploy at Bloomingdale's in New York—began filling up with names and numbers of Italian-American actors, Hell's Angels, producers, drug dealers, rock stars, and, as 1981 began, a foreign-born businessman who became his Buzzy Scioli-type friend in California.

The new friend was a legitimate entrepreneur who came from a well-to-do family. He was young, single, smooth, and living a fast life in Los Angeles. Dominick nicknamed him right away because he did not want to get in a habit of using his real name, for fear his identity might somehow get to Brooklyn and expose him to a strong-arm visit. He settled on "The Armenian," not because he was, but because during a silly drunken moment they shared a laugh over an ethnic joke about an Armenian.

The Armenian was the first person in California to hear the story of Dominick's life and times in New York. The saga now included the news (which Dominick learned in a telephone chat with Buzzy) that Anthony Gaggi had manufactured a story to explain his nephew's hasty exit from Brooklyn: Dominick had stolen a quarter-million of his dollars. After the shock, Dominick understood why. Taking off during an unresolved dispute with another family over Matty Rega's restaurant, he had embarrassed his uncle. Nino could not just say he ran away; that implied his nephew did not respect him. It had to be something that made Dominick look bad, and what was worse than stealing from your family?

"I know my uncle," Dominick told The Armenian. "He was pissed off and embarrassed, so he told a story. Someday, to make it look real, he'll try and make me disappear. Probably after my grandmother dies. He wouldn't want to upset her."

"Some family you come from."

"That's always been my problem. I was able to choose my friends, but not my family."

The bodyguard job lasted nearly a year, until Dominick collected enough money and knew enough people to go off on his own, as a drug dealer. In mid-1981, he thought he had finally arrived. He moved his family into a house to rival Paul's, Nino's, and Roy's, a big house in a private enclave known as Westlake, a section of Thousand Oaks, one of the San Fernando Valley's most upscale communities. The house was on the market for one million, seven hundred thousand dollars, but a cocaine partner of Dominick's concocted a lease-buy plan that gave him occupancy on only ten thousand down. The house came with a pool, a dock and gilt-edged furniture—"our own 'White House,' " he told Denise.

"Can we afford this?" she asked, marveling at the silk drapes, marble floors, and baby grand piano in the formal living room.

"It's only fifty-five hundred a month, no problem."

Of course, with the vagaries of the cocaine business, it was a problem, every month. Though the last year as Gorio's bodyguard had hardly been a tame time, the Westlake house marked the start of a wilder, more corrupt journey—and an even more puerile and promiscuous life than his former Hole-in-the-Wall life.

Determined to hold onto the house, he went into the cellar fast. A couple of times, short of money to buy cocaine, he sent acquaintances from The Daisy to steal it from dealers he knew had it; with his friend The Armenian, a handsome and debonair performer on the nightlife stage, he again rampaged for days at a time.

In the middle of it all, through a brother of hers, he contacted his old girlfriend, now a fugitive, Cheryl Anderson, and flew her to Los Angeles. He picked her up in a limousine and took her to the house in Westlake, where she stayed a few weeks; under Denise's nose, they relit their fire.

Cheryl, still a would-be Ma Barker, proposed a score—a robbery of her own father, a well-to-do contractor who kept sixty thousand dollars in his home on Long Island. Dominick informed Denise he was going to New York with Cheryl, but not why. She complained, but only about the risk of him being seen.

"Don't worry, in and out," Dominick said.

In Garden City, Long Island, he broke into the Anderson home, tripped an alarm, fought off a watchdog, found the money, got stuck in a locked garage on the way out, but managed to escape seconds before the police arrived.

The score was forty, not sixty thousand. He suspected Cheryl had taken twenty before she came to see him in California and set up the robbery to cover her tracks. She denied it, said she loved him and wanted him to leave Denise. He said forget about it, and flew back to Los Angeles alone, after stopping at his half-sister Michele's house to say hello. Michele was now happily married and living on Long Island. She still loved her half-brother, but her picture of him had changed. Her childhood hero was a man to pity too. He had been contaminated as a boy and now as a man the virus was fully developed. Because of a lot of things—Nino's pull, his mother's death, his decision to leave the Army—Dominick had wandered down the wrong road in search of himself. The journey was still continuing; despite all, he was just a scared kid searching for an identity.

The close call in Garden City hardly had any effect other than purging Cheryl from the scared kid's system. But in the summer of 1982, she was replaced by another woman. It happened one Friday night when a cocaine partner who could not get into The Daisy without him telephoned him at Westlake and asked him to come play.

"Nah, I'm bushed."

"I got two girls."

''No thanks.''

''What if I told you one of them was Miss Penthouse 1980?''

''What time do you want to meet?''

The second Penthouse Pet of the Year to come into his life was named Danielle Deneux, at least for modeling purposes. Coincidentally, both women had appeared in the same issue, June 1980. Danielle was that month's featured Pet and Anneka di Lorenzo, the Pet he met in New York at Chuck Anderson's apartment in 1977, was pictured in a lesbian grope from the movie *Caligula*—as far as Anneka ever got in her pursuit of a star on Sunset Boulevard.

Twenty-two-year-old Danielle had run away from her home in Texas at fourteen. She was a pretty, leggy brunette, like Denise. When Dominick met her outside The Daisy, she was dressed like Pocahontas on her wedding day; he became her brave that night, and for the next six months they danced with wolves. He went so out of control, was away from home so much, he did not notice the disenchantment finally taking root there.

All he noticed was that without any help from Nino, he was making it on his own. Just as Paul, Nino, and Roy had for their families in New York, he had provided his family, outwardly at least, an upper-middle-class lifestyle, ill earned though it be.

The Montiglio family, however, survived by its patriarch's ability to make a big score each month somehow, and thirty-one-year-old Denise was growing tired of living on such a tightrope. She liked the posh house, but not much in it was theirs, and she liked the spending money, when Dominick had some. With a fifty-five-hundred-dollar monthly nut on the home alone, but a husband who did not have regular income, she always felt like an eviction notice was in the mail. To make ends meet at the end of one cash-short month, Dominick had already peddled Matty Rega's Mercedes, and was now driving a Cadillac Seville borrowed from his friend The Armenian.

Denise did not know her thirty-five-year-old husband felt he had to raise more than fifty-five hundred each month, because he was helping out his new moll, Danielle Deneux, who lived beyond her means in a four-thousand-dollar-a-month penthouse in Beverly Hills. Dominick usually made the nut, but in traditional working wiseguy fashion, usually at the last minute—and in modern wiseguy fashion, usually through some drug-related scheme.

The robbery of Cheryl Anderson's father's home was an exception, and so was another scheme early in 1983 that caused Denise, who lied to bail Dominick out of a jam, to resent her situation even more. On January 6, four days before Roy's murder (the news never reached Westlake) Dominick and two pals from his debauched crowd at The Daisy were arrested after they botched the robbery of a jewelry broker.

The victim worked out of his home, also in Westlake. Dominick had met him at The Daisy and bought fifty-five hundred dollars worth of jewelry on goodwill, plus a gram or two. He still owed the jeweler three thousand. These days, as during his runaround years in New York, he was not encumbered by many moral notions apart from thou shalt not kill except in war and self-defense. His first waking thought each morning was usually how to "get over" that day. The day he was arrested, the thought was to raise the money for the jeweler by robbing him.

The heist was not planned well. Dominick stayed outside the jeweler's house, playing lookout; a second accomplice was at the wheel of the getaway car; the third robber, armed with a pistol, went inside alone, but quickly lost control of the situation because four people happened to be in the house; while trying to herd them into one room, he lost track of one, who fled out a bathroom window.

A neighbor saw the man fleeing and telephoned the Ventura County Sheriff's Office. Dominick and his accomplices fled too, but were caught fifteen minutes later because the neighbor also saw the getaway car and it was spotted and pulled over. A young, excited sheriff's deputy put a shotgun against Dominick's head, then reflexively pumped it; an unexploded round jumped out the chamber. Dominick imagined his head as an exploding ball of red mist. "Easy man, no trouble here," he said.

At the sheriff's office, he identified himself as a Mercedes-Benz salesman, then got cocky, waived his right to remain silent and tried to improve on a would-be alibi that accounted for his presence in the getaway car but put him at home during the time of the robbery. Instead, he became confused and placed himself in the car at the time of the robbery.

The detective who interviewed him then went to Westlake to see Denise. At first, she was a calm stand-up wife. She said she did not know what time her husband's friends came to the house that day, or what time he left with them.

The detective smelled baloney. "Your husband will talk his way into prison without your help," he said, then began to leave.

"Okay, I was lying," Denise called to him. "I was scared and didn't know what to say."

"The truth," the detective said, but Denise lied again and said Dominick's friends had come to the house, then left for a while, then come back and picked him up. "The second time they came, they seemed upset and frustrated about something."

For a story made up on the spot, it was a good one. Because of it, and because none of the victims or other witnesses could put him at the scene, Ventura County officials decided the case against Dominick was unwinnable and ordered his release. With a large assist from Denise, he skated out of trouble again.

Denise lied because Dominick was her breadwinner, father of her three children, and husband—but for the first time she spoke up and complained about his antic and criminal behavior. All her resentment about the way they lived came tumbling out. She felt alone and trapped—the twin themes of the fights they would have over the next seven weeks.

"You're never home!"

"I'm out making money!"

"Holding up your coke customers? What a great life." As she continued to complain, Dominick for the first time began to wonder if he had used up all her patience and loyalty; some of her remarks could be interpreted two ways: "If it weren't for the kids . . . I'm not sure what I'd do."

Dominick was trapped too, in a dissolute web of his own weaving, but was having too much fun to change; he was a boy locked inside a candy store with all the chocolate he wanted. Even the constant pressure of making the monthly nut was a fun game to play.

Early in March, he, Danielle Deneux and another man hatched a money-making plot that involved a trip to New York. They knew the man only as "Val" and had met in a bar in Westwood; he was a prison escapee from Canada. He said he knew someone in Montreal with a large supply of Quäalude tablets. Dominick said he knew people in New York who would buy thousands. Danielle said she would smuggle them over the border—by sewing them inside the liner of the mink coat she received as Pet of the Year.

"Nice touch," Dominick said.

"It's not gettin' much use out here."

Danielle was unpredictable and frequently strung out on cocaine, but he was attracted to her in the same way he had been to Cheryl Anderson. She was funny and had balls—she had talked her way out of a serious Quäalude arrest in Ohio some months before and paid only a fine—and she was so sultry when she got made up in one of her Pocahontas-type outfits.

To finance the trip and drug purchase, Danielle also sold a luxury sports car she won in the Penthouse competition. She and Val flew to Montreal, got the drugs and went on to New York. The night before Dominick was to leave Westlake to hook up with them, Denise, as she had when he went there with Cheryl, told him that going to a city where people wanted to kill him was an unnecessary and stupid risk.

"It is necessary, and it is a big town."

"Not your part of it."

"I'll be back in no time."

CHAPTER 23

The Other Shoe

With more breakthroughs on the near horizon, the Gaggi task force kept at the tedious task of verifying Vito Arena's information and determining which of the crimes he described they could prove. Members of the task force came to the assignment as individuals, but were now a close-knit crew. All had won many citations for bravery and performance; they were the moral opposites of the cops who had helped make the crew strong. From Vito, the good cops began learning about the bad cops—mainly, the slain detective, Peter Calabro, and Norman Blau, the Canarsie patrol officer who helped Peter LaFroscia beat a murder.

Because Calabro was a former auto crime cop, John Murphy and Harry Brady felt particularly betrayed. So it was with a sense of poetic justice that Walter dispatched them to the NYPD's Internal Affairs Division in Brooklyn to get records on Calabro and Blau; the IAD knew little of Calabro, but had investigated Blau—and found him guilty only of failing to report that his informant, Willie Kampf, smoked marijuana.

A high-ranking officer at the IAD refused to turn the records over because Murphy and Brady were just "uniformed cops." They tried explaining that in this instance they were just messengers too—for Walter Mack, an assistant U.S. attorney.

"How dare he send two police officers to see me."

"We'll call him and tell him how you feel," Brady said.

"I'll be right over," Walter said.

Walter took the subway to Brooklyn and marched into the IAD boss's office with Murphy and Brady, prepared to shed his normal rectitude because this was one of those big moments he had been holding in reserve—a time to step on toes. "The reason I sent these two officers here is I don't want the IAD to fuck up this case like it did the Blau case!"

Murphy and Brady left the room, heard much yelling inside, then saw Walter come out with a smile and several folders under his arm. "Let's go, fellows!"

In a few months, Walter would haul Blau into the grand jury; Blau invoked his Fifth Amendment privilege against self-incrimination. A judge then granted him immunity from Southern District prosecution—but not NYPD departmental charges—and ordered him to testify. Blau made several damaging admissions. The IAD, however, never followed up and he stayed on the force. Police brass could never adequately explain why. Task force cops assumed that Blau possessed damaging information against higher-ups.

Though tired and practically bald now, John Murphy no longer complained that the case was taking so long. He and the rest were now on a mission; although the case was even bigger than they imagined, they saw it as one of those times in a career when something is worth doing not for the reward but the meaning.

Other than for his daughter's wedding, Murphy had not taken a day off in six months. And now Vito had heaped so much more on his plate—Richie DiNome, for example. Vito had identified Richie as a partner in the car deal, and Murphy decided to apply some indirect pressure.

One day, he and Frank Kollman, another auto crime cop on the task force, visited Richie's father in Brooklyn. "Your son's pals are going to kill him unless he comes in and talks to us," Murphy told Ralph DiNome.

"If that happens, I'll know it came from the Gemini, and I'll take care of it."

"Then we'll arrest you for murder. Why don't you save yourself the trouble and have your son call us?"

Heading back to Manhattan, Murphy began feeling faint; his stomach growled. "I feel woozy, I must be hungry," he told Kollman. They stopped at a McDonald's and he ordered what he always called the "cop's cure"—French fries, a Quarterpounder, and coffee. Later walking up steps leading to the Southern District offices, he felt a radiating pain shoot through his left arm to his chest. An hour later, in the task force war room, his face turned ashen.

"We're taking you to a hospital," Frank Kollman said.

At the hospital, doctors hooked forty-nine-year-old Murphy to an electrocardiogram. "Why did you wait so long?" one doctor asked. "You're having a heart attack."

A nurse came into the room: "Sorry, doctor, that machine has not been working properly."

Murphy was placed on another machine. "Doesn't seem to be a problem now, you're fine," the doctor said. Then, the nurse said she was not sure which machine was working and which was not.

"Give me my coat, I'm out of here," Murphy said.

Kollman drove Murphy to Murphy's own doctor, who put him in another hospital and diagnosed the heart attack. A week later, in the hospital, Murphy's heart failed again and took him right to death's door, but not past.

Months later, after he was well enough to leave bed, NYPD doctors refused to certify his return to active duty, and he retired on a disability pension. Walter invited him to stay on the task force in some administrative capacity. "I'll find some way to get you some money for it. You were instrumental in starting this case, you might as well finish it."

Murphy felt another radiating pain admitting he could not finish it. "Walter, I'd do it for free if I could, but I am just not physically able."

While Brady and the remaining auto-crime experts on the task force focused on the stolen-car aspects of the case, the homicide experts the NYPD had assigned to Walter, Detectives Frank Pergola and Roland Cadieux, worked the murders.

Frank was Italian-American but looked more Irish and, with his short graying hair, wiry build, and Camel cigarettes, like an active-duty drill instructor. He was forty-four years old, a cop for seventeen, a detective for thirteen. He dressed fastidiously—black leather topcoat over crisp shirts, immaculate suits, and polished shoes with stretch hose—"gangster socks," they say in Brooklyn. The gangster link ended there; Frank took the Mafia as a personal insult and hated its influence in Bath Beach, where he was born and raised and still lived—not far from the old Gaggi bunker.

The taller, heavier, dark-haired Cadieux would likely have been a drill instructor if he had remained in the Marine Corps, but at age forty-one, he already had eighteen years "on the job," thirteen as a detective. He was a raconteur and a sharp dresser too, but more in the style of a politician; he was an elected official of the Detectives Endowment Association, the bargaining unit for men and women of the NYPD who carry the gold shield of a detective. Although his first name was "Roland," friends called him "Ronnie" because he did not like the sound of "Rollie."

Frank and Ronnie had never worked together, but they became an effective team. Their styles were different, but complementary. Where Frank was reserved, Ronnie was gregarious; where Frank threw a question and listened, Ronnie threw one and expounded on it with a story, if the situation seemed right. Ronnie loved his stories—such as the time a big drug raid did not go as planned and he was caught alone with twelve heroin dealers in the dimly lit coal bin of a Harlem drug den and he talked them into giving up. "Believe me, make a move, and I will shoot at least half of you before you get me!" Or the time: "I was a young cop on a drug bust, I always liked to go up the stairs first. Then an old cop said, 'First guy in gets shot; second guy gets the medal'!"

Comparing Vito Arena's stories to old files, Frank and Ronnie became convinced he was for real; some details he could not have possibly known unless told by crew members. Because the RICO statute enabled him to make use of a case ending in acquittal, Walter already had begun looking at Andrei Katz's unholy demise again, and now he assigned it to Frank and Ronnie.

They tracked down a woman who had left New York in despair years before—Judy Questal, the former go-go-boots girlfriend of Henry Borelli destroyed on the stand by defense lawyers as she testified in state court that she was duped into luring the Rumanian immigrant to his death.

Judy, now a settled, happily married wife and mother in another state, agreed to tell them the story, but never to testify. "I will never go through that again," she said.

"I'm not going to give those people another chance to kill me." However, she took a liking to Frank—beneath the drill-instructor look, he had a gentle and charming way—and he stayed in contact with her. He told Walter she might change her mind someday: "But the more I talk to her about it, the more guilty I feel. She doesn't want to be humiliated again and who can blame her?"

"Keep holding her hand, we need her," Walter said.

Working from John Murphy's list of unsolved homicides, Frank and Ronnie also looked into cases Vito had not mentioned—such as the murder of another young man from Canarsie, Jerome Hofaker, in 1977. He was executed in front of his girlfriend's house after a fight with one of the notorious Testa brothers, Dennis. Joseph Wendling told Frank and Ronnie that the girlfriend's brother saw the murder, and knew the killers—Joey Testa and Anthony Senter, according to neighbors. However, he had refused to talk.

Frank and Ronnie interviewed the brother; he was mildly mentally disabled, but they were convinced his inability to recall details had less to do with that than his grasp of a canon of Canarsie: Talk to cops and your sister dies. Still, they urged Walter to put him before the grand jury; maybe he would crack under the pressure of testimony under oath. He did not. Meanwhile, outside the grand jury room, the brother's friend told Frank the entire story. "He saw it, but you'll never get him to say it."

"Imagine that," Frank told Ronnie later. "In Canarsie, even a retarded kid stays with the code."

Regularly, and always after a big event came along, the task force held brainstorming sessions. For instance, during the session following Roy's murder, Walter said: "By killing Roy, someone has exposed themselves to prosecution. How do we use that?" Simultaneously, many people in the room had the same thought: Freddy DiNome.

Roy's devoted friend was serving his Empire Boulevard sentence in a prison in Otisville, New York. Kenny McCabe and Artie Ruffels, particularly, were convinced that Freddy would feel so betrayed he might open up, maybe even become a cooperating witness if he realized that he too was a RICO target of the task force—and that as soon as he was released on parole in a year or so, he might have to go back to prison for life.

Kenny and Artie visited Freddy in Otisville on February 10, 1983. Freddy did feel betrayed, and said that a few days before the murder he warned Roy by telephone to be careful and that a few days afterward, a crew member telephoned him and said, "Roy was found in his trunk; Nino says there will be no retaliation; you are to report to him when you get out." Freddy added that a fellow inmate told him he might "have a problem" with the crew after he was released on parole, but he was not worried.

The meeting lasted twenty minutes. Freddy would not discuss anything but the murder, and it was difficult for him to face an old nemesis like Kenny. Still, Kenny and Artie came back with a positive report: With the threat of a RICO case and the lure of avenging a friend's death, Freddy could be coaxed along; he just had to come to terms with an alien idea, helping the government.

"We get Freddy to talk and Roy's murder begins to look like a colossal blunder," Walter replied. He already believed the killers blundered badly by giving up the body. If Roy had been made to disappear, the task force would have wasted much time and money searching for him—on the chance he was in the wind.

Seeking to coax Freddy and give Kenny and Artie more time with him, Walter arranged to bring him to Manhattan for several days in February. He was housed at the federal Metropolitan Correctional Center next to the Southern District offices. At the MCC, word of a new prisoner—most inmates are pretrial detainees in frequent contact with their lawyers—travels fast, so Nino and the crew learned that Freddy was back in town right away.

· Just as the murder and disposal of Roy were strategic mistakes, so was a visit a minor crew member now made to Freddy at the MCC. The messenger's manner was panicky and ominous. He said Vito Arena had "turned over a lot of rocks," and everyone had to hang tough, then reminded Freddy of his obligation to report to Nino at the Veterans and Friends social club after he got out.

It occurred to Freddy that maybe Nino planned to put him in a trunk too. He hardly knew Nino. Nino was just a man Roy used to report to, not him. "I'm not reporting to nobody,'' he said, ''because I'm not involved with nobody no more. My friend is dead.''

Freddy also received an unsolicited visit from Gerald Shargel, Roy's former lawyer; it also backfired. He told Freddy that Roy's death was a tragedy and that he knew it was a great personal loss for Freddy because they were such friends. ''Roy told me what a great guy you are and how much he thought of you.''

Shargel added that he would not be able to represent Freddy in the Southern District investigation because he was now representing another figure in the case, Nino Gaggi. He did, however, announce that another lawyer would represent Freddy and that he would ''take care'' of the lawyer financially. While in the crew, Freddy was accustomed to legal decisions being made for him, so Shargel's attempt to orchestrate his defense struck him as business as usual—exactly what he was beginning to resent.

During the visit, Shargel told Freddy he did not believe the government had a case, and at a second MCC meeting, after Freddy was visited by Kenny and Artie again, he asked his nonclient, ''You didn't say anything, did you?''

''No.''

''You sure?''

Freddy lied and said sure. The truth was, Freddy had begun trusting Kenny and Artie more than Nino and Shargel. He had already agreed to talk but did not want anyone to know because he was afraid his brother Richie might be killed. He told Kenny and Artie he would provide information but would never testify. The task force was jubilant; Freddy had more time with the crew than Vito Arena and had been the driver for the crew's boss, Roy.

Even so, Walter Mack was disappointed too. He was still wary of going to trial with calculating Vito as his main accuser. Vito on the stand would try and be clever, inviting defense lawyers to make mincemeat of him. On the other hand, Freddy DiNome might actually evoke a jury's sympathy. He was just a sheep who had followed his seemingly invincible shepherd around.

Kenny and Artie kept working on Freddy. His brother Richie, a target now too, would have to make his own decisions about who to trust, they argued. Moreover, Freddy had already sacrificed a lot for his brother by pleading guilty and covering up Richie's role in the Empire Boulevard case. It was time Richie stood on his own feet.

Finally Freddy said he might testify if his wife, son, and daughter would join him in the witness protection program—a condition whose difficulty soon became apparent. After a couple of more meetings, Kenny and Artie transported Freddy back to his familiar cage in Otisville. En route, they stopped at a motel because Artie had asked other agents to bring Freddy's wife and children there for a reunion.

The reunion did not yield the intended result; the situation was more complicated than getting Vito on board. It had been easy to give Vito what he wanted after his debriefings, a cell next to Joey Lee's, but the relationship between Freddy and Carol DiNome was not as harmonious. He had been physically cruel and unfaithful. She had grown accustomed to his absence and liked it.

"Freddy will do what he's going to do with his mob. Why does it have to involve me?" she asked Artie. "I'm not pulling the kids out of school. I don't want any part of it."

Kenny and Artie were frustrated but not defeated. On the road again to Otisville, they told Freddy they would continue talking to Carol. "So now we get to be marriage counselors," Artie groaned to Kenny.

They would become so sooner than they thought—with a couple from California, Mr. and Mrs. Dominick Montiglio.

Early in March, a day after telling Denise he would be home soon, Dominick left for New York to meet Danielle Deneux and the man they knew as Val so they all could complete the Quāalude deal they had hatched a few days before.

Danielle, who had left earlier with Val and gone to Montreal to buy the drugs, picked him up at LaGuardia Airport in a limousine and took him to a suite at a Hilton hotel in Manhattan. She said it was good to see him because she only had a couple of dollars left—and, by the way, she and Val had been suckered. The Quāaludes they bought with their last cash were actually aspirin tablets.

"You fuckin' cuckoo clock!"

"Hey, it was Val's connection."

"Where is he?"

"Probably out knocking off a Safeway. He's broke too."

By the time Val returned to the Hilton, Dominick had come up with another plot to make money. During his Studio 54 days with Matty Rega, he had given a friend of Rega's several thousand dollars to start a belt-buckle company in which Dominick was to be a silent partner. Rega's friend, however, was arrested a short time later in the same federal drug case as Rega and Cheryl and went to prison a while. Dominick was out the money; now he had telephoned around and learned that the man, Jeffrey Winnick, owned a small residential real estate brokerage in Manhattan.

"At normal loanshark rates, I figure the guy owes me twenty grand by now," he told Danielle and Val.

"Beautiful," Danielle said.

Dominick also figured that Winnick would never see him willingly because he once talked tough to him while collecting money Winnick owed Rega; Danielle and Val would have to get him to the Hilton somehow. Naturally, Miss Penthouse 1980 would be the bait.

Danielle telephoned Winnick and said she was a model new to New York and needed to find a safe Manhattan apartment. When he asked about her employment and income, she said she was not just a local beauty queen but a Penthouse Pet of the Year. "Did you see June 1980? That was me."

Winnick then volunteered to come pick her up and show her several apartments.

Danielle dolled up and met him on a street corner in her mink coat. She waited until he got out of his Mercedes and opened its passenger door for her; as he did, Val came up with a pistol and pushed Winnick inside as his fantasy foldout walked away. Val told him not to worry, someone just wanted to see him.

At the Hilton, however, Dominick changed his mind and stayed out of the room; he let Val do the talking. Val told Rega's shaking friend he owed a legitimate debt.

He made it seem the money involved was actually Matty Rega's, not Dominick's, and he was collecting it for Rega, who owed it to Roy DeMeo.

Dominick did not know Roy was dead and had told Val about him—so Val told Winnick he would tell Roy if the debt was not paid: "And you know how he'd handle it."

Dominick Montiglio had just pulled his last scam. Winnick ran to the police and complained he was the victim of an extortion plot. He told detectives he was still on federal probation for an old drug case but was living right now. They contacted Winnick's probation officer, Joseph Beltry, to ask if he knew a Matty Rega. Beltry did recognize the name—he had attended task force meetings. He told them Rega was in prison and cooperating with the task force; it had to be someone else behind the plot.

The detectives contacted the task force. Everyone came to the same conclusion; Dominick Montiglio had come home. Walter was ecstatic. The task force did not have a clue where the nephew of the main potential witness in the case had gone because no one they talked to knew. And now Dominick had fallen out of the sky, a mile or so uptown from Walter's office, and involved in a scheme ready-made for catching him red-handed and pressuring him to cooperate. If Dominick rolled over, the task force could start drafting indictments for the grand jury to vote on in—realistically, for once—"sixty-ninety days."

Frank Pergola, Ronnie Cadieux, Harry Brady, and others were delegated to devise a plan for snaring Dominick in a trap; Winnick agreed to cooperate and wear a secret recording device. At noon on March 7, 1983, he telephoned the Hilton and left a message for Val; the cops hoped Val would lead them to Dominick.

That day, Dominick had already left the hotel for one of his former East Side hangouts, P.J. Clarke's, a bar and restaurant. There, he ran into two former acquaintances of his Uncle Nino's—former world middleweight champions of the world, Jake LaMotta and Rocky Graziano.

The Lower East Side legends and former combatants were now close friends who lived nearby in swank Sutton

Place apartments and usually met for lunch. Talking to
Jake, whom Nino always had the most to say about,
Dominick wondered whether he dared telephone Bath
Beach and say hello, but the thought quickly passed. He
asked Jake to autograph a napkin for son Dominick, Jr.,
and as the old Raging Bull scrawled his name, Danielle
Deneux arrived and gave Dominick the telephone message from Winnick. "Just in time," he told her, "because I'm down to my last two dollars."

Dominick decided to surface and meet Winnick face
to face—Val had done the dirty work. To the joy of the
detectives, he returned the call, and the wired Winnick
told him he was ready to pay five thousand dollars. They
agreed to meet in twenty minutes at a nearby Hickory Pit
restaurant. Danielle, pumped up on coke, wanted to go
along.

"Not wise, since he already saw you once," Dominick said.

"Do I look the same today? And I'll sit far enough
away."

Without a special effort, twenty-four-year-old Danielle
was fairly ordinary looking. This day, the Texas native
was wearing gawky cowgirl boots, a studded Levi shirt,
jeans, and a down vest. Coked-up, she actually looked
unkempt. "Suit yourself," he said.

They entered the Hickory Pit separately. She took a
table near the front; he walked to one toward the rear,
where Jeffrey Winnick was. Several detectives—two inside the restaurant, two across the street in a Rodeo
Drive–type boutique, and one posing as a Yellow-cab
driver double-parked in front—watched every move.

"This is all I can get now," Winnick said, handing
over the five thousand. "You gotta be patient."

"I'm in town a while. I'll stay in touch. Count on it."

Winnick was nervous, but Dominick was not suspicious. Rega's friend had always been jumpy, like Rega.
Winnick left, and in a few minutes Dominick rose and
headed for the Hickory Pit door.

Harry Brady then confronted him. "Police officer!
Freeze!" Dominick turned and Brady stuck a pistol in
his left ear. "Move a fucking hair and your brains are on
the floor."

"Take it easy, take it easy—I don't have a gun."

As Brady said he was under arrest for extortion and others came up and handcuffed him and taunted him for being a jerk because everything he said to Winnick had just been recorded, many thoughts came to Dominick's mind, including how he once told Henry Borelli that their life was a losing proposition and how here on their old turf with two dollars in his pocket, he had finally lost. In a much bigger way than he yet knew, however.

Frank Pergola, Ronnie Cadieux, and others arrested a panicky Danielle as she tried to walk out like none of it had anything to do with her. The suspects were taken to a nearby stationhouse; as they were fingerprinted and photographed, Danielle became hysterical. Frank and Brady picked her off the floor a couple of times. The balls Dominick thought she had were gone.

"She didn't do nothing," he told the arresting officers. "She's just a friend, a high-class girl, a Penthouse model."

"She must photograph well," Frank said.

Brady and another officer took Danielle to a hospital until she returned to earth. Later, they took her to the intended drug distribution suite at the Hilton, to wait for Val; they wound up renting it two more weeks. Val, however, either smelled trouble or decided to ditch his friends, because he never showed and was never found. Danielle quickly realized she was a bit player and was not going to be held accountable. At the outset of the fourteen-day vigil, she began enjoying the nonromantic company of Harry Brady, who enjoyed the assignment more than he did his undercover search for Vito Arena in the gay bars of Manhattan. She gave Brady a signed copy of her *Penthouse* layout, which she had taken to New York.

Brady took it to the Southern District, where most of the task force members thumbed the pages—"strictly for investigative purposes," they all said, laughing. They were struck by the contrast between the confident beauty on paper and the scruffy girl who had fallen to the floor.

In the meantime, after the NYPD got his picture and fingerprints, Dominick was transferred to federal custody and taken to the Metropolitan Correctional Center. He

asked Frank to please not lose the Jake LaMotta autograph taken from him when he was searched.

Frank told him not to worry, Dominick had bigger
problems. In his economical way, the Bath Beach detective said, "The other shoe is about to drop, Dom-Boy."

CHAPTER 24

Class President

Having nearly talked his way into prison in California two months before, Dominick clammed up during his initial processing on the extortion charge at the Southern District on March 7. Assistant United States Attorney Barbara Jones conducted the first pre-arraignment interview because Walter was occupied with other organized crime unit duties. Dominick, who had used some of Danielle's cocaine that day, did answer personal questions for the "pedigree" report Jones was filling out. He said, for instance, he never used drugs, that he was an unemployed songwriter, and that though his parents were dead, Anthony Gaggi, an uncle in Brooklyn, was still alive so far as he knew. Before talking about his arrest, however, he wanted to consult a lawyer.

While waiting for a court-appointed lawyer to arrive, he was permitted to make telephone calls. His first was to his Buzzy Scioli–type friend in California, the young legitimate businessman he referred to as The Armenian, rather than by name, so no hitman from Brooklyn who might hear of him would have an easy time finding him. He told The Armenian he had been set up by a friend of an old accuser, Matty Rega, and arrested on a phony charge that "might take a while to clear up." He asked him to go to Westlake and stay with Denise and the children; he was calling there next.

On the telephone with her husband, Denise exploded. "I told you it was stupid to keep ducking back into New York!"

"I just caught a bad break."

"That's great, what am I and the kids supposed to do because your luck ran out?"

"Just sit tight. The Armenian will be there soon and so will I."

Dominick's lawyer arrived and huddled with Barbara Jones and then separately with him. Consequently, Dominick began to realize what Frank Pergola meant when he said "the other shoe" was about to drop. He had not stumbled into a smalltime extortion trap, but a bigtime racketeering case against his uncle and the DeMeo crew. He agreed to have Jones illuminate the situation further and was startled to learn it was a violation of some law called "RICO" just to be associated with an organized group that commits crimes. "That is a strange-ass law," he told her.

Frank and Ronnie Cadieux were then assigned to draw Dominick, if he agreed to look at it, a sketch of the investigation thus far. He did.

Frank, with his tough-guy-with-a-heart manner and Italian-American, Bath Beach pedigree, was an apt and deliberate choice. He had already mentioned his Bath Beach connection as the suspect was transported to the Southern District. Now, offering Dominick the brand he also smoked, a Camel, Frank said that while growing up in Bath Beach his mother was acquainted with a local boxing champ—Dominick's father, Anthony Santamaria.

If the detectives already knew who his father was, Dominick realized they must have been investigating him a long time.

"Vito told us a few things about you," Ronnie said.

"Matty Rega too," Frank said. "Would you like to see a picture of Joey and Anthony?"

Barbara Jones and others dropped in and out, but Dominick and the two homicide detectives talked until four in the morning. They kept tossing more surveillance photographs at him—pictures of Paul, Nino, Roy—and, finally, him.

Off his high horse now, Dominick acknowledged to himself that life in the Beverly Hills candy store was at an end. "I might have done a few things for my uncle," he finally said. "Maybe a few pickups, you know."

That was an admission to loansharking, one of the "predicate acts" under the RICO law. Only two were necessary to show that a defendant proven to be part of a criminal enterprise had engaged in a "pattern of racketeering" on its behalf. With what was already known about him, Matty Rega, and drugs, Dominick was a dead man, legally speaking. They told him his future involved at least twenty years in prison unless he became a cooperating witness.

The session ended with him calculating the warning and wondering if he could ever take the stand against anyone, especially Nino. He had never "ratted out" anyone—not in school, the Army, or "that life." He had observed this rule since he was a boy, since the fourth grade when Nino ordered him to resign as class president because "no one in our family can ever be a stoolpigeon."

Frank and Ronnie went home to their wives, and Dominick was taken to the Metropolitan Correctional Center vacated recently by Freddy DiNome. His clothes and other effects were vouchered and he was given an orange jumpsuit—the color reserved for dangerous or important inmates—and led to a cell in the high security wing. Cops always say only a guilty man sleeps when he is thrown in jail the first time, and he nodded off right away.

Later that day, during MCC meals, he met several fellow inmates and became reacquainted with a flashy drug dealer he met in clubs during his Manhattan-nightlife period—Gene Greene, a member of a notorious Harlem-based ring and another example of the eclectic range of Montiglio associations in New York.

"Man, I heard you split the city," Greene said, after they got over the irony of running into each other again in prison.

"I did, but I came back for a score."

"Not very cool."

"Thanks, Gene. You and my wife, you'd get along."

"Trouble at the crib?"

"Serious. Hey, Gene, don't tell anyone around here who I am. You know, my uncle, he doesn't know I'm back."

"That's cool, don't worry."

On an inmate telephone allowing only collect calls, Dominick dialed Denise again. He told her the situation was "a bit" more serious than he thought, but thinking it best not to elaborate, he kept talking about all the "famous criminals" he was meeting.

"I ran into Gene Greene. He was the biggest dopester in Harlem. I met some people from the Weather Underground who took out an armored car and offed some guards. I met—''

"Dominick, shut up. I'm sick of this crap. You've put yourself in a situation that drastically changes our lives. I warned you it was stupid; you wouldn't listen. What's going to happen now? How do I feed the kids? Where do I stay?''

"Relax, hang on. We'll figure something out."

Hanging up, Dominick realized the federal government was not his only immediate problem, but Denise was more upset than he imagined. After she hung up, she told The Armenian: "I'm supposed to be happy he's in jail with all those maniacs? He's screwed up and he's making like he's at a party. I'm sick of his attitude."

Later that day, Dominick was brought to the office of Walter Mack, who expanded on the cooperation pitches made by Jones, and Frank and Ronnie the day before. If Dominick decided to become a cooperating witness, he would have to tell the truth about anyone and everything. He would also have to plead guilty to belonging to a RICO enterprise; the prosecution would note his cooperation, but if a judge wanted, he could sentence him to prison—probably for not as long as he would if Dominick did not cooperate and was found guilty, but Walter could not say for certain. In the meantime, until after the trial, the United States Marshal's Service, the agency that ran the witness protection program, would find a safe harbor for him and his family in some distant city.

"If you do this, the trial will be in about six months and then you will be sentenced and will know what you have to do to get your life in order," Walter said.

Dominick asked what would happen to Danielle Deneux. Walter said he was not sure yet. Dominick said he needed time to think.

Later, he was taken before a federal judge for arraignment on the extortion charge. The task force had withheld news of his arrest because it wanted him to decide whether to cooperate before Anthony Gaggi learned he was in the MCC and sent someone like Gerald Shargel in to see him.

In court, however, in front of several defense lawyers, a young assistant United States attorney on arraignment duty that day identified Dominick as a special kind of defendant, in that he was the nephew of a captain in the powerful Gambino organized crime family. No one had clued the assistant in, and all he did was read from the pedigree report that was given to him.

Dominick got more time to think about his situation because a judge set bail at twenty thousand dollars; month-to-month Dominick never had that kind of money laying around, so he went back into the MCC. Word of who he was arrived there sometime that day. By the next day, it was common knowledge among the inmates. Gene Greene, who had kept his promise and not told anyone, now warned him: "I am hearing ugly talk. Your uncle wants to ice you; some of your Italian friends are gonna do it. My man, be careful."

The next day, a lawyer (not Shargel) that Dominick had not asked to see, asked to see him. It was a brief meeting.

"Do you want me to call your uncle?" the lawyer asked.

"How do you know who my uncle is?"

The lawyer shrugged. Dominick got up and walked out. "If I want him, I can dial the fucking phone myself, pal."

Dominick returned to his cell. He asked himself whether Nino was capable of killing him, and quickly decided yes, he was. Nino had accused him of stealing a quarter-million of Nino's cash when he left the city. To prove he was not lying about the money, just to save face, Nino would try to kill him as soon as he made bail on the extortion charge—if not beforehand, right in the MCC. People were murdered in prison all the time.

That night, Dominick did not sleep. If he did not co-operate, he would either be murdered or have to sit at a defendants' table with Nino and several people from Canarsie whom he did not fondly recall, especially Joey and Anthony; if he lost at the trial, he would be gone at least twenty years. If he cooperated, he might be gone a few years, after which he might start over with Denise and their children. As bad as he had been, life with them looked good now. The correct course to take began seeming obvious, and if there was a recurring theme to his life, it was that he was a survivor.

Early the morning of his fifth day in custody, a Saturday, he stood in line at the inmate telephone, then dialed a man from the old neighborhood who had given him his number. "I'm not dyin' for nothin'," he told Frank Pergola. "If I die, I want to die for somethin'. I don't want to go down the tubes with these guys."

"No reason why you should," Frank said.

"What's going to happen to Danielle?"

"Don't worry about her. We're cleaning her up. We'll make sure she gets home." The task force never intended to prosecute Danielle, but kept it from Dominick until now; Frank also did not admit until later that the hidden recording device on Jeffrey Winnick had failed to work. That meant a judge could have tossed the extortion case for lack of evidence, and Dominick would have been free to go because a RICO case was not ready to be filed.

"Okay, come and get me," he said. "We've got things to talk about."

He and Henry Borelli had once given each permission to kill the other if they ever informed on anyone, but he had also once characterized his penchant for surviving crashes and explosions in Vietnam and Brooklyn to Buzzy Scioli this way: "I walked."

Dominick was not afforded much time to change his mind. On March 12, he was yanked out of the MCC on the pretext of a bail-reduction hearing on the extortion case; the hope was that snoopy inmates and lawyers would believe he had posted a lower bail and was released. Instead, he was taken to Walter's office, where he agreed to give a sworn statement for the grand jury.

After asking Dominick a series of questions designed to show he had been advised of his rights and understood what was happening, Walter's first question about the case was: "Now, did you at some occasion come into the employment of a gentleman by the name of Anthony Gaggi?"

"Yes." With one word, the long tug of war between Dominick and his uncle entered the home stretch. For the first time ever, Dominick had an upper hand. As he continued answering questions, the task force members present began to appreciate what a peculiar relationship it was: "My uncle didn't want me to get arrested for pornography. He said my grandmother wouldn't like it. Everything else was all right."

Though holding the advantage, Dominick did not bury Nino as deeply as he could. He said he did not know much about Nino's relationship with Roy, but for loan-sharking. He also found it hard to burn Paul Castellano, who was more avuncular to him than Nino. He said he never heard Paul and Nino discuss their relationship, and that while Roy took illegally earned money to Nino, he did not know if Nino took it to Paul.

When asked about Buzzy Scioli, Dominick, rather than fudge an answer, said he could not talk about Buzzy because he was too close a personal friend; besides, Buzzy was not a member of the crew.

"You have to recognize that somewhere down the road your agreement is to tell the truth about all things," Walter said.

"I know, but Buzzy, he's more than a friend."

"That's something you're going to have to resolve, okay?"

"Right."

He was not asked about Henry Borelli—not then—but he had resolved Henry long ago—on the day after Danny Grillo was murdered, when Henry assumed he was next and his friend Dominick was going to do it on orders from Nino and Roy. That meant ice-cold Henry was capable of killing him, despite their supposed friendship.

Walter told Dominick the detectives would be debriefing him extensively before his first actual grand jury appearance—to get him "to do a lot of thinking."

"A lot of remembering," Dominick replied. "Because this is stuff I took three years to forget."

The session lasted only seventy-five minutes, but committed him to an official record and made him begin to feel comfortable with the process. Suddenly, a man whose sister Michele thought of him as just a kid searching for an identity had begun to shed one skin and grow another—secret federal witness. He was hustled out of Walter's office and stashed in a motel on Long Island.

His new journey would be a series of emotional upheavals. At the outset, he thought Denise would be pleased when he telephoned to tell her his decision. Instead, she had her own announcements to make. She and the children would not join him in the witness protection program. It was obvious she would have to leave Westlake, but she would leave the marriage too. She would come to New York, but only to be with relatives until she got on her feet.

"I have fallen out of love with you," she said.

"C'mon, we can work this out. Let's give it a try."

"No, the time has come to say what I feel. I am not going to hide out with someone I don't love; I'd hate myself for it."

"Just think about it. I need you."

"I'm sorry."

Camarie Montiglio, now almost nine years old, was in the room when Dominick telephoned. Denise did not conceal her feelings. "I am going to call it quits with your dad because he has been a bad man," she said. "He left us alone all the time." Camarie, a smooth-faced, silky brunette image of her mother who had also inherited her father's musical talent, was angry at her dad too and unhappy about leaving California but unsure her mother was making the right decision. When he was home her dad was fun to be around. Denise informed the younger children, Dominick, Jr., and Marina, they would be taking a vacation to New York; Marina had never met relatives on either her mom's or dad's side.

Knowing he deserved the treatment Denise was giving him did not make Dominick feel any less bad. "I have treated her like shit, but I do love her," he told Frank Pergola. "I want to get back with her and resolve this mess I got my family into."

Hoping to stabilize their new witness's emotions, and becoming marriage counselors, as Artie Ruffels predicted they would, task force members telephoned Denise too and spoke on his behalf. He wanted to save the marriage and be a good husband and father, they told her. None mentioned Danielle, a bridge he would have to cross on his own.

It did not matter. Denise was adamant. Dominick's sentiments were of dubious sincerity; the time for saving was past.

Artie and the others were concerned about her and the children's safety when they returned to New York. On the night their plane arrived in Newark, New Jersey, a few days after Dominick's decision, Artie and another agent watched them as a relative met the fatherless family and drove them to a sister's house in Queens.

The next day, Artie visited her and asked if she would come to the motel on Long Island where Dominick was and listen to what he had to say. He added, "I don't want to frighten you, but many people will be very angry at Dominick. You need to be safe. Why don't you see if you can patch it up with him?"

Dominick and Denise spent two hours talking it over. He did not tell her about any of his girlfriends, but promised to stop using drugs and to be a better husband and father. "I'm ready now to walk away from all that. My head's already gettin' clear. Being arrested was the best thing for me. I have been saved."

Denise was still dubious. "You've made promises before. The problem now is, I don't know when to believe you. I don't think you will ever change." Before returning to her sister's home, however, she said she would think it over.

While Denise pondered a week, the security-conscious Gaggi task force kept moving Dominick to motels on Long Island and in Connecticut. The detectives did not want to release him to the United States marshals in charge of the witness protection program until he was debriefed at length and they knew whether they were handing over a witness or an entire family.

The FBI, perturbing Walter, had continued to refuse to commit more agents to the case because bureau bosses, despite all the graves the Gaggi task force was digging up, believed their John Gotti case was more important. Artie Ruffels tried to compensate by using his bureau credit card to pay for the care and feeding of Dominick and several detectives around the clock. He quickly became alarmed at the size of the bills—seven hundred dollars one day.

Ronnie Cadieux proposed an alternative whose only effect on Artie's credit card would be the cost of food and gas. A friend of his operated a campground in upstate New York. It had cabins, trails, a recreation center, and was so far in the still wintry woods, no one would even know they were there. "She says as long as we don't tell anyone she let the cops use it, it's okay with her," he told the task force.

At about the same time, Denise made her decision: Yes, but reluctantly, she and the children would relocate with Dominick. She told Artie she did not believe the marriage was salvageable, but was concerned what her husband's former associates might do when they learned he was cooperating. "I don't want this to be permanent, but I understand the danger to my kids. I will go."

Artie told her to be positive, things might work out. He now thought the campground was an inspired idea. The debriefing could continue under relaxed conditions, and the Montiglio family would have time to begin healing itself before the certain shock of deposit by the marshals' service into a city certain to be unlike New York or Southern California.

The only problem with the campground, as everyone discovered after a caravan of government cars wound its way north, was that only one cabin was heated. The witness, his wife and children got that one, and the detectives began taking turns staying in an unheated one—when keeping tabs on the family—or in a nearby motel. Every morning, the detectives in the unheated cabin lined up with their rifles outside the heated one to use the bathroom.

Despite the cold and inconvenience, the camp was a perfect place for people to get to know one another—again, or for the first time. When done debriefing for the day, Dominick and the detectives swapped stories, jogged, and shot pool. They took Denise and the children—the younger two had never seen snow—on long walks through the forest and to a movie theater in a town not far away. Denise, a gourmet cook, came up with great meals for all each night.

Denise was still distant toward her husband, however. They slept together, but did not make love. He wanted her absolution; she would not give it. He also wanted her to see his decision to cooperate the way he did: It was an act of survival, not of betrayal of family. "I didn't do this to sell my uncle out, but there was a serious threat to my life if I stayed in prison," he said. She said, "That's what you say; like I said, I don't know what to believe anymore."

Around everyone else, Denise was warm and appeared to be enjoying herself. "This is great," she told Ronnie early on. "This is the first time in nine years this family has sat down and had three meals in the same day with sane people." After only a few days, the detectives put their rifles back in their cars. No one was going to try anything, or go anywhere.

After others went to bed, Frank and Dominick began staying up to talk and to have more than a couple of drinks. The witness had promised to stop using drugs, but had not mentioned alcohol—and Frank became astounded by his ability to drink heavily and rise with a seemingly clear head the next morning. "If I keep this up, that kid is going to put a fucking hole in my stomach," he told Ronnie.

At times, Dominick became introspective. He was tormented by the notion that Nino's pull on him had proved stronger than his ability to resist it. This implied a fundamental character flaw that was painful to try to understand. "What are you supposed to think when the man who's your role model always cheers the TV bad guys, like my uncle always did? By the time I realized what a disastrous fucking life 'that life' was, it was too late—I was in too deep. And then I got off in the drugs and the broads. I knew it was gonna end some day, but what was I going to do, sell shoes?"

Frank was a homicide detective, not a psychologist. He did, however, give colleagues this early assessment of Dominick: "He was pushed into that life. He didn't jump, but once he was in it, he went whole hog. That's the kind of guy he is, whole hog. His uncle manipulated him, but he became a total wiseguy. I've never met anyone like him, he's a piece of work."

One of the key questions in debriefing Dominick and preparing him to be a witness was determining that, apart from Vietnam, he had never killed anyone—as he maintained in his sworn statement. At the outset, he told the detectives about his role in the grenade attack on Vincent Governara and admitted he was with Nino and Roy when they later shot and killed the neighborhood kid who broke Nino's nose. When a check of records of interviews of witnesses indicated that the youngest of the three men at the scene did not fire his weapon, Frank and the others in the task force began to believe in Dominick.

"I don't think he's capable of killing anyone," Frank

said to Ronnie. "He doesn't have that look in his eye, you know, like Joey and Anthony do."

Frank and Ronnie stayed with the family the entire time, ten days. Others came and went, and became part of the bonding taking place. One Sunday, Artie Ruffels brought along his wife Inger, a teacher, so she could assess the intellectual ability of the two oldest Montiglio children; Dominick had told Artie he knew Camarie was bright, but he was not sure about Dominick, Jr., whom he was just getting to know because he was such an absentee father while in Southern California. Inger Ruffels gave the children intelligence-quotient tests used in her school. Camarie and Dominick, Jr., zipped through. "Don't worry about your son," Artie told Dominick afterward. "He is off the Richter scale."

With his instinct for quick familiarity with people he enjoyed, Dominick began calling the FBI agent and former amateur boxer, "Uncle Artie." He told his kids, "You listen to what my Uncle Artie has to say. He knows what he is talking about."

Despite the serious business, at times a kind of campground-holiday-horseplay mood prevailed. One night, Kenny and Artie came up after several days back in Manhattan, and Frank and Ronnie enlisted Dominick to help them get even with Uncle Artie because he had gone to the comfort of the nearby motel. So had Kenny, but as Frank said, he was NYPD and "too big to get even with."

While Artie was finishing his evening meal and a few cocktails, they broke into his room, short-sheeted his bed and filled it with cereal flakes.

"First crime I ever did with a cop," Dominick said.

"First one I ever did with a gangster," Ronnie teased back.

Near the end of the campground stay, Walter Mack arrived to catch up with the debriefings and become acquainted with his new star witness. They had little in common but the trauma of combat, but Walter did not try to foster a relationship by appealing to shared experience. In the clutter of Walter's office, however, Dominick had noticed the Iwo Jima sculpture and Marine Corps watercolor, and he began to ask questions. When a veteran asked about Vietnam, Walter answered, and

Dominick was the most unusual, if also most wayward, veteran he had ever met. The former Green Beret and the former company commander established a respectful, friendly rapport.

"Let me tell you one thing, Dominick," Walter said. "If you screw up while on the program, I will personally come after you and make sure you go to jail. Even if you die doing whatever it is and come back as a ghost, you will do time."

"I ain't gonna fuck up."

The detectives' update on the debriefs pleased Walter. The information surpassed expectation. Dominick had given more information on the Gambino family than any witness in history—including how Nino did report to Paul, a crucial step up from Dominick's sworn statement two weeks before. Legally, with what Vito had already said about the car deal, Paul was now the indictable leader of a criminal enterprise. A minor stolen-car case against Patty Testa was headed to the top of the Mafia. The Gaggi task force became the Castellano task force.

Getting clearer all the time, Dominick got into his role. For the second time since Vietnam, the first while with Nino, he began feeling like a point man again, only this time he was the eyes and ears of an aboveground army. Despite the scoundrel he had become, he was still an inherently patriotic person—and this rose to the surface as he shed a skin and grew another. He volunteered to visit Henry Borelli in prison and talk him into cooperating. "He and I were close once. Maybe he'd see it the way I do now."

Walter nixed the proposal; if it failed, the targets would know for certain Dominick was cooperating. It was better to keep them guessing. "Don't worry—Henry will get a chance to decide whether to cooperate or go down with the rest."

At the end of his visit, Walter said that the family would be turned over to the federal marshals in a couple of days. He did not know to what safe harbor the marshals would take them; no one on the task force was supposed to know. Dominick and Denise began to realize how isolated they would be when Walter said further contacts between them and their new government friends, even telephone calls, would be arranged through the marshals.

Walter then invited everyone to dinner at a restaurant in a nearby town. They piled into two cars and left the campground as a snowstorm began to swirl. Dominick was with the detectives and Uncle Artie, Denise and the children with Walter. On an interstate highway, Dominick was looking in the rearview mirror of the lead car when the headlights of Walter's disappeared from view.

"Stop, turn around, they've crashed!"

Walter had hit a patch of ice and skidded completely around. Dominick and the others came back and saw everyone was okay. The children were laughing because Walter had said he was just practicing "evasive driving." Dominick smiled at Walter. "I told you I was on your team, you don't have to threaten my kids."

In the restaurant parking lot, after the meal, the detectives built the children a snowman, and everyone threw snowballs at one another. "It's going to be shitty giving these people to the marshals," Ronnie told Frank. "We've got a Stockholm syndrome here, the hostages and their takers have become one happy family."

The family was turned over in the parking lot of a Howard Johnson's restaurant and service area along the interstate. The children began to cry; the adults felt like it. Marina Montiglio, not yet three years old, was too young to write, but Camarie and Dominick, Jr., gave the detectives poems and elaborately decorated cards. "Roses are red, violets are blue, you are nice friends and I'm sorry to lose you," Camarie wrote. Dominick, Jr.'s message was as unabashed as his father's: "I love you."

CHAPTER 25

Wally's Pet Shop

Federal marshals, who tended to play it more by the book than the FBI, accompanied the reunited but hardly healed Montiglio family to an anonymous city in a wholly unfamiliar region of the country. Fourth-grader Camarie, a sharp Southern California kid, began feeling depressed as their airplane descended in a clear sky; for miles around, all she saw were wheatfields. Dominick and Denise tried to keep their children upbeat, but they felt marooned on another planet too.

The marshals helped them find an apartment, then provided a couple of hundred dollars, some fake identity papers, and a number to dial if they needed any more help. Dominick was expected to work, an alien idea for many years, but he took a job loading and unloading a Pepsi-Cola truck. Denise looked after Marina and tried starting a household from zero. Camarie and Dominick, Jr., enrolled in public schools; she got in a fight with some local nitwits who poked sticks in the spokes of his new bicycle. In no time at all, everyone was completely miserable.

But they hung in. Dominick kept his word and tried to be a good husband and father. At night, he also began doing something he had meant to do since Vietnam—write about it. Because he became casually acquainted with many people in the movie business while cavorting in Beverly Hills, he chose the screenplay as his form. The first words he wrote, inspired by the effect of moonlight on damp Vietnam vegetation, were: "The Glass Jungle."

Once started, he could not stop. He finished in two months and mailed it to The Armenian, who knew a film producer. Having heard a few Hollywood horror stories at The Daisy, he worried his work might be stolen, so he registered it first with the United States copyright office. Prudence aside, it was unlikely anyone would try and steal it; although poignant and clever in several scenes, it was a raw amateur's work. It also was unlikely it would ever be made into a movie, not with the way it ended.

It was a dark story about a highly decorated Vietnam veteran who returns home to New York and becomes a bum. He begins to have dismemberment nightmares, checks into a VA hospital and falls in love with a nurse. Bobby Russo (the last name was an old alias of Nino's) then cleans himself up, but a dope pusher claims he owes him money. They have a fight; the pusher pulls a knife, but Bobby kills him with a lead pipe. In a Hickory Pit restaurant, he tells the nurse it was self-defense, but the police will never believe it. As Detectives Furgola and Cordol close in, he jumps off a roof. Head first. End of movie.

Someone who read the screenplay urged Dominick to junk the ending. Bobby was too strong to commit suicide, and why send the audience home feeling bad? Through several rewrites, he did drop the ending, but could never come up with another. Suicide seemed the only way to resolve Bobby's torment and the plot. Nothing else felt right. He told Denise, "It's what I would do, if I were Bobby." Without an ending, "The Glass Jungle" was filed away.

Although they still had a long way to go, Denise began feeling closer to her husband and they became lovers again. Conveniently deciding it made no sense to disturb the progress they were making, he did not reveal any sexy skeletons in his closet, but also behaved himself when a woman along his Pepsi-Cola route seemed charmed by his way-out-of-state accent.

Gradually, the couple tried becoming part of their new surroundings. He joined a health club and they began sampling what nightlife there was—mostly restaurants and movie theaters. Denise adapted better than he did. He found it frustrating to remain silent about his past with strangers—as the marshals had warned. Despite having changed his ways, he was hubristic about his past; it was a better story than anything he could invent.

He began ignoring the marshals' warning, as it applied

to his army life. It was simply too much self-identity to give up; the paratrooper tattoo on his right forearm made it impossible anyway. Much as he hated it, he remained careful when someone, because of his accent, guessed he was from Brooklyn. Inevitably, the stranger would make a joke about gangsters, or ask: "Did you ever meet anyone in the Mafia?"

"Nah, people make more of it than it is. I knew a guy once; people said he was, you know, connected, but all he ever did I think was swipe a few cars. Big deal."

Many times, he held his tongue as people he just met felt compelled to tell the new guy in town from Brooklyn that he had a cousin whose uncle once robbed a gas station. "Can you believe these people?" he would later laugh to Denise. "His cousin's uncle robs a gas station and he thinks he's Dillinger!"

"Most people haven't lived the way we have," Denise would say. "Thank God."

Unsurprisingly, he soon tired of the Pepsi-Cola route. "I need something more challenging," he complained in a telephone call to Uncle Artie.

"Please, just make it legitimate."

"I will, I will. That part of me is over, I told you."

Just when he needed an outlet for his energy, he found one. He met a prominent local citizen with a few investment dollars who said he always wanted to own a restaurant. Dominick said he always wanted to run one, and furthermore his wife was a gourmet cook. "Something tells me this town never had a real Italian restaurant," he added.

In not much time, he and Denise became managers of a small restaurant specializing in Southern Italian cuisine, according to the debut advertising. In not much more time, it became a popular spot. This made them a highly visible couple—and much easier to find, if some Brooklyn nasty learned what city they were in—especially because they were still using their first names.

Dominick and Denise, however, thought they were so far away it did not matter, even when the food critic of the local newspaper came by and wrote: "The souls of the day to day operation are Dominick, whose Sicilian heritage shines throughout the menu, and his wife Denise, daughter of a New York restaurateur." The souls of the operation were "refreshingly unabashed," and their specialties included a Sicilian egg roll, lasagna, baked ziti, and "New York–style cheesecake."

Now and then, the male half of the operation disappeared for a few days—not to visit ailing relatives, as was claimed, but to make grand jury appearances in New York or to travel incognito to other cities for more debriefings with the Castellano task force. He did not know where he was going until a marshal walked him on an airplane, and usually his first stop was only to catch a connecting flight. At the actual destination airport he would be met by another marshal who would usually deliver him to Artie Ruffels or Kenny McCabe and Frank Pergola or sometimes Walter Mack.

More than Vito Arena—and Vito gave a lot—Dominick provided information that meant more work for the task force. He gave work to federal agents in Los Angeles too—the names of several major cocaine dealers in Southern California. Happily for him, he never had to confront his reluctance to speak about Buzzy Scioli; with so much else to do, the task force forgot about Buzzy because he was not a crew member.

Being who he was, Dominick knew more than Vito about Paul and Nino, the main targets now that Roy, whom Vito had known best, was dead. He also knew more about Gambino family rules and customs, its history, structure, and relations with other groups—information of use against other family capos and other criminal enterprises, such as the Irish-American Westies. Westies leader Jimmy Coonan and sidekick Mickey Featherstone had gone to prison but not on RICO charges, and they were due out soon.

"Ever since Carlo died, even though Paulie is the boss, our family has really been like two families," Dominick said one day. He then went on to explain how and why Paul Castellano gave the Manhattan faction under Aniello Dellacroce a wide berth. The detectives could hardly believe their ears when Dominick added, "Did I tell you they made Paulie the boss at my house? I was there. My uncle told me to go upstairs and shoot everybody who came out of the house if the meeting didn't go our way."

As Nino's eyes and ears, Dominick also had more history with the DeMeo crew than Vito Arena did, and the more history he gave, the more task force members came to believe they were investigating not just one serial killer—Roy—but four more: Chris Rosenberg, Henry Borelli, and Joey and Anthony. Dominick added so many murders to the crew's toll—among others, the five Cuban Crisis victims, Danny Grillo, the young unknown man who insulted Roy at the Gemini one night—that the task force made plans to excavate sections of the Fountain Avenue dump relevant to the time period; ultimately, the plans were dropped as impractical given the cost and the improbability of meaningful identifications of bones.

Walter, however, did spend two hundred thousand dollars digging up the underground tanks of a gasoline station that Roy once pointed to, saying to Dominick, "They ought to erect a tombstone there because we buried two bodies there." No bodies were found, although a section of a blue tarpaulin of the type used to cover swimming pools was found. The task force concluded that for some reason the crew removed the bodies; building records showed the station was under construction at the time, so a midnight exhumation would have been a simple if ghoulish matter.

Dominick understood why the detectives kept going over what he knew about the murders of such sympathetic victims as Vincent Governara, Cherie Golden, father-son amateur drug dealers Charles and Jamie Padnick, and vacuum cleaner salesman Dominick Ragucci. These were murders with "jury appeal." He was surprised, however, his interrogators wanted to know every detail about every victim, no matter how unworthy the person was while alive.

"I don't understand why you're so hot on some of these," he told Frank Pergola one day. "Sometimes, it was just one criminal killing another criminal over some beef. By the rules, they had the right to do it."

Frank and Dominick now talked to one another like brothers. "Don't be a shithead," Frank said. "Nobody has the right to kill. Nobody has that right, not for anything."

"Not in Nino's book."

"You ain't with Nino no more."

Meanwhile, task force members kept collecting evidence elsewhere too. The crew had long since cleaned out Roy's arsenal in the basement of the Gemini Lounge, but a search of Dracula's clubhouse-apartment turned up some forensic clues. "I betcha I you ain't gonna find a fuckin' thing," the failed bank robber said as a task force raiding party, armed with a search warrant, began ripping up walls and floors with saws and hammers. "I'll give you hundred-to-one odds."

"Hundred to one?" Ronnie Cadieux said. "You're not much of a street guy are you? How easy do you think it would be for me to lay a gun on the floor and say it's yours. But this is your lucky day: We're all straight guys—you got that going for you." By the time the raiders were done, they had recovered several dozen bullets embedded in the walls and floors—some right where Freddy DiNome, though not officially on board, had said to look.

Artie Ruffels and the detectives also searched Freddy's home in Shirley, Long Island. They found a videotape from a Fourth of July party at Roy's house—and hanging on the inside of a door to a hallway closet, a poster-size photograph of a nude and unusually well-endowed Freddy posing at his Broadway Freddy's Diagnostic Center. "He is a very strange person," Artie said to the others, "to have that hanging in a closet his kids use."

Working with Kuwaiti government officials, Harry Brady and John O'Brien, an auto crimes lieutenant, spent three weeks in the desert emirate identifying cars stolen from New York. Kuwait did not have a sophisticated national automobile registration system—or an auto-theft problem; the year before, only one car in the entire country was stolen. Still, Brady and O'Brien returned to New York with enough VIN plates to show major shipments—but not the cars; logistically and under international law, it would have been virtually impossible to accomplish.

The case itself, however, was looking more possible all the time, and it was still growing. Because he was part of it, Dominick provided an inside story on the fix at the Eppolito trial—a particularly satisfying revelation for Ronnie Cadieux, still much disturbed by Nino's acquittal and the murder of Patrick Penny, whom he had unsuccessfully urged to leave New York. Dominick told how he was part of a team sent to Penny's brother Robert to offer Patrick a payoff. This meant Nino was vulnerable to a new charge, obstruction of justice, a predicate RICO act. It also suggested Nino might have "reached" a juror—what Ronnie and prosecutor Steven Samuel thought from day one.

"I think you guys should go question everyone on the jury," Walter told Frank and Ronnie. "See what went on in that jury room."

"Is that legal?" Ronnie asked.

"Ask the questions, we'll worry about that later." With an attitude such as that, plus his commitment, Walter had gained the admiration of everyone on the task force. Many times in their careers, Artie Ruffels and the cops were teamed with prosecutors whose initial instinct was negative. They fixed on why things could not be done; Walter fixed on how to get them done. His first instinct was positive—and on the question of whether it was legally proper to interview the Eppolito jurors, entirely correct.

"Walter's got the biggest balls I ever saw in a prosecutor," Ronnie, the ex-Marine, told Frank. "I'd follow him into combat any day."

Kenny McCabe felt the same way. Many times he told his colleagues the biggest mistake the crew made was killing Roy and not Walter. "That's the only way they could have stopped this case," he would say. One day he told Walter his bosses in the Brooklyn DA's office were giving him grief for spending so much time on the task force, and he was tired of NYPD politics. He would even quit if he could find another job.

Walter reached into a desk drawer and, retrieving an application form, said, "How'd you like to be an investigator for the United States Justice Department, Southern District?" Kenny, now thirty-five years old, was a little over the age limit for applicants, but Walter pushed and though it took two years, Kenny got the job—basically, more of what he was already doing on the task force.

Frank and Ronnie interviewed the Eppolito jurors; after also checking records related to a home that Judy May and the man who led her into Nino's clutches, Wayne Hellman, had purchased after the verdict and after their marriage, the task force became highly suspicious of them and Wayne's father, Sol. Dominick identified Sol as a loanshark customer of Nino's. All three Hellmans were added to the already crowded target list.

As always, as much as possible, Dominick was checked against facts. As to his Eppolito bullet-switch story, Walter examined records of the Rikers Island infirmary and learned that the day before Nino handed over a bullet he claimed fell out of his neck, Dominick Montiglio was listed as a visitor.

Artie and the detectives stayed in regular contact with Dominick. They furnished news that the media in his city would never report, such as the shooting, in September 1983, of former 21 Club maître d' Chuck Anderson by armed robbers who held up the Manhattan restaurant he recently opened. The robbers believed Nino's long-time loanshark customer was lying when he said he did not have the combination to a safe, and they shot him in the head. "Mr. New York" died a few months later.

By the federal marshals' rules, task force members were not supposed to know what city Dominick was in, but they did; neither were they supposed to telephone him without setting it up with the marshals, but most also did. Breaking the rules was part convenience, part personal concern. They were rooting for him and Denise to survive as a couple, and were worried what their mercurial witness might do if a domestic crisis occurred. He frequently telephoned them, at the office or at home, with facts that came to him in the middle of the night—or to say hello. Over the telephone, he became friendly with their wives, including Sarah Lawrence graduate Consuela Mack, a rising talent in television news. "Hi Muffy," he would say. "Is Buffy there?"

By the fall of 1983, Walter Mack was getting ready to write a memo outlining the case and recommending who to ask the grand jury to indict and on what charges. The task force war room was now brimming with evidence, but to minimize every risk of legal combat, Walter still wanted Freddy DiNome on board; Freddy could corroborate Vito Arena on the stolen-car angle of the case that Dominick knew little about. He also could fill in gaps in crew history created by Dominick's flight to California in 1979 and Vito's defection in 1980.

The problem with getting Freddy to cooperate was still

his wife, not him. Kenny and Artie had arranged to take Freddy out of his cell again for another visit with her. In the meantime, Artie had also talked his Gambino squad supervisor Bruce Mouw into assigning another agent to help out with the paper trails and witnesses, and so the task force got its second Harvard graduate—Special Agent Marilyn Lucht, thirty-two-year-old native of Ohio, expert on RICO law, and member of the Gambino squad. Artie asked for her because she was a careful investigator and might be able to develop a better relationship with Carol DiNome.

Freddy's wife, however, was still pleased with life without Freddy and again refused to agree to join him in the witness protection program. Marilyn actually made a bigger impact on Freddy—who made some lewd remarks about her to Artie—than Carol. "It's not easy convincing someone who's spent their whole life in New York that they're going to be happy in Kansas," Marilyn told disappointed Artie. "Especially if it means getting back with someone she's been terrified of her whole marriage."

In their private meetings, Carol apparently gave Freddy another line of reasoning. "She says I can't be a rat," Freddy told Artie.

It was a setback, but these days the task force won, sometimes only in small ways, more than it lost. For example, while visiting Freddy in the federal prison in upstate Otisville, Kenny and Artie became acquainted with a prison official whose office computer showed where every inmate in the federal system was housed. "I'm curious, where's Henry Borelli?" Kenny asked.

The computer revealed that Henry, convicted with Freddy in the Empire Boulevard case, was in a minimum-security, camplike facility near the maximum-security federal prison in Lewisburg, Pennsylvania, a few hours by car from Brooklyn. "I know it was just a car case they got him on," Kenny said, "but the guy has killed fifty or so people. Why such a soft joint?" Within days, Henry was transferred from the camp to a hellhole in Arkansas, making it much more difficult for family and friends to visit.

In his wallet, Walter began carrying a color snapshot of a happy-looking young man, his adoring wife, and infant child. The young man was Peter Waring, a smalltime Canarsie cocaine dealer who, exceeding his reach, did a deal with the crew and became one of the first to die during the crew's foulest year, 1979. Waring was among those victims sent to the Fountain Avenue dump after the crew decided they were threats—in Waring's case, because they learned he was going to meet with narcotics detectives.

The task force learned about him after Waring's widow refused to let authorities forget her husband's disappearance, and detectives found a journal he kept in which he had written about his minor drug relationship with the crew.

Walter acquired the photograph after interviewing the widow. He carried it because it symbolized what the case was about—the crew's brutality and trail of tears, its defiance of authority—and his belief that any murder in the case should be probed to the maximum, regardless of who the victim was, because it might be the one that nails a conviction.

Some in the Southern District thought Walter had become obsessed with the case and that it was interfering with his supervisory duties as chief of the organized crime unit; Walter saw it differently. Many cases against the city's other criminal enterprises had begun since he took over. He believed he managed them all, and worked harder than everyone else—often eighteen hours a day, seven days a week. He was not going to turn the case over to someone. "If ever a case deserved to be finished, this is it," he told wife Consuela, whose television reporter's job kept her away from home a lot too. "The people in this are the worst we've ever seen, or even heard about."

Finally, in December 1983, after two years of putting off his superiors, police brass, and the FBI for "sixty-ninety days" more, Walter began the countdown to indictment. The statute of limitations governing the time frame in which the government is allowed to bring charges after learning of a crime was expiring on some of the stolen-car matters.

Thinking they might crack, Walter sought to isolate Richie DiNome and car-deal maven Ronald Ustica by moving against them first. He secured arrest warrants alleging the same crimes that Richie's brother and Henry Borelli were imprisoned for three years earlier.

Kenny McCabe, John O'Brien, and Harry Brady knocked on Richie's door early on December 4, a Sunday morning, a favorite time to arrest a suspect seen as a potential cooperating witness because, in theory, the suspect has more time to mull a deal without worrying if his criminal associates know he has been arrested. In theory, word travels slower on Sunday. Kenny and Ronnie had visited Richie's house in Brooklyn only a week before to warn him that the crew intended to kill him and Freddy as soon as Freddy was released. Richie laughed them off; he had survived a shooting six months earlier and believed his only problem now, like then, was cocaine dealers. Richie too had fallen in love with cocaine in the last two years and had separated from his wife.

"You're under arrest, come with us," Kenny said when Richie opened his door. "Maybe we can save your life. You're gonna wind up getting killed if you don't come on board."

"Like I told you before, that shooting had nothing to do with Joey and Anthony. They're my friends. I got no problems."

The arresting officers took Richie to Walter, who gave his standard opening remarks: "I'm the prosecutor in your case. Now we're charging you with serious crimes, but I'd be happy to hear your side of the story, if you'd like to talk to me about it. I'd like to ask you a few questions; you don't have to talk to me if you don't want to, but if you do, anything you say could be used against you in a court of law. . . ."

Richie was the last person in the world to match wits with Walter, but he tried anyway. While attempting to deny crimes he actually admitted some and while saying he would not cooperate actually provided some details about the crew.

O'Brien and Brady, with fellow auto crime cop Frank Kollman, picked up Ronald Ustica the next evening. Ustica's used-car business on Long Island was now bankrupt, and the lot formerly filled with stolen cars was now a parking lot for suburban railroad commuters. Brady tried softening him up for Walter. "Schmuck, they took you for everything, your business is down the tubes, and we got you involved in murders. Roy's dead. Don't spend the rest of your life in jail.''

In Walter's office, Ustica, also way over his head, denied wrongdoing but admitted being friendly with crew members and having done business with them. He, like Richie, also said he would never cooperate.

Paul Castellano and Anthony Gaggi were now virtually certain their former fair-haired boy Dominick was a cooperating witness. They had become suspicious when he abruptly made bail and was released from the MCC, seemingly into thin air, and grew more alarmed as detectives began turning over dirt piles such as the Eppolito case. They also feared that another former Green Beret, Mickey Featherstone of the Westies, had grown weak. A few months into his parole from prison, he was saying he was done with crime.

The family captain who had replaced Roy as Gambino liaison to the Westies was ordered to evaluate Featherstone's state of mind. The pair met in a Manhattan bar. "I know why I'm here, and I'm not the stoolpigeon," Featherstone said straight off. "I believe it's Dominick, Nino's nephew."

"How do you know?"

"You guys are saying it's an ex-Green Beret, and the only one I know besides me is Dominick."

Featherstone also had run into Nino at the Rikers Island jail a couple of years before, when Nino was brought from prison for a court appearance. "When I bumped into Nino in Rikers, he said Dominick was missing a few years already. So the stoolpigeon has got to be Dominick. It's not me."

As Featherstone spoke, Dominick was huddling with Walter and Artie on another debriefing, and on December 19, 1983, he met them in Atlanta for one more. This time, the task force invited Denise and the children to come along as a kind of pre-Christmas vacation; with all the trips her husband was taking, Denise was feeling left out.

In January 1984, for different reasons, some corners of the federal law enforcement establishment also began saying Paul should not be included in Walter's case. Rival prosecutors in the Eastern District and FBI agents based in Queens were the most outspoken—and if Paul had been privy to why, he would have been worried less about Dominick and more about what he had been saying around his white house lately.

The same team of prosecutors and agents working on the drug-dealing case against the John Gotti crew had succeeded in placing a hidden listening device inside Paul's Staten Island home. Gambino squad boss Bruce Mouw, his superiors, and many others did not want Walter to include Paul in the indictment, mostly because they wanted to be the ones to nail Paul.

The Brooklyn-based federal team thought the Manhattan-based team was about to bring a case against Paul that paled in comparison to the one they could bring. Walter told his counterparts in the Eastern District to relax, the Justice Department in Washington, which approved all major RICO indictments, was not going to approve his plan to put Paul into his case, and that he had made such a request only on a pro forma basis.

In fact, Walter believed in the strength of his case against Paul and was confident Justice Department higher-ups would agree. The reason was that a Justice Department higher-up Rudolph Giuliani, had recently been appointed United States Attorney for the Southern District. Less than a year before, Giuliani, a Brooklyn native who aspired to elective office, held the number-three job in the Justice Department, chief of the criminal division. More than his counterpart in Brooklyn, he had Washington's ear, and Walter was telling him the indictment could be drawn in such a way that Paul would be charged with being only the boss of the DeMeo crew criminal enterprise, not the Gambino family. That way, the Brooklyn prosecutors could bring their own case against Paul.

The irony of the situation was ample: the Manhattan faction of the Justice Department—the Brooklyn wing of the Gambino family in its sights—squaring off against the Brooklyn faction of Justice, which was trying to make the most of a case that began as an attack on the family's Manhattan branch.

Waiting for the turf issue to play out, the task force kept making moves. Following their arrests, Walter got his grand jury to indict Richie DiNome and Ronald Ustica, legally isolating them from the crew for the moment. Both again refused to cooperate, then made bail.

Kenny told Richie it was a bad move: "You're on the street now. Don't be stupid all your life; make a deal."

"Stop believing all that crap about my friends," he said.

The next day, February 4, 1984, in the Brooklyn neighborhood known as Gravesend, Richie was assassinated in the living room of an apartment he leased after leaving his wife for cocaine. Two men who lived nearby who happened to be visiting at the time were also executed. Richie had let people he knew well into his home; they did not forget their silencers or shoot themselves in the hand, and whoever they were, they thoughtfully locked the doors on the way out.

If the crew was behind the murders, and no one doubted it, it was another desperate and dumb move. The task force brought Freddy back to the MCC to work on him, and on February 16, Joey and Anthony visited him and tried to do the same; Anthony had recently finished serving several months in jail for his Canarsie gun and coke case. They told Freddy how sorry they were and how blameless too. Freddy listened but in disbelief. He thought he was listening to the men who murdered his brother.

Now came time to begin arresting the other targets. Several cops had been constantly keeping the Canarsie contingent under surveillance the past several days, hoping to catch them in the middle of a drug deal—a big pile of cocaine always makes a telling trial exhibit. The cops had seen new crew member Carlo Profeta, an acne-scarred heavy who had begun helping Joey Testa collect Roy's old loans, accepting a package from Joey and Anthony, but held off that time because the circumstances were not to their liking.

On February 17, however, the day after Joey's and Anthony's visit to Freddy, and after an informant said the crew would move drugs that day, a large task force team was positioned around R-Twice Collision, the Canarsie body shop where, in the post-DeMeo era, Joey and Anthony and other crew members hung out. The stakeout included two federal officers unaccustomed to drug raids—Artie's FBI partner, Marilyn Lucht, and Leslie Lauziere, a postal inspector—but Walter had imposed the task force model on his team.

In several two-way radio-equipped cars and a van, the team took turns picking up and handing off Joey as he drove out of R-Twice, then drove back and parked in front. Sergeant Joseph Coffey from homicide and Lieutenant John O'Brien from auto crimes, the operation's ranking officers, had picked up his trail last. Harry Brady was with them. "Joey took a package from the trunk! Let's move!" Coffey screamed over his radio.

As Coffey's undercover car screeched up, Joey bolted inside R-Twice. The three cops jumped out with unholstered pistols and ran right in after him as other undercover cars roared to life. Gunning his toward R-Twice from a gas station across the street, Frank Pergola hit a speed bump, blew out a tire and lurched the rest of the way on shredded rubber.

Inside, the first cops to arrive pointed pistols at Anthony and other crew members—"Don't anybody get excited!" Brady shouted. "Don't anybody move a fucking muscle, or I'll blow your fucking brains out!"

Having wanted this moment a long time, some of the cops were pumping more adrenaline than the crew. Especially Joseph Coffey, as he chased Joey into a bathroom and saw him flushing what appeared to be cocaine down a toilet. "You motherfucker!" he yelled, then rapped Joey in the head with his gun, grabbed him by the back of the neck and shoved his head into the toilet bowl. "You flushed the coke down, asshole. Now go get it!"

"Are you fucking nuts?" Joey gargled, squirming back up.

Coffey dragged Joey back into the body shop as Brady ordered the well-dressed suspects to lie face-down on the grease-streaked floor.

"What about our fucking clothes?" Joey protested.

"Fuck you and your clothes!" Coffey barked. "Lie down!"

After everyone calmed down, Kenny McCabe asked Coffey, a good friend, about the supposed package he said he saw Joey taking from the car. From the look on Coffey's face, Kenny concluded there was no package, that whatever Joey flushed away was a personal-use amount, and that Coffey had not seen a package and had just decided it was time to arrest these particular crew members. "You fucking guys," he said to Coffey and O'Brien.

Kenny was disappointed because he had hoped to snare Joey's new buddy Carlo Profeta in a drug deal. Profeta had been with the crew since Freddy was jailed in 1981. Under the pressure of drug charges, Profeta might have filled in more gaps in crew history. "Carlo," Kenny said, "could have given us some more bodies."

Coffey, however, insisted he did see a package. He and Brady visited the home of a nearby federal judge and obtained a search warrant for R-Twice based on Joey's frantic dash to the bathroom. No drugs or package were found. The other cops kept the suspects handcuffed in the grease a while, then took them to see Walter, who gave them his ritual greeting and invitation to be cooperative. All declined.

Ronald Jivens, another auto crimes officer, tried changing the mind of crew member Ronald Turekian, the man who had helped Vito Arena and Richie DiNome bury Joseph Scorney in cement five years before. Other than that, Turekian was not a big fish, but he did come up with a memorable reply to Jivens's pitch on behalf of Walter Mack.

"What am I, a canary? That guy Mack is a flag-waving son of a bitch. I ain't gonna work for no Wally's Pet Shop."

CHAPTER 26

Lassie Comes Home

The situation was again ripe for dying on the street with a gun in his hand—but on February 25, 1984, the day the task force chose to arrest Anthony Gaggi, he was unarmed. He was grabbed as he left a Bensonhurst diner and walked to a small clothing store his wife and daughter now owned and operated a few steps away.

Had he been armed and begun shooting, he would have died a hero, in the minds of some Bath Beach–Bensonhurst legend-makers, because of the way the cops came upon him. Ronnie Cadieux nearly ran him over as he drove his car up on a sidewalk and down it to block Nino's path, as another undercover car boxed him in from behind.

"Stop, Ronnie, stop!" screamed Cadieux's partner, Frank Pergola, as their car barreled down the sidewalk. Ronnie, eager for action because he was away during the R-Twice arrests, braked to a stop within a couple of feet of the startled suspect.

From the second car on the sidewalk, an old Gaggi adversary jumped out and delivered the news: "You're under arrest, Nino," Kenny McCabe said.

"State or federal?" was fifty-eight-year-old Nino's only reply, probably because he thought the Brooklyn District Attorney was coming after him for the Eppolito fix.

"This is the big one," Kenny said.

Other than that, handcuffed Nino had nothing to say on the ride to Walter's office. There, he also sat in stony silence, impressing his captors as a man who would hold up well as a prisoner of war.

The arresting officers then escorted Nino out of Walter's office for further processing at FBI headquarters, a short walk across Foley Square in downtown Manhattan.

It was raining, so they decided to drive. Frank Pergola saw there would not be enough room and began walking.

"No, get in, Frank," said Kenny. "I'll put Nino in the trunk."

Nino managed a tight smile. In FBI headquarters, he relaxed a bit more. Seeing Artie Ruffels cleaning his eyeglasses, he uttered his first words since being taken into custody many hours before. "You ought to try a pair with lighter frames. My son's an optometrist. He's on Madison Avenue—stop in and see him."

Artie and Nino then tried on each other's glasses. "I see what you mean," said Artie. Like the others arrested so far, Nino was arraigned and released on bail to await certain indictment by the grand jury.

It was now time for Freddy DiNome to fish or cut bait. Kenny and Artie took him out of the MCC and placed him in a motel on Long Island. Marilyn Lucht talked his wife Carol into going there for three days of talks. Carol, Freddy's second wife, told Marilyn she would listen, but she was not going to change her mind and go with him to Kansas or any state like it. "Without his friends, he'll just have me to beat up on."

On the last day of the meetings, Artie poured it on: "Look, Carol, this is your last chance. These people we're dealing with might grab you, they might grab one of your kids. How do I know this? This is Paul Castellano, head of the Mafia, we're talking about. If we take your husband back to the MCC—his friends already know we took him out—he's going to get killed. You can't do that to him, as a wife and as the mother of his kids."

Carol did not reply. Artie took that as a waiver. "All right, let's go," he said. He brought more agents to the scene, bundled everyone up in government cars, drove to a ferry crossing to Connecticut, declared a national emergency at the dock, ordered several other cars off the ferry, and sailed away into the witness wilderness with Freddy, Carol, and their children.

After a couple of weeks of debriefings, Freddy officially came on board on March 14, 1984, and testified to the grand jury on that day—the third and last major witness against Paul, Nino, and the crew. He was an exclamation point to Vito and Dominick, but also a supplier of many missing puzzle pieces—among them, rogue cops such as Avenue P graduate John Doherty and Gemini Lounge drinker Thomas Sobota. In time, Doherty would be called before the grand jury, where he pleaded the Fifth Amendment; because the statute of limitations had run out on some of his alleged crimes and because other evidence against him was weak, the task force assigned him a low priority and eventually forgot about him because he had already resigned from the NYPD. Sobota, who had quit drinking after Patrick Penny was killed, would make a deal and become a cooperating witness.

Freddy still had to complete the remaining few months of his Empire Boulevard sentence, but before he was transferred to a new prison with a witness-security unit, and before his wife and children were turned over to the marshal's service, Kenny, Artie, and Marilyn treated the family to several days of vacation.

At first, Freddy was in a buoyant and crass mood. He cracked a sick joke about his clumsiness in the dismemberment murders of Ronald Falcaro and Khaled Daoud— "After them, Roy demoted me from cutter to wrapper"—and lasciviously told Artie, "I'd like to fuck that bitch Marilyn." Ridiculous as the idea was, he tried flirting with her. "Oh, Freddy," Marilyn would say with remarkable patience, "you're not my type, and you're a married man!"

The agents treated Freddy and his family to dinners, movies, and trips to a museum and historical places. They tried to choose events that might benefit Freddy's sixteen-year-old daughter and eleven-year-old son, who, like a son from Freddy's first marriage was named Freddy, Jr. After a few days of such sights, Freddy fell into a deep funk and stopped talking. Only in hindsight did Artie and Marilyn realize why: Freddy had spent most of his life in the company of skels and was beginning to see how different he was from normal people. The cultural trips made him feel inadequate, a social loser. Carol DiNome had told Marilyn that their children were not allowed to have books around the house, because if Freddy could not read, neither could they.

On the last night of vacation, before Freddy was to return to prison, Artie's wife Inger joined everyone for a farewell dinner. Mostly, Freddy sat and stared at the ceiling. "Freddy could be pleasant if he wanted, he's not such a bad guy," Inger told her husband, "but he's freaking out. I'd worry about him."

Near the end of March, with the pivotal support of his influential new boss Rudolph Giuliani (who had pulled the right levers in Washington) Walter won his turf battle with the Eastern District. He got permission to include Paul in his case.

Alarmed by Nino's arrest, Paul dispatched a Machiavellian New York attorney, Roy Cohn—the communist-hunting wonder boy of the Senate Army-McCarthy hearings in the early 1950s—to tell Walter and Giuliani what a wonderful meat salesman Paul was. "Do you really believe a man such as Mr. Castellano is involved in auto theft?" Cohn asked.

Joseph Coffey, attending the meeting in his role as chief of the NYPD organized crime homicide squad, felt like tossing Cohn out a window, but the government lawyers politely listened and let Cohn earn his promotional fee without giving him anything useful or comforting for Paul.

Soon Walter's grand jury voted a massive firepower seventy-eight count RICO indictment against Paul, Nino, and twenty-two crew members or hangers-on and sometime associates—such as paralegal Judy May Hellman. For being Nino's ringer on the Eppolito jury, pretty, doe-eyed Judy, and her husband and father-in-law, would stand trial with several of the most notorious killers in United States criminal history. Because so many victims were never found and evidence in other homicides was not up to legal requirements, the indictment alleged only twenty-five murders; still, it was the most ever charged in a federal case.

As part of the turf-war settlement, Walter did not include John Gotti in his indictment. While investigating loanshark Sol Hellman, the task force had come across crimes for which Gotti was vulnerable, but the Eastern District desired Gotti for yet another case in the works, so Walter threw his rival prosecutors what was then a comparatively insignificant bone.

Walter's indictment was kept secret until March 30, when the task force arrested Paul, who unlike the others, was allowed to surrender at the Manhattan office of his trial attorney, James La Rossa—Nino's lawyer in the Eppolito case.

The agents and detectives were against the special treatment for Paul. They wanted to arrest him on the street like the others because a surprise arrest often yielded new information—a telephone number in a wallet, a diary in a jacket pocket—but Giuliani and Walter decided to grant Carlo Gambino's successor the dignity of an orchestrated, consensual arrest.

Task force members got together beforehand and elected Kenny McCabe as the one to say the magic words—"you're under arrest"—to Paul at La Rossa's office. In two cars, Kenny and seven other team members then escorted Paul to Wally's Pet Shop. Paul, unlike Nino, was courteous and seemingly relaxed from the start, but his message to Walter was the same: Take a hike.

As handcuffed Paul was escorted to the FBI, Kenny on his left, Joseph Coffey on his right, other task force members trailing behind, Coffey happened to recall how he once met Carlo Gambino.

"He was a real gentleman," added Kenny.

Paul turned and gave Kenny a wounded look, as if concerned Kenny believed he did not measure up to Carlo, his late cousin and brother-in-law. "What? I'm not a gentleman!"

"I didn't say that," Kenny said diplomatically.

Later that day, new United States Attorney for the Southern District Rudolph Giuliani took the spotlight at a press conference and announced the indictment. Never before had the government accused so many members of an organized criminal enterprise at once. Giuliani described it as "the most important chapter" in the history of the federal government's war against the Mafia, and veteran reporters noted with interest that Giuliani lavished praise on the NYPD before mentioning the FBI and other federal agencies.

The story made the national newscasts and dominated local late news shows. Retired auto crimes intelligence officer John Murphy watched them in silent satisfaction. Walter had invited him to the press conference, but Murphy was still too laid low by his heart attacks to endure Manhattan stress. "We did it, didn't we, Walter."

"We did, but it isn't over yet."

Henry Borelli, Dominick Montiglio's good friend once upon a time, was among those defendants eventually arraigned on the indictment. He was brought from prison to Walter's office, where he growled his way through the pedigree. As it happened, on a prison document, he had read that Kenny and Artie were behind his transfer from a camplike facility in Pennsylvania to a maximum-security dungeon in Arkansas.

"I know it was you guys," he said with an ice-cold stare.

Kenny and Artie just stared back, waiting for Henry to make a threat—and pick up another predicate act. Henry turned away.

All the defendants pleaded not guilty—except two who could not be found: Joey's brother Dennis, believed to have gone with the wind, and Joseph Guglielmo, aka Dracula, believed to have been murdered, probably to pieces, because he knew too much about the paint jobs on the floor in his Gemini apartment. Everyone was granted bail.

Walter's statement to Murphy that the case was not over yet contained more truth than even the most cautious prosecutor could have ever imagined. The road to the end of the case would feature sudden curves and deep ruts that knocked him and the task force off course several times. Right after the indictment, from the prison where he was doing time for his robbery spree, Vito Arena telephoned the *New York Post* city desk, described himself as the case's "star witness" and announced he was not going to testify because the government was treating him shabbily.

In reality, Vito was just upset because Dominick and Freddy were now on board and the case did not hinge on him anymore. He had lost some of his leverage, but eventually Walter got him some Bruce Springsteen music tapes and new tennis shoes, and he calmed down—for a while.

Then, six months after the indictment, to all of Walter's friends' anger and dismay, Rudolph Giuliani named Barbara Jones, the assistant U.S. attorney who first interviewed Dominick, to be the new chief of the Southern

District's organized-crime unit, replacing Walter. Jones, a veteran organized-crime prosecutor, was respected by all members of Wally's Pet Shop, but in their minds the demotion was about politics, not performance; Giuliani did not want independent-minded Walter running all the other high-profile cases against other Mafia families that were about to break. All of these had begun on Walter's watch, and would attract tremendous publicity. With Walter out of the way, the politically ambitious Giuliani could grab the glory for himself.

Walter kept his own counsel about the demotion. Outwardly, he was angrier about a tragedy that had occurred half a world away: the slaughter of two hundred thirty-nine Marines in a terrorist car bombing of a barracks in Beirut. He could not believe Marine commanders had placed so many men in a compound so poorly guarded a civilian car drove right inside. The risk to the Marines could have been minimized with rational planning; their commanders let them slip into a predictable routine; they forgot their greatest enemy was habit. Meanwhile, the most he would say on his demotion was that he and Giuliani had "differences of opinion" over how to proceed on cases—including the Castellano-Gaggi-DeMeo case. Giuliani thought Walter was taking too long.

Though he did mind the loss of title, Walter did not mind the loss of personal publicity that went with it. Unlike Giuliani, he did not try to curry favor with the press; he did not leak. Though married to a reporter, he felt the press should report on a criminal case on only two occasions: when an indictment was announced and when a jury returned a verdict. Intellectually, he understood that such docile scrutiny invited government abuse, but in his experience a nosy press added too many impurities to the process.

Giuliani told confidants he was merely exercising a right to place assistants of his own choosing in key positions. Whatever, Walter refused to criticize him publicly and dove into the Castellano case. In a similar situation, most assistant U.S. attorneys with his experience and credentials would have resigned and doubled their salary by taking a job with some establishment Wall Street firm. Walter, however, had promised John Murphy that he would stay with the case until the end.

Apart from all the pretrial legal wrangling with the battery of expert defense attorneys retained by Paul, Nino, and the crew, keeping the witnesses on an even keel became Walter's biggest worry. For example, before Freddy was released from prison to join wife Carol in the witness protection program, she made a request of her federal marshal: "Do we have to tell Freddy where me and the kids are? I'm afraid of him. I want a divorce."

The marshal sought the guidance of supervisors in Washington, who decided that a woman afraid of her husband had a right to live apart from him—so suddenly Freddy was looking at going into the program by himself, a scary journey for even the most well-adjusted person. Beforehand, however, he began speaking on the telephone from prison to his first wife, Peggy; they became close again. She was not keen on joining him in the program, but at least he was saved from feeling unloved.

The task force kept in tune with Freddy's emotional lows and highs during breaks in many pretrial appearances he made to bolster an effort by Walter to throw one of the defendants' lawyers out of the case. The effort had begun after Freddy testified in the grand jury that he was along when his boss Roy DeMeo gave defense attorney Gerald Shargel one hundred thousand dollars in a brown paper bag, to press an appeal of Nino's conviction in the Eppolito case and other legal business.

Since that time, Shargel had represented seven other DeMeo crew members and was now attorney of record for a minor defendant in the task force case. Walter subpoenaed him to appear before the grand jury and provide records showing fees paid to him by the crew. Shargel fought the subpoena, but eventually it was ruled enforceable. He then told the grand jury he had destroyed his fee records to avoid a situation such as this: being forced into providing sensitive information about clients. He also said that Roy's brown bag contained only two thousand dollars.

"Roy carried that much around in his shirt pocket," Freddy scoffed to Walter.

The sideshow dragged on a long time, and Freddy gave more secret testimony about the hundred-thousand-dollar payment and those times in the MCC when Freddy was thinking of cooperating and Shargel came on like he was his attorney, though Freddy had not asked him to be. Although it was not the same as testifying in a public courtroom, Freddy did fine in his grand jury appearances. Although smarter than he sounded, he seemed incapable of invention. Eventually, Walter prevailed. Judge Abraham Sofaer ruled that Shargel's actions suggested he was "acting in effect as a 'house counsel' for the enterprise." Shargel was off the case.

Midway through the Shargel matter, Freddy pleaded guilty to his RICO crimes. Like the other cooperating witnesses, he would not learn his penalty until after the case was over; as Vito also was, he was more vulnerable than Dominick to a sentence including some time in prison because, if not ever the actual shooter, he was on the edges of many murders—Scorney, Todaro, Rosenberg, Mongitore, Scutaro—and right in the perverse middle of Falcaro and Daoud.

In his plea, Freddy referred briefly to each murder; officially, he finally broke with Roy DeMeo. Describing Roy's actions in one killing, he said: "Mr. DeMeo was the shooter all the time. He wanted to do all the shooting. He was the killer."

Near the end of 1984, Freddy completed his Empire Boulevard time and was whisked into the witness program by marshals. He was renamed "Freddy Marino" and deposited in San Antonio, Texas—as foreign to Freddy as the moon, but he hunkered down and went to work fixing junk cars.

In a few months, he talked first wife Peggy into joining him in the program; she was unhappy at the time because of a tragedy in her family. They rented a cookie-cutter home in a subdivision on the western edge of San Antonio known as Emerald Valley; all the street names suggested a paradise of rolling hills and lush forests, but it was flat and barren as an overworked pasture.

Freddy and Peggy tried to mesh with the customs and rhythms of life deep in the heart of Texas, but their hearts were not in it. They wanted to relocate as soon as Freddy finished testifying at the trial. In time, however, they did become regular patrons of a drab pancake house twenty minutes away, a twenty-four-hour place called the Kettle; waitresses got to know the couple and were impressed that though Freddy and Peggy said they had been married a long time they pampered each other like newlyweds.

Often, Freddy came back at night by himself; a lot of young pot-smoking auto mechanics and gas-station jockeys also showed up then. The Kettle became a kind of Gemini Lounge, minus the murder suite next door. Freddy became ''buds'' with many of the young men, who called him Pops. He eventually told his new friends he was a hitman on the run from New York. Nobody believed Pops, not then.

Early in June of 1985, just when they began believing Freddy had found peace of mind in the program because of Peggy, the task force learned of trouble in the Montiglio household. At a neutral-site debriefing in Oklahoma City, Dominick told Frank Pergola and Uncle Artie that Denise was acting distant lately.

''It was great until a few weeks ago—she even told me she had fallen back in love—but then all of a sudden, she changed and said she didn't love me. It's weird.''

Frank and Artie got an uneasy feeling. The trial was only a couple of months off. Testifying against his uncle, and Paul, and Henry, in a courtroom sure to be packed with Rose Gaggi, and every other family member the defense lawyers could muster, each with the word ''rat'' in their eyes and on their lips, Dominick was due for the emotional test of his life. Nothing added more pressure than a wife whose love had waned, even if she had a lot more justification than she knew.

''What's her beef?'' Frank said, raising an eyebrow.

''No, no, I haven't done that. I've been like Beaver Cleaver for over a year. Not once.''

''Did you hit her?''

''C'mon, I've never done that. I don't understand it. For all those years, she complained because I wasn't around enough. Now she says I'm suffocating her, I'm around too much.''

Frank and Artie, without telling Dominick their intention, decided to bail out of the debriefing a day early—a prosecutor interested in another New York case stayed on—and they flew to where Denise was.

Denise seemed a different person from the one they saw at the Christmas vacation they arranged for her in Atlanta. Speaking directly and frankly, she said Dominick's assessment of the relationship was correct, it had deteriorated. "I'm just tired of everything, tired of living with this trial over our heads, tired of him. I was against this from the start. It was you guys who made it seem like I had no choice; I still resent that."

"If you're tired of the pressure," Frank said, "imagine Dominick. He's going to court against his uncle."

"He made his own life."

Her last remark left little else to say. "Just try to hold on a little longer," Artie said. "If anything happens, if you guys fight and he takes off, let us know, will you please?"

Denise said she would and Frank and Artie took the disturbing news back to New York.

Dominick came home the next day. Denise thought he had sent his task force friends to talk to her and was angry. They began arguing. In front of Camarie, she told him he was smothering her and she hated it because she did not love him, so why didn't he just leave? He did. He hugged his three children, took a few hundred dollars saved from the restaurant and got on a flight to Los Angeles—a major infraction of the marshals' rules, but he was flying away from everything, including being a witness.

After two weeks went by with no telephone call from Dominick, who always called at least once a week, Frank and Artie got on a telephone line to Denise.

"He left," she said. "I don't know where he is."

"You said you'd let us know!" Artie protested.

"I thought he'd call you. He calls you all the time."

"Denise, so much is at stake here. We're going to trial in three months and we don't even know where our main witness is. You said you'd call."

Denise was not bearing anyone's burdens anymore. "Look, I don't have any obligation to you. I don't have to explain anything. Goodbye."

In Los Angeles, Dominick jumped off the cocaine wagon and burned himself out until he was broke and had only two options: be a bodyguard for cocaine dealers he had already told FBI agents in Los Angeles about or keep the bargain he had made. He telephoned New York a day after Frank and Artie spoke to Denise.

"Uncle Artie," he said, "Denise kicked me out. I'm standing at a pay phone on a street corner in LA. I'm fucked up. I could take off with these drug guys I met if I want, but I don't. It's the same dead end I walked away from before. I need help."

"Give me the address, I'll have someone there in half an hour."

Artie called bureau friends in Los Angeles and two agents picked Dominick up and took him to a motel. Frank and Artie flew to Los Angeles to calm him down, then explain the facts of life. He had made a deal, and if he did not live up to it, the government would hound him forever.

A few days later, on June 20, 1985, he was brought back to New York, where Walter reminded him of a two-year-old threat to put him in jail if he ever violated his deal, even if he had died and come back as a ghost. Feeling guilty and cementing his relationship with the government, Dominick then pleaded guilty to his RICO crimes—extortion; loansharking; robbery; drug dealing; because of his role in Nino's one-way grudge match against Vincent Governara, attempted murder and murder. It was the last two crimes that most interested the judge accepting his plea, William C. Connor.

Recounting, in response to a question from Connor, the second attempt on the victim's life, Dominick said, "I had a pistol on me. I was supposed to shoot like everybody else, but I didn't."

"Was there any particular reason why you didn't?"

"Yes, your honor. I never shot anybody in the street."

Afterward, the task force turned Dominick over to the marshal's service, which was not happy to take him back. Denise did not want him back either, so the marshals took him to Jacksonville, Florida, but the local marshal there determined that Florida was a "hot" state for someone from New York City and shipped him to another marshal in Springfield, Illinois, but that marshal checked his computer and learned that another witness in the program who might know Dominick was there, so he shipped him to a marshal in Birmingham, Alabama.

All the frequent-flyer miles did nothing for Dominick's

morale. He was more afraid and more lonely than he had ever been before. He telephoned Camarie and his other children every night to say hello, and to try and win Denise back. "We're blowing our family apart over this, let's just try and make it work."

Denise would not budge. "I just want to be left alone."

"It's those trips with the government, you think I was fooling around? Do you think Walter Mack would let me fuck around on those trips?"

"I don't care about those trips anymore. Some private detectives from New York came by here after you left. They had a lot of things to say about you."

By the sudden sarcasm in Denise's voice, Dominick knew the marriage really was over—and that somehow Nino and the others he was soon to face had found out where he had been living and sent private investigators to collect some dirt for cross-examination.

Each word that now came out of Denise's mouth was a blunt instrument: "Dominick, they said something about a girl named Danielle. Seems you were arrested with her."

There was a long silence, in which she let him hang. "So that's it, I guess," he finally said.

"That's it, you'll get the divorce papers in the mail."

He hung up the telephone and began drinking. As he always told friends, Denise was the best woman a man ever had, but he chased her away. She gave him her complete trust, and he turned it into complete hate. As he kept hitting the bottle, it was impossible not to dwell on the not-so-fictional character of Bobby Russo taking a nose dive off a tall building in the original final scene of "The Glass Jungle." With the trial less than two months away, Dominick was a basket case.

Denise was not the only woman in Dominick's life contacted by the defense as the trial date neared. One night on Long Island, his half-sister Michele was stunned to pick up the telephone and hear Nino's voice on the other end—the first time he had called her since her mother died fifteen years before.

Nino made it seem like he was passing through the neighborhood and had telephoned on the spur of the moment to invite her to dinner. Michele, now twenty-three and tough-minded about her Bath Beach relatives, almost burst out laughing, but decided to go hear what Nino had to say. She knew it had to be about Dominick.

"This should be fun," she told her husband Chris on the way to the restaurant where Nino was waiting, ten minutes away. "Unless Nino wants something, you are a pile of shit. He thinks he's the king, and we're just little people from Levittown."

Nino, sipping a glass of wine, ordered a couple of drinks for Michele and Chris before asking if Michele would consider testifying for the defense about Dominick's relationship with Nino.

"You know the only thing Dominick ever did for me was drive my car."

Michele smiled. She wanted to hear more. Her husband said, "If that's all he did, you got nothing to worry about, not from him anyway."

Nino focused on Michele. "You know, we could subpoena you as a defense witness, ask you about that time Dom stopped over your apartment after he knocked off his girlfriend's father's house. We know all about that. We already talked to her."

Michele put her anger and resentment on the table. "You want to subpoena me? Great! Go ahead. What do you think I'll say about you—that you're a wonderful, warm human being? Go ahead, take a chance!"

"Okay, okay, calm down."

"I don't owe you shit!"

"Will you at least meet with my lawyers? They just have a few questions."

Michele said she would, but did not tell Nino it was because she wanted to tell them off too, which she eventually would. Nobody ordered dessert and Nino's first and last trip to Levittown came to an awkward end.

Early in September 1985, the judge who was to preside over United States v. Castellano ambushed Walter. Acting on defense motions, Judge Kevin Duffy ruled essentially that Walter had put too much firepower into the indictment: too many defendants were accused of too many crimes to sort it all in one trial. The judge, whose reputation was that he was hard on prosecutors, then hard on defendants convicted in his courtroom, further said that a series of trials would be necessary, perhaps as many as five, depending on what crimes how many defendants ultimately decided to plead guilty to. Walter was looking at a minimum of five years' more work.

Almost worse, Judge Duffy peeled off the twenty-three counts of the indictment relating to stolen cars and ruled that they be tried first—as a relatively straightforward conspiracy case, not as a RICO case, meaning that the illegal-enterprise theory of the task force investigation was down the tubes, at least insofar as the stolen-car matters went. Only five murders were part of the car conspiracy; all the others would have to be tried later. The judge set a September 30 opening for the conspiracy case, which involved only nine of the original twenty-four defendants.

The judge's rulings exposed a potentially fatal flaw in the task force investigation as it concerned lead defendant Paul Castellano. Since the aim all along was to portray Paul as the ultimate boss of the DeMeo enterprise and recipient of cash from all its crimes, those who debriefed Dominick—the only witness capable of putting cash from Nino and the crew in Paul's hands—had not asked him if he ever took money to Paul that was for stolen cars alone.

A week before trial, Walter, Frank, and Artie flew to Minneapolis to see a spurned and lonely man from Birmingham. "Yeah, I took money to Paul for the cars," Dominick said after everyone got together. "Actually, that money was handled special. When I got money from Roy for porno and stuff, I'd keep it if Nino wasn't around and he'd square with Paul when he got back. But the car money, I took that straight to Paul."

"Dominick, you could have told us this before," Artie said.

"I answer every question you ask me! We've had so many of these get-togethers, I can't keep tabs on every little detail. You told me I wasn't a big witness for the car stuff."

The interrogators flew home with a hasty patch for the case flaw. Walter was keenly aware how bad it would look when, as required to do under trial rules, he gave defense lawyers a report saying a witness cooperating for two and a half years first put car money in Paul's hands one week before trial. Duffy's rulings had laid waste to a lot of Walter's rational planning.

Dominick flew back to Birmingham. Emotionally, he was still in bad shape; he missed his children and was dreading his date in court, tentatively set for midway through the trial. He followed the beginning of the trial on a national television report, then learned a private detective working for Paul and Nino had found and tried to question The Armenian; he began to believe it was only a matter of time before he was found—but not just to be asked a few questions.

He began drinking. He imagined hitmen invading his dreary apartment while he slept. He went to an electronics store and bought fifteen radio transmitters that properly converted made excellent trip-wire alarms for doors and windows. Then, from the only friend he had in Birmingham, a man he met at a gym, he borrowed an M-16 machinegun and seven hundred rounds of ammunition.

He went home and while drinking another bottle of whisky, rigged a nighttime perimeter of trip-wire alarms. He started on another bottle, wrapped a jungle bandana around his forehead, put the M-16 on full automatic, barricaded his bedroom door, and telephoned Denise. He started crying, but she still felt the same way about the divorce. He hung up, hit the bottle again, then decided to make another call—to Uncle Nino's house.

His godson Michael Gaggi, now twenty-three, answered the call. Nino and Rose were not home. "Mike, I'm going to make it easy for your dad," Dominick said, then gave Michael his address and telephone in Birmingham, the make and model car he was driving and its license plate. "Tell him to come any old time. I'll be waitin'." Michael just listened; Dominick hung up, then passed out before he died of alcohol poisoning.

The next day he woke up still drunk. He telephoned Frank, told him about the call to Nino's house, and said he was on the verge of a nervous breakdown. "Me and Artie have got to go down there before he kills someone, maybe himself," Frank told Walter.

Before departing, they asked the marshals in Birmingham to check on him. The marshals ducked when the wild-looking veteran opened the door with the M-16 across his chest. They stayed with him until Frank and

Artie arrived, then reported his behavior to their bosses in Washington. Dominick was then taken out of Birmingham to a meeting with marshal's service brass in the District of Columbia. They wanted to boot him out of the program and let him fend for himself, but Walter intervened and a three-week-long tussle between federal agencies began. Dominick was stashed in a ghetto hideout in Maryland while Walter went to bat for him.

During that time he had many heart-to-hearts with his task force friends, who realized that losing Denise was not the only trouble he was having. The closer the trial got, the more guilty he was feeling about testifying. "I know I said I would do this, but do you know how hard it is going to be, getting up on that stand?" he said to Frank.

"Of course I do, but it's the right thing," Frank said.

"I mean, in 'that life,' it is the worst thing, being a rat."

"Just think of the people you're getting off the streets. You should get a fuckin' public service medal."

"Yeah, but the bottom line is, I have to look at myself as a stoolpigeon."

"I'm tired of hearing that crap! You're not Nino's kid anymore. Look at what living by the code got ya. The code's a bunch of bullshit."

At the end of the three weeks, after Walter won the fight with the marshal's service and got him a new placement in Albuquerque, New Mexico, Dominick seemed to gain some strength. He made a promise to the task force and to himself: "This thing is not going to beat me. I'm fine now. I was just blowing out some bad feelings. I am not going to let this beat me."

In Albuquerque, at a health club, he met an outgoing woman who ran a tanning salon. She was hip, funny, and good-hearted. In a few weeks, they became a couple. He began to feel even better—though the fright and torment of going to court soon was never far away.

The witnesses in the case—and without electronic surveillance and murder weapons, it was basically a witness case—drove the task force crazy. Altogether, there were twenty-two cooperating witnesses, but the big three—

Dominick, Freddy, and Vito—were the most trouble-some.

The problem with Vito was his incessant demands for favors and perks, such as a barber's chair for his prison cell. Shortly before he was to testify, he made another demand: He mailed the task force a newspaper clipping about cosmetic surgery, across which he had written: "I want to get this done or else I won't testify. This is the answer to my problems."

Once he was in New York for the trial, the task force decided to humor him—and play a trick. Artie made an appointment for Vito with one of the city's top plastic surgeons, but asked the doctor to find some way to dis-courage the patient from going through with cosmetic surgery; the bill would look pretty silly on Artie's FBI credit card. The doctor put Vito in a chair and began drawing lines across his face with a grease pencil.

"By the way, when was your blood pressure last checked?"

"Don't know, long time probably."

The doctor checked Vito's blood pressure. "Uh-oh, it's off the scale. Mr. Arena, I wouldn't operate on you if you were dying. You're going to have to lose a hun-dred pounds first."

Looking the same as in crew days, Vito lumbered into court on October 31, 1985, a month into the trial, and promised to tell the jury, which was seated anonymously, the whole truth and nothing but. In his opening argu-ment, Walter had told the jury: "This is a case about murder, money, and stolen cars. It is a case about a large criminal organization which stole hundreds of cars from the streets of New York, chopped them into small parts for sale, sold them after changing their identification numbers, at great profit, and murdered those that got in the way of the business venture."

The jurors had already heard from Matty Rega and Canarsie car thieves Willie Kampf and Joseph Bennett. They had not heard the word "Mafia" or words like boss, underboss, capo, and the like. Judge Duffy had banished them from the courtroom; words like "business ven-ture," "president," and "manager" were being used.

Spectators at the trial, including all the hometown press plus reporters from around the country and abroad, had already noticed how during breaks Paul and Nino never chatted with the younger defendants like Henry and Joey and Anthony, all neatly shorn and dressed each day in a different and fine suit. During longer breaks, the younger men went into the hallways to smoke Marlboros and chat with wives, girlfriends, and family members. In some spectators' minds, the defendants had already acquired the sympathy a crowd reserves for underdogs; people hate criminals until the criminal comes to court with a history, a pretty wife, and a likable lawyer.

The case was not going well for Walter; his concentration had been sapped by his behind-the-scenes witness problems and his trial strategy torn asunder by Judge Duffy's last-minute decision to split the case up. Judge Duffy had bluntly questioned Walter's preparation and some of his evidence; he had even threatened to declare a mistrial if Walter failed, as he had once already, to promptly turn over material to which the defense was entitled under legal rules.

The judge, who liked to wisecrack with the lawyers, had described some early testimony as having the effect of a sleeping pill, but everyone woke up when Vito began testifying—and said Roy DeMeo had sent out for pizza and hot dogs as Ronald Falcaro and Khaled Daoud were dismembered in Freddy's garage. He also was the first witness to name Paul Castellano as overall boss of the "organization" that formerly employed him.

In cross-examination, the defense lawyers played to Vito's vanity and had a field day. Vito said he demanded so much from the government, tapes, tennis shoes, a barber chair, extra food, because he was the case's "star witness"; he was, he boasted, in discussions with an agent about selling rights to his story, and wanted Tom Selleck to star as him. He turned sour, however, when Nino's lawyer asked about sexually explicit photographs of Joey Lee and him that the NYPD seized in 1981 when they were arrested in a stolen car; many other times, he lost his temper as the lawyers badgered and baited him.

By the time Vito left the stand, it was hard to say whether he helped or hurt the case. The task force was convinced he told the truth, but feared the jury might believe he exaggerated—to up the price of his movie rights.

On December 4, that morning's *New York Times* included a curtain-raiser about the scheduled appearance that day of the case's real star witness. The article described how "Mr. Montiglio" was a Vietnam veteran, loanshark collector, and drug dealer who would testify that Paul Castellano was head of the car-theft conspiracy and Anthony Gaggi was second-in-command.

While the city's trial-watchers read the story over morning coffee, Mr. Montiglio was wringing his hands and trying to stay calm in a bunkerlike compound beneath the courthouse where protected witnesses were housed between appearances on the stand. He was wearing Nino-style tinted eyeglasses, having recently become slightly nearsighted. Frank Pergola told him the glasses made him appear slinky, but he said it was the only pair he had. In truth, he did not need them except for driving, but they made it harder for people to see the anxiety in his eyes.

As he was led from the bunker and up to a waiting room next to the courtroom, he tried to get to another plane of consciousness, a zone of detachment from the whirl of the moment. At a time like this in Vietnam, he would have started chanting about being a lion and fox, but that mantra had grown hollow. Now, he thought of the simple vow he made two months before—"I am not going to let this beat me"—and silently recited it right on up to the time a marshal came in from the courtroom because Walter had just said, "The government calls Dominick Montiglio."

He followed the marshal through the door to the courtroom and for the first time in six years saw Nino and Paul, sitting closest to the door like stone idols, and then Joey and Anthony, and, behind them with a killing smirk on his face, Henry Borelli. He looked beyond to the crowded spectator section, and as he sat down in the witness chair, he saw Rose Gaggi, his uncle Roy Gaggi, and a dozen other relatives, including the "captain"—his iron-willed, eighty-seven-year-old grandmother Mary, who had come to court on crutches. *I am not going to let this beat me.*

Haltingly at first, but then more smoothly as Walter moved him along, Dominick told his story. Nino took "stacks of bills" to Paul every Sunday night, when both were in town. He himself had taken car money from Roy directly to "Mr. Castellano." The witness tried to stay focused on Walter's questions, but could not avoid the stares that came from all directions—particularly from Nino, who, in an amusing role reversal, was the one wearing untinted eyeglasses, no doubt on his lawyer's advice.

"Always look a man in the eyes," Nino had always said, "the eyes don't lie." So, as he grew more confident and willful, Dominick stared right into Nino's. The kid forced to resign the class presidency because Nino said it was like being a rat came home to roost.

The next day, when it came time for a break, Judge Duffy excused the jury, then the witness. As Dominick was led off the stand and past the defendants' table, a spiteful inspiration overcame him; remembering how Nino once made fun of him when he returned to the Veterans and Friends social club with his tail figuratively between his legs, he said with vicious delight: "Hey, Nino, Lassie came home."

"Knock it off, Dominick," a marshal said, leading him away.

He never spoke to Uncle Nino again, but for a parting comment, his last five words carried a number of messages. It was, however, too early to rub his testimony in Nino's face, not with cross-examination still to come. Paul's attorney, James La Rossa, threw him a curve right off the bat by producing some handwritten notes Dominick had made nearly a year ago—a list of points he remembered from a conversation with Walter about how to conduct himself on the stand. The notes could have come from only one source; in her hurt, Denise had found a way to lash back.

La Rossa used the notes to imply that Dominick was acting. His portrayal of the witness in place, La Rossa moved on to the first sworn statement Dominick had given the grand jury—the one in which he held back on Nino and Paul—and got him to admit he had committed perjury.

Pounding away at how the most damaging information against Paul came in the last of many task force debriefs, La Rossa then made it seem the witness invented a story to bail the government out of a jam. Dominick squirmed and became nervous again. He had told the truth in his trial testimony, but began feeling like a liar, and looking like one to many spectators. La Rossa then got him to agree again that he had committed another perjury.

Later, an exasperated Walter told him: "What were you doing! Do you know what perjury means?"

"Not telling the truth."

"It's giving a willful and deliberately false statement. You didn't do that with Paul and the money! You just didn't say anything because you weren't asked the right question!"

The damage was done, however, and Paul left the courthouse that day feeling more confident about the car case than Nino did. Paul was a lot more worried about another case on the horizon—one in which he stood indicted with other bosses as a member of the Commission, the Mafia board of directors. He had been taped talking about the Commission on the listening device the FBI had planted in his house.

He was also troubled by an ongoing dispute with the Manhattan faction of the family—leaderless the last two weeks because underboss Aniello Dellacroce had died of old age and disease. He was thinking of making Thomas Bilotti—the capo who had replaced Nino in Paul's deepest affections—the new underboss; he was going to get rid of the family's factional structure too. Like everyone else, the Manhattan wing would have to report to him through Bilotti.

He was particularly perturbed at Dellacroce's protégé, John Gotti. The FBI's investigation of Gotti's crew—the one that had allowed the Gambino squad to assign only Artie and then Marilyn Lucht to the task force—had yielded indictments of Gotti's brother Gene and other top crew members on charges of dealing heroin—a violation of Paul's rules. Paul had demanded copies of transcripts of tape-recorded evidence in that case that had been turned over to the defense; until he died, Dellacroce, on behalf of Gotti, had put Paul off. Gotti had enough troubles. The Eastern District had brought a RICO case against him, and he was also facing minor assault charges in Queens.

When a two-week holiday recess in the car case came, Paul focused on his family's disarray. On December 16,

1985, he and Bilotti drove to a steakhouse in Manhattan for a scheduled sit-down with several crew leaders. As they stepped out of Bilotti's Lincoln on Forty-sixth Street in congested midtown, several men in trench coats and fur hats came up and shot them dead.

CHAPTER 27

Nine South

Dominick learned about the murders of Paul and Bilotti the day after he returned to Albuquerque for a reunion with the new woman in his life. For several hours he paced the apartment they now shared, feeling soiled but also victorious about his testimony and wondering if it provoked the crime; a couple of newspaper reporters had opined that despite La Rossa's cross-examination, his testimony had sunk Paul, and on national television newscasts, it also was being theorized that Paul was killed because some in the Gambino family feared he might cut a deal with the government.

In reality, Paul and Bilotti were simply victims of a power struggle akin to the one that resulted in Carlo Gambino ascending to the family throne in 1957. The murders generated such a media firestorm that the defense lawyers asked for a mistrial in the car case, which was renamed U.S. v. Gaggi; Judge Duffy denied the motion. When questioned, the jurors said they could still be fair toward the remaining defendants.

Roman Catholic Church officials in New York denied Paul a mass of Christian burial. Only personal-family members attended his funeral, a sure sign of betrayal and that his business family was falling in line behind a new leader—John Gotti. Unlike the statelike sendoff for Carlo, Paul was buried quietly near his childhood home, in Gravesend, the same Brooklyn neighborhood where Richie DiNome had come to his end.

After Gotti was publicly identified as the new boss, most media stopped covering the car case on a daily basis; most reporters never returned. They moved on to courthouses in Queens and Brooklyn where the new boss, a former hijacker with an antiheroic flair for the spotlight, was a defendant in two cases. Eventually, he won both, then another, and became the country's most infamous celebrity gangster.

U.S. v. Gaggi was far from over, however. The main business left was Freddy DiNome's testimony. The woman who had joined him in the program, his first wife Peggy, was glad to see him leave San Antonio for New York. During the Christmas holidays, Freddy had reverted to his abusive way with women and had hit her after they fought over her spending some of his once-again few dollars, talking long-distance to friends back home.

On the witness stand, however, Freddy came across as a docile and humble man and someone plainly uncomfortable testifying. Because he could not read, he also was a hard person to cross-examine. Defense lawyers were denied a favorite tactic—asking a witness to read from a grand jury document or other statement and contradict what he had just testified to. He was a good witness for Walter, but did say that Joey and Anthony, apart from the Falcaro-Daoud murders, had nothing to do with the Kuwait operation, the heart of the stolen-car conspiracy.

With some newspaper clippings about his testimony and Paul's murder under his arm, Freddy went back to San Antonio—to an empty house in Emerald Valley. Peggy, angry because Freddy hit her, had packed her bags and gone to New York. Freddy went into another funk; he began drinking and using drugs with his motley young friends at the Kettle, the forlorn pancake house that was his Gemini Lounge–type hangout. He told them his wife had left him; he did not say why.

One night he made a drunken pass at Judy Totter, a Kettle waitress. "Why don't I pick you up after you get off?"

"I can't go out with you! I'm married!"

"No problem. I'm a hit man—I'll wipe him out."

"Get out of here."

"I'm a hit man. I'll kill him."

Totter told other regulars that Freddy was getting strange.

Late in January 1986, he invited another Kettle regular to live with him in Emerald Valley. It was like taking in a stray cat: Jack Knight was thirty-three years old, unemployed, recently divorced, and had been living in his broken-down Chevrolet Vega.

Knight's presence in the house did not lift Freddy's depression. He telephoned Peggy at a sister's house in New York twice a day, but she did not want to live with his temper again. He told Knight all about his past as the two-year anniversary of brother Richie's murder came on February 4. The Kettle was no escape from his gathering gloom; the first selection on its jukebox was a Merle Haggard song called, "I Don't Have Any Love Around." As part of its humdrum decor, the Kettle also featured a caricature of a sad-eyed fool saying, "I'm pretty good at most things, but being alone in San Antonio isn't one of them."

In New York, aware of Freddy's fragile mood, Kenny, Artie, and Marilyn asked Peggy to stay in a hotel a few days and talk the matter through with them. They needed Freddy, like Dominick and Vito, for further trials. Peggy said she might try a week-long stay with Freddy, but wanted to think more.

Kenny and Artie flew to San Antonio to massage Freddy. He met them at the airport and drove them to the Davy Crockett Hotel, where they chatted in the lobby. They noticed his eyes appeared glazed, like he was under the influence of some drug. "We saw Peggy yesterday," Artie said. "She said she'll come out next week, stay a week and see how it goes. If you play your cards right, and have a little patience, it might work out."

Freddy grew agitated; he wanted Peggy back now. A desk clerk came up and asked him to move his car; it was blocking access to the hotel entrance. Kenny and Artie walked out with him and told Freddy, who was wearing a jogging suit, to go home, get dressed for dinner and come back, but he barely heard them.

"I'm calling Johnny Gotti right now and I'm going to get that bitch killed. I'm going to get this all straightened out."

"Freddy, take it easy!" Artie said.

Freddy got into his car and as Kenny and Artie stood on either side, opened the doors and urged him to relax, he jumped on the accelerator and roared away—in reverse, with the doors still open, and Kenny and Artie barely got out of the way. Several yards later, he braked the car, then zoomed forward as they jumped out of the way again.

"Freddy, Freddy, Freddy," Artie lamented.

"Let's go to our rooms," Kenny said. "He'll be back by six."

Freddy went to the Kettle and met Jack Knight. He told him he might be going to New York soon. The pair then drove to the house in Emerald Valley, but Knight left to visit friends and Freddy was home alone.

He took off his jogging suit, and lay down on a canopied king-size waterbed that he had built on an especially high platform. Two wandering jews hung on either side of the headboard, attached to the ceiling by macrame rope. After a time spent in some interior hell, Freddy rose and took one of the plants down and unfurled its macrame hanger; it was six feet, three inches long. He got back on the bed and, standing on the rolling mattress of water, removed a mirror from the canopy and put it on the floor. He tied one end of the rope around one of the canopy's two- by six-inch support beams; he tied the other around his neck, its brass ring snug against his windpipe. He bent his legs behind him at the knees and let his body sag, tensing the rope.

Then, as a purplish Texas twilight closed in on the house in Emerald Valley, Freddy DiNome jumped knees-first off the waterbed and into his own black night.

After Freddy had sped away from the Davy Crockett, Artie had telephoned Marilyn Lucht in New York and asked her to move Peggy to another hotel because Freddy had made a threat and who knew what he would do. Marilyn did as requested, but felt guilty she and the others were going to such lengths, for the good of the case, to get a woman back with an abusive man.

Kenny and Artie did not know Freddy's address in San Antonio. At eight-thirty p.m., with no one answering the telephone at Freddy's house, they went to dinner. Beforehand, they made sure the guns they carried were loaded, then stayed alert through the meal. They now thought it was possible Freddy was so completely flipped he might try to kill them.

Three hours later, Kenny and Artie were back in their rooms. As he was falling asleep, the telephone in Kenny's began to ring. Jack Knight had come home, found the man he knew as Freddy Marino and telephoned the Bexar County Sheriff's Office, whose detectives found Kenny's name and local number in Freddy's bedroom.

"Kenny McCabe?" a Texas drawl said. "This is Detective Hernandez of Bexar County. Do you know a Freddy Marino?"

"You got him under arrest?"

"I got him dead."

Kenny and Artie flew home the next morning. Marilyn picked them up and they went to Peggy's hotel to tell her the news. On the way, Artie stopped and bought a bottle of Jack Daniel's.

At first, Peggy thought Artie was joking. In another hotel just a few days before, she had told him how she had just seen a movie about a witness whose death was faked by the FBI so he could disappear.

"I'm sorry I'm not kidding. He's dead," Artie said.

Peggy began screaming and crying. Over several hours and a few drinks, she passed through all the inevitable emotions: "I'm so mad at him, that he would do this to me—make me feel it's my fault, that son of a bitch."

Freddy's suicide made the New York newspapers a day later; the jurors in the car case were already deliberating the verdict. Walter felt battered; the case had been a disaster since it was broken up and watered down. His lead defendant had been murdered, one of his main witnesses had killed himself and then, near the end of the trial, his own elderly mother had become gravely ill. His coprosecutor Mary Lee Warren gave the final argument. She did a superb job, but so did the defense attorneys, who were betting each other they would beat parts of the case, and on March 5, a few days after Walter's mother died, they did.

The biggest winners were Joey and Anthony—acquitted of the stolen-car charges and recipients of a hung jury on the Falcaro-Daoud murder counts. The biggest losers were Henry Borelli and Ronald Ustica, convicted of everything. In between, with Peter LaFroscia, was Anthony Gaggi—convicted only of conspiracy to steal cars. From the task force view, the verdict was a disappointing wash, and, as to Joey and Anthony, an egregious defeat.

Frank Pergola put the best face on it. "Don't worry,"

he told Dominick, "Nino and Joey and Anthony are going to have to come back and stand trial again for about fifty more murders." Frank was exaggerating, but not by much.

One juror later wrote in a guest newspaper column that had it not been for Dominick's testimony, Nino Gaggi would have left the courthouse as completely acquitted and delighted as Joey and Anthony. As it was, however, Nino was already in the MCC pending his sentencing; Judge Duffy had jailed the convicted defendants immediately. Reading the clipping days later and visualizing Uncle Nino in an orange jumpsuit and sneakers, brooding in the same prison he once was, Dominick was certain there was no doubt now; Nino would put Lassie to sleep, if he ever got the chance.

A month later, Nino, still the defiant raging bull, was led into court to be sentenced. Before being jailed, he had been the only Sicilian capo in the Gambino family who had not hastened to kiss the Neapolitan feet of John Gotti—according to Gotti, who was talking on a secret government listening device in his Queens social club. In one conversation, Gotti complained to an underling about the way Nino had told one of his underlings to bring Gotti to him for a meeting—about an unspecified problem at a restaurant that was eventually torched. "He told you to bring me? He's under me! Yeah, tell him to get his ass up here to see me."

At the sentencing, Nino's attorney Michael Rosen strenuously objected to a pre-sentencing report prepared for the judge by the probation department. In it, Nino was described as someone unable to live by "socially acceptable standards." Judge Duffy, however, true to his reputation for being tough on prosecutors and defendants, turned a stony ear on Rosen and gave Nino and all but one of the other convicted defendants maximum sentences and ordered that they begin serving them immediately. In Nino's case, maximum meant five years.

"I am quite sure that your family will be hurt no matter what I do," Judge Duffy told Nino. "I just hope that you recognize that whatever hurt is brought on them is brought to them not by me but by your own actions."

Nino's prominent vein seemed permanently engorged nowadays, and he had nothing to say. Unlike the Eppolito case, his lawyers also could not get an appeals judge to let him stay free on bail while they appealed his conviction. After being allowed a brief moment with Rose, his mother Mary, and four grown children, sixty-year-old Nino was taken right to Lewisburg, Pennsylvania—to the maximum-security prison there, not the adjoining camp. He did not look like a man who was going to do his time easily.

Henry Borelli had a lot to say when he stood before Judge Duffy, but disingenuous Henry, convicted of several murders related to the car conspiracy, was facing life in prison. First, he quoted from a book, *The Goals of Democracy—A Problems Approach,* that he probably discovered in a prison library while serving his Empire Boulevard sentence: "The safeguards of our liberty are not so much in danger from those who openly oppose them as from those who, professing to believe in them, are willing to ignore them when found convenient for their own purposes."

Then, he said that the Roman Catholic Church's decision to deny Paul Castellano a funeral mass hurt him, a Catholic, in the eyes of jurors and that he was only "guilty of being an Italian." Finally, he said he was a fool for believing he would get a fair trial.

"You did get a fair trial and you will get, to my mind, what is a fair sentence," Judge Duffy said. "You have been convicted of being what is generally called a contract killer."

Fair ended up being life, plus ten years for each of sixteen car-conspiracy counts. The judge urged that Henry never receive parole. "Henry Borelli, you profess Roman Catholicism. I would suggest that what you should do is beg God for forgiveness."

Henry smiled and turned his back on the judge.

Ronald Ustica, the used-car dealer who became suddenly lethal once he suddenly began prospering with Roy DeMeo, got a life sentence too. Peter LaFroscia, who escaped culpability for John Quinn's murder a second time, but was convicted on a car count, got five years.

The only defendant in the conspiracy who got a break from Judge Duffy was Ronald Turekian, the crew member who coined the term "Wally's Pet Shop." His knack for words was what saved him with the judge. He told of an impoverished Canarsie childhood in which his mother died and his father rejected him and how now he had met a woman who loved him and had "a chance not to be alone." He added, "There may be grease on my hands, but there's no blood on my hands."

Judge Duffy gave Turekian five five-year sentences, but ordered them to run concurrently, meaning Turekian would be eligible for parole in thirty months. "When I came out here they were going to be consecutive sentences," the judge said.

On that lenient note, U.S. v. Gaggi came to an end—but all the other elements of the original indictment, the other murders, the drug dealing, prostitution, pornography, loansharking, and bribery, the fraud and obstruction of justice in the Eppolito case, remained to be tried.

Happily for Walter on August 7, 1986, after Patty Testa and several other of the original twenty-four defendants decided to plead guilty, Judge Duffy consolidated the charges into a single trial, not four as was once feared. It would be the RICO trial Walter wanted from the start.

The lead defendant would be Anthony Gaggi, boss of the Roy DeMeo criminal enterprise; and nine other defendants would include Joey and Anthony and the Hellman family. A redrawn indictment upped the murder counts to thirty. "There are at least twenty-five more homicides I could list," Walter would say in a sidebar remark to Vincent Broderick, the judge who got the second installment of U.S. v. Gaggi. "They were not put in this indictment for a variety of reasons. We figured thirty was enough."

Pretrial maneuvering would take a year and a half. The trial would begin on February 22, 1988, and last an agonizing sixteen months—longer than any other federal racketeering case. It would amount to the bloodiest story ever told in a federal courtroom.

Walter and the task force tried to leave no stone unturned. A vast cast of witnesses took the stand to tell what they knew about the DeMeo crew and its victims. Overcoming her reluctance to get involved again because of her humiliating experience on the stand in state court, Judy Questal—with Detective Frank Pergola of Bath Beach holding her hand between breaks—testified in disguise and relived her Andrei Katz nightmare. Victor Katz,

Andrei's previously afraid brother, also found the courage to come forward and take part in the mournful parade.

Dr. Todd Rosenberg also recalled his brother Harvey, as Robert Penny did his brother Patrick, and Youseef Najjar his brother Khaled Daoud. Harry Beinert remembered his adoptive son Joseph Scorney, as Giuseppe Mongitore did his son Charles, and Matthew Scutaro his son Daniel. Brian Todaro spoke about his father Frederick. Donna Falcaro recalled her husband Ronald, as Barbara Waring did husband Peter. Muriel Padnick remembered both her husband Charles and son Jamie.

Most of the victims' relatives talked willingly; a few, such as Angellina Grillo did not, even though Walter had made it possible for her to finally collect on husband Danny's half-million-dollar life insurance policy, by telling the insuror her husband was dead, not missing. Roy DeMeo's son Albert was in the same reluctant group, as was Roy's friend Frank Foronjy.

Gladys DeMeo got a pass so far as being called to testify, because Walter was unsure what she knew or tolerated and what the stone-cold widow might say on the stand; in a written statement, she was allowed to "stipulate" to some fuzzy details about who her husband was.

One of the defense lawyers, in a sidebar comment, described Roy's childhood friend Frank Foronjy as a "loose cannon," which caused Judge Broderick to comment on what was an atmospheric characteristic of the courtroom on many days: palpable fear. "If I were sitting there looking at this lineup of defendants, I might be a loose cannon, pretty much a frightened loose cannon. It's been in the trial from the beginning, and it's one of the things that makes this a very tough trial."

Later, with Foronjy still on the stand and acting like a loose cannon, Broderick said at sidebar: "This witness has been either frightened or strongly persuaded by somebody to change his testimony. It is crystal clear to me that this witness is coloring his testimony in a conscious effort to aid the defendants on trial in this case. Why he is doing it, I don't know. But he is lying to this jury."

* * *

Anthony Gaggi sat impassively during the RICO trial's early months. He was awaiting another stare-down, the moment his nephew would come back to testify about much more than hot cars. In the meantime, for the trial's duration, he was housed in the MCC, on a high-security floor known as Nine South. After nearly two years at Lewisburg Penitentiary, he did not look well, and he did not even pretend to be a *Wall Street Journal* reader anymore. His lawyer Michael Rosen had tried and failed to win time off his five-year, car-conspiracy penalty. "His wife Rose, four children—and now his grandchildren—visit him regularly and keep his spirits up," Rosen had written Judge Duffy. "But Anthony Frank Gaggi is not doing his time easily. The time he serves is 'hard time,' mentally and physically."

On Nino's behalf, Rosen blamed it all on Dominick and gave Nino's version of an old event at the Gaggi bunker. "The hard time I refer to exists as a result of an uncle who knows he was framed by his no-good nephew, whose life he actually once saved when he was choking on a quantity of narcotic pills. Even the most hardened, insensitive judge must realize how extraordinarily difficult it must be to languish in prison, separated from loved ones, because of the word of a desperado such as Montiglio."

Sixty-two-year-old Nino was also mourning the death of the woman with whom he lived all his life, his mother Mary, who had died at ninety, with him at Lewisburg. By the time he reached the MCC, even though he had been so fastidious about his health all his adult life, he had also developed—just like his father Angelo, the Lower East Side barber—a heart ailment for which he took medication four times a day.

The trial dragged on. More witnesses kept going on the stand and hurting Nino, the remaining mainstays of the DeMeo crew, Joey and Anthony, and the Hellman family. Ex-detective Thomas Sobota, describing himself as a recovering alcoholic, and Housing Police officer Paul Roder told parts of the Eppolito–Patrick Penny saga. Even ex-Westie Mickey Featherstone, whose West Side friends had framed him for a murder, turned up. Becoming the second ex–Green Beret to make a Southern District deal, he described the Westie-Gambino connection and told the jury how Nino and Roy had painted themselves as his superior officer and supervisor.

In April 1988, just prior to Dominick's appearance, another person from Nino's past took the stand: Dr. Jesse Hyman, a Brooklyn dentist and insurance-plan schemer who had tried to bail Nino, Paul, and Carlo out of their shaky loans to the Westchester Premier Theater by arranging a bank bailout. Hyman had also agreed to cooperate, after receiving a thirty-year hammer in an unrelated case.

Nino's impassive air wilted as Hyman described visits to Nino's house and said he saw Dominick giving Nino loan collections. Nino squirmed in his chair as Hyman put Rose Gaggi in the trial transcript and identified her in a photograph and, doing so, gave a nod toward her in the spectator section.

One of the Hellman-family defense attorneys, Lorin Duckman, was struck by how red Nino's face became, how his chair seemed to vibrate, and later he told colleagues he thought Nino was on the verge of a heart attack. "That was against all the rules, pointing out the wife," he said.

The incident occurred late on a Thursday afternoon, and the trial was adjourned to Monday. In between, on Saturday morning, April 16, 1988, Nino rose from a lower bunk in his cell on Nine South and went to the rooftop recreation area to take a walk. He was joined by a legendary MCC inmate, Joseph Doherty, a soldier in the revolutionary Irish Republican Army; Doherty had been in the MCC longer than anyone in history—the result of a topsy-turvy court fight in which the United States was trying to force his deportation to Great Britain, where he was badly wanted for alleged crimes in Northern Ireland.

Doherty was on Nine South too, in a cell directly opposite Nino's, and they had become friendly. Nino would tease him about how tough the Irish cops on the Lower East Side were when he was a kid; Doherty would say how tough British-backed cops in Northern Ireland were when he was a Catholic kid in Belfast. Although they had little else in common and Doherty was only thirty-three, they regularly exercised together. Mostly, Nino talked about his family and his R&A Sales food brokerage—only rarely about his case, which was so ignoble, compared to Doherty's.

On this Saturday morning, Nino began to complain of physical discomfort. "My stomach really hurts, I got indigestion."

"If it's a stomachache, it'll go away," Doherty said. "Come on, keep walking, maybe it'll go away."

Nino's discomfort did not go away. He spent most of the rest of the day in his cell; his cellmate was Ronald Ustica, who also was standing trial again in the second task force case.

After lockdown at eleven p.m., Doherty heard Ustica banging on the tiny plexiglass window of the cell opposite his. "Nino's sick!" Ustica screamed. "Call the guards!"

Doherty and other inmates began banging on their cell doors to attract the attention of prison guards studying a television set several yards away. After a few moments, the guards arrived.

"The man has a heart complaint!" Ustica said, as Nino lay on his bunk clutching his chest. "You've got to get this man to the hospital!"

"What do you mean, heart?" one of the guards said.

"Get the doctor, will ya!" Doherty yelled.

Across several crucial moments, the guards debated whether to ask a prison doctor on duty several floors below to come up, or to take Nino down to him; the guards chose the latter option and escorted a stricken Nino down a flight of stairs leading to an elevator.

"Wait a minute," one of the supervisory guards said. "We can't take him down if he ain't wearin' his jumpsuit."

Absurdly abiding by prison rules at a time of clear emergency, the guards ordered Nino, dressed in a warm-up outfit, to walk back up the steps to his cell and put on his prison-issue orange jumpsuit. From the tiny windows in their cells, Doherty and the other inmates looked on furiously and helplessly.

Nino walked back down, got in the elevator and was escorted into the prison infirmary about two a.m. He lay down on an examining table and as he was being attached to an electrocardiogram, Anthony Frank Gaggi balled his fists, moaned softly, then closed his eyes for the last time. He died at sixty-two, the same age his father had.

Death's shadow, which had hung over the witness stand from the start, now fell on the defendants' table in U.S. v. Gaggi, which was adjourned ten days, then renamed U.S. v. Testa. Several defense lawyers attended the wake for Nino at Cusimano & Russo's funeral home— the parlor where Carlo Gambino and Marie Montiglio were waked—and gave their condolences to Rose, who, when she saw Kenny McCabe and Artie Ruffels on surveillance across the street, gave them a mocking salute.

Eventually, Rose filed a negligence suit against the prison, the guards, and the government. Prison officials had waited until late the next day to inform her of Nino's death. Four years later, judging by documents submitted in the suit, it appeared the only issue remaining was how much the government would have to pay Rose Gaggi for contributing to Anthony Gaggi's death.

Dominick was preparing for his appearance in the case when Frank Pergola telephoned with Nino's obituary. He took it as one takes the unexpected death of a distant relative—regretful news, but not devastating. In the last two years, still in love with the same woman he met in Albuquerque and beginning to recast himself as a legitimate businessman in the field of merchandising, he had ceased feeling much emotion, love or hate, for Nino, now just a memory of a former life. "In Nino's mind, dying like that would mean he beat you guys," he told Frank.

CHAPTER 28

Clean Slate

Anthony Gaggi's former eyes and ears went on the stand two weeks after Nino died, and stayed there two weeks. Because Walter had gotten his chance to throw the kitchen sink at the crew in a RICO case, Dominick got to tell more of the story this time, but the rules of admissibility removed most of the interior emotions and shadings—the area between the lines. Nino's lawyer stayed on the case to help all the other lawyers subject the witness to the usual brutality of cross-examination, but Dominick was stronger than before—and did not make any smart-aleck remarks to the remaining defendants.

On weekends and between breaks, he relaxed with his friends on the task force. One day, he visited Uncle Artie's home in Connecticut, and Artie gave him a tour of his competition sailboat, *The Bootlegger*. It was a lazy day, a time to reminisce about the unlikely road they had traveled the last six years.

"You know what is strange?" Artie said. "If someone ever tells this story, no one is going to believe it happened."

"When you live it, it doesn't seem so unbelievable."

U.S. v. Testa played out to an almost empty courtroom. The parade of witnesses—including Vito Arena again—continued. Vito pulled another stunt, this time right on the stand, where he announced a sudden case of amnesia and refused to continue testifying until a recess was called and he extracted some pampering by the task force.

Walter and his coprosecutor Arthur Mercado put on a relentlessly detailed case, dotting every point in the dense indictment. The defense lawyers challenged every move. The trial transcript swelled to more than thirty thousand pages and the evidence included many hundreds of exhibits. Jurors got sick, lost loved ones, and quit jobs. The trial was a legal triathlon, the longest federal criminal case anyone could remember. Seeking relief, Joey Testa and Anthony Senter brought cocaine to court one day and were arrested and hit with more charges as they departed a snorting break in a hallway bathroom.

Near the coda, Judge Broderick ruled that Walter lacked the evidence to prove that Joey helped killed Roy DeMeo as the indictment charged—but since Joey was accused of so many other murders it mattered only technically. The judge also dismissed the bribery counts against the Hellman family but kept them in the case on fraud charges related to the Eppolito fix.

Closing arguments began the first week of June 1989— more than a year after Nino died. One by one, the nine defense lawyers got up and put their best spin on the million or so facts strewn across the trialscape. "This is the ninth defense summation," Anthony's lawyer, Benjamin Brafman, told the jury. "I feel a little bit like Elizabeth Taylor's seventh husband on his wedding night. I know what to do; I know how to do it. The trick is to make it interesting for you."

Brafman went on to spin a brilliant web, so preposterous yet so cleverly woven as to be plausible, that laid blame for all the murders in the case on the witnesses, mainly Vito Arena—frequently as if they related somehow to Vito's homosexual lifestyle.

In his rebuttal summation, normally just properly aggressive, Walter delivered the most emotional argument colleagues had ever heard. Some neck veins rising out of his Christian Dior collar appeared inflamed. He ridiculed Brafman's web and marched the jurors quickly through the horror of the case one more time. "We ask that you resolve the facts in this case," he concluded, "that you find the truth in the spirit of complete fairness and impartiality. Now is the time for justice. Godspeed."

The jury deliberated two weeks. Some defense attorneys took that as a good sign, but on June 22, the jurors hammered the rest of the DeMeo crew into oblivion. They found them and the Hellman family guilty on every single count left in the indictment. It was a complete and shattering victory for the task force.

Judge Broderick, a former commissioner of the NYPD,

thanked the jury for enduring the ordeal, then said, "The story of systematic murder that has come before the jury in this case is something that I am sure was beyond the ken of anybody in the jury. It certainly was beyond my previous ken."

The judge denied bail to Joey and Anthony and their crew mates pending appeals. He said, "I am so sure that the jury's verdict was correct with respect to those defendants alleged to have been involved in the murder activities of the DeMeo crew that I can see no possible argument that could be put forward before me that would justify continuing any one of them for a single day at liberty."

He allowed the Hellmans to remain free pending sentencing, and when that came he said that by the standard of a sentencing hearing—preponderance of the evidence, rather than reasonable doubt—he believed that Judy, Wayne, and Sol Hellman did tamper with the jury process in the Eppolito case, and gave them two, three, and five years respectively.

Joey and Anthony were sentenced on September 14, 1989. With one side of the courtroom packed with their relatives and friends and the other side with task force members and their supporters, Broderick gave Joey and Anthony what Henry Borelli had gotten, enough time for several lifetimes in prison. Joey's attorney, Herald Fahringer, found himself in the legally logical but incredibly insensitive position of arguing that it was wrong for the probation department to have included in the presentencing report letters from relatives of victims in the case describing the impact of the crimes on their lives.

"They are not the victims, they have not had the crime committed against them," he said.

Try telling that to Dominick Ragucci's parents, or Ronald Falcaro's daughter, or Peter Waring's wife, or Cherie Golden's grandmother, or any of dozens more relatives, everyone on the task force side of the courtroom said to themselves. Fahringer's words hung in the air like noxious fumes.

Joey smiled that wide mocking smile of his through most of the sentencing. He knew the time had come to pay the hangman; so did Anthony. Neither ever gave anyone on the task force side a glance. In one of those moments too good to be true, the bells of a church adjacent to the courthouse began pealing through the open windows just as Broderick lowered the boom on the Gemini twins. When he added fines to Anthony's life sentence, Anthony sneered out loud. "I'll send you a check."

Joey and Anthony were permitted to say goodbye to their wives along the well of the court. Old neighborhood friends came up and slapped them on the back. "Can you imagine what heroes they would be if they had won?" Frank Pergola whispered to Artie, as they watched Joey's and Anthony's fans gather around.

The marshals then took the pair away—and off to different prisons to live out their lost lives; for the first time since childhood, Joey and Anthony were not inseparable.

On December 18, 1989, it was Dominick's turn to discover what punishment he would get for his guilty plea to one RICO count in June 1985. His sentencing had been delayed until the case ran its course, and it was still up to Judge William C. Connor to determine whether he should serve some time in prison.

Under law, he was a murderer for being along when Nino and Roy shot Vincent Governara to death. He had pleaded guilty to that, and to attempted murder for rigging a grenade to Governara's car, and to a raft of other crimes: robbery, extortion, loansharking, and drug dealing. His court-appointed attorney intended to ask Judge Connor for probation, but it was expecting a lot to walk away from such a record without any time behind bars, even considering—as Walter had always reminded him— his contribution to the destruction of the crew.

Prior to meeting his federal marshal and leaving for New York from yet another new hideaway, Dominick sat down at a personal computer and composed a statement he intended to read to the judge. His friend The Armenian offered to fly in from Los Angeles and address the court on his behalf.

They were reunited in an office at the Southern District, where Walter Mack, Kenny McCabe and Artie Ruffels had gathered. They saw a new Dominick—tan, fit, and bursting out of a camel-colored sportscoat because he had bulked up his arms and upper body pumping iron in a gym. The old fireplug physique that once provoked his Army friends to nickname him Stubby was back. He looked a lot more like Anthony Santamaria than Anthony Gaggi now—except for the tinted eyeglasses.

"Take those fucking things off," Detective Frank Pergola of Bath Beach growled when he came into the room.

"They're prescription!"

"They make you look like a fucking hood."

"You must be Pergola," cracked The Armenian, who had never met Frank before. Everyone laughed; Dominick had obviously provided an accurate account of his relationship with Frank.

The tension he was feeling gave way a bit as everyone chatted, but began building again as the entourage made its way to Judge Connor's courtroom. Whatever came, he was anxious to get it over with; since Albuquerque in 1985, the marshals—keeping him on the go for fear someone might find him—had sent him and the special woman he met in Albuquerque to Cheyenne, Wyoming; Denver, Colorado; and Seattle, Washington. He had been in the program longer than most anyone in history. He wanted to put it all behind and live where he wanted without federal intervention, and hoped to get to know his children again. He had not seen them in four years.

Judge Connor invited The Armenian to take a seat at the defense table with Dominick—a good sign—and got the hearing underway. In the case of a cooperating witness, judges normally determine sentence by applying a three-tier test. Has the witness acknowledged his crimes and shown contrition? To what degree has he rehabilitated himself? Has he fully cooperated with the government?

Dominick's court-appointed attorney, Lee Richards, a former prosecutor, got straight to these points:

"On each of these important tests, your honor, I have to say that Dominick Montiglio presents the most remarkable picture of a defendant that I have ever encountered. No defendant I have ever met or heard of has ever faced mistakes and changed his life so completely or contributed so much to law enforcement. Your honor this morning has the power to put the final piece of the puzzle for Mr. Montiglio in place and to allow him to complete what I really believe is a remarkable transformation."

As to the violence Dominick committed, Richards attributed it to the "extraordinary influence" of Nino Gaggi and the men around Nino. "Those people made what I call the old Dominick Montiglio. Since then, Dom has remade himself."

Judge Connor asked to hear from the defendant. Dominick rose and spoke in a voice that cracked, then grew steady. "I make no excuses, your honor, for crimes I committed in the past, here in New York or afterward, in California. Everything I did was of my own accord, and I fully understand that I am to be held accountable for my actions." Four words in the statement came straight from the Latin motto of Airborne Rangers—*sua sponte,* of my own accord.

Dominick shifted his feet, fiddled with his prepared statement, then ad libbed. He said he wanted to particularly mention how Frank Pergola, Kenny McCabe, Arthur Ruffels, Walter Mack, and other "good guys" had helped him salvage something of his life.

He recalled how Frank had told him "nobody has the right to kill" and how Kenny once was the "enemy outside our club taking pictures" but was now "one of the few men I trust in my life." He "couldn't say enough" about Uncle Artie and said Walter had "made only one deal with me and that was to tell the truth." He added: "What I learned from these men was that family isn't necessarily one of blood, but trust and respect. They are the family I have now."

He concluded with a simple plea for mercy: "I have a good job, a nice apartment, a future that I can look forward to. I have been with the same woman four years. I do realize I committed serious crimes. Whatever your judgment may be, your honor, all I want is for this all to end and to have a clean slate."

Walter stood next and told the judge that Dominick had been of "extreme value to the United States" and met all his obligations as a witness. Uncle Artie added, "I have found Dominick to be forthright and honest in all the dealings I have had with him." Frank Pergola spoke last: "The New York City Police Department and the people of the City of New York owe Dominick a great deal. He has cleared up a lot of mysteries for families of victims."

As Judge Connor began speaking directly to him, Dominick grew more relaxed with each word:

I think you are what we sometimes refer to as a situational offender. You got into criminal activity because of the situation in which you were raised. . . . When you were arrested you immediately agreed to cooperate to an extent which has rarely been exceeded. . . . You have been separated from your children for a number of years and from friends. . . . You have been in a form of prison for a number of years and will continue to be so in the sense you will always be looking over your shoulder wondering whether your identity and your location have become known to those who I am sure would like to get retribution against you. . . . You have turned your life around. I think your rehabilitation is complete.

The proper punishment, the judge concluded, was five years—on probation.

The judge left the bench wishing Dominick health and safety, and Walter, Kenny, Uncle Artie, and The Armenian took turns slapping his back and shaking his right hand. But the last scene was of Frank Pergola and Dominick, with the Great Seal of the United States on the maple wall beyond them, embracing like brothers who had grown up together in a normal house in Bath Beach, Brooklyn.

EPILOGUE

Special Update for the Paperback Edition

Gladys DeMeo had no comment when approached for an interview about her late husband. "No," was all she would say, closing the door to her new home, and to that part of her life, the way she always had.

Rose Gaggi did not have anything to say either. Approached in a courthouse hallway after a hearing on her negligence suit against the government for the way her husband died in prison, she was more ironic than she may have intended to be when she smiled and said through clenched teeth, "The record speaks for itself." Months later, the negligence suit was quietly settled. The details were kept a secret, but sources said Rose got what she wanted most, a pledge by the federal Bureau of Prisons to implement new medical-emergency rules, including one requiring a doctor to be on duty at the MCC at all times. "Rose insisted throughout that she was not interested in a financial settlement," a person involved in the proceedings said, "only that procedures be put in place that would make it less likely no one suffer the way Nino did. So Nino, through Rose, ends up contributing something to society."

Denise Montiglio did not want to be bothered either. "I will no longer be a part of what is an embarrassment to me and my family," she said.

It is hardly surprising the women wanted to keep all skeletons in the closet. Besides, they all grew up in Brooklyn where, in the neighborhoods that incubated the DeMeo crew, legend has it that people mind their own business, or else.

Early in 1991, co-author Jerry Capeci visited the former Gemini Lounge and clubhouse in Flatlands; he was accompanied by Richard Scheslinger and Alan Goldberg of the CBS Television program "48 Hours," which was preparing a segment featuring a look at this story. The three journalists found one person willing to talk—Debbie Doyle, who had moved into Dracula's old clubhouse-apartment next to the bar. Some walls in her apartment still bore the damage from the task force raid of several years before.

After moving in, she had learned a little history about the apartment from a newspaper story. Still, she said, living there was disturbing in only one way, and that was "all the blood that went down the drain from the bodies. You know, I kind of felt eerie when I took a shower. But other than that, it really didn't bother me because I feel when people are dead, they're dead. I mean, it happens. You know, it's life."

As the interview was taking place on the street outside the apartment, another woman came out of the old Gemini Lounge, now Justin's Pub, and listened to Debbie Doyle's remarks. She then introduced herself as a former Gemini patron and barmaid. She knew Roy, Joey, and Anthony and all the rest and knew they were accused of terrible crimes, but they were always pleasant to her, so she always minded her business. "You know how it is," she said, "this is Brooklyn." (And in Brooklyn, about two years after older brother Joseph was sentenced to prison for life, Patrick Testa, the former teenage genius-with-cars who had served only a few months for his DeMeo-crew activities and then joined the Luchese crime family, would be shot dead in his body shop by an unknown gunman.)

As the hardcover edition of this book was being published, co-author Capeci, accompanied this time by reporter Steve Dunleavy and producer Cynthia Fagen of Fox Television's "A Current Affair," returned to the bar. The owner of what was now Justin's Pub wasn't too pleased to see them. He tried to block the show's cameramen from filming the exterior and screamed at Fagen, "I had nothing to do with those guys!"

Police from the Six-Three Precinct were called in to soothe over everyone's feelings, but not before Debbie Doyle came out of her haunted house to say, "Just because one hundred people got killed in my apartment—what's the big deal?"

Eventually, Doyle invited Dunleavy and Fagen in for

a look-around, and thus a national television audience got a guided tour of Dracula's cutting-room floors. The old DeMeo crew clubhouse-apartment looked too oddly banal for the horror that went on there.

Meanwhile, the cops, agents, and lawyers who worked on the Testa-DeMeo-Gaggi-Castellano task force got together at Tavern on the Green in Central Park for a victory party. Walter gave out red T-shirts with white letters—"I Worked in Wally's Pet Shop" on the front, "U.S. vs. Castellano" on the back.

To the twenty-eight members of the task force who attended, Walter also presented silver bowls—a replica of one struck by Paul Revere to commemorate a band of Revolutionary War patriots who, according to an accompanying note, stood up to corruption and "the violent menace of villains in power."

The FBI gave out commemorative cocktail glasses, inscribed somewhat haughtily with the date the Bureau had entered the investigation. Joseph Coffey, now an investigator for a state organized-crime investigative agency, got up and said: "If anyone wants to say thanks for this dinner, you should say it to John Murphy, because if it wasn't for him, none of us would be sitting here."

Multiple heart-attack victim Murphy, who was there, was stunned and embarrassed. He was a bit stronger these days and doing some private investigative work with the Fort Zinderneuf graduate, Joseph Wendling, who had since retired from the NYPD with a serious back injury after a car slammed into the rear of his as he transported a prisoner.

Ronnie Cadieux had retired from the NYPD too, and opened his own private detective agency; he would soon help solve a brutal double homicide of two ordinary Bath Beach women—a case the NYPD had bureaucratically fumbled until Ronnie showed that the victims, a mother and a daughter, had wandered, completely innocently, into the web of a connected man.

Uncle Artie Ruffels, still a champion sailboat racer at age fifty-five, was about to launch an enterprise akin to Ronnie's because, incredibly, the FBI was kicking him out the door. Though the stupid policy was soon to change, the bureau was at that time enforcing a mandatory-age requirement for brick agents. Meanwhile,

Marilyn Lucht was off working on another big FBI case. Kenny McCabe was still an investigator for the Southern District, and Danielle Deneux's platonic buddy, Harry Brady, was applying for a similar job he would eventually get. Frank Pergola was now attached to the NYPD major-case squad based at NYPD headquarters at One Police Plaza, a few steps from Walter Mack's office.

In his wallet, Walter was still carrying the photo of DeMeo-crew victim Peter Waring; now and then, he still got telephone calls from around the country from people who had heard about the case and were looking for relatives missing in New York. The head of the organized crime squads at the FBI in New York, Jules Bonavolonta, had publicly said the crew might have killed in excess of two hundred people. The NYPD did "clear" seventy-five homicides by attributing them to the crew.

The NYPD clears a homicide when it believes it knows who is responsible but cannot go further with the case because the suspect is dead or because of other insurmountable problems. Considering the nature of the crew, and the years of crew history for which no cooperating witness was available, its victim toll is probably higher than seventy-five. But even Joey, Anthony, and Henry could not be precise, because they were not always around when Roy got the urge. Roy would not know either, because the crew kept killing after his murder. Not long after the hardcover edition of this book came out, one of Roy's relatives called to tell us: "Roy certainly was the black sheep of the family. He brought a lot of shame to the family, but we never knew how bad he was until we read about it. I'm glad he got it. Many of us would like to exhume his body and dump it on the street."

Walter was investigating a new case—the murders of Paul Castellano and Thomas Bilotti. He saw the murder of Paul, a task force defendant at the time, as a last bit of task force business. Eventually, he gathered enough evidence to recommend indicting Gambino family boss John Gotti under a RICO theory that the murder was a racketeering act to achieve power in a criminal enterprise. Meanwhile, however, prosecutors in the Eastern District had assembled a broader case against Gotti, based partly on yet another listening device agents had secreted

in a place he felt safe to talk—a widow's apartment above
Aniello Dellacroce's old Little Italy hangout.

This led to another turf war over which district would
indict Gotti. This time, because Rudolph Giuliani had
resigned to run unsuccessfully for mayor of New York,
Walter did not have a powerful lever to pull in Washington. The Eastern District won. Not long afterward, Walter resigned from the Southern District and took a big job
on Wall Street. Eventually, the Eastern District would
win its case against Gotti—thanks partly to the Dominick-
like testimony of an insider, Salvatore Gravano, the man
Gotti had appointed underboss after taking over the family from Paul Castellano, whose murder he was convicted
of orchestrating. Bruce Mouw, Artie's and Marilyn's boss
on the FBI's Gambino squad, would get the Justice Department's highest award for achievement for his role in
assembling the case that ended Gotti's winning streak in
courtrooms.

Gravano also provided information that bore directly
on a major scene in this story—the murder of Roy. Gravano told Mouw and other agents that he was visiting
Paul's White House the day after Roy's body was found
when Paul showed him a newspaper account of the recovery and asked for his reaction; Gravano knew some
members of Roy's crew. "If you're not mad, I'm not
mad," Gravano said he told Paul. As 1993 dawned, we
were trying to persuade Gravano—who pleaded guilty to
nineteen murders as part of his plea bargaining with the
government—to help us tell the story of Gotti's reign and
fall, the subject of our next book.

On February 15, 1991, a major, if grating, figure in
Walter's case made the news again. Vito Arena, released
early from prison because of his testimony, had gone
back to the robbery game, only this time he played with
the wrong people in Houston, Texas. Armed with a gun,
he held up a convenience store. He would have gotten
away with some cash if he had not stopped on his way
out and come back to demand some music tapes too. A
clerk reached below a counter and came up firing into
Vito's face with a .357 Magnum, definitely ending his
cosmetic-surgery dreams.

Today, of the case's major witnesses, Dominick is the
only survivor. He was pleased to hear in early 1992 that

an appeals court upheld the convictions of all of the defendants except for the jury-rigging Hellman family. The court said the Hellmans should have been tried separately. (And when that took place in December 1992 only Wayne and Judy Hellman were in the dock because Judy's father-in-law, Sol, had died in the interim. Even though Judge Broderick had said after Judy's original conviction that he believed she had thrown a case for Nino, she was acquitted this time around. Her husband, Wayne, was not, and he faced three years in prison as the softcover edition of this book went to press. He was convicted of fraud related to financial transactions he made after Nino Gaggi's acquittal, in which he lied about the sources of his income.) In disguise, and while wearing an "America's Most Wanted" baseball cap, Dominick would make his national television debut on "A Current Affair" with Debbie Doyle and talk about what it was like testifying against his uncle— "I'd rather do three more tours in 'Nam," he said, among much else.

His romance with the woman he met in Albuquerque had ended, but he had met another woman and had fallen in love once again. Today, they and his daughter Camarie live somewhere in the great expanse of the country he grew to know during his turbulent time in the witness protection program. Camarie, a pretty seventeen-year-old with a heavenly voice, came to live with him six months after he received probation.

In the immediate wake of the publishing of the hardcover edition, the authors received a letter from someone who got to know Dominick's father, Anthony Santamaria, after Nino chased Anthony out of the Gaggi bunker when Dominick was three years old. The letter, which was passed along to Dominick through government channels, painted a poignant portrait of Anthony. It was a bittersweet reminder of what might have been, if Dominick had grown up with "The General" as the man of the house. But it also gave Dominick something to cherish—his father's affirmation. Here is an excerpt:

For many years I helped "The General" deal with the hurt and pain of losing his son Dominick and the guilt held inside wondering what Dominick thought of him, and further wondering what had become of him. Many times I watched The General cry over the mistake of losing Dominick and hearing him repeatedly say that Nino was "no good" and would eventually ruin Dominick's life. Knowing The General's constant battle with alcoholism and the pain harbored within him made me especially sad. To see a man so powerful in so many ways and powerless in other ways was truly a tragedy. The General always preached high moral values, demanding that people be honest, law abiding, and good natured, which were truly his values. When he heard Dominick was a decorated war hero, he was so proud that Dominick had not become part of "that life." I know if The General were alive he would also be so proud and would admire the courage that Dominick displayed in separating himself from a life that is worse than cancer.

By the time Dominick received the letter about his father, he had repaired his relationship with his other two children, Dominick Jr. and Marina; Denise allowed them to live with him in the summer of 1990. Fourteen-year-old Dominick Jr., like his father was, is rather stubby and large for his age, and a promising football player and math wizard. Marina, age eleven, sounds like she is going to be a talented singer like Camarie is. All the children live under new names. Dominick even gets along better with Denise these days; he says she still doesn't want to talk publicly about her harrowing life with him, but has read this book and was surprised to find that their relationship had been accurately portrayed.

Despite the torment he still feels for testifying, Dominick seems happy. He has found his identity; it was there all along, waiting for the virus to be purged. The proof was when he told his sentencing judge, "Your honor, I never shot anybody in the street." He makes a comfortable living in the merchandising of entirely legitimate products. Once in a while at parties, friends will badger him to get up and sing, and after a few drinks he might. He has been crime-free for ten years now. In a couple more, he will be off probation; his slate with society will be clean.

He will live the rest of his life, however, looking over

his shoulder. He fully expects that someday friends and relatives of the people he helped send away will come calling. Without saying too much about his defensive preparations, he is ready for them.

Acknowledgments

Many people helped us tell this story. The effort that many characters in it showed during their troubling times inspired us during ours. We begin with Walter Mack and the detectives, cops, agents, and government lawyers involved in the law enforcement thread of the story— particularly Kenneth McCabe, Arthur Ruffels, Frank Pergola, Roland Cadieux, John Murphy, Harry Brady, Joseph Wendling, Anthony Nelson, and Marilyn Lucht— and also Bruce Mouw, Gil Childers, Charles Meade, Mary Ellen Luthy, Barbara Jones, Mark Feldman, Joseph Coffey, Bill O'Loughlin, Steven Samuel, Jules Bonavolonta, and Nick Akerman.

In addition, we received assistance from the Federal Bureau of Investigation, the New York City Police Department, the United States Attorney's office in Manhattan, the United States Attorney's office in Brooklyn, the Brooklyn District Attorney's office, and the Bexar County Sheriff's office in San Antonio, Texas.

We also salute New York City Councilman Herbert Berman, who gave us an insider's tour of eastern Brooklyn, the officials and employees of James Madison High School and Saint Thomas Aquinas School, both in Brooklyn, and Mary Help of Christians School in Manhattan. A large number of those who helped have to remain anonymous. Many of them live in Bath Beach, Canarsie, and Flatlands, Brooklyn, particularly on or around Avenue P in Flatlands and Cropsey Avenue in Bath Beach. Some folks in the vicinity of Whitewood Drive and Park Place in Massapequa Park, Long Island, were also helpful.

Some people were not wild about helping us, but treated us courteously and offered some information, people such as Judith Questal and Professor Albert DeMeo of Brooklyn Law School.

For being friends, or for lifting a hand and answering a question when we asked, we thank Eliot Wald, Jane Wald, Dominick Marrano, Gail Collins, Patrice O'Shaughnessy, Michael Lipack, Helen Peterson, Vera Haller, Edward McDonald, Laura Ward, Douglas Grover, Charles Healey, Michael Pizzi, Ralph Parente, and members of the Montiglio family, Anthony, Michele, and Camarie.

All through the usual trauma of bringing a book home, our cheerleading literary agent Faith Hampton Childs was always there to hold our hand and, near the end, Senior Editor Laurie Bernstein of E.P. Dutton saved the day.

As we noted in the prologue, we owe a special debt to Dominick Montiglio. May he live happily, return to college, and become class president.

INDEX

TRUE CRIME AT ITS BEST

From *New York Times* Bestselling Author
Joseph D. Pistone

His real-life story.

DONNIE BRASCO
My Life Undercover in the Mafia

Twice on the *New York Times* bestseller list.
You've seen the movie, now read this
unforgettable eyewitness account of the
chilling world of wiseguys and the Mob.

Penguin Group (USA) Online

What will you be reading tomorrow?

Tom Clancy, Patricia Cornwell, W.E.B. Griffin,
Nora Roberts, William Gibson, Robin Cook,
Brian Jacques, Catherine Coulter, Stephen King,
Dean Koontz, Ken Follett, Clive Cussler,
Eric Jerome Dickey, John Sandford,
Terry McMillan, Sue Monk Kidd, Amy Tan,
J. R. Ward, Laurell K. Hamilton,
Charlaine Harris, Christine Feehan...

You'll find them all at
penguin.com

*Read excerpts and newsletters,
find tour schedules and reading group guides,
and enter contests.*

Subscribe to Penguin Group (USA) newsletters
and get an exclusive inside look
at exciting new titles and the authors you love
long before everyone else does.

PENGUIN GROUP (USA)
us.penguingroup.com